# A MORE EQUAL SOC

## New Labour, poverty, inequ and exclusion

Edited by John Hills and Kitty Stewart

2007 London

First published in Great Britain in January 2005 by

The Policy Press
University of Bristol
Fourth Floor
Beacon House
Queen's Road
Bristol BS8 1QU
UK

Tel +44 (0)117 331 4054
Fax +44 (0)117 331 4093
e-mail tpp-info@bristol.ac.uk
www.policypress.org.uk

British Library Cataloguing in Publication Data
A catalogue record for this book is available from the British Library.

Library of Congress Cataloging-in-Publication Data
A catalog record for this book has been requested.

ISBN 1 86134 577 1 paperback

A hardcover version of this book is also available

**John Hills** is Director of the Centre for Analysis of Social Exclusion (CASE) and Professor of Social Policy and **Kitty Stewart** is a Research Fellow at CASE, London School of Economics and Political Science.

Cover design by Qube Design Associates, Bristol
*Front cover:* photograph supplied by kind permission of Mark Power/Magnum Photos
Printed and bound in Great Britain by Hobbs the Printers Ltd, Southampton

# Contents

# List of figures and tables

## Figures

## Tables

# Acknowledgements

This book was made possible by the Joseph Rowntree Foundation, whose funding supported our work as editors and contributors, as well as the work of Tom Sefton and Elizabeth Washbrook. We are very grateful for this support, linked to the centenary of the Foundation. Many of the contributors work at the Economic and Social Research Council (ESRC) Research Centre for Analysis of Social Exclusion (CASE), at the London School of Economics (LSE). We are grateful to the ESRC for their support for the centre, which allows the research on which this book draws to take place; to the Suntory and Toyota International Centres for Economics and Related Disciplines at LSE for their support for Tania Burchardt and Abigail McKnight's inputs through their Toyota Fellowships; and to the Nuffield Foundation for their support for Helen Willmot's research. The opinions and views expressed here, however, are those of the contributors and not of any of our supporting bodies.

Several of the contributions draw on analysis supplied by the UK Data Archive at Essex University and by government departments, none of whom bear responsibility for the analysis or interpretations reported here. In particular, the analysis presented in Chapters Seven, Eight and Eleven of this volume using the POLIMOD model from the Microsimulation Unit at Cambridge University uses data from the Family Resources Survey, 1999-2000, made available by the Department for Work and Pensions through the UK Data Archive. The analysis in Chapter Twelve of spending patterns uses data from the Family Expenditure Survey. Material from the Family Expenditure Survey is crown copyright and has been made available by the Office for National Statistics through the UK Data Archive and is used by permission. All of the contributors are also grateful to Irina Verkhova and Nic Warner for their IT support that allows this kind of analysis to take place.

We are also grateful to Blackwell Publishing for permission to reproduce Figure 5.2, and to the Institute for Fiscal Studies to reproduce Figure 15.1.

Many people have helped us as editors and authors. We would particularly like to thank Jonathan Bradshaw, David Piachaud, John Micklewright, Brian Nolan, Jane Waldfogel, and all of our fellow contributors for their comments on specific chapters, Peter Townsend for assistance with Chapter Four of this volume, Robina Goodlad and Eithne McLaughlin for interesting and useful discussions about policy differences with Scotland and Northern Ireland, and two anonymous referees for their very helpful suggestions on the structure and content of the book as a whole. Where mistakes and omissions remain as a result of our failure to take this always constructive advice, the responsibility is ours.

We owe most to those who have helped us prepare the manuscript for publication with great good humour despite a tight timetable. Without the inputs of Leila Alberici, Jane Dickson, Nicola Harrison, Lucinda Himeur, and Hannah

Loizos, the project could not have been completed on time, or possibly at all. We are greatly in their debt.

*John Hills and Kitty Stewart,*
*London School of Economics and Political Science,*
*August 2004*

# Notes on contributors

**Tania Burchardt** is a Research Fellow at the Centre for Analysis of Social Exclusion (CASE). Her interests span welfare and employment policy, and theoretical frameworks for understanding poverty and social exclusion. Recent publications include 'Capabilities and disability: the capabilities framework and the social model of disability' (*Disability and society*, 2004), *Enduring economic exclusion: Disabled people, income and work* (2000) and 'Degrees of exclusion: developing a dynamic multi-dimensional measure' (with Julian Le Grand, and David Piachaud) in *Understanding social exclusion* (2002).

**Maria Evandrou** is Reader in Gerontology at Kings College London and Co-Director of the ESRC Research Group Simulating Social Policy for an Ageing Society (SAGE). She has written widely on social policy and older people. Recent publications include 'Family, work and quality of life: changing economic and social roles through the lifecourse', and 'Combining work and family life: the pension penalty of caring' (both with K. Glaser in *Ageing and Society*, 2003); 'Demographic change in Europe: implications for family support for older people' (with Jane Falkingham) in P. Kreager and E. Schroeder-Butterfill (eds) *Elderly without children* (2004).

**Jane Falkingham** is Professor of Demography and International Social Policy within the School of Social Science at Southampton University, and Co-Director of the ESRC Research Group SAGE. She has written widely in the field of population ageing and social policy. Recent publications include 'Pensions choices for the 21st century: meeting the challenges of an ageing society' (with Katherine Rake, in *Social Policy Review*, 2003), and 'British pension policy in the 21st century: a partnership in pensions or a marriage to the means test?' (with Katherine Rake and Martin Evans, in *Social Policy & Administration*, 2000).

**Howard Glennerster** is Professor Emeritus of Social Policy at the LSE and Co-Director of CASE. He has written widely on many aspects of social policy although he has specialised in the economics and finance of social policy. His recent books include *British social policy since 1945* (2nd edn, 2000) and *Understanding the finance of welfare* (2003).

**Paul Gregg** is a Professor of Economics at the University of Bristol and a member of the Council of Economic Advisers at HM Treasury.

**John Hills** is Director of CASE and Professor of Social Policy at the LSE. His research interests include the distributional effects of tax and welfare systems, income distribution, social security and pensions. Recent publications include

*Inequality and the state* (2004) and *Understanding social exclusion* (co-editor, 2002). He is a member of the Pensions Commission.

**Ruth Lupton** is a Lecturer at the Institute of Education, University of London, and was formerly a Research Fellow at CASE. Her research interests include understanding the problems and dynamic processes of high-poverty neighbourhoods, trends in the geography of disadvantage, urban policy and regeneration and education. Her recent publications include *Poverty Street: The dynamics of neighbourhood decline and renewal* (2003), which reported on the findings of CASE's longitudinal study of low-income neighbourhoods.

**Abigail McKnight** is the Toyota Research Fellow at CASE. She is a labour economist and her research interests include low-wage employment, inequality, evaluation of welfare-to-work programmes and education.

**Coretta Phillips** is a Lecturer in Social Policy at the LSE. Her research interests focus on ethnicity, racism, crime and criminal justice, minority perspectives and issues around community safety policy and practice. Recent publications include *Racism, crime and justice* (2002, with Ben Bowling) and articles in the *British Journal of Criminology*.

**Anne Power** is Professor of Social Policy and Deputy Director of CASE at the LSE. Her research interests include change in poor neighbourhoods, the impact of poor neighbourhood conditions on families, European, American and international urban problems, community involvement and sustainable development. Recent publications include *East Enders: Family and community in East London* (with Katharine Mumford) (The Policy Press, 2003).

**Liz Richardson** is a Research Officer for LSE Housing, based in CASE. Her research interests include community self-help, public participation, adult learning, social housing, regeneration and neighbourhood dynamics. She has provided developmental evaluation support for organisations providing community development and adult learning. Publications include *Developing residential learning* (2003), 'Community, neighbourhood and social infrastructure' in *Understanding social exclusion* (2002) and *Low demand for housing* (2004).

**Franco Sassi** is a Lecturer in Health Policy in the Department of Social Policy at LSE. He is a former Harkness Fellow in Health Care Policy (2000-01) and adviser to the European Office of the World Health Organisation. His research interests include the economic evaluation of health interventions, trade-offs between equity and efficiency in health care, inequalities in health and in access to health care.

**Tom Sefton** is a Research Fellow at CASE. His research interests include the distributional impact of public spending, fuel poverty, income dynamics, attitudes towards the welfare state and the economic evaluation of social welfare interventions. Recent publications include *Poverty in Britain: The impact of government policy since 1997* (with Holly Sutherland and David Piachaud, 2003).

**Holly Sutherland** is a Research Professor in the Institute for Social and Economic Research at the University of Essex. She specialises in building and using microsimulation models for the analysis of the effects of policy changes on poverty and inequality and coordinates the EU-wide EUROMOD project.

**Kitty Stewart** is a Research Fellow at CASE. Her research interests include child poverty and disadvantage, international comparisons of policy and outcomes relating to poverty and exclusion and employment trajectories for the low skilled. Recent work has examined patterns of social exclusion at regional level in the EU.

**Jane Waldfogel** is a Professor at Columbia University School of Social Work and a Research Associate at CASE, where she visited during the 2003-04 academic year. She has written extensively on the impact of public policies on child and family well-being. Her current research includes studies of family leave, early childhood care and education and child abuse and neglect.

**Elizabeth Washbrook** is a Research Assistant at the Centre for Market and Public Organisation, University of Bristol, and a research student at the University of Oxford. Her interests are in the intra-household allocation of resources and the determinants of children's development.

**Helen Willmot** is a Research Officer with CASE's Families Study. She leads the research in Sheffield and Leeds, working in conjunction with the London-based research officer to investigate how families experience and respond to living in low-income areas. Her recent focus has been on how such areas impact on parenting – for example, how parents cope with the additional pressures of disadvantaged areas, and whether New Labour's child and family-focused initiatives have helped with child-rearing. Her other research interests include the dynamics and meaning of intimate relationships.

# ONE

# Introduction

*Kitty Stewart and John Hills*

The Labour government that took office in 1997 inherited levels of poverty and inequality unprecedented in post-war history. More than one in four UK children lived in relative poverty, compared to one in eight when Labour had left office in 1979 (DWP, 2004a). Poverty among pensioners stood at 21%[1]. Income inequality had widened sharply: in 1979 the post-tax income of the top tenth of the income distribution was about five times that of the bottom tenth; by the mid-1990s that ratio had doubled (Hills, 2004a, Table 2.5).

In opposition, the new government had been careful to avoid major commitments to addressing social and economic disadvantage. In practice, it has implemented a broad and ambitious social policy programme, taking on a wide range of social ills, including child poverty, worklessness, area and neighbourhood deprivation and inequalities in health and educational attainment. How much has this programme achieved? Shortly after the election, one of New Labour's prominent strategists had challenged "the doubters" to "judge us after ten years of success in office. For one of the fruits of that success will be that Britain has become a more equal society" (Mandelson, 1997, p 7). There is some time to go before that particular deadline, but as Labour nears the end of its second term in office, this seems a good moment to take stock. This volume aims to assess the impact of government policies since 1997 on poverty, inequality and social exclusion. Is Britain indeed becoming a more equal society than it was when Labour was elected?

## The scale of the problem

Figures 1.1 and 1.2 place the changes in poverty and inequality that Labour inherited in the perspective of longer-term historical trends. Levels of poverty and inequality show fluctuation during the 1960s and decline in the 1970s before the sustained increases of the 1980s. By the early 1990s, the lines on both figures have flattened out at what appears to be a new plateau high above the original plain. Unlike every other post-war decade, in which the gains of economic growth were shared across income groups, growth in the 1980s benefited the richest most and the poorest least. Indeed, on one measure, the incomes of the very poorest were *lower* in real terms in 1994/95 than they had been in 1979 (Hills, 2004a, Figure 2.7).

**Figure 1.1: Poverty in the UK: share of the population with below half average income (BHC) by household type (1961-97)**

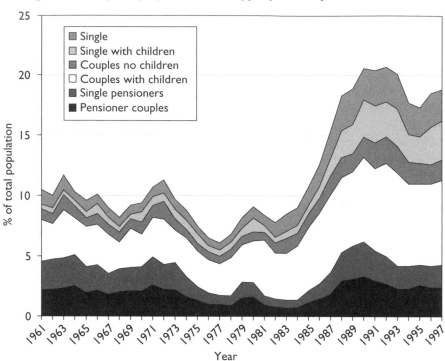

Source: Hills (2004a, Figure 3.1); based on Goodman and Webb (2004) and DWP (2003a) and earlier equivalents

Unemployment was high by historical standards in 1979, and indeed had played a part in the Conservatives' election victory, with 'Labour Isn't Working' posters featuring prominently in the campaign. However, unemployment soared during the 1980s (see Figure 1.3), passing the 3,000,000 mark in 1983. After a sharp fall during the late 1980s' boom, male unemployment peaked at nearly 14% in 1993, before another period of growth brought it back down towards 1979 levels. At 8% for men in 1997, and 3% for women, unemployment was relatively low in international terms. However, the allocation of jobs across households had changed, with growing polarisation between households with two earners and those with no member in work. By 1997, more than 16% of households were workless, more than twice the 1979 level (Gregg et al, 1999).

In part, these developments can be attributed to global changes which led to falling demand for unskilled labour and increasing premiums for skills and qualifications. These pressures affected many countries, but the UK was hit harder than most. Long-term factors, such as the high proportion of the workforce with low qualifications, arguably made the UK particularly vulnerable. However, government policy under Margaret Thatcher exacerbated the effects. Curbs on trade union powers, an end to the minimum wage protection provided through

**Figure 1.2: Inequality in the UK: the Gini coefficient (BHC) (1961-97)**

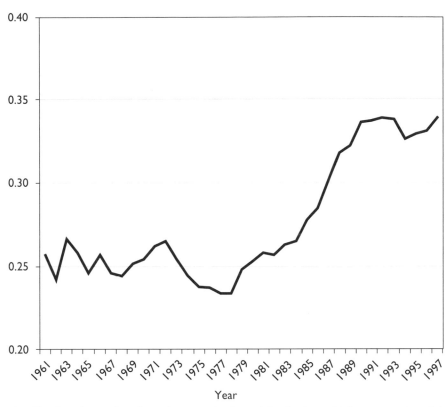

*Note:* The Gini takes a value of zero for a completely equal distribution and 1 if one person has all the income and the rest none.
*Source:* IFS (HBAI) series from Clark and Taylor (1999)

the wages councils, the move to linking benefits to price levels rather than to incomes and changes to tax policy which shifted the burden from those with high to those with low incomes all played a significant part.

Certainly the UK's relative performance on poverty and inequality deteriorated sharply during this period. Figure 1.4 shows the change in the Gini coefficient between the start of the 1980s and the mid-1990s for the UK and ten other industrialised countries with available data. While the most equal countries saw slight increases in inequality over this period, the biggest changes took place in Australia, the US and – most strikingly – the UK. By the mid-1990s the Gini was higher in the UK than in any other country represented except the US.

A comparison of child poverty in the same 15 countries placed the UK third from bottom: only the US and Italy had a higher percentage of children living in relatively poor households in the mid-1990s (UNICEF, 2000). And while three other European countries (Finland, Belgium and France) had higher rates of household worklessness in 1996, among households with children, worklessness was higher in the UK than anywhere else in the industrialised world (see Figure

**Figure 1.3: UK unemployment rate (claimant count) (1971-97)**

*Source:* ONS, dataset Imsum 11

**Figure 1.4: Changes in the Gini coefficient across countries during the 1980s and early 1990s**

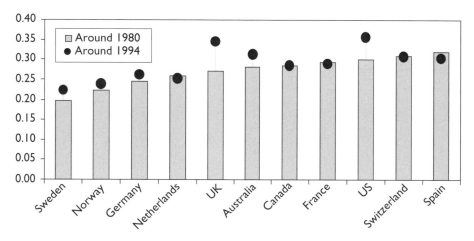

*Note:* Data for each country as follows. France and US 1979, 1994; Norway and UK 1979, 1995; Spain 1980, 1990; Australia, Canada and Germany 1981, 1994; Sweden 1981, 1995; Switzerland 1982, 1992; Netherlands 1983, 1994.
*Source:* Luxembourg Income Study (www.lisproject.org, 23 May 2004)

1.5). Nearly 20% of such UK households had no adult in work, more than double the OECD average.

This was a tough legacy for a political party traditionally concerned with the poor and dispossessed. In addition, the incoming government faced public services

**Figure 1.5: Workless household rate by country for households with children (1996)**

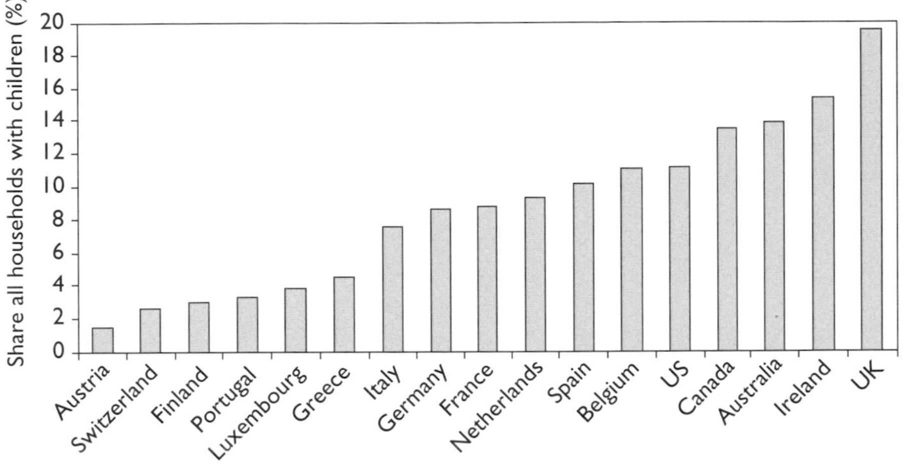

*Source:* OECD (1998, Tables 1.6, 1.7)

that had suffered from two decades of declining investment, a process which had begun with the visit of the International Monetary Fund (IMF) in 1976 and continued under Thatcher and into the 1990s. Overall public expenditure changed little as a share of GDP during the late 1970s and 1980s. However, net public sector *investment* fell from an annual average of 5.9% of GDP between 1963 and 1976 to an average 3.1% between 1976 and 1980 and 1.3% between 1985 and 1995 (HM Treasury, 2000). Relative public sector pay had also fallen significantly, with nurses, teachers and manual workers hardest hit: a young male teacher would have been ranked in the 72nd percentile position in the late 1970s (that is, he would have earned more than 71% of the population), but only 63rd between 1995 and 1999; a young female manual worker (such as a hospital ward assistant) fell from the 55th to the 39th percentile over the same period (Nickell and Quintini, 2002). This meant low morale, staff shortages and high rates of staff turnover in some of the most important areas of the public sector.

Surveys of public opinion at around the time Labour took office showed strong support for tackling many of these trends. In 1995, 87% of those interviewed for the British Social Attitudes (BSA) Survey agreed that "the gap between those with high incomes and those with low incomes [in Britain] is too large"; up from 72% in 1983 and high by international standards (Spencer, 1996). Similarly, 71% of those interviewed in 1994 agreed that there was "quite a lot" of "*real* poverty" in Britain, up from 55% in 1986 (Hills, 2002). And 73% of respondents in 1998 thought it "definitely" or "probably" the government's responsibility to reduce the income differences between rich and poor.

When it comes to considering *how* the government might do this, opinion is more divided. The British Election Survey finds slow decline to 1992 in those agreeing that "income and wealth should be redistributed towards ordinary working people" (54% in the mid-1970s down to 47% in 1992), followed by a sharp increase to 60% in 1997 (Heath et al, 2001, Table 2.9). The BSA shows falling support throughout the 1990s for the statement that "government should spend more on welfare benefits for the poor", although in 1997 more people (40%) still agreed than disagreed (Hills, 2002, Figure 1). But there is overwhelming support for the extension of public services, including health, education and welfare, even if this would mean higher taxes – 72% in favour in 1997, compared to 7% who would have cut taxes even at the expense of reducing services. In 1979, both options had received 34% support (Heath et al, 2001, Table 3.8).

Would the new government be able to harness public opinion to bring about real change?

## The government's strategy

### A radical dawn?

The initial euphoria which greeted Labour's General Election victory on 2 May 1997 masked the fact that most people had had low expectations for the new government – fewer than three quarters of the electorate had turned out to vote, for instance. The wave of excitement that swept the country may have been explained by a general expectation of change; it was unlikely to have been driven by any clear new strategy or specific pledges made by the Labour Party in opposition. In an interview shortly before the election, Tony Blair claimed he was going to be "a lot more radical in government than many people think" (*The Observer*, 27 April 1997), underlining the cautious promises with which the party had approached the election.

Given Labour's recent electoral history their approach was understandable. As early as 1985, Neil Kinnock had argued that "the harsh electoral reality" was that Labour could not rely "merely on a combination of the dispossessed, the 'traditional' and increasingly fragmented working class and minority groups for the winning of power", but needed to broaden its appeal (quoted in Heath et al, 2001, p 101). Kinnock initiated a major policy review which led to the party abandoning many of the policies believed to have cost it votes in 1983, including commitments to unilateral nuclear disarmament, to the extension of public ownership, to restoring trade union collective bargaining rights and to withdrawal from the European Community (Seyd, 1998). These changes brought modest electoral benefits: Labour's share of the vote rose four points to 35% in 1992 – still less than it had achieved in 1979 after the winter of discontent (Heath et al, 2001).

In the aftermath of the 1992 General Election defeat, the need to reposition the party grew in urgency. Many shared Giles Radice's view that social and economic trends were gradually eroding Labour's traditional core support in the trade unions, on council estates and among manual workers (Radice, 1992). When Tony Blair took over the leadership on John Smith's death in 1994, he made it clear that he intended the party to "build a new coalition of support, based on a broad national appeal that transcends traditional electoral divisions" (Blair, 1994, p 7). The new target voters were to be those in "middle income, middle Britain"; the strategy was to appeal to those with economic and social aspirations, not just to the poor and disadvantaged (see Seyd, 1998; Heath et al, 2001). From the start, Tony Blair continually emphasised the idea that he was leading a new and different party. In his speech to the 1995 Labour Party Conference, he used the word 'new' 59 times, 16 of them with reference to 'New Labour' (Seyd, 1998).

The 1992 defeat left Labour with a particular concern – almost an obsession – about the issue of tax. As Blair's strategy adviser, Philip Gould, put it in 1998:

> We were certain that we had lost elections in the past partly because of tax, and we were determined not to let it happen again this time. (Quoted in Heath et al, 2001, p 44)

As shadow chancellor, John Smith had proposed the restoration of a 50% tax rate on incomes over £40,000 and the extension of national insurance contributions on incomes over £22,000. An analysis of poll data had found no evidence that these proposals had cost Labour the 1992 election (Heath et al, 1994), but after four successive defeats the Labour Party were not willing to take risks. In January 1997, Gordon Brown made a public commitment to stick to the Conservatives' spending plans for the first two years of a new Parliament, and not to raise either the basic or top rates of income tax. This pledge seems to have registered with the public: for the first time, 1997 saw roughly as many people (31%) place themselves to the left of Labour on taxes and spending as to the right (34%) (Heath et al, 2001, Table 6.4). In 1992, 19% had put themselves to Labour's left, against 57% to the right.

The commitment on spending was not simply about getting elected. Heath et al (2001) argue that Labour had failed in the past due to a lack of realism and effectiveness in managing the economy, and that the modernisers accepted this. Labour administrations in the 1960s and 1970s had spent heavily in the first years in office and paid the price later on. New Labour was determined to be different. Sticking to Conservative spending plans at the start would enable the new government to prove its competence, while getting the economy ready for increased expenditure in the second half of the Parliament.

So the party that took power in 1997 promised little in the way of major change for those living in poverty. It had abandoned the traditional tax and spend commitments associated with the Labour Party. It had distanced itself from the unions and shed any commitment to securing full employment. The 1997 election manifesto contained just two references to reducing poverty, one in the context of tax and benefit reform to reduce welfare dependency, and the other about helping people into jobs. There was one (very general) reference to tackling inequality, but no mention of social exclusion or the excluded. The manifesto did place a strong emphasis on the importance of addressing educational disadvantage. It also promised to introduce a national minimum wage and to tackle long-term unemployment, particularly among young people: one of the five much trumpeted 'early pledges' was to get 250,000 under-25s off benefit and into work, using money from a windfall tax on the privatised utilities. However, the biggest changes proposed were arguably the constitutional reforms, including the reform of the House of Lords and devolution for Scotland and Wales.

Although never appearing high on the agenda, Blair's rhetoric prior to the General Election had made reference to the dispossessed. In January 1996, he had proclaimed that "for the new Millennium we need a war on exclusion and a determination to extend opportunity to all" (Levitas, 2000, p 363). In July of the same year he wrote in the *Independent on Sunday*:

> If the next Labour Government has not raised the living standards of the poorest by the end of its time in office, it will have failed. (Blair, 1996, p 21)

But under some definitions, the living standards of the poorest had risen slightly even under Thatcher, so this could hardly have been more modest an ambition. However, as Labour Minister Margaret Hodge would put it in 2000, "in the latter days of Opposition, few Labour politicians chose to promote equality for fear of losing electoral support" (Hodge, 2000, p 34). "Have faith" was Blair's message to his critics on the left (Blair, 1996, p 21). It was impossible to know whether goals would become more ambitious once Labour was safely in office.

## New Labour in office

In their analysis of Labour's first term, Toynbee and Walker point to Blair's visit to a Peckham estate in June 1997 as the first clear indication that poverty and disadvantage were on the government's agenda. In what was particularly significant for being his first major speech as Prime Minister outside the House of Commons, Blair promised "no forgotten people and no no-hope areas", committing the government to addressing "the dead weight of low expectations, the crushing belief that things cannot get better" (Blair, 1997a). As Toynbee and Walker describe it:

> cheers went up from those hanging out of tower-block windows but also around the country from those who had voted Labour but had been waiting for a clear statement of intent. (Toynbee and Walker, 2001, p 10)

Within months, social exclusion had become a central government concept. In August 1997, Peter Mandelson announced the creation of the Social Exclusion Unit (SEU), denouncing the "scourge and waste of social exclusion" as "the greatest social crisis of our times" (Mandelson, 1997, pp 6, 9). Social exclusion would never receive a clear definition, but it was clear from the series of attempts to define it that the government's concern was with multiple deprivation. At the SEU launch in December, Blair described it as:

> about income but ... about more. It is about prospects and networks and life-chances. It's a very modern problem, and one that is more harmful to the individual, more damaging to self-esteem, more corrosive for society as a whole, more likely to be passed down from generation to generation, than material poverty. (Blair, 1997b)

Later, he would define it as:

> a short-hand label for what can happen when individuals or areas suffer from a combination of linked problems such as unemployment, poor skills, low incomes, poor housing, high crime environments, bad health and family breakdown. (DSS, 1999, p 23)

The SEU was seen as important precisely because of the interrelations between these different problems: it would be able to coordinate policy across departments and with local authority and voluntary organisations, "helping government to work in a more coherent, integrated way", so as to provide "joined up solutions" for "joined up problems" (Blair, 1997b).

While those who had called for action to tackle deprivation were pleased (perhaps relieved) that this was clearly a New Labour priority after all, there was concern that talking about social exclusion was a way of disguising the fact that nothing was being done about income inequality and material poverty. Fairclough (2000) points out that Blair's first definition given above moves seamlessly from defining social exclusion as about 'more than income' to a formulation in which exclusion is contrasted with material poverty – in other words, it is not about income at all. Similarly, Levitas (1998) notes that Mandelson speaks of achieving a more equal society through many routes, "*not just* the redistribution of cash from rich to poor" (Levitas's emphasis), but that he goes on to make it clear that these other routes – promoting employment and improving educational standards – must take priority (see Mandelson, 1997, p 8). The announcement of the SEU's programme for the first six months made it clear that income poverty was not part of its brief: the first areas to be looked at were school exclusions, rough sleeping and poor areas; to be followed by teenage pregnancy and 16- to 18-year-olds not in education, training or employment. In the week of the 1997 Labour Party Conference, 54 professors of social policy and sociology wrote to the *Financial Times* welcoming the establishment of the SEU but expressing concern that its agenda did not include the adequacy of benefit levels. They argued that, by ignoring the need for income redistribution, the government was trying "to tackle social exclusion with one hand tied behind its back" (Lister and Moore, 1997, p 20).

However, the fact that redistribution was not part of the SEU's brief did not necessarily mean that material poverty was being ignored. The Treasury kept firm control of tax–benefit policy from the start, and the SEU agenda is consistent with a strict division of labour between the two bodies. In fact, one of Gordon Brown's first priorities at the Treasury was a welfare-to-work programme. As had been promised in the Labour Manifesto, the first Labour budget in July 1997 announced that the windfall levy on privatised utilities – the only major source of additional funds available during the first two years in office – would be used to fund a New Deal for Young People, with some of the money set aside for a New Deal for Lone Parents. Alongside programmes helping the workless into jobs, Brown was also keen to ensure that paid work made financial sense: on the day after the election, he told the Treasury to start developing plans for a tax credit scheme for the working poor (*The Guardian*, 26 November 1997), formally announced in the March 1998 budget as the Working Families Tax Credit (WFTC). A commission to investigate a starting level for the national minimum wage was also established in these first few weeks.

The emphasis on work-based policies reflected Brown's belief that "the most serious cause of poverty is unemployment" (Pre-Budget Report, November 1997) and that "the answer to social exclusion is economic opportunity" (1998 Budget Speech). However, while the WFTC received a cautious welcome as a means of boosting the incomes of low-paid workers, it did not allay the concerns of those worried about people unable to work for a wide range of reasons: it did not address the points expressed in the Lister and Moore letter to the *Financial Times*.

The row which broke out in late 1997 over cuts in benefits for lone parents reinforced the impression that work was considered the only solution to poverty and did serious and lasting damage to Labour's reputation as a government genuinely concerned about the least well-off. The outgoing government had proposed the cuts, eliminating top-ups to income support and child benefit received by single parents, and Labour pressed ahead with them to keep their commitment to stick within Conservative spending limits. The decision provoked huge outrage and led to a back-bench rebellion of 47 MPs just seven months after election victory. The March 1998 budget would subsequently leave the majority of lone parents better off overall as a result of universal increases in child benefit and higher income support allowances for all children under 11 years of age, but many people's attitudes to New Labour's social policy had been set and would prove difficult to shift.

The increase in income support for families with children was significant, as it represented the first move to raise benefits for those out of work. The Spring 1999 Budget would raise income support for young families again, and more sharply, while also increasing the generosity of the prospective WFTC. The government appeared to be quietly beginning to address some of the concerns expressed by its critics on the left.

Then, shortly after Budget Day 1999, Tony Blair made an unexpected announcement. At a lecture in memory of William Beveridge, he committed the government not just to reducing but also to eliminating poverty among children:

> Our historic aim [will be] that ours is the first generation to end child poverty forever.... It is a 20-year mission, but I believe it can be done. (Blair, 1999, p 7)

The pledge was followed up with a concrete interim target: the Treasury and the Department for Work and Pensions were instructed to reduce the proportion of children living in relative poverty (with incomes below 60% of the contemporary median) by a quarter by 2004.

Despite the gentle overtures of the 1998 and 1999 budgets, it is widely agreed that Blair's Beveridge speech marked a sea change in both the government's language and its policy approach (Lister, 2001a; Deacon, 2003). There is less consensus about where this change appeared from, and why it happened when it did (see Deacon, 2003). One theory is that, with the two-year commitment to the Conservative spending plans coming to an end, the government was now able to declare openly the goals it had had all along. Alternatively, the announcement may have been a reaction to the rebellion over lone parent benefit cuts.

Both factors are likely to have played a part, but a third element was almost certainly the growing recognition of the extent to which opportunities available to adults are diminished by the experience of poverty in childhood. In a pamphlet on the Third Way in 1998, Blair had declared the four values 'essential to a just society' to be "equal worth, opportunity for all, responsibility and community" (Blair, 1998, p 3), and since then 'opportunity' had become a government watchword. At about the same time as the Beveridge speech, the Treasury released a report based on research into the dynamics of opportunity (CASE/HM Treasury, 1999). The message was clear:

> Children who grow up in poverty are much less likely to succeed as adults.... Childhood disadvantage has long term scarring effects. (HM Treasury, 1999, pp 3, 26)

If the government was serious about providing everyone with real opportunities, it had to begin by tackling child poverty.

Early 1999 also saw the government announce an annual audit of poverty and social exclusion. When the first report was published in September of the same year, it was called *Opportunity for all* (OFA), underlining the framework within which the attack on poverty was understood (DSS, 1999). *Opportunity for all* represents an excellent summary of government thinking and intentions on poverty and social exclusion in 1999 – a sort of second manifesto, and one offering a vision hugely different and more ambitious than the manifesto for the 1997 General Election.

Starting from the commitment to tackle poverty and its causes, the report outlined what the government saw as the "complex, multi-dimensional problems" of poverty and social exclusion (DSS, 1999, p 2). The key features were listed as lack of opportunities to work; lack of opportunities to acquire education and skills; childhood deprivation; disrupted families; barriers to older people living active, fulfilling and healthy lives; inequalities in health; poor housing; poor neighbourhoods; fear of crime; and disadvantage or discrimination on grounds of age, ethnicity, gender or disability. The report promised "an integrated and radical policy response" to these combined problems (1999, p 23), and emphasised the importance of long-term solutions, and of flexible action geared to local needs.

Tackling childhood deprivation lay at the heart of the strategy outlined, with three essential policy areas highlighted: education, including pre-school education; policies to tackle family worklessness and poverty through changes to the tax–benefit system and improvements to childcare provision; and policies supporting young people in the transition between childhood and adulthood, including increasing educational participation and achievement by 16- to 18-year-olds, improving outcomes for children leaving care and action on teenage pregnancy.

The second theme was employment. In language by now familiar, the report asserted that "worklessness is the main cause of poverty and social exclusion" (DSS, 1999, p 78); "work for those who can" (DSS, 1999, p 7) is therefore key to the solution. Again, the response was to be multi-pronged: welfare-to-work programmes; changes to incentives to make work pay; policies to promote 'lifelong learning' to improve skills; and action on health inequalities.

Employment was also a central part of the strategy for combating poverty among future generations of pensioners. For current pensioners, OFA highlighted increases to benefit income and action to eradiate fuel poverty, as well as action on health, housing, transport and crime; all aimed at improving opportunities for pensioners to live "secure, fulfilling and active lives" (DSS, 1999, p 113).

Finally, OFA contained a chapter on the importance of area-based solutions to social exclusion, identifying "the increasing polarisation between thriving communities on the one hand, and deprived ones on the other" as "one of the key problems of our society over the past 20 years" (DSS, 1999, p 11). The report promised area-based programmes to improve the quality of life in the most deprived communities by improving job prospects, tackling crime, raising educational achievement and reducing poor health.

Four annual OFA update reports have now been published, each re-emphasising the themes identified earlier, although the most recent reports have given slightly more central roles to the provision of support to those unable to work (in particular the disabled) and to "tackling inequalities by improving public services" (DWP, 2002a, p 14). Labour's Election Manifesto for 2001 echoed many of the OFA themes, with "opportunity for all children, security for all pensioners" one of the ten goals listed for 2010. In contrast not just to the 1997 Manifesto, but to election manifestos throughout the 20th century (see Kenway, 2003), poverty is mentioned 19 times in a domestic context; all are references to children and pensioners. Opportunity or opportunities (in the relevant sense) are mentioned no less than 42 times.

Since then, the government's language on these issues has had periods of both expansion and retrenchment. At the 2002 Labour Party Conference, Gordon Brown made a pledge to abolish pensioner poverty – "Our aim is to end pensioner poverty in our country" (cited in Goodman et al, 2003, p 2) – although, unlike the child poverty pledge, this was not accompanied by explicitly quantified targets. In 2002, Tony Blair also referred to redistribution for the first time, calling for a Britain "in which we continue to redistribute power, wealth and opportunity to the many not the few" (Blair, 2002). But the furore which developed in June 2003 when Labour Minister Peter Hain called for a public debate about raising income tax for those with very high incomes made it clear that the government was not prepared to contemplate any major explicit shift in direction. In March 2004, Social Exclusion Minister Yvette Cooper appeared to set new boundaries in announcing that "if we are to achieve social justice in the next generation, we have to tackle inequality as well as exclusion"; but she went on to make it clear that her concern lay with inequalities in life chances, not outcomes (Cooper, 2004).

## Assessing the impact

*Opportunity for all* and the child poverty pledge laid the groundwork for what has become a wide-ranging and ambitious set of policies. This volume aims to assess the overall impact these policies have had to date on the situation of groups and individuals living in poverty or at risk of exclusion when the government came to power. Before going any further, however, it may be helpful to clarify the terms under which our assessment will be made. Are we assessing the government's success in meeting their own objectives, or in meeting an alternative set of objectives that we believe they ought to have had? And if the latter, is it reasonable to be judging progress towards goals that the government itself might not accept as legitimate?

This government has been very good at setting itself targets. *Opportunity for all* contains 'indicators of success' in each of the areas it has set out to tackle; the annual OFA updates report on progress towards these goals. Overall reported progress has been good: the 2003 results show that 32 of the 43 outcome indicators for which there are data have been improving, not just over the most recent year but in the medium-term (roughly since Labour came to power), while only two have got worse in the most recent year, and *none* have got worse over the full period (DWP, 2003b).

Assessing the government's success in meeting its own objectives, therefore, could be a relatively straightforward task, with a lot of the work already done, although the tricky question of whether the targets set were sufficiently ambitious remains. A more fundamental question is whether we accept the government's objectives; that is, whether we accept their understanding of the key elements of poverty and social exclusion. An overview of alternative discourses on social exclusion is helpful here.

## Concepts of poverty and social exclusion

Perhaps the most useful place to start is with Levitas (1998), who identifies three different approaches to social exclusion used in contemporary political debate, each with its own implications for policy solutions. The first, which Levitas labels the redistributionist discourse (RED), sees social exclusion as a consequence of poverty: it is income that the excluded lack, so raising benefit levels would be one effective policy response. The second, the social integrationist discourse (SID), sees inclusion primarily in terms of labour market attachment. The excluded are those who are workless, leading to a focus on policies which encourage and enable people to enter paid work. The third approach is labelled by Levitas as the moral underclass discourse (MUD) and places responsibility for social exclusion on the 'moral and behavioural delinquency' of the excluded themselves.

Levitas (1998, p 128) argues that: "Labour understands social inclusion primarily in terms of participation in paid work"; it is an understanding based heavily in SID. (She also suggests that certain policies, such as benefit cuts for lone parents, have undertones of MUD, but there is little hard evidence of any genuine belief in a moral underclass.) As we have seen, employment takes centre stage in OFA alongside tackling childhood deprivation, and Labour's rhetoric has consistently emphasised employment as the route out of poverty and exclusion. However, the simplification that the Levitas position inevitably represents is unfair to Labour in 2004. While early language and policy suggested welfare-to-work programmes would be the main plank of Labour's social policy, subsequent developments have resulted in a much richer set of policies than would have been predicted in 1998, as discussed earlier. There is much in OFA – and there has been extensive policy action – concerning non-employment barriers to participation, including poor health, poor housing, high levels of crime and poor neighbourhoods.

Still, this leaves the question of whether Labour's approach has any foundations in RED. On the one hand, while the language of redistribution has clearly been downplayed, there has been considerable 'redistribution by stealth' to non-workers, and not just to families with children but also to pensioners and to some disabled claimants. 'Security for those who cannot work' may have received less attention than many would like but it has not been ignored altogether.

On the other hand, it can be argued, first, that the interpretation of 'unable to work' has been narrow: there has been little sympathy for workless adults without children who are not registered disabled. Working-age adults without children tend to be overlooked in poverty assessments: poverty among all working-age households is tracked in OFA, but this includes (and hence figures are strongly affected by) households with children.

Second, where redistribution has taken place it has been clearly (and often explicitly) limited to improving the situation of those at the bottom relative to the middle, with the position of those at the top considered irrelevant. Equality has been redefined as equality of opportunity, with a sense that this can be achieved without tackling income inequality overall. This is a convenient position for New Labour, as Margaret Hodge acknowledged in 2000 (p 35):

> [Equality of opportunity] allows us to position ourselves as promoting both individual ambition and prosperity, while still tackling inequality. That appeals to middle Britain.

But does it make sense? Is it possible to "create equality through public services" (Hodge, 2000, p 39) against a background of huge inequalities in income and accumulated wealth, which allow many people to opt out of those services? As Lister (2001b, p 438) argues, "equality of opportunity in the context of economic and social structures that remain profoundly unequal is likely to remain a contradiction in terms".

A working definition developed by Burchardt, Le Grand and Piachaud (BLP) provides a second perspective on social exclusion (Burchardt et al, 2002). Synthesising a number of previous formulations, BLP define social exclusion in terms of non-participation in key activities. For the UK in the 1990s, they identify four dimensions:

- *consumption* (the capacity to purchase goods and services);
- *production* (participation in economically or socially valuable activities);
- *political engagement* (involvement in local or national decision-making); and
- *social interaction* (integration with family, friends and community).

Participation in every dimension is regarded as necessary for social inclusion.

The first two of the BLP dimensions can be seen as rooted in RED and SID respectively, although the type of productive activity that brings about social integration is understood more widely here than elsewhere, going beyond the paid labour market to include, for instance, caring activities and volunteering. However, the third and fourth dimensions broaden the concept to include ways of participating that are often overlooked. In particular, this conceptualisation highlights the importance of empowerment – of having a voice in decisions that affect one's life. This is not a concept that features explicitly in the government's understanding of social exclusion. Neither political nor social participation is mentioned in OFA as important in its own right; 'partnership' is promoted but because it is likely to result in more successful programmes: "real progress can only be achieved by working together" (DSS, 1999, p 3).

Finally, we consider the most comprehensive recent attempt to choose indicators to monitor social inclusion at the European level. Social exclusion has been growing in importance on the European agenda, and the European Council Summit in March 2000 led to the development of a common set of indicators to track progress towards tackling the problem. *Social indicators* (Atkinson et al, 2002) was written as a key part of the consultation process.

The Atkinson report is similar to OFA in taking a pragmatic approach to defining social exclusion: given the aim of contributing to policy, it sidesteps the definitional minefield and opts simply to accept the terms social inclusion and social exclusion:

> as *shorthand* for a range of concerns considered to be important in setting the European social agenda. There is, we believe, broad agreement about the list of such concerns, which encompass poverty, deprivation, low educational qualifications, labour market disadvantage, joblessness, poor health, poor housing or homelessness, illiteracy and innumeracy, precariousness and incapacity to participate in society. (Atkinson et al, 2002, p 3)

Thus, like OFA, the report focuses on key features commonly accepted to be important though not within any particular framework.

The starting points of *Social indicators* and of OFA are naturally rather different, as the former aims to identify indicators appropriate across the EU, but a comparison of the indicators chosen is still informative. The *Social indicators* list is smaller and more limited in scope, with indicators of five broad areas:

* financial poverty and income inequality;
* education;
* employment and unemployment;
* health; and
* housing.

But while the list is inevitably less rich overall, it finds space for a number of measures not included in OFA. All of these relate to financial circumstances: low income and financial hardship are given much greater prominence than they receive in OFA. In particular, first, where the OFA employment measures focus on rates of employment and joblessness, the *Social indicators* list includes indicators assessing the relationship between employment/unemployment and low income: measures of low pay among employees and the share of the workless living in poverty are included, with clear implications for policy. Second, the *Social indicators* list includes a measure of overall income inequality, the quintile share ratio. It should be noted that most of the indicators mentioned, including the quintile share ratio, feature in the final list adopted at the Laeken European Council Summit in December 2001 by all member states including the UK. So the UK government has signed up to being monitored on an income inequality measure as part of its commitment to furthering social and economic cohesion in the EU.

## Outline of the book

This volume also takes what might be deemed the key features approach. It includes chapters that cover what the BLP framework sees as dimensions of social exclusion, chapters that examine causes or risk factors, and chapters that focus on particular groups where poverty or social exclusion was high when the Labour government took office. Up to a point, the layout and themes of the book reflect the OFA 'key features' listed earlier. Most of these have one chapter dedicated to them; all but one of the others is covered somewhere in the book. (The exception – disrupted families – is rather different in that it lies largely beyond the reach of the state.)

However, our assessment goes beyond the terms of the government's framework in a number of ways. First, our interpretation is broader, giving more space to aspects of social exclusion that receive little attention in OFA but which are central to other understandings of the concept. Two elements in particular stand out, reflecting the two gaps in the government's coverage identified above: the book includes a chapter (Chapter Five) on social and political participation; and it gives greater focus to income poverty and income inequality, with Chapter Eleven considering the overall impact of policy on the income distribution.

Second, the aim is not just to evaluate the government's success in achieving particular policy goals, but also to consider the overall impact in contributing to a fairer and more equal society. This means considering policies that may have had an adverse effect on the wider goal: the introduction of tuition fees for higher education might be an example. It means considering groups overlooked or ignored by the government: hence Chapter Ten on vulnerable minorities looks at what happened to asylum seekers as well as to those groups targeted by the SEU. Finally, it involves assessment – though this is usually very difficult – of how far policies are in fact responsible for outcomes: in some cases other factors, such as broader macroeconomic changes, may have contributed to apparent successes or, alternatively, made objectives more difficult to attain.

Following this introduction, the book is divided into four parts. The chapters in Part One each explore policy and outcomes relating towards a particular cause or aspect of social exclusion. In Chapter Two, Abigail McKnight examines employment, at the heart of the New Labour project. The chapter considers the combined impact of macroeconomic policy, the New Deals, the National Minimum Wage and changes to the tax-credit system on employment, unemployment and inactivity. In Chapter Three, Abigail McKnight, Howard Glennerster and Ruth Lupton look at changes to policy affecting compulsory and post-compulsory education and whether these have had an impact on inequalities in educational attainment. In Chapter Four, Franco Sassi examines health inequalities, an area subject to considerable prominence, a number of targets and several government enquiries, but where policy action has been less clear. In Chapter Five, Liz Richardson asks whether the government has given disadvantaged people a greater say over decisions affecting their lives. She looks at attempts to improve formal political participation, but also at changes that have affected both informal participation and social participation with a social benefit, such as community self-help activities.

Part Two focuses on groups at particular risk of social exclusion, or among whom poverty was especially high when Labour came to power. In Chapter Six, Ruth Lupton and Anne Power consider the government's attempts to regenerate poor neighbourhoods and ensure that "no-one ... [is] seriously disadvantaged by where they live" (SEU, 2001, p 8). In Chapter Seven, Kitty Stewart looks at policy towards child poverty and child deprivation. She asks whether the government is on track to meet its first child poverty target before going on to consider the impact on disadvantaged children of the government's early years policies.

Chapter Eight turns to the other end of the age spectrum, examining policy affecting poverty and social exclusion among older people. Jane Falkingham and Maria Evandrou look in turn at policies affecting each of the priorities for older people outlined in OFA. In Chapter Nine, Coretta Phillips examines Labour's strategies to reduce ethnic inequalities. She argues that there have been few initiatives directed specifically at minority ethnic groups; rather, broader policies aimed at reducing disadvantage in general have been expected to lift minority groups with them. She assesses the impact of this approach on long-standing inequalities in education, employment and policing. Chapter Ten turns to the role of the Social Exclusion Unit (SEU). Tania Burchardt considers the success of the SEU in coordinating better responses to the problems of a number of disparate vulnerable groups, including truants, teenage parents and rough sleepers. But she also notes that not all vulnerable groups have been targeted by the SEU. For one set of people in particular, asylum seekers, policy has been actively exclusionary; the chapter traces developments under New Labour for this group.

Part Three contains chapters that take a step back from individual policy areas to examine the combined impact of policy or to provide a wider perspective. In Chapter Eleven, Tom Sefton and Holly Sutherland look at changes in overall poverty and income inequality. Chapters Twelve and Thirteen, in very different ways, each give a more detailed insight into what policy changes have meant in reality for families with children. In Chapter Twelve, Paul Gregg, Jane Waldfogel and Elizabeth Washbrook use recently available expenditure data to examine how increases in family income resulting from tax–benefit and employment changes have affected household spending patterns. For instance, have low-income families been able to increase their spending on items likely to promote children's health, learning and development (fruit and vegetables, toys and books)?

Chapter Thirteen, by Anne Power and Helen Willmot, presents results from a CASE study which has tracked 200 families in four deprived areas since 1999.

This chapter is rather different to most of the rest of the book in presenting qualitative findings. It offers a unique opportunity to see how reforms are viewed on the ground: respondents (mostly mothers) explain in their own words whether and how they have been affected by recent policy changes in the areas of employment, education, neighbourhood renewal and community empowerment.

The last chapter in Part Three (Chapter Fourteen) provides an international perspective: Kitty Stewart looks at how levels of poverty and inequality in the UK now compare to those in other industrialised countries, and at the factors that might explain remaining differences.

In Chapter Fifteen, we pull together the threads of the book with the aim of reaching an overall assessment of the government's record. Does the evidence of the previous chapters add up to a substantial assault on the levels of poverty, inequality and social exclusion inherited in 1997? As this becomes the first Labour government in history to complete a full second term in office, how much of a difference can it be said to have made?

Finally, a word on devolution. One of the most significant reforms of Labour's first term was constitutional, with separate assemblies and greater powers over a number of areas of domestic policy for Scotland and Wales. With the Northern Ireland experience included, there are therefore three or four variants across the UK for many of the policies discussed in this book. In some cases, this means little more than different names and details for policies moving largely in the same direction, but in other cases the differences are of more substance. The volume is unable to do full justice to the wide variety of experience, and discussion is often confined to the situation in England, but chapters aim to draw attention to the most significant policy differences, particularly where these appear to have led to differences in outcomes.

## Note

[1] In both cases, the poverty line is 60% of the equivalised contemporary median, and both are given for a Before Housing Costs income measure. After Housing Costs, child poverty was 34% in 1996/97 and pensioner poverty 27%.

# Part One:
# Aspects of exclusion

# Employment: tackling poverty through 'work for those who can'

*Abigail McKnight*

## Introduction

Labour's strong focus on employment is rooted firmly at the historical heart of the party. Full employment is still clearly an aspiration. However, New Labour's approach to employment policy represents a departure from previous Labour governments: both the approach to achieving full employment and arguably the motivation have changed. After the high levels of unemployment in the 1980s and early 1990s recessions, Labour was cautious about pledging a commitment to full employment. However, shortly after Labour came to power, a new definition was put forward. In a speech launching his first pre-budget report in November 1997, Chancellor Gordon Brown stated that:

> We need a new approach – Employment Opportunity for All – to face the challenges of today's dynamic labour market, creating a modern definition of full employment for the 21st century. (HM Treasury, 1997)

The emphasis, therefore, shifted from employment for all to employment *opportunity* for all.

Brown identified five vital elements needed to meet the new challenge:

- a framework for macroeconomic stability;
- a flexible and adaptable labour market, underpinned by minimum standards;
- skilled and adaptable people;
- policies which encourage people to move from welfare to work; and
- a tax and benefit system that makes work pay.

One of the main departures is the greater emphasis on supply-side policies; for example, helping people become more employable, search for work, equip themselves with marketable skills, provision of financial incentives to seek and remain in work and more conditions placed on many out-of-work benefits with greater coercion to find work. In the past, Labour placed more emphasis on demand-side policies, viewing unemployment as a problem of lack of demand which could be stimulated through a variety of policies. Indeed, as we shall see, Labour adopted and strengthened many of the supply-side policies developed and introduced by previous Conservative governments.

In this chapter, we examine the progress of Labour's Employment Opportunity for All agenda, identifying areas where New Labour's approach diverges from previous approaches, and we assess the appropriateness of Labour's emphasis on employment in its bid to reduce poverty. After outlining Labour's inheritance, we assess Labour's performance by first looking at macroeconomic trends in the labour market before turning to specific groups.

## Background and Labour's inheritance

Most individuals and families rely on earnings from employment to provide them with an independent income; income-poor families are often work-poor families. Therefore, it is not surprising that Labour put employment policy at the heart of its (undeclared) 'War on Poverty'. Where reduction in poverty is a key policy objective, tackling the overlap between poverty and worklessness poses one of the greatest policy challenges.

While a whole raft of policies can be introduced to reduce levels of worklessness, it is inevitable that some individuals (usually the most disadvantaged) will experience periods of non-employment and for others work is simply not an option (either in the short term and sometimes in the long term). Through the safety net objective of the UK welfare state, these individuals (and, where applicable, their dependants) are provided with an income through social security benefits. The challenge is to provide sufficient out-of-work income for people in need without creating a disincentive to seek and remain in work, where work is an option. As many individuals have very low earnings potential, there can end up being very little difference between in- and out-of-work income where benefit incomes are high enough to keep workless individuals and families above a relative income poverty line (this is even harder where inequality of earnings and incomes is high). Chapter Fourteen of this volume shows the relationship between Income Support entitlements and the poverty line for different family types.

The incentive to find and remain in work can be improved through supplementing the in-work incomes of individuals with low earnings potential and the qualification rules for receipt of out-of-work benefits can be tightly defined and systematically monitored and enforced (assessments of ability to work and, where appropriate, active search for work). These challenges and the policy responses are not new and New Labour's response built on existing initiatives (discussed later in this chapter).

The association between worklessness and poverty among working-age adults is shown in Figure 2.1. These data cover 1996/97 and represent the situation when Labour came to power. It is clear that working-age adults with children are at greater risk of living in poverty (less than 60% median contemporary equivalised income) than those without children and after housing cost measures record a greater risk of poverty than before housing cost measures. A larger share of households with no adult in work is in poverty. The highest share is in households where the head or spouse is unemployed, irrespective of family type. However, it is also apparent that work does not always protect a household from poverty, particularly when there is no adult in full-time work. Clearly work will not be enough to alleviate relative income poverty in all households unless income from work increases.

When New Labour came to power, the economy was recovering from the early 1990s' recession. The party inherited an improving labour market and strong macroeconomic environment. The economy was growing, unemployment was falling and the workforce was becoming more skilled. However, all was not rosy. Earnings inequality and income inequality were high and rising, unemployment and economic inactivity were still high, general job insecurity and deteriorating job quality for the low skilled in particular were problematic, work was increasingly polarised across households, inactivity rates among older men were high and rising (see, Gregg and Wadsworth, 1999).

The Conservative government's onslaught on the trade unions and the continuing shift away from manufacturing to services saw a decline in union density – from around 50% in 1979 to 35% in 1989 and 27% in 1997 (ONS, 1999; DTI, 2004). There was further erosion in employment protection of low-skilled workers as a result of the decline and final abolition of the Wages Councils in 1993; which had set minimum wage rates in a selection of industries. There were also major reforms to the administration of unemployment benefits. There

**Figure 2.1: Percentage of working-age adults living in poor households by economic status (1996/97)**

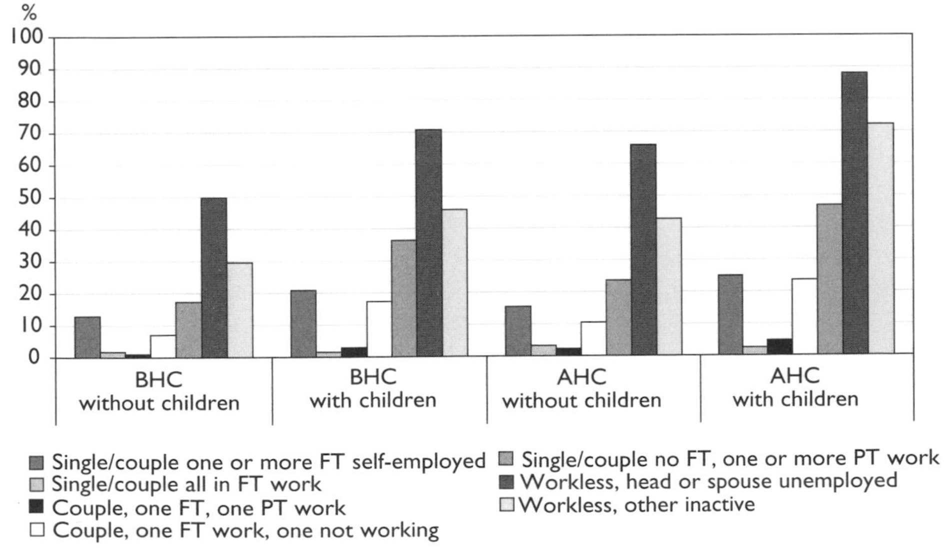

Source: DWP (2004a)

became a growing division between the 'active' (claiming unemployment benefit) and the 'inactive' (claiming Income Support and Incapacity Benefit). The inactive did not count as part of the unemployed and were not offered any assistance to find work. A major reform of unemployment benefit was introduced in 1996 with the introduction of Jobseeker's Allowance (discussed later in this chapter).

Overall, the economy seemed trapped in a cycle of boom and bust and this undoubtedly led to higher levels of insecurity which have a negative effect on employers' investment decisions (in physical and human capital) and on individuals' well-being. There were fears that Labour would be weak on economic management and through high levels of spending would once again take the economy into a recession.

## Policies

This section outlines some of the labour market policies which Labour introduced, focusing on those which are targeted at the most disadvantaged. While the independence of the Bank of England and, with it, monetary policy through the setting of interest rates to meet inflation targets has been important, this was not targeted specifically on the labour market. Responsible fiscal policy is also clearly important. Undoubtedly monetary and fiscal policy have a significant impact on the macroeconomy and therefore on employment. These will not be covered specifically in this chapter but their effects will have influenced the labour market outcomes discussed later in this chapter.

Probably the largest employment policy initiatives undertaken by New Labour have been changes to the administration of welfare benefits and investment in welfare-to-work programmes. During the first two years following election success in 1997, Labour stuck to Conservative spending plans but levied a windfall tax on the privatised utilities, the proceeds from which were spent on the New Deal (£5.2 billion). They have continued to invest in the programme and it has now become an integral part of the system. The New Deal programmes (the main ones covering lone parents, young people of 18 to 24 years, long-term unemployed aged 25+ and disabled people) are based on personalised support provided by Personal Advisers in Jobcentres who help benefit claimants with job search and work preparation. The programmes vary for different claimant groups and in some cases are compulsory (young people and adult long-term unemployed) and very structured while others are voluntary (lone parents and disabled people). More detail on specific New Deal programmes is provided in later sections of this chapter. Under the New Deal, unemployed benefit claimants have more conditionality and scrutiny in terms of meeting their work search eligibility criteria and more assistance with finding work than at any other time. In addition, for the first time, individuals claiming out-of-work benefits for which receipt is not conditional on actively seeking work, were given help with searching for and preparing for work (lone parents on Income Support and disabled people on Incapacity Benefit). There has been a further evolution of support and administration of benefits for those not in work. All benefit claimants are now required to attend Work Focused Interviews (WFIs), although active search for work is still not required for all benefit claimants, such as lone parents on Income Support. In addition, the Benefits Agency (who administered claims for benefits) and the Employment Service (who provided assistance to job seekers and monitored unemployment benefits claimants' search for work) are gradually being merged to form Jobcentre Plus (to be completed by 2006).

While dependent partners of unemployed benefit claimants had previously been ignored, two policies have specifically targeted this group. The New Deal for Partners was introduced in 1999 on a voluntary basis and offers, through Personal Advisers, assistance in the preparation and search for work. From 2001 childless couples (some age restrictions apply) making a joint claim for unemployment benefit are both required to meet the associated employment conditions and are both offered assistance. Since April 2004, both partners of relevant benefit claimants are required to attend a WFI after six months of receiving benefit.

Labour introduced a number of measures to increase the financial incentives to find and remain in work for individuals with low earning power. For the first time, albeit at a low level, a National Minimum Wage was introduced in April 1999. A number of changes were made to income tax and National Insurance rates and schedules to reduce the tax burden on low-wage workers, allowing them to keep a higher share of their earnings. Some changes also reduced the tax burden on employers of low-wage workers which softened the impact of the National Minimum Wage. The pre-existing system of in-work benefits has been made more generous and extended to new groups. In 1999, the more generous Working Families Tax Credit (WFTC) replaced Family Credit for working families and the Disabled Persons Tax Credit replaced Disability Working Allowance for working disabled people on low incomes. In April 2003, WFTC was divided into two elements: the 'working element', Working Tax Credit (WTC), and the 'child element', Child Tax Credit (CTC). Eligibility to WTC was extended to singles and couples without children and CTC was made more generous and paid to working and non-working main carers of children. Where applicable a childcare element was made available to working families with children. Additional credits were also introduced for working disabled people and persons aged 50+ years of age returning to work after claiming benefit for at least six months. The impacts of these changes on income distributions are examined in Chapter Eleven of this volume.

## Employment: a macroeconomic success story?

It is easy to get lost in a sea of statistics: the picture can be complex and political parties naturally highlight statistics which cast the most favourable light on their performance. For example, unemployment rates based on entitlement to unemployment benefit can be affected (or even manipulated) by changes in eligibility for such benefits. Changes made by the Conservative government reduced the number of out-of-work people who qualified for the benefits used in the claimant count measure of unemployment. Equally, Labour's active labour market programmes affect the record of 'continuous spells' of unemployment for those who cycle through the New Deal programmes, which affects both the claimant count and measures of long-term unemployment. While a whole series of statistics could be examined, we shall concentrate on unemployment, inactivity and jobs. These three series in combination overcome the deficiencies in any one series examined in isolation and present a more complete picture of changes in the labour market.

It would be difficult to refute the claim that employment has been one of Labour's big success stories. In May 2004, registered unemployment reached a 30-year low. Figure 2.2 shows the unemployment rate measured in terms of individuals claiming unemployment related benefit. While this is not the government's preferred measure of unemployment (they favour the International Labour Organization [ILO] measure[1]), it has the advantage of being available over a longer historical period. The two severe recessions presided over by the Conservative governments of Thatcher and Major are clearly evident. Under Labour, claimant unemployment in spring 2004 had fallen to a rate not seen since before autumn 1975. While the fall in unemployment had started well

**Figure 2.2: UK unemployment rates – based on unemployment benefit receipt and ILO definitions**

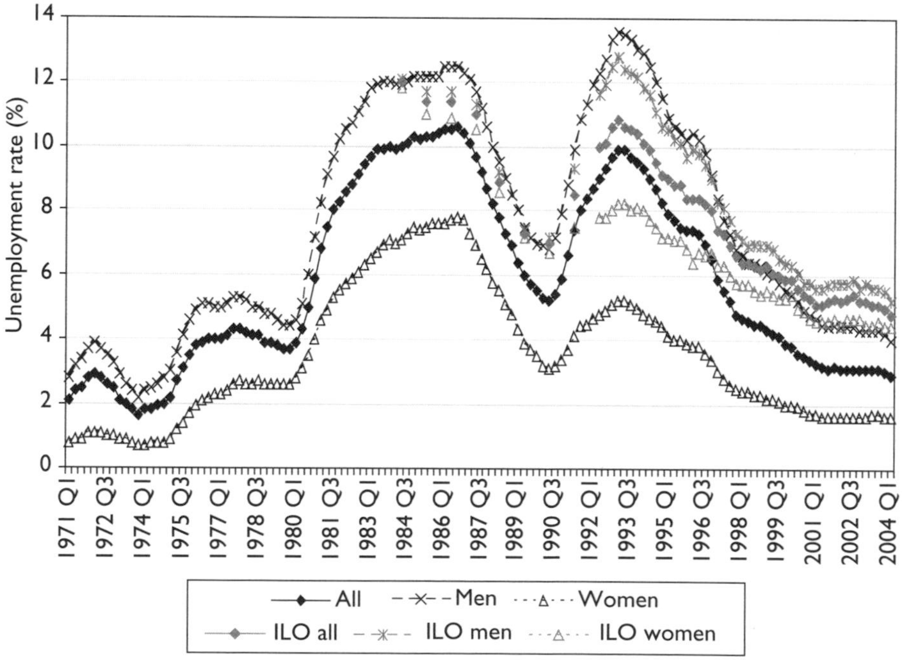

*Source:* National Statistics (www.statistics/statbase/tsdlistfiles.asp)

before May 1997, it is hard to argue that the sustained fall cannot be, at least partly, attributed to Labour's management of the economy and labour market policies. In fact, unemployment continued to fall through the turning points of the previous two pre-Labour recessions. In Autumn 1997, unemployment broke through the turning point into the early 1990s' recession (5.2%) and in spring 2002 it continued falling beyond the turning point into the 1980s' recession (3.7%). In addition to the overall unemployment rate, Figure 2.2 shows the separate rates for men and women. The fact that the registered unemployment rate for women is below that for men in the UK is well known; it is interesting, however, to note the much greater impact of the early 1990s' recession on men.

Contrasts between the claimant count measure of unemployment and the ILO measure reveal some interesting findings. For women, the ILO measure identifies a much higher rate of unemployment than the claimant measure. This is likely to be driven by their ineligibility for unemployment benefit either because they have not built up sufficient entitlement through National Insurance contributions or because their entitlement to benefit is through their partners' entitlement. In addition, lone parents with dependent children usually qualify for Income Support; therefore, this group of women do not appear in the claimant count. After a divergence in ILO unemployment rates between men and women during the early 1990s' recession, the rates have once again converged.

Since May 1997, it does appear that there has been a divergence between the claimant and ILO measures of unemployment. The ILO measures of unemployment have not fallen nearly as much as claimant unemployment, which suggests that around two percentage points of the ILO unemployed are not entitled to unemployment benefit. Whether this is because of changes in the eligibility rules for benefit, a higher proportion of the unemployed claiming benefits which are not included in the count (for example, because they receive Income Support or Incapacity Benefit) or because they do not have contribution based entitlements and are living in higher income households, is not clear. For the first time since both series have been available from the early 1980s, all ILO unemployment rates are above the claimant count unemployment rate for men.

Over the years, under both Conservative and Labour governments, there has been concern that unemployment statistics (claimant-defined and ILO-defined) mask the true extent of joblessness in the UK economy. In Figure 2.3, we show the jobless and inactivity rates since 1984 covering part of Thatcher's government, Major's government and part of Blair's government. The jobless rate is defined as the share of the working-age population who are not in work. The inactivity rate represents the share of the working-age population who are not in work or unemployed and searching for work according to the ILO definition. The difference between the jobless and inactivity series represents the share of economically active men and women who are unemployed and seeking work under the ILO definition. There is no evident break in the trends following Labour's election with all series continuing in the direction that began after the 1990s' recession under the John Major government. Jobless and economic

**Figure 2.3: Joblessness and economic inactivity in the UK (% of working-age population)**

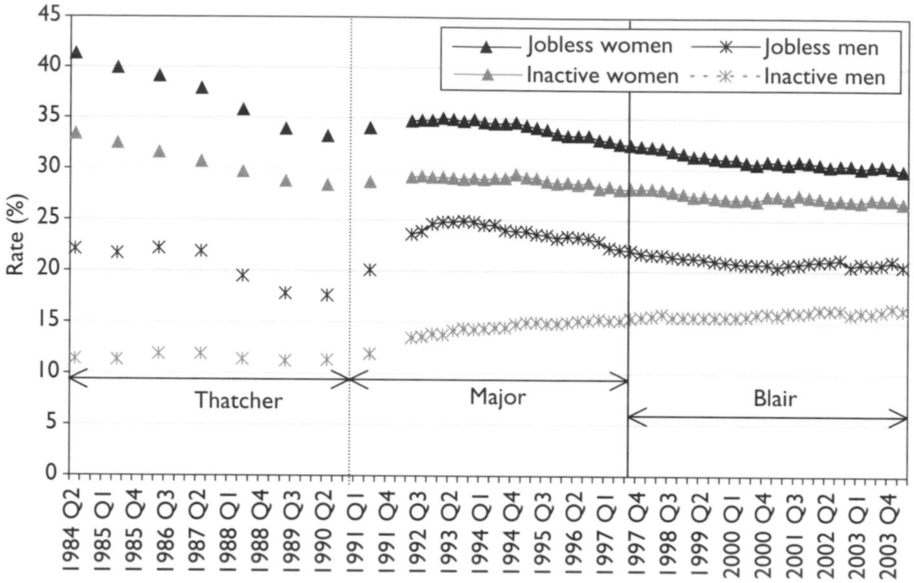

Source: National Statistics (www.statistics/statbase/tsdlistfiles.asp)

inactivity rates are higher among women than men reflecting the higher rates of women's activity in child raising. However, there has been a convergence in inactivity rates between men and women with women's inactivity rates falling and men's inactivity rates rising. Over this 20-year period female economic inactivity rates fell by around seven percentage points while male economic inactivity rates increased by five percentage points. The increase in male inactivity rates could be partly explained by increased staying-on rates in post-compulsory schooling and further and higher education and early retirement from the labour market, but prime-age men (25 to 54) in the bottom skill quartile make up the majority of the increase for this group and a much larger share of the inactive now report a limiting health problem than in the 1970s (Faggio and Nickell, 2003). Overall this means that the fall in the unemployment rate is less impressive when the increase in inactivity is taken into account.

Figure 2.4 takes a slightly different perspective, showing the number of workforce jobs in the UK over a longer time period going back to the beginning of the 1960s. These statistics are based on a job count and are not adjusted for hours of work. The number of jobs in the UK grew by around five million over this 45-year period, but the number of jobs held by men changed very little. Over the Conservative years (1979-97), the number of jobs held by men fell by over one million. Even with the growth of the late 1980s' boom, the number of jobs held by men never fully recovered from the 1980s' and early 1990s' recessions. Under the Labour government since 1997, the number of jobs held by men has recovered,

**Figure 2.4: Total workforce jobs**

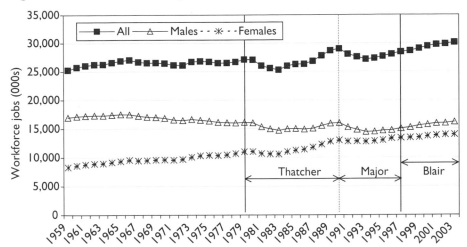

*Source:* National Statistics (www.statistics/statbase/tsdlistfiles.asp)

increasing by just over one million. The big growth in jobs over this period is accounted for by the growth of jobs held by women and, even though many of these women will be in part-time jobs, it still represents a significant increase – 2.4 million between 1979 and 1997, and a further 0.6 million since then.

## Specific groups

So far we have examined changes over time in aggregate employment trends which, with the exception of inactivity rates among men, appear to be largely positive. However, these aggregate trends can mask changing fortunes for different groups of individuals. Non-employment, poverty and labour market disadvantage are not randomly distributed across the population so in this section we look behind the aggregate trends to assess how different groups have fared since 1997. Specific policies and programmes have been targeted at particularly disadvantaged groups and we will to a large extent follow these groupings in the assessment that follows. For example, we look at young people, the long-term unemployed, lone parents, disabled people and older workers.

### Young people

High unemployment rates among young people were a major concern when Labour came to power in 1997. There was discussion of a serious collapse in the youth labour market as high quality alternative routes into employment largely disappeared over the 1980s and 1990s. The apprenticeship system, which was mainly associated with the manufacturing sector and the trades, gave way to poorer quality government-funded youth training programmes[2] which were much shorter in duration (one or two years compared with five years). Some attempt to return to the higher quality apprenticeship system had been tried under the Major government through the Modern Apprenticeship system introduced nationally in 1995. Young people under the age of 18 were not usually entitled to unemployment benefit but had a guaranteed place on a training scheme. Eighteen to twenty-four year olds were entitled to unemployment benefit, the entitlement rules for which were considerably tightened when Jobseeker's Allowance (JSA) replaced Unemployment Benefit and Income Support in October 1996.

In 1997, Labour pledged to reduce the number of young unemployed people by 250,000. It introduced the New Deal for Young People (NDYP) in April 1998, which is by far the most structured and well funded of all the New Deal programmes and is compulsory for 18- to 24-year-olds who have been unemployed and claiming JSA for six months[3]. Unemployed young people entering the programme are assessed and given a tailored package of support through a Personal Adviser (PA) for the first three months (maximum of four months). This is known as the Gateway period. If, at the end of this period, they are still unemployed, they are required to take up one of four options (remaining solely on JSA is not an option). The options are:

• full-time education or training for up to 12 months;
• a six month job in the voluntary sector;
• a job on the Environmental Task Force; or
• a subsidised job which must include at least one day a week of training.

Benefit sanctions apply to those who do not comply with the programme. The programme was seen not simply as a welfare-to-work programme but as an investment programme that would lead to improved longer-term outcomes for these young people.

An extensive evaluation of NDYP has been undertaken both of a pilot programme and the national programme, funded by the Department for Work and Pensions and undertaken independently by academics (see, for example, Blundell et al, 2001; Riley and Young, 2001a, 2001b; Van Reenen, 2004). Youth unemployment fell fairly rapidly over the recovery to the extent that the client group was greatly diminished in size even between the inception and introduction of NDYP. This meant that it was easy to exaggerate the estimates of young people helped by NDYP as many of the young people who found work during the Gateway period would have done so anyway, but also meant the programme faced a greater challenge as the young people who remained on the programme for longer were arguably more disadvantaged. The best estimate suggests that NDYP raises employment by about 17,000 a year (Van Reenan, 2004). Unemployment among the target group has fallen but many of the young people have taken up the education and training option (which clearly could have much longer-term beneficial effects on labour market outcomes) so the employment to population ratio among 18- to 24-year-old men with low levels of qualifications has not increased (Blundell et al, 2003). Blundell et al (2003) conclude that NDYP has led to modest improvements in employment, and the social cost per job is outweighed by the social benefit.

Other policies affecting young people include the National Minimum Wage (NMW) introduced in April 1999 (although workers under 18 are not currently covered[4] and 18- to 21-year-olds are only entitled to a lower rate). Assessments of the impact of the NMW suggest that it did not result in the much-feared job losses or lead to substitution of 18- to 21-year-olds with 16- to 17-year-olds (LPC, 2000, 2004). As many young people are in low-wage employment, they appear to have benefited from wage gains from the NMW without job loss. Other policies have largely sought to increase the incentive for young people to remain in education (arguably the NMW exemption of 16- to 17-year-olds also fits into this category), such as the financial assistance provided through the Education Maintenance Allowance (to be introduced in September 2004) and changes to the post–16 curriculum (see Chapter Three of this volume).

While a number of statistics could be explored to assess the changes in the youth labour market since 1997 we focus here on the change in unemployment (using the ILO definition). Unemployment among economically active 18- to 24-year-olds started falling at the beginning of 1993 (from a peak of 18%) and continued falling after Labour came to power and after the introduction of NDYP, but since autumn 2000 has remained static at around 10% (twice the rate for all working-age people in winter 2003) (Figure 2.5). Economically active 16- to

**Figure 2.5: Trends in ILO unemployment rates for younger workers**

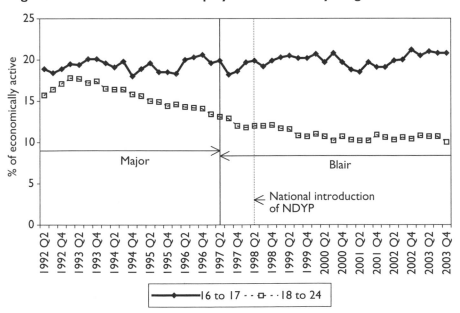

*Source:* Labour Force Survey, National Statistics (www.statistics/statbase/tsdlistfiles.asp)

17-year-olds have not fared so well. As noted earlier in this chapter, this group is not usually entitled to unemployment-related benefit and does not qualify for any active labour market programmes. The unemployment rate for 16- to 17-year-olds has actually increased over the recovery from the early 1990s' recession and has marginally increased since 1997 (from 20% to 21%).

Young people have benefited from the NDYP and some have benefited from the NMW. However, although fewer 16- to 17-year-olds are economically active as more are staying on in full-time education, those that are active have not benefited from the economic recovery and have so far been left behind in terms of active labour market programmes[5]. For these young people, who are likely to be some of the most disadvantaged, we could well be storing up trouble for the future.

## Long-term unemployed

Long-term unemployment is clearly more of a problem than short-term unemployment. It can indicate problems around employability and lack of demand. There is now a wealth of research that suggests that the longer people remain unemployed the harder it is for them to return to work (see, for example, Narendranathan and Stewart, 1993; Arulampalam et al, 2000). Long-term unemployment is clearly detrimental for the individuals concerned and for the economy. Long-term unemployment became a feature of the UK labour market in the 1980s and a number of specific programmes have been introduced over the years. Some of the policies have reduced entitlement to unemployment benefit – such as the reduction in entitlement to contribution based benefit from 12 to six months introduced by the Conservative government as part of the introduction of JSA in 1996. The frequency and amount of contact required as part of entitlement to unemployment benefit has also changed over time, with the onus on checking claimants' efforts to find work and assistance with job search and preparation for work. The most notable changes under the Conservative government were the introduction of Restart Interviews in 1988, which take place every 13 to 26 weeks[6] with employment advisers at Jobcentres to review job search activities and the stricter work search criteria associated with JSA (see Smith et al, 2000, for evaluation evidence on the impact of JSA). Even with all of these efforts, the share of unemployed people unemployed for 12 months or longer remained high and when New Labour came to power in 1997 over 40% of the unemployed had been unemployed for 12 months or longer (Figure 2.6).

The New Deal for 25 plus (ND25plus) was introduced nationally in June 1998. (A so-called re-engineered version of ND25plus was introduced in April 2001.) As with all the New Deal programmes, it has evolved over time, but the basic core model remains a tailored programme of work search assistance and preparation for work. Unemployed people claiming JSA for 18 months (reduced from 24 months in April 2001) or longer qualify for the programme and, from April 2001, those who have been unemployed for 18 of the last 24 months also qualify. The New Deal for 25 plus is similar in design to NDYP, but at the end of a Gateway period they enter a mandatory Intensive Activity Period (up to six months) where they are offered a tailored package of support and/or 6 months' subsidised employment, and, exceptionally, 12 months' education/training while remaining on JSA.

In response to the recognition of the difficulties associated with helping the long-term unemployed back into work and the need to innovate, the government introduced a set of Employment Zones (EZs). The first set of contracts for EZs were awarded in 2000 in parts of the country characterised by persistently high levels of long-term unemployment. The welfare-to-work programmes for the relevant client groups in the Zones are run by private sector organisations, some voluntary sector organisations and sometimes in partnership with Jobcentre Plus. New contracts for EZs took effect from Spring 2004. In the first round, EZs were focused solely on long-term unemployed benefit claimants aged 25+. In the EZs, it is compulsory for these benefit claimants to attend the welfare-to-work programme offered by the contractor rather than ND25plus. The contractors are given an allowance per client (the Personal Job Account) based on their benefit entitlement plus funds that would have been made available through ND25plus, work-based training for adults and a number of other smaller funds. Apart from paying the client an allowance at least equivalent to their benefit entitlement while they are out of work, the contractor has no further restrictions on how the money should be spent. Evidence from an evaluation of the first round of EZs suggests that they have been successful in helping some groups into work. Outflows from unemployment increased by a little over one percentage point and participants were less likely to return to unemployment than their counterparts in a set of comparison areas. The impact of the EZs was strongest in the first year of operation with only weak evidence in the second and third years (Hasluck et al, 2003). The decline in the effectiveness of EZs over time may be a problem associated with short-term contracts given to the providers or a larger effect at the start of the programme as those easiest to help are selected first by the contractors. There definitely seemed to be a problem with contractors classifying eligible benefit claimants into 'employable' and 'unemployable' with much more focus and resources being spent on the 'employable' group (Hirst et al, 2002). A comparison between EZs and ND25plus based on the aggregate flows[7] into work also suggests that EZs have poorer outcomes for disabled people, but better for people aged 49+ and ethnic minorities (TUC, 2003).

In the second round of EZs, eligibility is being extended to lone parents (on a voluntary basis) and 18- to 24-year-olds who have already participated at least once in NDYP (their participation in EZs is mandatory).

Figure 2.6 shows the increase in the share of unemployed who had been unemployed for 12 months or more over the early 1990s' recession before falling. However, the share had already started to fall before Labour came to power in 1997. The greatest percentage point drop (ten) occurred in the year between Labour winning the election and the introduction of ND25plus in June 1998. A

**Figure 2.6: Share of unemployed 25- to 49-year-olds who have been unemployed for 12 months or longer**

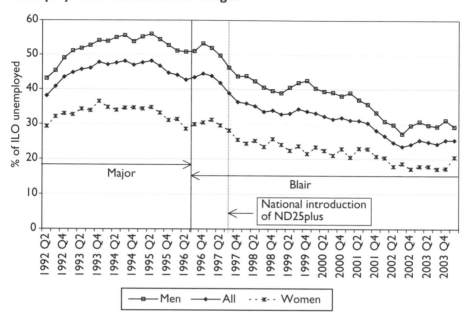

Source: Labour Force Survey, National Statistics (www.statistics/statbase/tsdlistfiles.asp)

further 10 percentage point drop occurred between Summer 1998 and Spring 2002, but since then the share has remained static at around 25%.

## Lone parents

Lone parents increasingly came under the policy spotlight over the 1980s and 1990s as their numbers increased and their attachment to the labour market fell, leading to an increase in the number of children living in workless households and, by association, growing up in poverty. The number of lone parent families increased from around 0.5 million in the early 1970s to one million in the early 1980s and 1.5 million in 1997 (Holtermann et al, 1999). This represented an increase in the share of all families headed by a lone parent from 13% in the early 1980s to around 25% in 1997. In 2000, employment rates among UK lone parents were one of the lowest among OECD countries (see Chapter Fourteen of this volume) and the gap between employment rates of married and lone mothers is one of the highest (OECD, 2001a). This had not always been the case. In 1979, married mothers and lone parents had similar employment rates (at around 50%), but increases in employment among married mothers (70% in 2003) have not been matched by lone parents (53% in 2003). Employment rates among lone parents actually fell between 1979 and the early 1990s; since then, they have increased (Gregg and Harkness, 2003). A complex set of factors underline this divergence, some of which is due to changes in the composition and characteristics of lone parent families. There are probably three main reasons why lone parents have lower employment rates than married mothers. First, they are most usually the sole carer of their children. Second, on average, they are more disadvantaged, have lower levels of education and face greater barriers to employment. Third, they face the difficulty of earning enough (particularly given the first two points) to better their out-of-work benefit income. Married mothers are often the second earner in a household and, on average, face fewer barriers to work.

The number of lone parent families dependent on Income Support increased steadily from the early 1970s reaching around one million in 1996. Since then, there has been a fall associated with the increase in employment. All of these factors contributed to the higher rates of poverty among lone parent families (see Chapters Seven and Fourteen in this volume).

The Conservative government tried to tackle the poverty trap associated with the difficulty of bettering out-of-work benefit income through employment income. They replaced the in-work income supplement which had been in existence since 1971 (Family Income Supplement) with the more generous Family Credit in 1988 and reduced the minimum qualifying hours of work from 24 per week to 16 in 1992 (for more details see, Ford and Millar, 1998). They were also in the process of developing a pilot programme designed to give dedicated employment assistance to lone parents when they lost the general election in 1997.

New Labour set two targets which directly affected lone parents. The first was to raise employment rates among lone parents to 70% by 2010. The second was to eliminate child poverty by 2020 (with interim targets to reduce child poverty by a quarter by 2004/5 and a half by 2010/11; see Chapter Seven of this volume). They have tackled the low employment and high poverty rates among lone parents in a number of ways. In 1998, they introduced the New Deal for Lone Parents (NDLP), a voluntary employment programme which is now available to all non-employed lone parents and those working less than 16 hours per week[8]. It is now run by Jobcentre Plus and delivered through PAs. Under NDLP, lone parents are offered a package of support around preparation for work, assistance with work search, training, childcare, application for tax credits and in-work benefits designed to help them find employment for at least 16 hours per week[9]. There are no opportunities for subsidised employment under NDLP and overall the programme is run at a much lower cost than NDYP or ND25plus. While participation in NDLP has remained voluntary, since 2001 lone parents have been required to attend WFIs (PA meetings) at the start of a claim for Income Support and, since October 2002, every six months throughout the duration of a claim.

To help remove some of the barriers to work, the government has put in place a National Childcare Strategy and increased coverage of nursery places for pre-school-age children. Lone parents living in poor areas have also benefited from childcare places made available under the Neighbourhood Nurseries Initiative and through the expansion of 'wrap-around' care to fit around the school day and in the school holidays, although both remain insufficient (see Chapter Seven of this volume).

To improve the financial incentive to find and remain in work, and reduce in-work poverty, the introduction of WFTC and then WTC/CTC particularly benefited lone parents (see Chapters Seven and Eleven). Low-paid lone parents will also have benefited from the introduction of the NMW in April 1999 and from lower taxes due to changes in the income tax and National Insurance schedules and rates.

Right from the start, NDLP was received positively by lone parents. Results from the evaluation of a prototype programme, which ran between July 1997 and October 1998, showed that NDLP had a positive effect on moving lone parents off Income Support. It was estimated that six months after joining NDLP, the stock of eligible lone parents claiming Income Support was reduced by 1.5%, and flows off Income Support were increased by 15% (McKnight, 2000). The New Deal for Lone Parents was rolled out nationally from April 1998. Current evaluation evidence from the national programme suggests that nine months after joining NDLP approximately 26% of lone parent participants left Income Support who would not have done so otherwise (24% into jobs). The New Deal for Lone Parents approximately doubles employment chances of participants (Lessof et al, 2003), although this estimate appears high given other evidence and may be revised in the future. This evidence suggests that overall 1.1% of the eligible population of lone parents left Income Support due to NDLP. The much smaller overall effect on the eligible Income Support population in contrast to the impact on participants highlights the fact that only a minority of eligible lone parents on Income Support participate in NDLP (approximately 10%) (Lessof et al, 2003). The introduction of compulsory WFIs has led to an increase in participation in NDLP (Evans et al, 2003), but it is not clear to what extent increasing participation in the programme (perhaps through compulsion) will have a detrimental impact on its effectiveness. Outcomes for lone parents entering NDLP from a PA meeting/WFI are lower, but this is not surprising as these lone parents are likely to be less work ready.

The introduction of the NMW in April 1999 appears to have been met with little impact on jobs (Dickens and Manning, 2003). As many lone parents are employed in low-wage jobs, they are likely to have been significant beneficiaries, although the extent to which higher wages lead to higher net incomes depends on adjustments to in-work income supplements and housing benefit, among other things.

Gregg and Harkness (2003) assess the overall effectiveness of the full range of policies in raising employment rates among lone parents between 1998 and 2002. By assessing the counterfactual using a number of comparison groups they estimate that employment rates among lone parents are approximately five percentage points higher then they would have been in the absence of New Labour policies. Actual employment rates among lone parents increased by 6.6 percentage points over this period. However, these types of estimates are fraught with difficulty as they rely on finding a suitable comparison group. By using their comparison groups (single women without children and women in couples with children), they assume that there would be virtually no growth in employment rates (1.6 percentage points) among lone parents over this period because of the limited growth among their comparison groups. However, their comparison groups had much higher initial employment rates and therefore relatively less room for further increases. In addition, given the upward trajectory in lone parents' employment rates in the first half of the 1990s, it would seem unlikely that this would have stopped in 1997.

Figure 2.7 shows the increase in lone parents' employment rates between 1992 and 2003 and the projected required annual increases between 2004 and 2010 if New Labour is to meet its 70% target. The government is clearly faced with a considerable challenge if it is to meet this target. It would require larger annual increases in lone parent employment rates than they have managed to achieve since 1997. At this stage, it is not clear what significant policy initiatives could lead to such large increases in employment among lone parents, although other countries do achieve such rates (see Chapter Fourteen of this volume).

**Figure 2.7: Actual employment rates among lone parents (1992-2003) and projected required increases to meet the 2010 target of 70%**

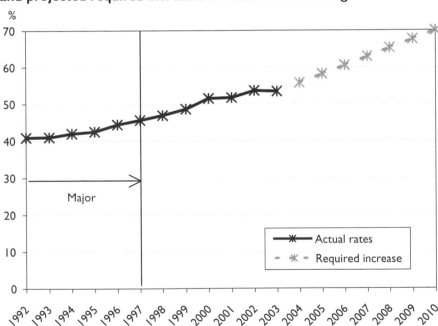

*Source:* Lone parent employment rates 1992-2003, Spring Quarter Labour Force Survey, adapted from *Employment opportunity for all,* 2003

## Disabled people

Over the last 20 to 30 years, we have seen some major changes occurring among long-term sick and disabled people. Findings vary a little depending on the data source and the definition of limiting illness and disability used but three main trends seem to emerge. We have seen:

- increases in the share of the working-age population reporting a limiting health problem or a disability;
- increases in the share of the working-age population claiming a sickness- or disability-related benefit; and
- increases in the share of the working-age population with a limiting health problem or a disability who are economically inactive.

How much of the rise in disability among the working-age population is due to greater recognition and less stigma associated with disability and how much is due to a genuine increase is a hotly debated topic (Burchardt, 2000). Faced with these three 'facts', it is very easy to jump to uninformed conclusions. For example, it could be claimed that increases in long-term sickness and disability has meant increases in benefit dependency and inactivity among this group. However, alongside the increase in inactivity has been an increase in the share of disabled people who are in employment. This highlights the fact that explanations for the trends are much more complex than they might initially appear to be.

Disabled people face a number of disadvantages which contribute to a much higher than average probability of living in poverty. They are disadvantaged in the labour market because their earnings potential is reduced by lower than average levels of education and work experience, and in some cases the type of work they can undertake. Even when these factors are taken into account, disabled workers' wages are lower then non-disabled workers' (Burchardt, 2000). Most published figures also underestimate the share of disabled people living in poverty as the extra costs associated with their disabilities are rarely met through social security benefits (Zaidi and Burchardt, 2003).

When Labour came to power, there were a number of policy dilemmas. On the one hand, the growth in the disabled population along with the growth in public expenditure on disability-related benefits and concerns that disability status was being used as a means to early retirement and a cover for long-term unemployment suggested that the criteria used to assess eligibility for disability-related benefits needed to be reviewed and possibly tightened up. On the other hand, disabled people's needs were clearly not being met, and, for some at least, benefit income needed to be increased to avoid high levels of poverty, barriers to employment and discrimination in the labour market needed to be reduced and financial returns to work needed to be improved.

Labour's response has been to reform disability-related benefits (for details, see Burchardt, 1999), continue with the implementation and enforcement of the

1995 Disability Discrimination Act, introduce an active labour market programme designed for disabled people (the New Deal for Disabled People, or NDDP) and improve the financial incentives to work in the form of a tax credit.

It is still too early to tell the impact of the benefit reforms on the caseload as rights have been preserved for existing claimants, but they have received a mixed reception among disabled people and disability groups. Many have criticised the delays around implementing the 1995 Disability Discrimination Act (DDA) and the fact that the onus is still on disabled people to bring action on those who fail to comply with the act. In addition, most employment cases relate to unfair dismissal when arguably the major problem is recruitment where the DDA has little to contribute. The NDDP has not been a great success; indeed, the take-up of the pilot programme was only 3% (Loumidis et al, 2001) making it impossible to undertake any meaningful evaluation. Take-up rates of tax credits have been a great improvement on those of the income supplement they replaced (Disability Working Allowance), and no doubt have increased the income and work incentives for a number of disabled people. However, inactivity rates among disabled people remain high (44% of men aged 25 to 54 and 70% of men aged 55 to 64 with a limiting health problem or disability were economically inactive in 2002; Faggio and Nickell, 2003) and there remains a large unmet demand to work and unacceptably high rates of poverty among disabled people.

## Older workers

Between the mid-1970s and the mid-1990s, employment and economic activity rates among men aged 50+ fell (see also Chapter Eight of this volume on this subject). Employment rates fell from 84% in 1979 to 64% in 1993 for men aged 50 to 64 (Atkinson et al, 2003). This fall in the participation rate was not unique to the UK but experienced by many developed economies. The fall was greatest among older men aged 60 to 64 (Campbell, 1999). Labour-force participation rates among women aged 50+ remained fairly flat suggesting that the factors affecting increased participation rates among all women counterbalanced the forces leading to falling activity rates among older workers. However, participation rates among older women remain at a considerably lower level than among older men. The dramatic fall in participation rates among older men has attracted much attention but analysis has uncovered a complex picture without one single dominant factor explaining the observed trend. It would appear that the main contributory factors are a demand shift in favour of younger workers (which could be skill/technology driven), increased private pension coverage (although forces operate in both directions), institutional discrimination, the operation of the benefit system (particularly Incapacity Benefit for the long-term sick and disabled) and voluntary early retirement (Disney, 1999). Clearly these factors can interact, for example, firms wishing to shed workers can find it easiest to offer redundancy to older workers with pension provision. The 1980s' and early 1990s' recessions are also likely to have taken their toll on older workers made unemployed over these periods who find it particularly difficult to find work after prolonged periods of unemployment, with firms and individuals finding retraining less attractive as returns are lower than for younger workers. Older workers appear to have been disproportionately affected by the recession as they were more likely to be employed in the declining sectors. Loss of employment among older workers is not just likely to lead to lower contemporary income and greater reliance on benefit income, and by association greater dependency on tax receipts of younger workers, but there is also evidence that lack of employment among low-skilled men in their 50s is associated with low income and poverty in old age (Bardasi and Jenkins, 2002).

Around the mid-1990s, just before Labour came to power, the fortunes of older workers, particularly those in their 50s, appear to have improved. Employment rates among men and women aged 50 to 54 have steadily increased. By 2002, they had equalled the rates observed at the peak of the last economic cycle in 1990 for men and were seven percentage points higher for women. In fact, between these two points, employment rates have increased for women aged 55 to 59 and 60 to 64 and men aged 55 to 59 but decreased for men aged 60 to 64 (Disney and Hawkes, 2003). A little under two thirds of men aged 60 to 64 were not in employment in 2002.

New Labour has introduced a range of policies to improve employment rates among older workers. The New Deal 50plus (ND50plus) was introduced in Spring 2000. People aged 50+, and their dependent partners, who have been claiming a range of out-of-work benefits for six months or more, qualify for the programme[10]. Participation is voluntary, but those claiming JSA for 18 months or more are required to participate in ND50plus. The ND50plus offers advice and guidance on finding work through a New Deal PA and, if on a low income, an in-work income supplement. Prior to April 2003, ND50plus participants could qualify for Employment Credit which was paid for one year at a fixed rate (£60 for full-time workers and £40 for part-time workers). Since April 2003, older workers can qualify for the WTC and ND50plus participants can qualify for an additional over-50s element, which is withdrawn after a year. A Training Grant of up to £1,500 (£750 before April 2002) is also available for those in receipt of the income supplement.

While the income supplement increased the financial incentive to accept low-wage employment, there were fears that its time-limited nature would affect employment retention or lead to financial hardship once it had been withdrawn. We have not found any quantitative evidence of the impact of the supplement, but the qualitative evidence suggests that most remain in work and cope with the fall in income associated with its withdrawal by cutting back on expenditure or increasing income through working longer hours (Atkinson et al, 2003). Clearly the evidence needs to be treated cautiously as individuals self-select onto the programme.

Unemployed older people, subject to meeting the eligibility criteria, can also qualify for Work Based Learning for Adults and Training for Work, New Deal for Disabled People and Work Trials.

The findings from a review of 'what works' for 'clients' aged 50+ conducted by the Department for Work and Pensions suggest that there is still a lot to be learnt about helping older people in the labour market but recommends that more focus should be given to the 'inactive', more work should be done with employers to overcome age discrimination and that there needs to be a review of training (Moss and Arrowsmith, 2003).

Flat participation rates among older women mask the countervailing forces and it would be dangerous to conclude that there is not a low participation problem among older women. The dramatic fall in participation rates among older men attracts attention but it is important that the policy response is not male-biased.

## Conclusion

The longest period of economic growth for over a century (200 years according to Gordon Brown) is a clear indication of the health of the macroeconomic environment. If we look back over the five vital elements identified by the Chancellor of the Exchequer we can see that the first (macroeconomic stability) would appear to have been met. Independence of the Bank of England is likely to have been an important contributory factor. Unemployment has fallen considerably and is now at a level that has not been seen since the early 1970s. On the second, it is difficult to assess whether the labour market is more flexible and adaptable. The fact that Labour has managed to avoid a recession may indicate that this is the case. So too may be the extent to which the economy has embraced new industry, but time will tell. Some minimum standards in the labour market have been introduced. Under Labour we have seen the introduction of an NMW, the Working Time directive, improvements in rights to maternity and paternity leave and regulations preventing less favourable treatment of part-time workers. On the third, the workforce has become more educated, but it is not clear whether it has become more adaptable. Finally, the New Deal programmes and more widespread job search assistance have undoubtedly helped encourage people to move into work. The introduction of tax credits, changes to income tax and National Insurance rates and schedules and the NMW have helped to make work pay for some low-paid workers.

So what has been the overall impact on poverty? In Table 2.1, we repeat the information shown in Figure 2.1 for 1996/97 and add information for 2002/03 on the percentage of working-age adults living in poor households by household type. Working-age adults living in workless households remain the most likely to be living in poverty and most likely if the head or spouse is unemployed. For working-age adults without children, the risk of living in poverty has remained constant or has increased in all household types between 1996/97 and 2002/03.

**Table 2.1: Risk of working-age adults living in households below 60% contemporary household equivalised income by economic status (1996/97 and 2002/03)**

|  | BHC | | AHC | |
|---|---|---|---|---|
|  | 1996/97 | 2002/03 | 1996/97 | 2002/03 |
| *Without children* | | | | |
| Single/couple one or more FT self-employed | 13 | 13 | 15 | 16 |
| Single/couple all in FT work | 2 | 3 | 3 | 4 |
| Couple, one FT, one PT work | 1 | 2 | 2 | 3 |
| Couple, one FT work, one not working | 7 | 9 | 10 | 13 |
| Single/couple no FT, one or more PT work | 17 | 19 | 24 | 24 |
| Workless, head or spouse unemployed | 50 | 56 | 66 | 64 |
| Workless, other inactive | 30 | 34 | 43 | 47 |
| *With children* | | | | |
| Single/couple one or more FT self-employed | 21 | 20 | 25 | 22 |
| Single/couple all in FT work | 2 | 3 | 2 | 4 |
| Couple, one FT, one PT work | 3 | 3 | 5 | 5 |
| Couple, one FT work, one not working | 17 | 13 | 24 | 20 |
| Single/couple no FT, one or more PT work | 36 | 31 | 47 | 43 |
| Workless, head or spouse unemployed | 71 | 77 | 88 | 93 |
| Workless, other inactive | 46 | 50 | 72 | 74 |

*Notes:* Economic status of benefit unit.
Source: DWP (2004a)

The exception is a slight fall among workless households where the head or spouse is unemployed (AHC) but this remains the highest risk household type. In contrast, working-age adults with children have experienced constant or falling risks of poverty as long as they live in a household where someone works. Working-age adults living in workless households with children have experienced increased risks of poverty. The only exception is single/couple households where all are in full-time work where the risk has increased marginally, but the risk of poverty remains extremely low for this household type. These figures highlight the impact of policies that have increased the incomes among families with children (tax credits, child benefit, and so on) particularly among working families. However, very high risks of poverty remain in workless households (although the chance of living in these household types has decreased) and in-work poverty is far from being eradicated.

A closer examination of specific groups reveals that although great gains have been made in terms of falling unemployment a number of policy challenges remain for the future. Increasing inactivity rates and falling jobless rates among working-age men remain a concern. Sixteen- and 17-year-olds have largely been ignored, and young people (most likely disadvantaged) entering the labour market have high and rising unemployment rates. These young people appear to have slipped through the net and we could be storing up trouble for the future. The New Deal programmes have been a success, but indicators such as the stagnant unemployment rates among 18- to 24-year-olds (twice the average rate at 10%) and the fact that one in four unemployed 25- to 49-year-olds have been unemployed for 12 months or longer suggest that a major review or new initiatives need to be considered. Lone parents have benefited from the NDLP and continue to volunteer in large numbers and speak positively about this programme. They have also benefited from the additional financial incentives to enter work offered through tax credits and the NMW. However, it looks unlikely that the government will reach its target of 70% lone parents working by 2010. It would seem counterproductive to meddle too much with the success of NDLP by making participation compulsory. New initiatives need consideration or perhaps the target is too ambitious?

## Notes

[1] The ILO definition of unemployment identifies people who are: out of work, want a job, have actively sought work in the previous four weeks and are available to start work within the next fortnight; or out of work and have accepted a job that they are waiting to start in the next fortnight.

[2] Various government-funded youth training schemes have been in operation including: the Youth Opportunities Programme, Youth Training Scheme and Youth Training (see Roberts, 1995).

[3] Dependent partners aged 18 to 24 without children are also offered a place on the programme.

[4] The government has accepted the Low Pay Commission's recommendation of a £3.00 rate for 16- to 17-year-olds (not in recognised training) from October 2004.

[5] Economic activity rates among 16- to 17-year-olds fell from 60% in Spring 1997 to 53% in Winter 2003 (Labour Force Survey, National Statistics, http://www.statistics/statbase/tsdlistfiles.asp).

[6] Evaluation evidence showed that Restart Interviews had a positive impact on reducing unemployment benefit claims (Dolton and O'Neill, 2002).

[7] Differences in definitions and time periods make the comparison imprecise.

[8] Eligibility for NDLP has been gradually widened. Initially, NDLP was only available to lone parents claiming Income Support and was specifically targeted at those whose youngest dependent child was of school age.

[9] While the core programme has remained largely unchanged a number of changes have been made in terms of what PAs can offer participants such as the Adviser Discretion

Fund introduced in 2001 to help with costs associated with finding work, a childcare subsidy and a training premium.

[10] Jobseeker's Allowance, Incapacity Benefit, Severe Disablement Allowance or Income Support, or receipt of National Insurance Credits.

# Education, education, education
# an assessment of Labour's success in
# tackling education inequalities

*Abigail McKnight, Howard Glennerster and Ruth Lupton*

## Introduction

Labour signalled that education was a policy priority well before the 1997 General Election. In his now famous Labour Party Conference speech in 1996, Tony Blair announced that the three highest priorities in government would be 'Education, education, education'. In December 1996, Blair outlined Labour Party thinking on education policy; themes, which, as we shall see, have continued to be important since 1997:

> I believe there is the chance to forge a new consensus on education policy. It will be practical not ideological. And it will put behind us the political and ideological debates that have dominated the last thirty years. The foundations of the consensus are clear. Early support for children under the age of five. Primary schools delivering high standards of literacy and numeracy. Rigorous assessment of pupil and school performance, and action based upon it. Improved training and qualifications for teachers, especially Heads. Early intervention when things go wrong. Support from all sections of the community to ensure that all our children are given the best possible start. And we must never forget that education is not a one-off event for the under 18s. The new consensus must be based on wide access to higher education and continual opportunities for all adults to learn throughout life. (Tony Blair MP, Speech given at Ruskin College, Oxford, 16 December 1996)

Education also featured in both the 1997 and 2001 election pledges. In 1997, as one of the five 'early pledges', Labour promised to cut class sizes to 30 or under for five-, six- and seven-year-olds by using money from phasing out the assisted places scheme. In 2001, Labour pledged to increase the number of teachers by 10,000 and improve standards in secondary schools. Even more recently, Tony Blair reaffirmed Labour's commitment:

Education was, is, and will continue to be our top priority for as long as we are in office. (Speech to the National Association of Head Teachers in Cardiff, 3 May 2004)

In this chapter, we assess the impact of Labour's education policies focusing particularly on those designed to tackle educational inequalities. We look at a number of policies targeted at schools, including reducing class sizes, literacy and numeracy hours, Key Stage tests, Education Action Zones (EAZs), Excellence in Cities and post-compulsory education policies such as the Education Maintenance Allowance and changes to the post-16 curriculum. We also explore how changes to Higher Education financing have affected the socioeconomic make-up of university entrants and consider prospects for the future.

Lifelong learning, once a government priority, seems to have fallen by the wayside. We examine the success of policies intended to tackle low levels of adult literacy.

With limited space, it is not possible to include everything. Some topics are examined in other chapters. Chapters Nine and Ten cover truancy from school and school exclusions, and Chapter Seven pre-school-age children. Some topics, although important, are not covered. For example, further education policy and training are important topics in their own right, but would require more space than is available here. We have not been able to examine changes in the structure of school provision or curriculum content and pedagogy. We have mainly focused on England, as this is where Labour has been able to have the most influence, but contrasts, where relevant, are made with Scotland, Wales and Northern Ireland.

## Differential rates of achievement

Differential rates of educational achievement are not necessarily problematic. A range of factors, including genetic differences in ability, ill health and pure hard work, can determine achievement. What is undesirable is underachievement for social reasons, children achieving well below their academic ability and at levels that make their full participation in society and its prosperity difficult.

Higher income is often associated with higher earnings due to education and therefore low-income families tend to be characterised by lower levels of parental education. Separating out the independent influences is not straightforward. Low income is often associated with a range of factors that could contribute to children's attainment such as worklessness, lone parenthood, unstable families, large families, young parents, ill health, and so on. A low level of family income can directly affect children as:

- it can determine the quality of childcare;
- it can limit the resources available to families to purchase additional tuition if the child is having difficulty;

- it can limit school choice by preventing moves to catchment areas of higher performing schools;
- it can affect a child's health (poor diet, poor living conditions, for example); and
- in the presence of capital market failures or where there is uncertainty about the returns to education, family income can affect the chance of continuing in post-compulsory education.

A low level of parental education can be important for a number of reasons:

- it can affect the extent to which parents help their children with school work and their interest in their children's education;
- it can influence children's motivation and aspirations; and
- it can affect child development.

Investigation of the relative importance of these factors has not produced agreement. Feinstein (2000), Chevalier and Lanot (2002), Jenkins and Schluter (2002) and Bratti (2002) broadly find that, although family income has a positive and significant effect on children's educational attainment, other family characteristics, such as parents' education and their interest in the child's schooling, are more important. Other researchers find quite large income effects and argue that fewer controls should be used (see Blanden et al, 2004: forthcoming).

Whatever the precise relationship, recent research has shown that the association between income and attainment has increased, with children from higher income backgrounds experiencing greater increases in attainment relative to children from lower income backgrounds (McKnight, 2002). More detailed analysis confirms that this correlation cannot be readily explained by other factors (Blanden et al, 2004: forthcoming). Moreover, the gap between educational performance of children from different socioeconomic groups is wider in the UK than elsewhere (OECD, 2003a). It is not just that disadvantaged children start school at a disadvantage; rather, recent research has uncovered the finding that young children with similar levels of competence diverge as they progress through school according to their socio-economic background (Feinstein, 2003).

A second problem is that disadvantaged children are more likely to live in deprived areas. Where children live can affect attainment for a number of reasons:

- high levels of unemployment and poor job quality can influence aspirations and motivation;
- an unattractive area and poor performing school can put off high-quality teachers or more generally all teachers leading to retention and recruitment problems affecting costs and the continuity of education;
- a poor physical environment can hamper learning;
- it can result in a culture of low achievement and negative peer group pressure both in the classroom and the neighbourhood (truancy, crime, and so on); and
- it can mean limited extra-curricular activities.

The fact that many of the poorest performing schools are located in some of the most deprived areas is now well established (Lupton, 2003a). The composition of the school intake is an important explanatory factor. Richer families moving to catchment areas of higher performing schools compound the association between advantaged neighbourhoods and high-performing schools (Gibbons and Machin, 2001). However, the fact that some schools with similar intakes perform better than others suggests that other factors are also important. Gibbons (2002) shows how the rankings of English counties and wards based on average performance of constituent primary schools change when adjustments are made for intake. In addition, the new school league tables based on a value-added measure show how rankings differ from the raw statistics[1].

## Policies affecting compulsory school-age pupils

In this section, we assess the effectiveness of Labour's policies in raising achievement and reducing educational inequality among children aged 5 to 16. We begin by outlining the main policies affecting this group. The discussion includes assessment as we go of any direct outcomes following from policy (for example, the impact of policy to reduce class sizes, and evaluations of particular initiatives, such as the literacy hour). We then turn to consider the combined impact of the package of policies on Key Stage test results and GCSE (General Certificate of Secondary Education) examination results.

*Funding*

When Labour came to power spending on education as a share of GDP had fallen to historically low levels. Labour pledged to stick to Conservative spending plans during the first two years in office. The result was that UK public expenditure on education as a share of GDP fell to its lowest figure since the early 1960s (see Glennerster, 1997, for earlier figures). In 2000, UK public expenditure on education as a share of GDP was less than in the majority of OECD countries (17 countries were spending a higher share) (OECD, 2003a). Table 3.1 shows how education spending has changed since 1990, along with planned spending up to 2007/08 as announced in the 2004 Comprehensive Spending Review. The expenditure share planned for 2007/08 was last seen in 1980/81 (see Glennerster, 2001).

The share of expenditure going to schools has increased under Labour, rising from 53% in 1996/97 to 62% in 2000/01 (Glennerster, 2001). The later historically large increases in government expenditure on schools coincided with changes in the way resources were allocated. The revised school funding system introduced in 2003 increased the share going to local authorities with the most deprived populations. However, in its first year at least, this had limited visible impact since much of the extra money was swallowed up by additional salary costs as a result of the introduction of performance related pay and higher National Insurance

**Table 3.1: Public expenditure on education as a percentage of GDP**

| Year | % GDP |
| --- | --- |
| 1990/91 | 4.8 |
| 1991/92 | 5.1 |
| 1992/93 | 5.2 |
| 1993/94 | 5.2 |
| 1994/95 | 5.2 |
| 1995/96 | 5.1 |
| 1996/97 | 4.9 |
| 1997/98 | 4.8 |
| 1998/99 | 4.5 |
| 1999/2000 | 4.5 |
| 2000/01 | 4.8 |
| 2001/02 | 5.0 |
| 2002/03 | 5.1 |
| 2003/04 | 5.3 |
| 2004/05[a] | 5.4 |
| 2005/06[a] | 5.5 |
| 2006/07[a] | 5.5 |
| 2007/08[a] | 5.6 |

*Notes:* [a]planned spending announced in the 2004 Comprehensive Spending Review.
*Source:* Glennerster (2001, Table 2); 2002 and 2004 Comprehensive Spending Reviews

and teacher pension contributions. Some schools actually lost funds because a wide range of special funding that schools had previously bid for individually became wrapped up in the single formula (many gained, but their voices were not heard above those who had lost out). The government also acknowledged that even the additional funds were only sufficient to meet half the unmet needs identified during the research it commissioned to inform the development of the formula.

There have also been additional grants to disadvantaged schools. In 2002/03, all secondary schools in 'challenging circumstances' and achieving under 25% GCSE A★-C grades received additional funding, and from 2003, 1,400 schools in disadvantaged areas have received a Leadership Incentive Grant. However, there is still a long way to go before school funding is sufficiently differentiated to adequately meet the additional needs of the most disadvantaged pupils. Two new initiatives may help indicate the form that a more appropriate response would take. The Department for Education and Skills (DfES) is currently working with eight schools in challenging circumstances to develop and test measures for raising attainment, and it has also introduced a programme of 240 'extended schools', offering facilities for specialist support, such as speech therapy, and services for families such as community education and health. Evaluation of these initiatives may produce some vital clues for future policy.

### National Curriculum, tests and examinations

The Conservative government introduced a number of major education reforms, particularly in its latter years. Possibly the biggest for England and Wales was the introduction of a National Curriculum in 1988. Scotland has a separate school curriculum and a different system of monitoring pupil performance.

The National Curriculum standardised children's education in the state sector and progress was monitored through a series of Key Stage (KS) tests. The results from these tests allowed teachers to compare the progress of individual pupils with a benchmark and schools to compare their attainment levels with national averages, while published results gave parents more information that could be used to select schools. Before the introduction of KS tests in 1995/96, publicly available information on the performance of individual students and schools was not available until the pupils sat public examinations at age 16. The first performance tables for English schools were published in 1995, although not all schools collaborated. Table 3.2 shows the relationship between school-year groups, pupils' age and the corresponding KS. Pupils take the KS test in the final year of each group.

Labour has continued to develop the National Curriculum and publish KS test results at the school level. Since 2002, they have also included a 'value-added' measure in the tables for secondary schools, and from 2003 for primary schools. The National Assembly for Wales has abolished the publication of secondary school league tables. In July 2004, it announced that by 2007/08 it would abolish testing of 11- and 14-year-olds in Welsh schools; testing of seven-year-olds was abolished in 2001. Northern Ireland has also abolished secondary school league tables, and Scotland is considering abolishing such tables.

It was believed that universal testing of pupils would raise standards due to the extra information available to teachers and parents and the incentive for schools to increase their performance. However, concern has been expressed that schools would 'cherry-pick', either through the selection of pupils or through concentrating on borderline cases, potentially increasing educational inequality.

Examinations marking the end of compulsory schooling in English and Welsh schools were significantly reformed in 1988 under the Conservative government when the General Certificate of Secondary Education (GCSE) replaced Ordinary Level (O Level) and Certificate of Secondary Education (CSE) examinations. The curriculum was changed and coursework assessment was introduced. Pupils began to take a larger number of examinations covering a broader range of subjects. In the early 1990s, GCSEs were supplemented with a system of vocational qualifications (GNVQs) offering students a wider range of options. Labour has continued to develop and enhance provision of vocational qualifications.

**Table 3.2: The relationship between age, school year and Key Stages**

| Year group | Reception | I | 2 | 3 | 4 | 5 | 6 | 7 | 8 | 9 | 10 | 11 |
|---|---|---|---|---|---|---|---|---|---|---|---|---|
| Age of pupils at end of year | 5 | | 6 | 7 | 8 | 9 | 10 | 11 | 12 | 13 | 14 | 15 | 16 |
| Key Stage | | Key Stage 1 | | | Key Stage 2 | | | | Key Stage 3 | | | Key Stage 4 | |

## Class size reduction

While teachers, parents and many politicians share a common-sense assumption that small classes positively affect children's achievement, the research evidence is much less conclusive (for a review see Wilson, 2002). The most serious attempt to assess the impact of class size on pupil attainment was conducted in the US[2]. It is difficult to know if it is possible to generalise these results, but the main findings show a positive effect associated with smaller class sizes, although classes have to be 20 or less to have an impact on achievement. Greater effects are found for children from less advantaged backgrounds. In addition, small classes have been found to be associated with lower rates of drop-out, exclusion and absence (Finn and Achilles, 1990; Nye et al, 1992; Krueger and Whitmore, 2001).

There is little UK evidence that class size has a significant effect (Dolton and Vignoles, 2000), which may be due to data quality and the difficulties associated with identifying the correct counterfactual. It is difficult to identify the direct causal effect of class size on pupil performance as class sizes can vary for a variety of reasons such as resources and/or demand. However, there is some evidence that smaller class sizes increase staying-on rates and future wages (Dustmann et al, 2003).

When Labour came to power, average class sizes in English primary and secondary schools had been rising since the late 1980s (see Figure 3.1). A much higher share of primary school children were found in larger classes than children in secondary schools. In their 1997 manifesto, Labour pledged to reduce class sizes to 30 or less for 5- to 7-year-olds within five years. They have been successful in reducing the share of primary school pupils in classes larger than 30, although

**Figure 3.1: Class sizes in English schools**

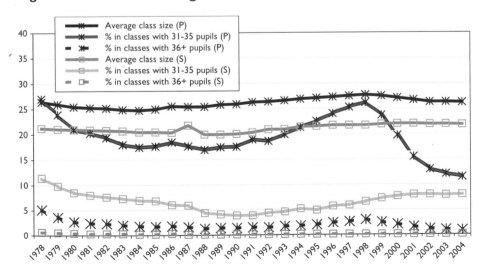

*Notes:* Classes taught by one teacher.
*Source:* DfES Bulletin 01/03, 1978-2002; DfES Statistical First Release 08/2004, 2003, 2004 (provisional)

in 2002 13% of pupils were still in classes with 31 to 35 pupils and just over 1% were in classes with 36+ pupils. Both shares have continued to fall up to 2004. However, we are not aware of any evaluation of the impact of this reduction. Average primary school class sizes are still well above the required size which has been shown to have an improvement on children's attainment. The share of secondary school pupils in classes of 30+ has continued to grow.

### Literacy and numeracy hours

In 1998/99, the government introduced a daily literacy hour in English primary schools in response to low levels of literacy among both school children and the adult population. This strategy had been developed by a literacy task force under the previous administration but was taken forward and implemented by Labour.

Until recently, there have only been qualitative evaluations with little in the way of hard statistical evidence, but the first quantitative evaluation of the literacy hour is now available and provides some very positive results (Machin and McNally, 2004). The research evaluates the forerunner to the National Literacy Strategy, the National Literacy Project (NLP), which was introduced in two cohorts of Local Education Authorities (LEAs) in 1996/97 and 1997/98 before the roll-out of the national programme in 1998/99.

The pilot programme in a select number of LEAs allowed the evaluators to compute robust estimates of the programme impact by matching NLP schools with otherwise similar schools without NLP.

Machin and McNally find significant improvements in KS English test results and some (weaker) evidence of improvements in GCSE performance in English. They also find that NLP had a greater impact on boys' performance, leading to a narrowing of the gender gap at KS2 English. They conclude that the low relative cost of this programme has made it an extremely cost-effective means of improving pupil attainment in English.

Machin and McNally are also evaluating the numeracy hour, which was introduced in English primary schools around the same time. Early unpublished evidence suggests that this too has been a success.

### Targeting deprived areas and lowest-attaining schools

When Labour came to power, there was plenty of evidence that deprived areas were associated with a higher concentration of poor performing schools. A number of programmes have been introduced that are aimed specifically at the areas and schools with the lowest levels of attainment, or the highest levels of social disadvantage.

The first of these were Education Action Zones (EAZs) implemented in two rounds in 1999 and 2000. Seventy-three EAZs were set up, each comprising two or three secondary schools and their feeder primary schools – about 1,300 schools. The idea was that partnerships would use innovative approaches to tackle attainment by addressing six issues:

- the quality of teaching;
- the quality of learning;
- social inclusion;
- support to families;
- support to pupils; and
- work with businesses and other organisations.

The zones were also expected to draw in additional money from private sector partnerships. An OFSTED report on EAZs (2003) found that they had implemented some useful initiatives on inclusion, such as homework and breakfast clubs and adaptations to the KS4 curriculum, which had the effect of improving the motivation, attitudes and self-esteem of pupils, with some effect on the number of permanent exclusions but no significant effect on attendance overall. The EAZs' work on raising standards was effective at KS1, mainly because of effective support for improvements in the teaching of literacy and numeracy. However, they had a patchy effect on standards at KS2, and no real impact on KS3 or higher grade GCSE. Lower grade GCSE results improved in the EAZs because of their focus on inclusion. Overall, the report found that despite innovative activities, strong working relationships and improved management, EAZs had mixed success, and did more to tackle inclusion than standards.

In 1999, the EAZ initiative was succeeded by a bigger programme aimed at schools in disadvantaged urban areas – Excellence in Cities (EiC). In contrast to EAZs, EiC was not a competitive programme but was targeted at specific areas: 25 LEAs were included in the first phase and another 33 in the second (altogether, about one third of LEAs and schools). It also focused only on secondary schools initially, extended to some primary schools in the second phase, and to some post-16 providers. The funding was much more substantial (about £350 million per year) although less targeted, aimed at all the secondary schools in an area, and not just two or three. This was also a more prescriptive programme, with specific funding available for particular purposes, namely employing learning mentors, making provision for gifted and talented pupils and providing learning support units and City Learning Centres.

Evaluation of the impact of EiC on attainment in KS3 Maths and English tests over the first two years suggests that the programme had a modest but positive effect (Machin et al, 2004). The effects are greater for Maths than for English and there is some evidence to suggest that for Maths boys experienced a greater improvement than girls. The greatest improvement was for pupils with lower levels of attainment (Machin et al, 2003). There is also evidence that EiCs reduce pupil absence.

OFSTED (2003) also looked at the management and performance of EiC and found positive effects on attainment and attendance. It also found EiC to be a more effective initiative than EAZs, mainly because it was largely managed by schools themselves and concentrated on a small number of improvement strategies underwritten by clear planning and guidance, in contrast to the EAZs, which had to concentrate on establishing partnerships and raising funds, and tended to adopt a large number of innovative schemes rather than concentrating on a small number of core objectives. However, OFSTED's review of both programmes found that the effects were very variable. Some schools had "little to show in terms of performance for the money ... spent" (2003, p 68). Perhaps just as significantly, it noted that, even where the special funding had made a difference, the attainment gap was still too wide and rates of exclusion and absence too high. Two thirds of the schools affected by the initiatives and surveyed by OFSTED had not managed to improve their attendance and were still struggling with regular attendance rates well below 90%.

## Outcomes: Key Stage test results

We now turn to examine the combined impact of the policies discussed on overall educational attainment and inequality, as measured by national Key Stage (KS) test results in this section and, in the next section, GCSE examination results. Table 3.3 shows the percentage of pupils in English schools who achieved expected standards between 1996 and 2003. It is difficult to assess Labour's inheritance and subsequent achievements in a systematic way as data are not available for more than one year before they were elected and this year does not provide a realistic benchmark (see later in this chapter). There has been a general improvement in all subjects and at all levels between 1996 and 2003. Some of this improvement is to be expected, as teachers become more familiar with the material and in their preparation for tests and as pupils get used to preparing for and sitting examinations. This is likely to explain part of the much larger gains between 1996 and 1999 than in any subsequent three-year period. There was also much more room for improvement: by 2003, very high percentages of pupils were achieving the expected standards in some subjects and KSs.

The well-documented gender gap in performance is plainly evident. Girls consistently outperform boys in English (and the gap increases with each KS level). There is some evidence that boys have been able to narrow this gap over the last seven years. Girls and boys performance in Maths and Science tests are much more equal.

Evidence that some of the initial gains may have been in some sense artificial can be seen by tracking the progress of a number of cohorts. Cohort 1, shaded dark, sat KS1 tests in 1996 and KS2 in 2000. Cohort 2, shaded light, sat KS1 tests in 1999 and KS2 in 2003. While there was a notable improvement in KS1 test results between 1996 and 1999 (between Cohorts 1 and 2), these did not translate into similar improvements in performance at KS2 for Cohort 2 compared with Cohort 1. A similar comparison can be made between KS2 and KS3 progression.

**Table 3.3: Percentage of pupils achieving expected levels in Key Stage tests**

| Boys | | 1996 | 1997 | 1998 | 1999 | 2000 | 2001 | 2002 | 2003 |
|---|---|---|---|---|---|---|---|---|---|
| Key Stage 1 | Reading | 73 | 75 | 75 | 78 | 79 | 80 | 81 | 80 |
| | Writing | 74 | 75 | 75 | 78 | 80 | 82 | 82 | 76 |
| | Maths | 81 | 82 | 82 | 85 | 89 | 90 | 89 | 89 |
| Key Stage 2 | English | 50 | 57 | 57 | 65 | 70 | 70 | 70 | 70 |
| | Maths | 54 | 63 | 59 | 69 | 72 | 71 | 73 | 73 |
| | Science | 61 | 68 | 70 | 79 | 84 | 87 | 86 | 86 |
| Key Stage 3 | English | 48 | 48 | 56 | 55 | 55 | 57 | 59 | 61 |
| | Maths | 56 | 60 | 60 | 62 | 64 | 65 | 67 | 69 |
| | Science | 57 | 61 | 57 | 55 | 61 | 66 | 67 | 68 |
| **Girls** | | | | | | | | | |
| Key Stage 1 | Reading | 83 | 85 | 85 | 86 | 88 | 88 | 88 | 88 |
| | Writing | 85 | 85 | 86 | 88 | 89 | 90 | 90 | 87 |
| | Maths | 84 | 85 | 86 | 88 | 91 | 92 | 92 | 91 |
| Key Stage 2 | English | 65 | 70 | 73 | 76 | 79 | 80 | 79 | 80 |
| | Maths | 54 | 61 | 58 | 69 | 71 | 70 | 73 | 72 |
| | Science | 63 | 69 | 69 | 78 | 85 | 88 | 87 | 87 |
| Key Stage 3 | English | 66 | 67 | 73 | 73 | 73 | 73 | 76 | 75 |
| | Maths | 58 | 60 | 59 | 62 | 65 | 67 | 68 | 72 |
| | Science | 56 | 60 | 55 | 55 | 58 | 66 | 67 | 68 |

*Note:* Expected levels are KS1 (level 2 or above); KS2 (level 4 or above); KS3 (level 5 or above).
*Source:* DfES Statistical Bulletin No 03/2000; DfES Statistics of Education 2001 No 03/02; DfES Statistical First Release 21/2004

Nevertheless, the gains at KS3 are still significant and have been growing since 2001.

We are particularly interested in the relative performance of disadvantaged pupils. Glennerster (2001) used data on test scores for rich and poor schools according to the percentage of pupils who qualify for Free School Meals (FSMs) (up to 5% and over 40% respectively). These figures have been updated to include 2001 (Table 3.4). While there remain significant differences in performance at KS1 and KS2, there has been a narrowing of this gap between 1997 and 2001. Gibbons and Machin (2001) show similar evidence confirming catch-up of schools at the bottom of the performance distribution. However, there continues to be extremely poor performance of pupils in poor schools at KS3.

Unfortunately comparable figures are no longer published. However, since 2002 it has been possible to examine pupils' individual performance. In Table 3.5, KS test results are shown according to FSM eligibility, gender and ethnic minority status (in Reading and English). Results are also available for Maths and Science but have not been reproduced here.

Pupils eligible for FSMs perform, on average, considerably worse in KS tests than their counterparts. The differences are greater at higher KS levels. Girls outperform boys irrespective of FSM eligibility or ethnic status (the difference is greater for English/reading than for Maths). Poverty has a greater impact on boys' English/reading test scores than that of girls (there is no difference for Maths). There is variation in KS test performance for pupils according to ethnic

**Table 3.4: Median share of pupils reaching expected levels in Key Stage tests within rich and poor schools**

|  | Rich | | | | Poor | | | |
|---|---|---|---|---|---|---|---|---|
|  | 1997 | 1999 | 2000 | 2001 | 1997 | 1999 | 2000 | 2001 |
| *Key Stage 1* | | | | | | | | |
| Reading | 91 | 93 | 94 | 93 | 62 | 67 | 70 | 70 |
| Writing | 92 | 94 | 94 | 94 | 62 | 68 | 71 | 73 |
| Maths | 94 | 91 | 98 | 97 | 70 | 76 | 81 | 82 |
| *Key Stage 2* | | | | | | | | |
| English | 80 | 87 | 89 | 89 | 37 | 48 | 55 | 55 |
| Maths | 79 | 85 | 86 | 85 | 37 | 49 | 53 | 52 |
| Science | 85 | 92 | 95 | 97 | 45 | 60 | 70 | 76 |
| *Key Stage 3* | | | | | | | | |
| English | 75 | 84 | 83 | 85 | 0 | 8 | 0 | 0 |
| Maths | 78 | 82 | 83 | 85 | 0 | 9 | 14 | 14 |
| Science | 79 | 78 | 79 | 86 | 0 | 5 | 13 | 13 |

*Notes:* Rich=up to 5% with Free School Meals; poor=over 40% with Free School Meals.
*Source:* DfES Statistical Bulletins 04/1998, Table 19; 04/2001, Table 18; 03/2002, Table 18

**Table 3.5: Percent of pupils achieving expected levels in Key Stage tests by ethnicity, gender and Free School Meal (FSM) eligibility (2003)**

|  | Non FSM | | FSM | | Difference | |
|---|---|---|---|---|---|---|
|  | Boys | Girls | Boys | Girls | Boys | Girls |
| *Reading Key Stage 1* | | | | | | |
| White | 85 | 92 | 61 | 74 | 24 | 18 |
| Mixed | 86 | 93 | 70 | 80 | 16 | 13 |
| Asian | 80 | 87 | 67 | 76 | 13 | 11 |
| Black | 80 | 87 | 66 | 76 | 14 | 11 |
| Chinese | 86 | 93 | 86 | 87 | 0 | 6 |
| Any other ethnic group | 78 | 83 | 60 | 68 | 18 | 15 |
| All pupils | 84 | 91 | 63 | 75 | 21 | 16 |
| *English Key Stage 2* | | | | | | |
| White | 75 | 85 | 46 | 60 | 29 | 25 |
| Mixed | 78 | 87 | 55 | 70 | 23 | 17 |
| Asian | 69 | 78 | 53 | 65 | 16 | 13 |
| Black | 68 | 79 | 51 | 65 | 17 | 14 |
| Chinese | 77 | 87 | 78 | 84 | -1 | 3 |
| Any other ethnic group | 67 | 75 | 48 | 59 | 19 | 16 |
| All pupils | 74 | 84 | 48 | 61 | 26 | 23 |
| *English Key Stage 3* | | | | | | |
| White | 68 | 81 | 35 | 50 | 33 | 31 |
| Mixed | 69 | 82 | 41 | 58 | 28 | 24 |
| Asian | 66 | 78 | 44 | 62 | 22 | 16 |
| Black | 54 | 71 | 37 | 54 | 17 | 17 |
| Chinese | 76 | 86 | 60 | 80 | 16 | 6 |
| Any other ethnic group | 62 | 76 | 38 | 50 | 24 | 26 |
| All pupils | 67 | 80 | 36 | 52 | 31 | 28 |

*Source:* DfES Statistical First Release 04/2004

status. Black boys have one of the lowest levels of attainment and appear to fall steadily further behind as they go through school (but this might be a cohort effect with increases in attainment among younger black boys). Chinese pupils consistently outperform other groups[3]. However, while on average pupils eligible for FSMs perform less well than their counterparts, the relative difference between pupils with and without FSMs is greater for white pupils than for other ethnic groups. This usually results in white pupils eligible for FSM performing least well among all such pupils. It is not clear why this is the case. Chinese pupils, in contrast, generally suffer no poverty penalty.

### Outcomes: performance in compulsory school leaving examinations

General Certificates of Secondary Education (GCSEs), and their equivalents, mark the end of compulsory schooling and so provide a useful point at which to assess Labour's overall impact, although we must bear in mind that it is still early for assessment as Labour's policies will take some time to have an impact on school leaving examinations. Attainment of GCSEs had been improving under the Conservatives and Figure 3.2 shows how achievement in school leaving examinations has continued to rise under Labour. Unlike earlier evidence, this figure includes all countries of the UK. Only a very small fraction of young people now leaves school without any examinations (around 5% in 2002). This has fallen from one third of the cohort born in 1935-44 (Glennerster and Hills,

**Figure 3.2: Percentage of UK students at a typical age achieving GCSE and SCE S Grade/Standard Grade (SG)**

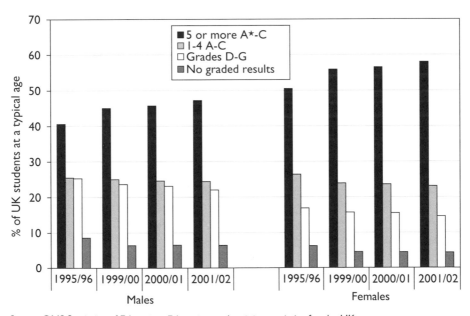

*Source:* ONS Statistics of Education: Education and training statistics for the UK

1998). There is a significant gender gap in GCSE attainment with girls outperforming boys. In 2001/02, boys were still not reaching the levels attained by girls in 1995/96. More up to date UK statistics are not available but results for England up to 2002/03 show continuing improvements in the shares gaining 5+ A*-C GCSEs and further falls in the shares leaving with no GCSE passes (DfES, 2003a).

However, it is difficult to attribute these changes to Labour policy as there has been a long-term trend increase in the proportion of pupils taking school leaving examinations and a rise in post-compulsory staying-on rates (Blanden et al, 2004: forthcoming). The continuing rate of attainment in these examinations has sparked debate about falling standards, an issue which has not been (and probably will never be) resolved and will not be covered in this chapter. It may be easier to distinguish a New Labour effect in examining changes in educational inequality.

Table 3.6 shows that Labour inherited a situation where there existed wide inequalities in GCSE attainment by social class background. These inequalities had increased under the Conservative government between 1989 and 1994 due to greater relative gains made by children from more privileged backgrounds.

Although we do not have the figures for 1997, comparing 1996 with 1998 and 2000 suggests that the share of children from unskilled manual backgrounds gaining 5+ GCSE A*-C has risen under Labour, after a fall between 1996 and 1998. The percentage point gap in attainment fell sharply between 1998 and 2000, taking it down to the 1989 level but at higher levels of attainment for both social classes.

After 2000, the socioeconomic classification changed, making comparisons difficult. Trends since then suggest improvements for all socioeconomic groups but no fall in the percentage point gaps in attainment. Table 3.7 gives a more detailed breakdown of GCSE grades by social class background in 2002. The figures show how children from more advantaged backgrounds are more likely both to take GCSEs and to gain higher grades. Pupils from higher managerial/ professional backgrounds are more than twice as likely to achieve 5+ A*-C GCSEs as pupils from routine occupation backgrounds.

Only a small fraction of pupils leaves school without any GCSE passes, but

**Table 3.6: 5+ GCSE A*-C by parents' social class (1989-2000)**

|  | 1989 | 1991 | 1992 | 1994 | 1996 | 1998 | 2000 |
|---|---|---|---|---|---|---|---|
| Managerial/professional | 52 | 58 | 60 | 66 | 68 | 69 | 69 |
| Other non-manual | 42 | 49 | 51 | 58 | 58 | 60 | 60 |
| Skilled manual | 21 | 27 | 29 | 36 | 36 | 40 | 45 |
| Semi-skilled manual | 16 | 20 | 23 | 26 | 29 | 32 | 36 |
| Unskilled manual | 12 | 15 | 16 | 16 | 24 | 20 | 30 |
| Other/not classified | 15 | 18 | 18 | 20 | 22 | 24 | 26 |
| Gap | 40 | 43 | 44 | 50 | 44 | 49 | 39 |

*Note:* The gap is the percentage point difference between Unskilled manual and Managerial/professional.
*Source:* DfES 2003, Youth Cohort Study (England and Wales)

**Table 3.7: GCSE grades by social class background (NS-SEC) (2002)**

| | 5 or more GCSE grades A*-C | 1-4 GCSE grades A*-C | 5 or more GCSE grades D-G | 1-4 GCSE grades D-G | None reported | All |
|---|---|---|---|---|---|---|
| Higher professional | 77 | 13 | 6 | – | 3 | 100 |
| Lower professional | 64 | 21 | 11 | 2 | 2 | 100 |
| Intermediate | 52 | 25 | 17 | 2 | 4 | 100 |
| Lower supervisory | 35 | 30 | 27 | 4 | 4 | 100 |
| Routine | 32 | 32 | 25 | 5 | 6 | 100 |
| Other | 32 | 29 | 26 | 4 | 9 | 100 |

*Note:* 'Other' includes children with no employed parent.
*Source:* Youth Cohort Study, ONS *Social Trends* 34, England and Wales

this is much more likely for pupils in receipt of FSMs and for some ethnic groups (see Table 3.8). While only one in 20 boys not eligible for FSMs leaves school with no GCSEs, one in seven boys eligible for FSM does so. As with KS results, the 'poverty penalty' seems to be higher for white pupils than for pupils from other ethnic groups. Once again, Chinese pupils do not appear to suffer a poverty penalty. A similar pattern emerges for 5+ GCSE A*-C (lower panel of Table 3.8). Around one quarter of pupils eligible for FSMs achieve 5+ GCSEs A*-C compared with over one half of ineligible pupils.

Overall, we have seen an improvement in the performance of children from the least advantaged backgrounds in compulsory school leaving examinations, but even in 2003 the chances of leaving school without any examination passes

**Table 3.8: Percentage of pupils with no GCSE passes and achieving 5+ A*-C by gender, ethnicity and Free School Meal (FSM) status (2003)**

| | Non-FSM | | FSM | | Difference | |
|---|---|---|---|---|---|---|
| | **Boys** | **Girls** | **Boys** | **Girls** | **Boys** | **Girls** |
| *No GCSE passes* | | | | | | |
| White | 4.6 | 3.2 | 16.6 | 11.5 | 12 | 8 |
| Mixed | 5.5 | 3.7 | 12.4 | 8.6 | 7 | 5 |
| Asian | 3.6 | 2.7 | 5.8 | 3.9 | 2 | 1 |
| Black | 7.4 | 5.2 | 9.0 | 7.1 | 2 | 2 |
| Chinese | 5.1 | 4.1 | 0.8 | 1.7 | –4 | –2 |
| Any other ethnic group | 10.0 | 8.5 | 13.3 | 8.6 | 3 | 0 |
| All pupils | 4.8 | 3.4 | 14.3 | 10.1 | 10 | 7 |
| *5+A*-C* | | | | | | |
| White | 50.2 | 61.1 | 17.1 | 24.2 | 33 | 37 |
| Mixed | 49.3 | 62.6 | 22.7 | 33.4 | 27 | 29 |
| Asian | 53.9 | 65.5 | 32.9 | 45.5 | 21 | 20 |
| Black | 33.1 | 48.7 | 21.5 | 31.7 | 12 | 17 |
| Chinese | 72.1 | 79.8 | 62.5 | 75.9 | 10 | 4 |
| Any other ethnic group | 49.4 | 58.3 | 27.8 | 38.4 | 22 | 20 |
| All pupils | 49.9 | 60.8 | 20.4 | 28.5 | 30 | 32 |

*Source:* DfES Statistical First Release 04/2004

or achieving below the expected level remains high for these pupils. There remains a gender gap in performance, with girls outperforming boys, and the poverty penalty is generally higher for boys. Results differ by ethnic background, with results for black children (especially boys) lagging behind other groups, but with white children suffering the highest poverty penalty. (Further discussion of disparities in attainment by ethnic background can be found in Chapter Nine of this volume.)

## Age 16 to 18 outcomes

Over time there has been an increased emphasis on encouraging young people to stay on in full-time education after compulsory schooling ends at age 16. There has long been concern that one of the factors which puts young people off is the strong focus on academic qualifications and the need to specialise within the A-level curriculum (a broader range of topics is usually studied for Highers in Scotland). In English and Welsh schools, the Conservative government broadened the post-16 curriculum through the introduction of National Vocational Qualifications (NVQs) in 1986 but left A-levels largely unchanged. Labour has broadly maintained the system of NVQs, but in 2000 they introduced wide-ranging changes to the post-16 curriculum. The introduction of AS-level qualifications usually taken after one year's post-16 study was designed to broaden the range of subjects studied and to attract more students to stay on in full-time education. In addition, Advanced GNVQs and Key Skills qualifications were introduced with a similar objective in mind.

The Office of National Statistics (ONS) are currently in the process of re-weighting population estimates in light of the 2001 Census, so, following their advice, precise figures and trends for post-compulsory staying-on rates are not presented here. What the evidence does suggest is that staying-on rates have continued to increase so that now the majority of 16- to 17-year-olds are in full-time education (over 70% of 16-year-olds and nearly 60% of 17-year-olds) (DfES, 2004a). However, the UK performs poorly on this measure when compared with other industrialised countries. In 2001, the UK ranked 27th out of 30 countries for participation rates among 17 year olds (OECD, 2003a), and the small increases since 2001 are unlikely to have changed this.

There is also a significant minority of young people who are not in education, employment or training (NEET) and young people from disadvantaged backgrounds are more likely to be NEET than their counterparts. In 1999, the Social Exclusion Unit (SEU) estimated that around 9% of 16- to 18-year-olds were not involved in any education, employment or training (SEU, 1999) but this figure varied across socioeconomic and ethnic groups and across regions. The SEU outlined a number of policies to reduce NEET but set no overall targets. The latest figure for the share of 16- to 18-year-olds who are NEET in 2003 is still 9% (DfES, 2004a)

Figure 3.3 shows the share of the 16- to 18-year-old candidates in England achieving various A-level (or equivalent) qualifications between 1994 and 2003. The shares achieving two/three or more passes are higher among young women than young men and the shares for both increased over this period. In addition, around 10% more young women enter these examinations than young men (DfES, 2004b). The impact of the introduction of AS-levels in 2002 in terms of broadening the post-16 curriculum can be seen by the significant increase in the share of candidates achieving three or more A-levels (or equivalents). Over this ten-year period, the number of candidates achieving three or more A grades also increased steadily. By 2003, the number of candidates increased by over 50,000, reflecting the increased rate of staying-on in post-compulsory education, but the results show that broadening participation at A/A-S levels has not led to a fall in levels of attainment (assuming constant standards).

Labour is currently introducing an additional policy, designed specifically to increase staying-on rates among less advantaged young people. The Education Maintenance Allowance (EMA) is a weekly cash allowance (up to £30) payable to young people (16- to 19-year-olds) from low-income families who remain in full-time post-compulsory education. It will be available from September 2004

**Figure 3.3: Share of 16- to 18-year-old candidates in English schools and FE sector colleges achieving GCE/VCE A/AS levels**

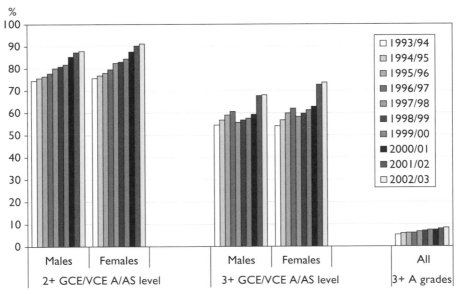

Notes: Age at start of academic year.
A candidate is someone attempting at least one of the relevant qualifications.
Each GCE/VCE AS counts as half of a GCE/VCE A level and each VCE Double Award counts as 2 GCE/VCE A levels.
From 2001 includes GCE/VCE A and Advanced Subsidiary levels, VCE Double Awards, GCE Advanced Supplementary levels and Advanced GNVQs and figures for 2002 onwards include GCE/BCE A/AS and VCE Double Awards.
*Source:* DfES Statistical First Release, SFR 24/2004

to all eligible UK students. Education Maintenance Allowances were piloted extensively and the evaluation of these pilots provided positive evidence that financial assistance could improve staying-on rates among young people from less advantaged backgrounds (an increase of around six percentage points was observed) (Ashworth et al, 2002). Of course we will not see the impact of this policy on national staying-on rates and inequalities in these rates until 2005/06 at the earliest.

## Higher education

Higher education (HE) has undergone some major reforms in recent times, many originating before Labour came to power. For example, Labour implemented many of the Dearing committee's recommendations[4] set up under the Conservative government. The shift in financing from general taxation to pupils and their parents and the growth in postgraduate education began before 1997, and has continued under Labour at varying paces. There is insufficient space to document these changes here (see, Smith et al, 2000; Glennerster, 2001; Blanden and Machin, 2004); instead we concentrate on the impact of these changes on education inequalities.

The shift from means-tested maintenance grants to student loans (completed in 1998) largely benefited students from more affluent families (Callender, 2003). Under the new funding system, students from poorer backgrounds left university with debts while more advantaged students who previously had not qualified for grants had access to very cheap loans. The introduction of top-up fees in 1998 should not have affected the least advantaged students as they paid no fees, while the maintenance loan became more generous.

The government has been struggling to balance HE financing with its widening participation agenda and its participation target of 50% by 2010. Analysis of participation rates by social class background over the last 20 or 30 years shows increases for all social classes but the relative rates for students from less advantaged backgrounds have not increased (Greenaway and Haynes, 2000) and have not improved since 1997 (Galindo-Rueda et al, 2004). Recent research has shown that HE participation was more sensitive to parental income in the early 1990s than in the late 1970s (Blanden and Machin, 2004). Blanden and Machin conclude that the expansion of HE has disproportionately benefited more affluent families.

There are a number of reasons why less advantaged students have lower HE participation rates. As shown earlier in this chapter, they have lower levels of educational attainment in pre-HE examinations. In part, this may itself be due to the disincentive created by the perception that HE leads to high debt and low financial rewards. The prospect of debt seems to have a much greater impact on the less advantaged (Callender, 2003). Higher education is a riskier investment for those from poorer backgrounds, who face higher drop-out rates, higher rates of unemployment and lower chances of finding a graduate job on leaving university (even after controlling for a range of factors) (Naylor et al, 2002).

Average rates of return frequently used to underpin HE policy have often ignored wide variance, ranging from close to zero to very high rates.

A recent study (Galindo-Rueda et al, 2004) has tried to identify the impact of tuition fees on the socio-economic gap in HE participation and shows that the relationship between income and HE participation increased between the early 1990s and 2001. In 1992, 40% of young people from professional/managerial/skilled-non-manual backgrounds participated in HE compared with 14% of young people from skilled-manual/partly-skilled/unskilled: a gap of 26 percentage points. The gap widened to 28 percentage points in 1998 and to 31 percentage points in 2001. Galindo-Rueda et al (2004) conclude that the steepening of the relationship after the introduction of tuition fees in 1998 is part of a longer-term trend, but this is a subjective assessment and it is not clear how to identify the impact of tuition fees on participation rates. They also find that prior educational attainment (which itself could be due to socioeconomic background) could previously explain differences in participation rates, but that by 2000 this was no longer the case. The expansion of HE and the widening participation agenda have done little to curb the widening socioeconomic gap in HE participation.

From 2005, universities will be allowed to vary tuition fees up to a maximum of £3,000 per annum. The current system of upfront fees will be replaced by an income contingent loan repaid after graduation. It is unknown what impact this new system will have on differential participation rates and subject choice.

## Adult basic skills

More British people lack basic literacy and numeracy skills than is the case in most other leading economies (ONS, 1997; OECD, 2003a). In 1995, one-in-five adults could not look up a telephone number and one-in-four could not work out the change they would get from £2.00 if they bought two cans of baked beans and a loaf of bread. The government set itself the target of 'helping' 0.5 million adults a year by 2002 (out of approximately eight million). A working group was set up to advise on how this could be done, chaired by Sir Claus Moser. As a result of his report (DfEE, 1999), an Adult Basic Skills Unit was set up in the DfES to develop and fund a national programme. This set itself the target of equipping 750,000 adults with better basic skills by 2004 and 1.5 million by 2007.

A number of policies have been introduced to tackle low levels of basic skills among the adult population but the high-profile failure of the Individual Learning Accounts caused damage and slowed further policy development. In 2004, the government announced a replacement scheme called Adult Learning Grants to help adults reach Level 2 qualifications, as well as an extension of apprenticeships to a wider age range (DfES, 2004c).

An experiment (Link Up) was started in 2003 in a sample of very poor areas, funded by the DfES and the Basic Skills Agency. It attracted volunteers who were local tenants, employees or members of community groups. They were trained to encourage colleagues or neighbours into contact with basic skills courses and to support them. This has begun to produce very encouraging early results though future funding will depend on support from local Learning and Skills Councils (LSCs). The scale of this task is daunting.

Although the government claims to be on track to meet its 2004 target, we do not know the starting skill levels of those adults passing tests, or whether those with the lowest levels of skill are being helped. A baseline study was undertaken in England in 2002/03 (DfES, 2003a), which gives us a much better picture of the distribution of skills in the population and some idea of progress since 1995. It suggests that just over one million people in England had literacy levels at or below Entry Level 1, meaning they could only 'understand short texts with repeated language patterns on familiar topics'. Numeracy levels were more worrying: 5% (1.7 million) were at Entry Level 1; that is, for example, they could only count reliably up to ten. Five million people were deemed not to be fully functionally literate.

Poor levels were strongly associated with lower social status, not having English as a first language and living in areas of high deprivation, holding these other factors constant.

It is difficult to compare these results with the less detailed earlier studies for a number of reasons, so interpretations have to be cautious. However, it does appear that there were probably fewer adults at very low standards of literacy in 2003. The National Child Development Study (NCDS) survey suggested there were 19% of 37-year-olds in this category in 1995 and 15% in 2002/03 (see DfES, 2003a, pp 142-3). However, levels of poor numeracy seem to be identical in the two years on all the surveys.

## Conclusion

One of the recurrent findings of educational research from the 1950s onwards has been that children from less advantaged backgrounds have lower levels of educational attainment. Such inequalities lead to lifetime inequalities due to the relationship between education, unemployment and earnings and a range of other adult outcomes such as general health and psychological well-being. Recent evidence suggests that since the 1980s this cycle has strengthened.

Labour have increased overall education funding and reformed funding mechanisms particularly to direct more resources to schools in disadvantaged areas. These increases did not take place until after 2000 and it is likely to be some time before their full effect will be felt, but the sums involved appear to be insufficient to meet the needs identified. Additional targeted initiatives aimed at schools in the poorest areas seem to have had a positive impact, but a great deal more still needs to be done.

The evidence suggests that the performance gap between rich and poor schools may need to be tackled by more radical reforms to mainstream school funding, rather than just by targeted initiatives. Such reforms could include three elements:

- a higher level of welfare support to directly address the social disadvantages limiting pupils' educational progress;
- a higher level of educational support to reflect the low starting point and esteem of pupils and their limited educational support at home; and
- different types and levels of staffing for schools with very disadvantaged intakes.

There has been continued improvement in KS test results at ages seven, 11 and 14, but progress has slowed down. There appears to have been some narrowing in the performance of rich and poor primary and secondary schools in terms of KS test results and a narrowing in the gender gap in English tests where traditionally girls have outperformed boys. It would appear that at least part of this can be explained by the successful introduction of literacy and numeracy hours. However, there remains a large gap in the performance of richer and poorer children and considerable variation between ethnic groups, with Chinese children doing well and black children underperforming, particularly at higher KSs. Poverty appears to have the biggest impact on boys' performance in English KS tests and white pupils tend to suffer a greater poverty penalty than other ethnic groups.

Class sizes in primary schools have been reduced, but there is no evaluation evidence that this reduction has led to improvements in educational attainment. Research evidence suggests that class sizes have to be reduced to a small size (20 or less) for there to be an impact on attainment and average primary and secondary school classes are still well above this level.

There is some evidence that there has been a narrowing in the gap between less advantaged and more advantaged pupils in school leaving examinations but poor pupils (particular boys) still have fairly high probabilities of leaving school without any formal qualifications and low probabilities of reaching the expected level of attainment. In addition, although the percentage point gap between the most advantaged and least advantaged social class groups has fallen significantly since 1998 the gap is the same in 2003 as it was in 1989.

The more advantaged students seem to have benefited most from the expansion and recent reforms in HE and evidence suggests that HE participation is now even more dependent on family income than it was previously. The socioeconomic gap in HE participation has widened. Some of this is undoubtedly due to the complexity of the funding system, to poor knowledge about the potential gains and to the uncertainties involved. One way of making the existing 'package' simpler and to send a clearer message to disadvantaged young people at the age of 14 might be to offer them an upfront deal (possibly in the form of a voucher). Conditional on GCSE results, this could guarantee financial assistance through the EMA to stay on at age 16; conditional on gaining a university place, it could guarantee to cover all fees and provide a small maintenance grant and a maximum value student loan. If this message does not get through we will undoubtedly see continuing increases in education and earnings inequality and falling intergenerational mobility.

## Notes

[1] Value-added school performance statistics can be found at (www.dfes.gov.uk/performancetables).

[2] The Tennessee Student Teacher Achievement Ratio, often referred to as Project STAR.

[3] There are only around 100 Chinese boys/girls eligible for FSMs at each stage.

[4] The National Committee of Inquiry into Higher Education, known as the Dearing Committee, was set up in 1996 and reported in 1997.

# FOUR

# Tackling health inequalities

*Franco Sassi*

## Health, poverty and social exclusion

*A dual causal pathway*

Much of the evidence on the relationship between income and health seems to point to a non-linear relationship, at least at the individual level, indicating that the association is much stronger when income is low (Deaton, 2003). Whether it is absolute income, or poverty, that matters, rather than relative income, or rank, a non-linear relationship with health indicates that reducing income inequality will improve overall health, as the health gain enjoyed by the worse off outweighs the deterioration suffered by the better off. Moreover, when a country reaches the level of wealth at which average income has negligible effects on overall health, improvements could still be achieved by reducing income inequality. And this is independent of any direct effects that income inequality may have on health (Wilkinson, 1996). The evidence would appear to strongly support the case for redistributive policies, and for policies to fight poverty, in a country like the UK. This would not just improve the health of the worse off, and likely reduce inequalities, but it would also improve overall population health. However, redistribution tends to produce its effects in the long term, and may have an opportunity cost in terms of reduced growth and average income. In the short term, health policy measures to improve the health of the worse off tend to require disproportionately large investments, and measures generally aimed at improving population health tend to have a greater effect on the better off, making the simultaneous achievement of a narrowing of inequalities and of an improvement in overall health difficult, if not impossible.

If the broader concept of social exclusion is considered, the case for policies targeted at the worse off appears strengthened. Poor health is a determinant of social exclusion along all its dimensions (Burchardt et al, 2002) as it imposes limitations in consumption, production (directly and through unemployment) and political and social participation. Poor access to health care, often associated with poor health, also contributes to social exclusion as an aspect of limitations in consumption, although one that does not derive primarily from low income. The hypothesis of a dual causal pathway between social exclusion and health is supported, for instance, by evidence on the impact of unemployment on health and mortality; and on the association between health and social networks, voting inequality and participation in unions. The concept of social capital has been widely adopted in recent research to explain the complex relationship between socioeconomic disadvantage, inequality and health (Kawachi, 1999).

### Equity and health inequalities: the concepts and ethical dimension

Concepts of equity adopted by national governments and international organisations often focus on health *care* and tend to be centred on notions of equality with respect to some relevant dimension, a common example being equal access for equal need. However, there is no consensus on what should be equalised, and in respect to what dimension. This is reflected in the confusion and inconsistencies among equity principles pursued explicitly (Donaldson and Gerard, 1993) and implicitly (Sassi et al, 2001) by governments. Approaches to promoting equity with regard to health *outcomes* have been more cautious, generally avoiding direct references to notions of equality, and rather focusing on the reduction of variations across population groups. There is generally recognition that health disparities are likely to persist as long as social structures allow some degree of inequality. It has been argued that health inequalities, at least to a certain extent, are acceptable, or even desirable (Collison, 1998). This is because of trade-offs between equity and efficiency, non-modifiable risk factors (for example, genetic heritage) and individual choice (such as lifestyle). The question for governments is which health inequalities should be tackled, and how much effort should be put into redressing them. Moral judgements are inevitable, but governments tend to operate within loosely defined ethical frameworks. Their approach to health inequalities tends to be pragmatic, and often entails the setting of targets simply in terms of improvement of the status quo. In a few instances, governments have proposed conceptual frameworks to justify their policies towards health inequalities (for example, in the Netherlands, see Programme Committee on Socioeconomic Inequalities in Health, 2001) but the normative link remains vague and open to judgement.

## Health inequalities in the UK: historical overview

### Evidence about health inequalities prior to 1997: socioeconomic inequalities

In 1977, the Labour government of the time launched an independent inquiry into health inequalities, led by Douglas Black. Its report received a "frosty reception" (Townsend et al, 1992, p 3) by the newly elected Conservative government. It depicted a stunning picture of inequality, particularly across the social class divide and across the north–south geographic divide. Infant and male adult mortality rates were approximately twice as large in social class V as in social class I, and standardised mortality ratios varied between 90 in the South East, 113 in the Northern region and 117 in parts of Wales, even after adjusting for age and social class. A review of trends in socioeconomic inequalities over the previous 20 years showed that inequalities had widened over time, with the higher social classes substantially improving their health while the lower ones showed little improvement and in some cases even a worsening. These findings were later confirmed by two further reports, *The health divide* in 1987 (Townsend et al, 1992), and the *Health inequalities* decennial supplement (Drever and Whitehead, 1997), although the use of social class as a marker of socioeconomic condition raised controversies, as changes in the size and composition of social classes may be at least partly responsible for the trends observed (Illsley and Le Grand, 1987).

When the current Labour government took office, most health indicators were on a long-term trend of improvement, but with a gradient in rates of improvement by socioeconomic condition, resulting in relentlessly increasing inequalities. Between the early 1970s and the early 1990s, average life expectancy at birth increased by 3.1 years for men and 2.8 years for women. The gap between social classes widened, particularly for men (see Figures 4.1 and 4.2). Overall inequality in life expectancy, as measured by the Gini coefficient, fell slightly but steadily for both men and women up to the early 1990s (Le Grand and Vizard, 1998) and began to increase in men in 1993, as shown in Figure 4.3. Infant mortality rates dropped substantially over time, from 13.3 per 1,000 live births in 1977 to 5.8 in 1997. The social class gap widened from the early 1990s, although official figures may underestimate this trend, because social class information is not available on many births outside marriage (Figure 4.4). Inequalities in child mortality also widened between the early 1980s and the early 1990s, for both boys and girls, despite significant improvements on average (Drever and Whitehead, 1997). A similar pattern was observed for adult male mortality up to the age of 64, with rates dropping by 44% over 20 years to the early 1990s in the higher social classes, but only by about 10% in social class V, with the latter showing significantly higher rates than all other classes. Cause-specific inequalities in mortality were particularly large for respiratory diseases, and for mental disorders (Figure 4.5). Aggregate data from the General Household Survey (GHS) appear to indicate an overall increase in both chronic and acute illness over the period 1974-94 (Le Grand and Vizard, 1998) but no consistent widening of inequalities (Figure 4.6). Behavioural risk factors, such as smoking, nutrition, obesity and lack of physical activity, also showed a clear social class gradient, which, at least in the case of smoking, increased over time (Drever and Whitehead, 1997).

A clear gradient in life expectancy was observable among health authorities with different average degrees of deprivation, which was even more marked for healthy life expectancy (Figure 4.7). A more detailed analysis of geographic inequalities in Britain is reported in Shaw et al (1999). Geographic inequalities were accounted for only to a limited extent by differences in social class composition:

> For England and Wales, the inclusion of social class reduces the number
> of excess [relative to expected] deaths by area per year by only 29%.
> (Shaw et al, 1999, p 259)

The extent of the inequalities reported is well beyond the reach of any health
care resource allocation formula. Their apparent widening over time was deemed
to reflect a socioeconomic 'polarisation', with widening gaps in income, income
inequality, wealth, unemployment and increasing rates of poverty in the most
disadvantaged areas (Shaw et al, 1999; Graham, 2000).

### Inequalities by ethnicity

Patterns of inequality vary substantially by country (or broader region) of birth,
which is often used in place of ethnicity because the NHS has so far failed to
collect the latter routinely. The social class gradient observed in the general
population is reproduced only in some groups (for example, Indian subcontinent,
or white minorities), with others showing a less clear pattern. After adjusting for
social class structures, standardised mortality ratios (SMRs) were as high as 137
for individuals born in East Africa, and 159 for those born in Bangladesh. Only
Caribbean-born individuals had an SMR below 100 (82), while Scottish- or
Irish-born residents in England fared significantly worse than average, particularly,
but not exclusively, in the manual classes (Drever and Whitehead, 1997). A
comparison between the results of an early study by Marmot et al (1984) and

**Figure 4.1: Trends in life expectancy at birth by social class and 95%
confidence intervals, women**

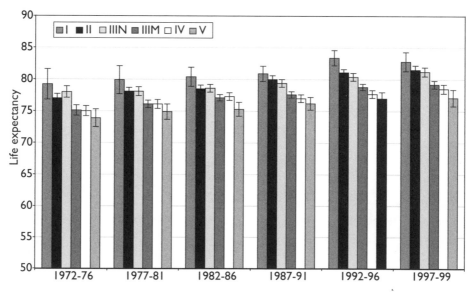

*Source:* ONS data

**Figure 4.2: Trends in life expectancy at birth by social class and 95% confidence intervals, men**

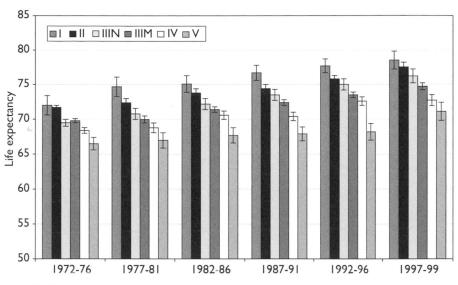

*Source:* ONS data

data presented in Drever and Whitehead (1997) shows that people born in the Indian subcontinent or Ireland further worsened their relative position between the early 1970s and the early 1990s, while people born in the Caribbean further improved theirs. Social class inequalities within groups increased across all groups, again except the Caribbean, who showed an inverse gradient in 1984.

Ethnic inequalities appear relatively small in younger individuals, and begin to widen beyond the mid-30s (Nazroo, 2003). Karlsen and Nazroo (2000) argued that:

> ethnicity as structure (both in terms of racialization and class experience), rather than ethnicity as identity, is strongly associated with health for ethnic minority people living in Britain. (p 55)

*Evidence about inequalities in access to and utilisation of health care*

A review undertaken in the early days of the Labour government could only support the conclusion that deprived groups are under-served, relative to their needs, in relation to inpatient procedures such as coronary angiography or cardiac revascularisation, or preventive services, such as screening or child immunisations (Goddard and Smith, 2001).

A more recent review distinguished between macro- and micro-studies of access, and attempted to explain apparent discrepancies (Dixon et al, 2003). Macro-studies, based on national survey or panel data, recently identified an inverse (pro-poor) social class gradient, the opposite of what previous similar studies had

**Figure 4.3: Trends in mean age at death by gender (age standardised, base 1974), and in overall inequalities in life expectancy (measured by Gini coefficients), England and Wales**

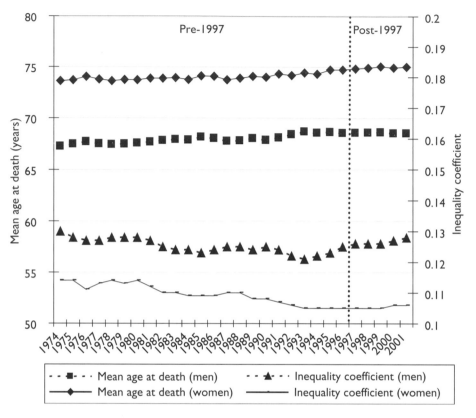

*Source:* 1974-94 figures from Le Grand and Vizard (1998); 1995-2001 figures based on author's analysis of ONS data

reported. The nature of the data used does not permit a detailed adjustment for need, and this may explain at least part of the differences. A recent study on pooled Health Survey for England data 1994-99, using a multidimensional adjustment for need, came to the conclusion that socioeconomic disadvantage is associated with poorer access (utilisation) of health care (Sutton et al, 2002). Dixon et al also reviewed a number of micro-studies, focusing on individual services or patient groups. These pointed more unequivocally to a social class gradient favouring the better off in access to care, for preventive as well as acute and chronic health care. They concluded that differences in 'voice', social networks and health-related beliefs need to be addressed, in addition to more material barriers (Dixon et al, 2003).

Attempts were made from 1975 to bring the geographic distribution of health care financing in line with variations in need among areas. The Resource Allocation Working Party (RAWP) formula for the allocation of hospital resources

**Figure 4.4: Trends in infant mortality rates (per 1,000 live births) in England and Wales, by socioeconomic condition**

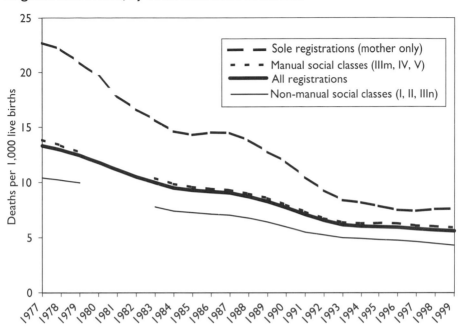

Source: DH analysis of ONS data

contributed to equalising health expenditure across NHS regions, although relative changes have been slow, and needs-adjusted inequalities still persist today.

## New Labour: government objectives and policies

*Campaign objectives*

Health inequalities were hardly a key issue in the heated campaign preceding the General Election of 1 May 1997. The Labour Party pledged to "tackle the division and inequality in our society" (Labour Party, 1997) but its Manifesto did not contain specific references to health inequalities. The party appeared more concerned about cutting waiting lists and ensuring an adequate growth of the financial resources available to the NHS. However, before the general election the Labour spokesman confirmed the party's intention of launching an independent inquiry into health inequalities, as the first stage of a long-term strategy to tackle the problem (BMJ, 1997).

By the 2001 election campaign, health inequalities had become a prominent feature in the party's programme. The new manifesto contained pledges to "close the health gap" (Labour Party, 2001, p 21) by tackling major causes of death, particularly heart disease, cancer and stroke, and by placing a new emphasis on prevention through screening, child nutrition and smoking reduction. Pledges

**Figure 4.5: Standardised mortality ratios for key disease areas, by socioeconomic group, England and Wales (1991-93)**

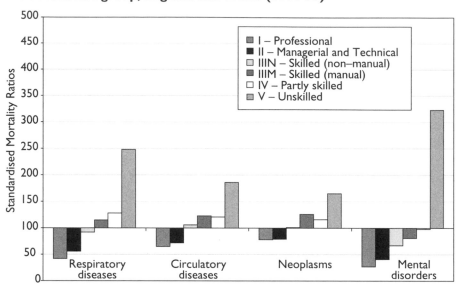

Source: Drever and Whitehead (1997)

were also made to tackle discrimination against the over-50s in health care. But even the more detailed 2001 Manifesto did not do justice to the government's elaborate strategy to tackle health inequalities.

### Setting the baseline: the Acheson Inquiry (1998)

An independent inquiry was set up in July 1997, under the leadership of Donald Acheson, which reported in November 1998. It concluded that:

> Inequalities by socioeconomic group, ethnic group and gender can be demonstrated across a wide range of measures of health. (DH, 1998b, p 25)

A socioeconomic model was used to interpret interactions between layers of health determinants and highlight possible intervention points. Thirty-nine recommendations were made, only a small minority concerning the provision of health care.

The central tenets of the future strategy to tackle health inequalities were all clearly identifiable in the Acheson Report. First, the emphasis on the need for cross-governmental policies, at the national and local levels, to address the multidimensional causes of ill health. Second, the emphasis on a life-course approach, recognising that the causes of health inequality in adult life often date back to childhood, or even before birth. Third, the emphasis on the need to

**Figure 4.6: Prevalence rates of acute sickness and limiting long-standing illness in selected years: ratios between social classes V and I**

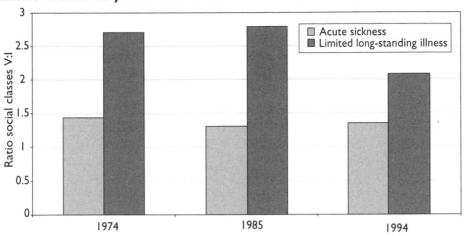

*Source:* GHS, data analysed by Le Grand and Vizard (1998)

address poverty and social exclusion as the primary objective of government policy, although recognising that health inequalities tend to be shaped as a gradient across all social classes.

Despite a generally warm reception, the Acheson Report attracted a number of criticisms. Many recommendations were seen as reflecting desirable goals more than concrete policy proposals. Their insufficient prioritisation was also a concern, as well as the failure to provide cost and cost-effectiveness evidence, and the lack of an explicit reference to a coherent ethical framework (Davey Smith et al, 1998; Macintyre, 1999; Macintyre in House of Commons, 2000; Oliver and Nutbeam, 2003). A key limitation of the Acheson Report is its failure to address explicitly trade-offs between equity and efficiency in relation to specific policies. It did not discuss how to prevent inequalities from being worsened by policies aimed at improving average health, which may benefit the better off to a greater extent. This would remain a crucial ambiguity in government policy in the following years.

## The strategy: tackling health inequalities

### Our healthier nation

The first comprehensive attempt by the Labour government to deal with the issue of health inequalities was the publication of the consultative Green Paper, *Our healthier nation: A contract for health*, in February 1998, which anticipated some of the analyses and proposals of the Acheson Inquiry. Emphasising the principle of "mutual responsibility for improving health" (DH, 1998a, p 29) between the individual, the local community and the state, the Green Paper signalled the government's determination to set its quest for a reduction of health

**Figure 4.7: Life expectancy (LE) and healthy life expectancy (HLE) in health authorities (1999 boundaries) ordered by average level of deprivation (IMD2000, income domain), England and Wales (1994-98)**

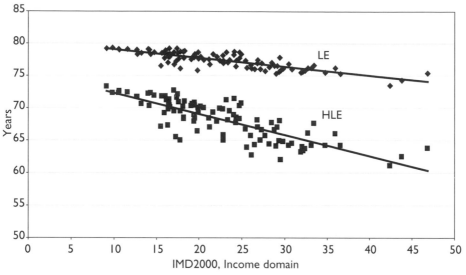

*Note:* HLE was calculated by adjusting Life Expectancy for health status, based on data from the General Household Survey (GHS)
*Source:* Author's analysis of HLE and LE data from Bajekal et al (2002)

inequalities in the context of policies aimed at improving overall health, failing to address the potential conflict between the two goals. National targets were set in four priority areas: heart disease and stroke, accidents, cancer and mental health; but the likely distributional effects of policies to reduce their incidence were not discussed.

The White Paper, *Saving lives: Our healthier nation*, and the joint document, *Tackling health inequalities: An action report*, followed one year later, setting out a comprehensive public health strategy. The commitment to reducing health inequalities by attacking "the breeding ground of poor health – poverty and social exclusion" (DH, 1999, p 3) was reinforced, although the government was committed to remaining firmly within existing social structures (Birch, 1999). Even Donald Acheson, while acknowledging the government's efforts, testified, "I should like to see some more redistribution of wealth" (House of Commons, 2000, question 116), two years after the publication of his recommendations. The action report provided a blueprint for action in all the areas of government where the inquiry identified scope for policy development. However, the extent to which individual recommendations were addressed and the level of detail of the proposed policies varied significantly. Also, the link between the Acheson Inquiry's "description of desirable outputs", and the government's "planned inputs" described in detail in the action report, was "missing", leaving no means of assessing the effectiveness and cost-effectiveness of the proposed policies (Macintyre in House of Commons, 2000, para 10).

## The NHS Plan and the national targets on health inequalities

The government's enthusiasm for its public health and health inequalities agenda was deemed to have reached a high point with the publication of the White Paper, *Saving lives*, and to have started to cool off thereafter (Whitehead in House of Commons, 2000). The NHS Plan 2000 addressed the issue of tackling health inequalities in a dedicated chapter, but did not give it high prominence elsewhere. The NHS Plan focused on changing the resource allocation formula as a means of tackling inequalities. It also set out a number of policies to improve the health of the most vulnerable groups in the areas of child health, nutrition, smoking, and drug and alcohol misuse.

Two national health inequalities targets, announced in the NHS Plan, were finally issued in February 2001, four months before the general election. The first was specifically aimed at children:

> Starting with children under one year, by 2010 we will reduce by at least 10 per cent the gap in infant mortality between manual groups and the population as a whole. (DH, 2001a)

The second target was broader:

> to reduce the difference in life expectancy between areas with the lowest life expectancy and the national average. (DH, 2001)

The first was consistent with a core aspect of the government's strategy, although the significance of the proposed reduction (in the region of one infant death averted every 20,000 births in the manual classes) may be debatable. The second target appeared to shift the focus towards geographic inequalities, which are not exclusively related to socioeconomic differences between areas, as previously discussed. This change of emphasis was probably linked to the government's renewed interest in resource allocation as a means to tackle inequalities, although most of the policy statements that preceded and followed the setting of the national targets were centered on socioeconomic, rather than geographic, inequalities.

## The increasing involvement of the Treasury

After launching a broad consultation exercise in the wake of its second electoral success, the government undertook a cross-cutting spending review in 2002. This marked the start of a substantial involvement of the Treasury in the area of health inequalities. The review aimed at developing the evidence base on the impact of interventions to tackle inequalities, and formulating a strategy for delivering the national health inequalities targets. The evidence base was little more than an abridged version of that provided by the Acheson Inquiry.

Interventions most likely to have an impact on progress towards the targets were identified as priorities. These ranged from reducing smoking in manual social groups to improving housing and road safety; from improving antenatal care to preventing teenage pregnancy.

A cross-government delivery plan, *A programme for action*, published the following year, included the first comprehensive assessment of progress made since the Acheson Inquiry. However, this was mainly in terms of targets set, spending commitments made and policies developed. Outcomes, even intermediate- or short-tem, were virtually absent. Indicators were identified only for future use. A detailed action plan followed, pinpointing departmental responsibilities and delivery mechanisms throughout. But, as in previous plans, many of the actions listed are, in fact, mere goals or targets.

In order to assess long-term resource requirements, the first Wanless Review, published in 2002, set out a vision of the NHS in 20 years' time. Its scenarios were all based on the assumption that a direct relationship exists between population health improvement and reduction of inequalities. Only at the end was it envisaged that good progress could be made "with the benefits of the high quality service disproportionately benefiting those most affluent and knowledgeable" (Wanless, 2002, p 65), thus eventually widening health inequalities. This scenario was dismissed as only possible in a country such as the US, where financing through general taxation is limited. The review failed to discuss why in fact this reflected so closely what had happened for a long time in the NHS, funded mainly through general taxation since its establishment.

The second Wanless Review, published in 2004, was aimed at identifying cost–effective approaches to the accomplishment of the most favourable scenario set out in the first review. Wanless had to conclude that suitable evidence did not exist, but that this should not be an "excuse for inertia" (Wanless, 2004, p 107) and advocated the immediate evaluation of current initiatives through a series of natural experiments. The review also recommended the development of a framework for using economic instruments such as taxes, subsidies and tax credits, on the model adopted for environmental protection (HM Treasury, 2002).

## Addressing health inequalities through the NHS

Disease-specific inequalities have been addressed through National Service Frameworks (NSFs), setting out targets, policies and resources to tackle major diseases. For instance, the NSF for coronary heart disease indicates that "resources will be targeted at those in greatest need and with the greatest potential to benefit" (DH, 2000, p 9). The first Wanless Review took this into account in its NSF costings, in recognition that the NHS could contribute to "substantial reductions" in inequalities. Similarly, the NHS Cancer Plan listed tackling inequalities among its major aims, particularly through a reduction of the prevalence of smoking, and of waiting times for access to specialist care. More recently, there has been increasing attention to ethnic inequalities (Sassi et al,

2004), an example being the consultation document on mental health issued by the Department of Health in 2003.

The National Institute for Clinical Excellence (NICE) was created in 1999, partly to end the phenomenon of 'postcode prescribing' through technology appraisals and clinical guidelines. The government placed an increasing emphasis on the mandatory nature of NICE's recommendations, but eliminating postcode prescribing remained difficult, due to financial constraints at the local level. To tackle broader geographic inequalities, the Advisory Committee on Resource Allocation (ACRA) was established in 1997 to review NHS funding arrangements. A new formula was implemented in 2003/04 with the aim of contributing to the reduction of avoidable health inequalities. Allocations for the years 2001/02 and 2002/03 included an interim Health Inequalities Adjustment, essentially based on a measure of premature mortality (the Years of Life Lost Index). This component was relatively small, £130 million in the first year, of which about half was to provide funding for Health Action Zones (HAZs), but the principle was generally welcomed (Whitehead in House of Commons, 2000; Shaw and Smith, 2001). Scotland and Wales developed separate formulae and policies for the allocation of health care resources to health boards (Box 4.1).

---

### Box 4.1: Health inequalities in Scotland and Wales[a]

When the New Labour government took office in 1997, health inequalities existed between and within countries in the UK. Wales, Scotland and Northern Ireland had consistently lower GDP per capita and higher mortality rates than England. Conversely, spending allocations, based on the Barnett formula, were substantially higher than in England. In this context, the devolution process set in motion by the government posed significant challenges in relation to health and health inequalities (Pollock, 1999). The evolution of the NHS in Scotland, in particular, has been progressively diverging from reforms implemented in England, with the return to a larger degree of command and control in the system. It is difficult to predict how this will impact on health inequalities in the long term. Policies directly aimed at tackling health inequalities in Scotland and Wales have mainly focused on resource allocation.

In Scotland, John Arbuthnott led a review of resource allocation arrangements. The final report, published in 2000, presented a new needs-based formula to allocate over £4 billion to 15 Health Boards, taking into account aspects such as inner-city deprivation. Although the principle that no Health Board should see their allocation cut down was maintained, an attempt was made to accelerate the realignment of resources to needs. However, evidence of poor progress towards health improvement and towards tackling inequalities in health and access to health care has recently become available (Irvine and Ginsberg, 2004). This prompted Arbuthnott himself to envisage a new review of the funding of Health Boards in 2005, as the strategy previously set out does not appear to be sufficient without a more structural reform of the system.

---

The National Assembly for Wales has embarked on a novel strategy. A National Steering Group to allocate NHS resources was set up in 2000. Its report in 2002 (Townsend, 2001) made three particular recommendations to reduce inequalities in health and access to health care: to adopt a direct needs formula for the allocation of NHS resources; to improve financial information; and to establish a dual strategy for health covering action outside as well as within the NHS. All parties in government accepted the report, and a Standing Committee was established to implement the recommendations. As a first step, early in 2004 most of an additional £30 million was allocated to the five Local Health Boards, among the total 22, whose funding was found to be significantly below the average required to meet the health needs of local populations. Further steps towards establishing equity of NHS resources by local area in future years are anticipated, together with joint action with professionals and organisations to reduce inequalities within areas.

As the basis for allocating funds, a new 'direct needs' formula was devised. It is based on the Welsh Health Survey, which provides detailed information about the conditions of health of a substantial representative sample (30,000) of the population of Wales. Among 18 indicators covered are arthritis, back pain, respiratory illness, heart problems, mental illness, cancer and diabetes. The survey is unique to the UK and is being extended to children. The formula displaces previous methods of using service utilisation as a proxy for need, and the data are considered to be more comprehensive, practicable and reliable than the alternatives (Gordon et al, 2001).

[a] Note prepared by Franco Sassi and Peter Townsend.

## Local level partnerships

Health Improvement Programmes, introduced in the White Paper, *The new NHS*, involve collaboration between health authorities, local authorities and other local organisations, towards the development of a local strategy for health improvement. When Primary Care Groups and Primary Care Trusts were introduced, these became the focal point of policies towards health inequalities at the local level within the NHS. The 1998 Green Paper called for local strategies and local targets for meeting national targets. Health Improvement Programmes were to play a key role in this process, identifying additional local priorities and, crucially, setting out strategies to tackle inequalities by addressing the problems of the most disadvantaged local neighbourhoods.

Health Action Zones (HAZs) were specifically aimed at developing programmes to tackle health inequalities through collaboration with social services, voluntary and business organisations and local communities. Twenty-six HAZs were established between 1998 and 1999, after a competitive bidding process. The results of interim national (Barnes et al, 2001) and local (Peters et al, 2002) evaluations indicate that HAZs should be seen mainly as 'agents of change', making possible partnerships and initiatives that would not otherwise have happened. Despite clear problems with the working of some partnerships and with community involvement, and although a direct impact on health outcomes was not yet observable, HAZs were generally regarded as a success. This contrasts with the view expressed by others that a limited geographic approach as that taken by HAZs will not address the problems of disadvantage, which is spread across communities (Shaw et al, 1999).

The NHS Plan called for an improvement of the collaboration between the NHS and local services, with the creation of Local Strategic Partnerships to "strengthen the links between health, education, employment and other causes of social exclusion" (DH, 2001b, p 111).

## Assessing the impact of government policies

Perhaps the best summary of the impact of the extraordinary policy machinery set up by the Labour government to tackle health inequalities is given in the second Wanless Review:

> After many years of reviews and government policy documents, with little change on the ground, the key challenge now is delivery and implementation, not further discussion. (Wanless, 2004, p 183)

Independent research, mainly based on a number of policy case studies, had reached similar conclusions in terms of a lack of apparent outcomes attributable to policy initiatives taken by the Labour government (Exworthy et al, 2003). It identified as an important achievement of the government's strategy the widespread, although not yet universal, recognition of the issue of health inequalities in the policy agenda, at the central and the local levels.

The approach taken by the Labour government to tackling health inequalities focuses on a broad array of determinants of health, some of which produce their effects during the course of a lifetime or even across generations; therefore, it is not likely to have a visible impact other than in the long term. National targets were set by the government only in 2001, to be reached in 2010. The measures to which these refer – disadvantage for manual classes in infant mortality and geographic variations in life expectancy at birth – actually worsened slightly in the early years of the Labour government, up to 2000 (Department of Health, 2002). Mortality gaps between social classes also widened in men, while they improved slightly in women, in the early years of the Labour government (Figure 4.8). Overall inequality in mean age at death continued to widen for both men and women from 1997 to 2001 (Figure 4.3).

The only assessment of progress made by the government to date is published as part of *Programme for action*. This contains very little evidence of progress. When evidence is presented, in fact, it often relates more to population health improvement than to the reduction of health inequalities. For instance, the report indicates that "in 2001-2, 120,000 people quit [smoking] at the four week stage"

**Figure 4.8: Trends in all cause mortality by social class, men and women aged 35 to 64, England and Wales**

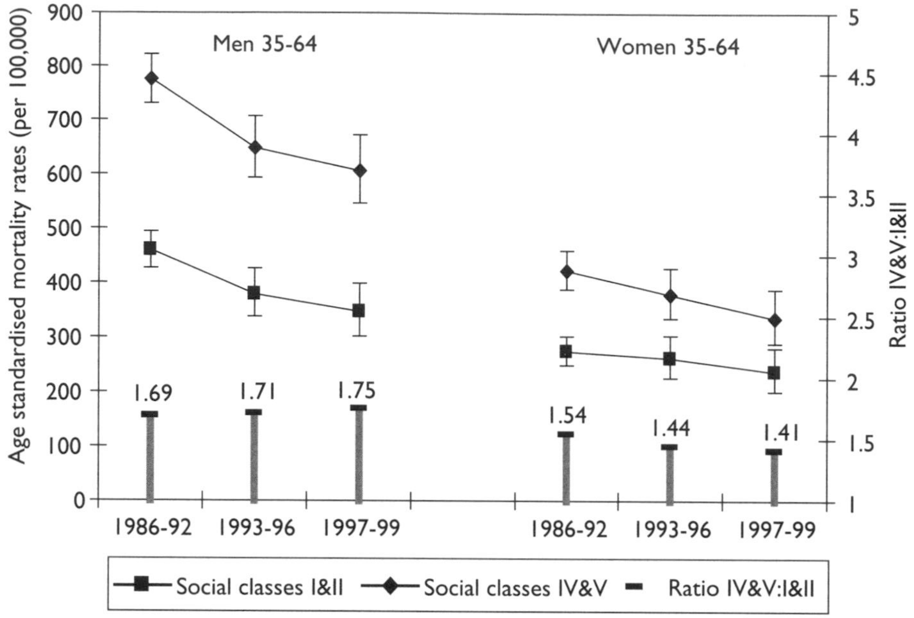

*Source:* ONS Longitudinal Study

(DH, 2003a, p 19). However, independent research shows that "services operating in deprived communities achieved lower cessation rates" (Bauld et al, 2003), even if those located within HAZs reached larger numbers of smokers. More consistent with the goal of tackling health inequalities are the outcomes reported with regard to child poverty (a reduction of 400,000 children in low-income households between 1998/99 and 2001/02; see also Chapter Seven of this volume), and with regard to housing (a reduction of homes falling below decent housing standards from 2.3 to 1.6 million, and a reduction of fuel-poor households from 4.3 to 1.8 million, between 1996 and 2001).

A comparison of GHS data on self-assessed health and long-standing illness before and after the Labour government took office shows diverging trends for the extreme income groups, resulting in an increased gap. The proportion of respondents indicating that their health was 'not good' over the previous year increased only in the bottom income group among working-age adults, and in the bottom two groups among pensioners, as shown in Figures 4.9 and 4.10. The pattern for long-standing illness was virtually identical. These findings are particularly interesting if read in conjunction with Le Grand and Vizard's analysis of GHS data (1998) covering the period 1974-94 (Figure 4.6), which identified similar disparities across socioeconomic groups, but concluded that "there is no obvious trend towards greater inequality over time" (p 114).

Some evidence is available on coronary heart disease (CHD) and cancer, two

**Figure 4.9: Proportion reporting less than good health by income fifth among working-age adults**

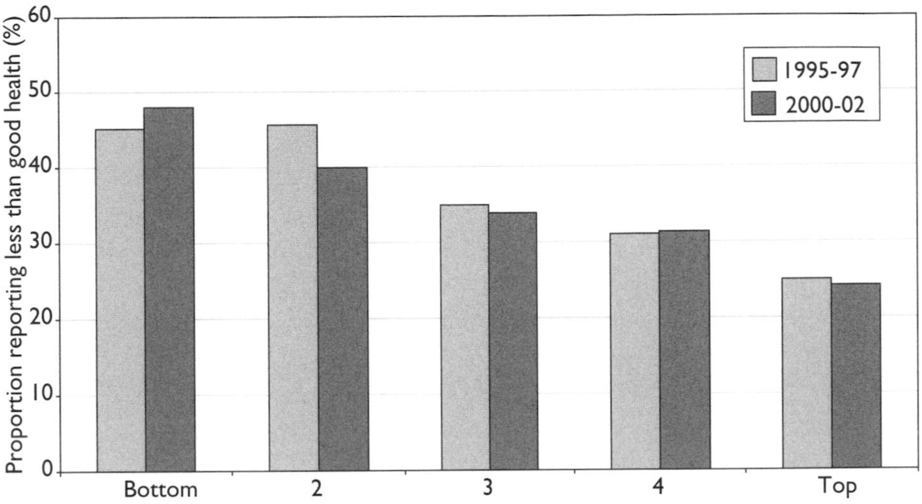

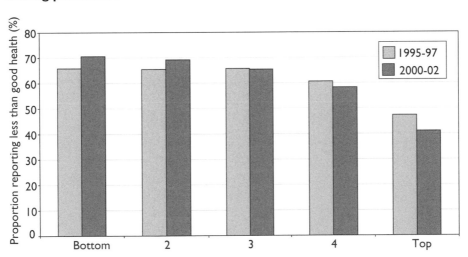

*Source:* GHS data, comparing pooled 1995/96 and 1996/97 data with pooled 2000/01 and 2001/02 data, Tom Sefton, CASE, LSE, unpublished

**Figure 4.10: Proportion reporting less than good health by income fifth among pensioners**

*Source:* GHS data, comparing pooled 1995/96 and 1996/97 data with pooled 2000/01 and 2001/02 data, Tom Sefton, CASE, LSE, unpublished

diseases with a disproportionately high incidence and mortality in disadvantaged socioeconomic groups. The 2004 progress report on the implementation of the NSF for CHD shows that the death rate for circulatory disease among the under-75s decreased by almost one quarter between 1996 and 2002, exceeding the trend planned in order to achieve the NSF target of a 40% reduction by 2010. Remarkable results were also reported in terms of reduction of waiting lists, access to thrombolysis within 30 minutes of arrival at hospital for victims of heart attacks (which improved from 38% in 2000 to 81% in 2004) and the use of statins for the prevention of CHD. However, the report does not provide any evidence of progress in tackling health inequalities, with the exception of one graph showing a positive correlation between the prescription of statins by area in 2002/03 and standardised mortality ratios. Taken in isolation, this is hardly evidence of any improvement. Time trends are not shown, the appropriateness of prescriptions is not examined, and whether increased prescriptions are simply in line with increased prevalence of risk factors, or higher, or lower, is not discussed. Data from the Public Health Observatories indicate that similar mortality reductions were achieved in all areas, and that the gap between areas with the highest CHD mortality and the national average was reduced by approximately 5% in the first three years of the Labour government (APHO, 2003), as illustrated in Figure 4.11. An analysis by social class indicates that the gap narrowed in men, but remained substantially stable in women (Figure 4.12).

Evidence of a widening of the mortality gap between socioeconomic groups, although covering only a short period of time after the publication of the NHS Cancer Plan, has recently become available from independent research. The study was undertaken on 2.2 million patients diagnosed with cancer between 1986 and 1999 in England and Wales, and followed up until 2001. It shows improvements in survival for most cancers and across all socioeconomic groups, especially in the late 1990s, but also an increase in the deprivation gradient in survival (Figure 4.13), which appears to be more consistent in male than in

**Figure 4.11: Trend in difference in age-standardised mortality rates for ischaemic heart disease between the fifth of local authorities with the highest mortality rates and the national average, England**

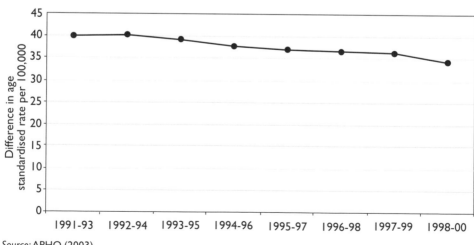

*Source:* APHO (2003)

**Figure 4.12: Trends in mortality from ischaemic heart disease by social class, men and women aged 35 to 64, England and Wales**

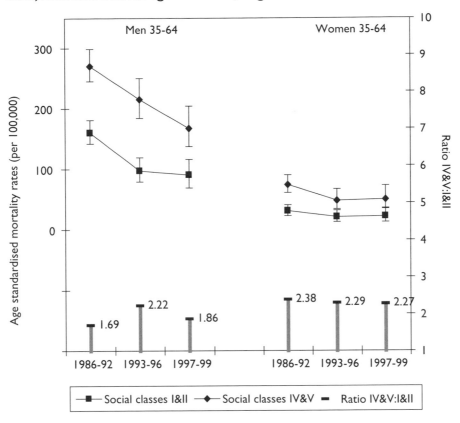

*Source:* ONS Longitudinal Study

female cancers (Coleman et al, 2004). Similarly to CHD, improvements in mortality were obtained in all areas in England, but there was virtually no reduction in the cancer mortality gap between the areas with the highest rates and the national average (APHO, 2003).

Limited evidence is also available on inequalities in access to health care in the early years of the Labour government. With regard to one of the priority areas for government action, the latest report of the Confidential Enquiries into Maternal Deaths indicates that "women from the most deprived circumstances appear to have a twenty times greater risk" of suffering a maternal death than more advantaged women (CEMD, 2001, p 42), suggesting that inequalities in access to antenatal care by socioeconomic group could be a major determinant. Poorer access to antenatal care was also observed in ethnic minorities (Petrou et al, 2001).

A socioeconomic gradient has historically been observed in low birth weight, a problem of crucial importance in the life-course perspective espoused by the government. The incidence of low birth weight increased in all groups in the

**Figure 4.13: Trends in cancer survival up to 2001, by period of diagnosis and deprivation category, England and Wales**

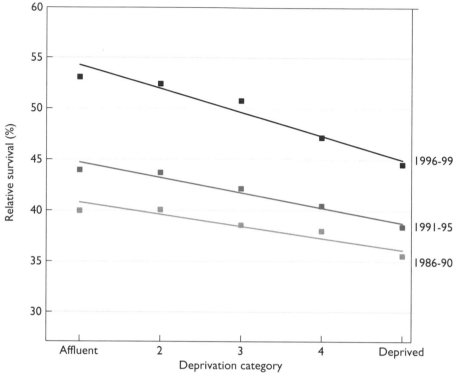

*Source:* Coleman et al (2004)

period between 1993 and 2002, but more in manual than in non-manual groups, although the increase in relative risk was not statistically significant (Moser et al, 2003).

On a more positive note, an analysis of the health of children up to the age of 15 based on data from the 1999 Health Survey for England (Saxena et al, 2002), which focused particularly on the health of ethnic minorities, failed to observe substantial inequalities in health and access to health care between children belonging to different socioeconomic groups. Health disparities by ethnic group were observed in favour of children with an Asian background, while Afro-Caribbean children suffered a disadvantage.

Controversial results have been achieved in the area of preventive health care, also at the centre of government action. The uptake of MMR vaccination began to fall in 1997, largely in association with "changes in the perception of the vaccine" (Middleton and Baker, 2003, p 854). Inequalities between areas with different levels of deprivation also fell, but only as a result of a proportionally greater decline in uptake in more affluent areas. Inequalities in the uptake of cervical cancer screening also reportedly decreased, with a 37 point increase in the proportion of GP practices achieving the 80% coverage target in more deprived areas (from 39% to 76% between 1991 and 1999), compared to an increase from 84% to 99% in more affluent areas (Baker and Middleton, 2003). However, the study does not investigate the socioeconomic condition of women who fail to receive screening even when the 80% coverage target is achieved, which is likely to reflect substantial inequality. Evidence to this effect has become available on breast cancer screening showing a larger proportion of deprived women among non-attenders, even with high coverage rates (Banks et al, 2002).

## The right policies? The right objectives?

*Discussion of findings*

The commitment made by the current Labour government to addressing the growing problem of health inequalities is unprecedented at home and almost unparalleled in an international context (Mackenbach and Bakker, 2003). However, the lack of consistent signs of progress to date, and the uncertainty about future progress resulting from the policies implemented, raises questions about the validity of this approach. In principle, each step appears worthwhile. In practice, a number of flaws become apparent.

Action could have been more prompt and incisive. One interpretation of the role of the Acheson Inquiry is that it helped the government to buy time, enabling it to resist pressures for immediate action after it took office (Shaw et al, 1999). The consultation exercise that followed the 2001 General Election could be interpreted in the same way. It could perhaps be argued that the production of review after review, consultation after consultation, action plan after action plan, was a deliberate strategy to keep the attention focused on health inequalities. If this is the case, however valid in principle, the strategy appears rather inefficient and potentially counterproductive.

The formulation of objectives and targets was virtually neglected by the Labour government until national inequalities targets were set during the 2001 General Election campaign. Objectives have always been defined very vaguely, referring at best to the general concept of 'reducing' or 'tackling' health inequalities. Similarly, the targets selected appear either limited in scope or not entirely consistent with the emphasis placed on the socioeconomic dimension of health inequalities.

The Labour government has never been clear about the sacrifices it would find acceptable in order to narrow health inequalities. In most policy statements, the emphasis is placed primarily on improving health overall, with reductions in health inequalities often seen as an outcome that will naturally follow, as long as targeted programmes ensure that the worse off are not left out. However different from the previous (Conservative) government's 'trickle-down' approach to addressing health inequalities, centred on economic recovery, the Labour government's approach does not seem to depart fundamentally from the controversial idea that overall improvements will address inequalities because those most in need will benefit the most.

The government deserves credit for having fully recognised the potential role of multiple forms of public intervention, well beyond health care, in tackling health inequalities. This led to a continued emphasis on collaboration in the development and implementation of policies. However, the government has not been able to prevent a certain degree of ambiguity and confusion with regard to institutional structures and accountabilities. With a newly appointed minister for public health, the Department of Health was a focal point for policies to tackle health inequalities throughout the first term. The second term was marked by the increasing involvement of the Treasury. Despite an appearance of coordination and complementarity, a dual leadership would inevitably become a source of duplication, conflict, ambiguity and blurred accountabilities in the delivery of the health inequalities agenda. In *Programme for action*, this issue was explicitly addressed with the creation of an elaborate structure, assigning ultimate responsibility to the Domestic Affairs sub-committee on Social Exclusion and Regeneration, chaired by the Deputy Prime Minister, although Public Service Agreements set responsibilities for the achievement of health inequalities targets within the Department of Health.

Tackling the root causes of ill health required the focus of government policy to shift away from health care. The measures adopted to make mainstream services more accessible and more responsive to the needs of disadvantaged groups have remained limited and vague, making their implementation difficult. Broader NHS reforms implemented by the Labour government may further jeopardise equity of access. Concerns have been raised, for instance, about the impact of the private finance initiative, likely to produce regressive distributional effects (Gaffney et al, 1999); the devolution of leadership on local action to tackle health inequalities to the recently created Primary Care Trusts, without the transfer of adequate means and resources to play this role effectively (Benzeval and Meth, 2002); and the creation of foundation hospitals, which may adversely affect equity of access and fairness in health care financing in multiple ways (Pollock et al, 2003). Even the exceptional financial strategy adopted by the Labour government, aimed at bringing health care expenditure in line with the European average, could hardly be expected to lead to reductions in health inequalities. A substantial share of the extra funding will be absorbed by the increasing cost of human, financial and physical resources. What is left will mostly be directed towards expanding capacity and improving quality, with no assurances that the distribution of such benefits will be skewed in favour of those who are presently at a disadvantage.

The development of policy to tackle health inequalities in England since 1997 appears to support Klein's view that "policy making about health inequalities takes place in a fog of disagreement about goals, controversy about causes and uncertainty compounded by ignorance about means" (Klein, 2003, p 55). The approach adopted by the Labour government is commendable, in many respects, and will certainly influence policy overseas. However, a fundamental lack of clarity about objectives and a number of flaws in the design and implementation of policies may prevent it from producing any impact on health inequalities, which may even continue to increase despite the government's efforts. The effective tackling of poverty, particularly among children, as discussed in other chapters of this volume, is likely to have an impact on the health of the worse off in the long term. However, this alone does not constitute a sufficiently aggressive redistributive policy to produce radical changes in many aspects of health inequalities.

# FIVE

# Social and political participation and inclusion

*Liz Richardson*

## Introduction

> It is not just representative democracy that needs to be strengthened....
> Every authority should set itself targets for improving voter turnout
> and strengthening local participation in the government of their
> community. (Tony Blair, 1998b)

> The ... freedom of citizens can only truly be realised if they are enabled
> to participate constructively in the decisions that shape their lives....
> Communities should be helped to form and sustain their own
> organisations, bringing people together to deal with their common
> concerns. (David Blunkett, 2003, pp 3, 6)

> I place such importance on the existence of a thriving voluntary and
> community sector [because] the community [where] I grew up
> revolved not only around the home but the church, the youth club,
> the rugby team, the local tennis club, the scouts and boys brigades,
> the Royal National Lifeboat Institution, the St Johns and St Andrews
> Ambulance Society.... (Gordon Brown, 2004)

The aim of this chapter is to investigate trends in political and social participation
since 1997 and to assess the impact of New Labour's attempts to increase the
quantity and quality of citizen participation. We look both at formal ways of
participating in political decision making processes – in this case, voting – and at
the more informal ways people influence decisions that affect the nature, level
and quality of public services they receive. We also look at social participation;
that is, people's involvement in activities of community or social benefit, like
volunteering and community organising.

Social and political participation is important for social inclusion because
deprivation is about more than income poverty. The ability to take part in decisions
that affect our lives is one way we are included in society. Political engagement
and social interaction are two of the four types of activity people should be able

to participate in to be considered socially included in the definition of social exclusion developed by the ESRC's Centre for Analysis of Social Exclusion (CASE) (Burchardt et al, 2002). Our participatory research has shown that residents in deprived areas also feel that "to be accepted as having useful ideas to contribute to society" and "to be involved in the community" are activities people should be able to participate in to be considered socially included (Richardson and Le Grand, 2002, p 13).

There has been a strong emphasis on all three forms of participation under New Labour, with participation at the centre of reform agendas for local government, public services and civil society more generally. The high priority and profile accorded to a range of forms of participation has been acknowledged as new and qualitatively different from previous administrations (Lowndes et al, 2001; Burton, 2003; Haezewindt, 2003).

The government's general policy statements on participation (including voting) have covered the whole population, and have not emphasised the importance of encouraging participation among certain groups in particular. In practice, however, specific New Labour policy actions and funding on social participation have been skewed towards tackling social exclusion. Involvement in regeneration by definition is targeted on areas of concentrated deprivation, while involvement in public services has a social exclusion dimension by default, for example, because of service delivery failures in deprived areas (Lupton, 2003b).

## Formal political participation

### New Labour's inheritance

Voting in general elections had been in decline over several decades by 1997, as shown by Figure 5.1 (Whiteley, 2004). Most European countries follow similar trends. Turnouts are much lower for those on low incomes, people in unskilled jobs, some minority ethnic groups and younger people (The Electoral Commission, 2003a). There has also been a decline over at least two decades in turnouts for local government elections, from an average of 41% between 1976 and 1996 to 32% in 1999, with no significant closing of the gaps in turnout by income, age or tenure (LGA, 2000; Rallings and Thrasher, 2000).

### Policy interventions from 1997

New Labour hoped that constitutional reform would restore public confidence in the political system and lead to improved turnouts. Reform included the devolved administrations, reform of the House of Lords and the 2000 Freedom of Information Act. 'Better public confidence' in democratic institutions was a Public Service Agreement (PSA) from 1999.

In addition, the option of a directly elected mayor was introduced, while the 2000 Representation of the People Act made possible local election pilots,

**Figure 5.1: Voter turnout in general elections, UK (1945-97)**

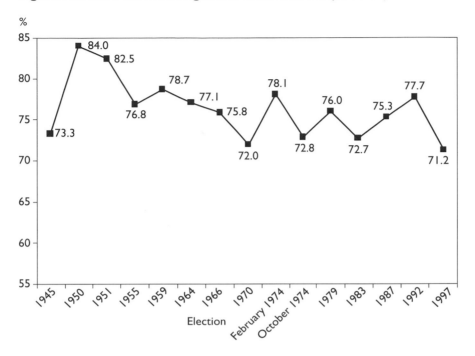

Note: Turnout calculated as percentage of registered voters.
Source: Whiteley (2004)

including changes to the opening times of voting stations, mobile ballot boxes, postal voting and e-voting. The majority could now vote without using a traditional ballot box for the first time since its introduction. There was no target for increased local turnout, but it is a 'Best Value' Performance Indicator (BV6) for local authorities.

## Results post-1997

The 2001 General Election seemed to confirm even worse levels of interest in voting. Turnout in 2001 at 59% was the lowest since 1918, down from 71.5% in 1997, and the first time turnout fell under 70% since 1945 (Figure 5.1). The profile of 2001 voters also shows continuing differences between groups: for example, 77% of owner-occupiers voted compared to 52% of social renters, and just over half of manual workers (54%) voted compared to 66% of professionals. Turnout by people from black and minority ethnic backgrounds was just 47% (The Electoral Commission, 2003a).

However, as we will see from the local election pilot results discussed later in this chapter, the dismal turnout for the 2001 Election does not mean that the relative failure of representative democracy is a fact of modern life. There was arguably not a strong enough policy agenda in Labour's first four years to encourage better national turnout. The public saw constitutional reform and freedom of information as a low priority (Bromley et al, 2001). One conspicuous gap was any attempt to change the tenor of political debate, and it has been argued that the 2001 turnout was particularly bad as people saw the election as uncompetitive (Whiteley, 2004). For many voters, New Labour's co-option of Conservative positions into its own agenda left little choice between the two parties. Therefore, New Labour's success in establishing the 'Third Way' actually undermined their own efforts to increase political participation.

Directly elected mayors have not revived interest in local democracy as evidenced by the initial referendum turnouts and average election turnouts below those for local elections (Rallings et al, 2002). The election in Peter Mandelson's Hartlepool constituency of H'Angus the Monkey as mayor, the mascot of the local football team, was widely acknowledged as a symptom of public disillusionment with party and local politics. (He did little to help by failing to deliver on his election promise to give all school children free bananas.)

However, there have been turnarounds in voting at a local level where there have been more accessible ways for voters to express their choices. Postal voting was the most successful in increasing turnout (The Electoral Commission, 2002). Postal voting had larger effects on potentially socially excluded groups: 43% of social renters voted by post compared to 25% of owner-occupiers. People with disabilities also responded to postal voting, as did people from minority ethnic backgrounds (MORI, 2003). In local authorities with concentrations of deprived areas, turnouts in relation to "previous comparable elections" increased with the use of postal voting; for example, from 31% to 42% in Middlesbrough and from 27% to 55% in South Tyneside (The Electoral Commission, 2002).

There is still some tweaking needed to improve the election pilots, particularly to make them as socially inclusive as possible. Postal voting can be more difficult for people with low levels of basic skills, and/or English as a second language. An Electoral Commission evaluation of all postal voting found only very limited evidence of any increase in fraud or electoral offences, but there have been concerns over allegations of vote rigging and the 2004 local elections also saw problems with poor implementation. There are Electoral Commission (2003b) recommendations to reduce risks for the future.

## Assessment

People do vote in large numbers when given more accessible ways to participate and a topic of interest to them. An "(all too) often" (Bromley et al, 2001) quoted example is TV polls like Big Brother:

> Over 10 million people are expected to vote in the Big Brother final – nearly as many as voted for Tony Blair in the last election. (*The Sun*, 22 July 2002)

A less frivolous TV poll example would be the 2.3 million votes cast to choose one historic UK building to restore in the BBC programme Restoration. This relates well to the government's work to raise the quality of the built environment, for example through the Commission for Architecture and the Built Environment (CABE). Other examples include average turnouts of 75% for housing stock transfers from the late 1980s (National Housing Federation, 2004), unsurprising perhaps given that the issue is of obvious relevance, and that there may have been local publicity and development over a long period. Surveys also indicate that electronic and other innovative ways to express views could increase rates of electoral participation (MORI, 2003).

People are not irreversibly cynical about politics but New Labour has failed so far to find sufficiently engaging issues. It has had a small amount of success in encouraging turnout by making voting more accessible. However, technical changes cannot compensate for lack of political content, debate or perceived relevance.

We look now at a second type of participation – social participation – before moving on to look at informal involvement in decision making.

## Social participation

### New Labour's inheritance

Overall, the UK seems to have had relatively stable and healthy overall levels of social participation since the 1950s when it was quoted as an example of good civic culture (Hall, 1999; Warde et al, 2003). Forms of participation have changed over time, notably the decline of trade unions and the Women's Institute, with membership of environmental organisations on the rise. However, between 1951 and 1998, the total volume of civic engagement remained steady (Hall, 1999; Warde et al, 2003). The UK compares well to other European countries and internationally[1]. In this sense, there was no serious 'problem' of participation for the general population to be dealt with in 1997.

However, the other relatively stable feature of social participation has been class, income and educational differences (Hall, 1999; Johnston and Jowell, 2002). Indeed, there is evidence that between 1991 and 1998 differences got worse, with the odds of being a 'joiner' decreasing for those on lower incomes, in lower skill jobs or with fewer formal educational qualifications (Warde et al, 2003). In 1997, middle class people were more likely to volunteer, be members of groups and take part in other semi-structured social activities (Smith, 1998). We look at more informal participation such as mutual aid later in this chapter.

Pre-New Labour policy on the voluntary sector was well developed, and already contributed to participation through funding programmes. Some continuing programmes, such as the Department of Health's Opportunities for Volunteering, began in the early 1980s. The other legacy for New Labour was a confusing array of organisations, funding sources and a patchy infrastructure for the voluntary and community sectors (Civil Renewal Unit, 2003). This issue was recognised by the government[2] (Active Community Unit, 1999), as were difficulties in getting sustainable funding, the need for new skills and lack of confidence and experience. The Centre for Analysis of Social Exclusion's own £1.45 million action research experiment, the Gatsby Project[3], started in 1996 as a result of these problems for 'bottom-up' community organisations.

## Policy interventions from 1997

Until 2001, the government's stated aim was only to make 'substantial progress' by 2004 towards getting one million more people actively involved in their communities. This was hardened into a PSA target in 2001 (Home Office PSA 8) to increase community participation (adults doing something at least once a month) and voluntary and community sector activity by 5% by 2005/06. A 5% increase would represent around a million people, assuming 47.5% of adults were already volunteering (Attwood et al, 2003). Policy interventions to reach this target have been spread over "at least 20 separate national programmes" (Dean, 2001) run by at least six government departments. There was no focus on social exclusion in the PSA until 2004, when the PSA was amended to include targeting efforts "especially among those at risk of social exclusion". Despite this, many government programmes are targeted on socially excluded groups. Some examples are given in Table 5.1. A review of voluntary and community infrastructure started in the second term (Active Community Unit, 2003).

The government has taken measures to create suitable neighbourhood contexts for social participation. High density mixed income urban design as promoted in the government's Sustainable Communities Plan may help facilitate social interaction (Cabinet Office, 2002). The government has argued that its work to maintain law and order is at the base of its attempts to stimulate social capital. We do not examine the evidence on social participation rates, social stability and neighbourhood contexts, but this demonstrates the government's rather rounded approach to community building.

## Results post-1997: overall levels of social participation

The message from government itself is that volunteering levels are now on the rise. Surveys done in 2000 and 2001 show that levels of social participation remained high (Krishnamurthy et al, 2001; Coulthard et al, 2002). New data sources such as the Home Office Citizenship Survey mean we can compare changes in social participation over time, which has been difficult until now[4] (Haezewindt, 2003; Whiteley, 2004). On the basis of these data, David Blunkett recently announced that the government has already exceeded its 2006 target of increasing community participation by 5%: the number of adults doing community activity rose by 1.6 million in the period 2001-03, a rise of more than 6%.

**Table 5.1: Examples of social participation schemes targeted on social exclusion**

| Scheme name | Organisation | Target areas/groups | Dates | Aim | Amount | Outputs |
|---|---|---|---|---|---|---|
| Fair Share | New Opportunities Fund and Community Fund (HM Treasury) | 77 deprived areas | 2002-05 | To bring target areas up to at least average levels of Community Fund allocations by 2005 | £179m over the period | **2002-03** – £31.4m awarded to 37 areas (90% of target) – £36.6m to 51 LA areas – £50m to CFN for 69 local area funds |
| Community Chest | Neighbourhood Renewal Unit, Office of the Deputy Prime Minister | 10% most deprived wards in the 88 Neighbourhood Renewal areas | 2001-06 | To fund volunteer led activities bringing communities together, and build capacity to tackle neighbourhood problems | £75m over the period £15m/yr | **2002-03** 5,835 awards to projects[a] |
| Community Club Development Programme | Sports England (Department of Culture, Media and Sport) | Community-based sports clubs | 2003-06 | To fund community club capital projects such as upgrading sports pitches and sports lighting | £60m over the period £20m/yr | **2003-04** half of the £20m allocated went to projects located in or benefiting the 20% most deprived wards |
| Millennium Volunteers | Department for Education and Skills | 16- to 24-year-olds, particularly those with experience of social exclusion | 1999-date | To get young people to complete 2,000 hours of volunteering in a year | – | **1999-2002** – over 53,500 young people – nearly half no previous experience of volunteering |
| Development Fund/ Volunteer Recruitment Fund (VRF from 2004) | Active Community Unit, Active Communities Directorate, Home Office | Volunteers who would not normally participate | 2001-date | To fund outreach work to recruit volunteers, and to increase group volunteering numbers. | £5.4m/yr | **2004-05** planned to support 90 projects |

*Sources*: NOF (2003); [a] Unpublished figures supplied by NRU, May 2004; Sport England (2004); Institute for Volunteering Research (2002); ACU (www.homeoffice.gov.uk)

*Levels of social participation by people and areas facing social exclusion*

New Labour has made inroads by creating social participation programmes targeted at socially excluded people and areas. Not all of the programmes have been successful; for example, the Experience Corps failed to achieve its target numbers of over-50s volunteers and had its government funding withdrawn. But there have been successes in targeting the 'non-joiners' (Table 5.1).

One significant New Labour success is the changes to the allocation of the Community Fund (National Lottery charities funding) (Table 5.1). Research mapping out charitable grants has shown that Community Fund funding and strategy strongly shapes the pattern of funding to geographical areas across several funding sources (Coombes et al, 2001). Following criticism by the Select Committee on Public Accounts that Lottery funding was failing to benefit poorer communities in 2000, 'Fair Share' ring-fenced funding was announced. There were also changes to simplify the application process.

The Community Chest scheme has also reached deprived people and areas. This is new government money targeted at areas facing social exclusion, although we do not know if the activities are wholly additional. Sport England has a new Community Club programme that has benefited deprived areas. The Department for Education and Skills (DfES) Millennium Volunteers scheme has been successful in involving young people not in work. New Labour has also put a programme of citizenship education projects in place for school pupils and 16- to 19-year-olds in education or training based on recommendations by Sir Bernard Crick. Citizenship education was introduced in 2002 as a statutory foundation subject for 11- to 16-year-olds.

This work to target the non-joiners is important to close the class, education and income differences in participation rates that were evident pre-1997, after three years in 2000/01 (Haezewindt, 2003; Summerfield and Babb, 2004) and again in 2003 (Munton and Zurawan, 2004). For example, in 2000, 18% of those in the 10% least deprived wards in England were active in a local organisation, compared to only 7% of those in the 10% most deprived wards. Differences between owner-occupiers and social renters were very similar (Williams, 2002). The Home Office Citizenship Survey shows that the vast majority of 'new' volunteers between 2001 and 2003 were people from the least deprived areas doing more informal volunteering (for example, favours for friends, house-sitting, babysitting), although this type of volunteering had also risen for people in the third worst of ten bands of deprivation, as had volunteering by Asian men (Munton and Zurawan, 2004).

There is a number of possible explanations for these disappointing numbers. Many Labour changes did not take place until the second term and have yet to show through. For example, only one of the examples in Table 5.1 started before 2001. 'Naturally occurring' and increasing social participation by better-off people also dwarf the scale of targeted government programmes. The relatively small scale of efforts to target social exclusion in participation is potentially a hindrance to them closing the gaps, and achieving the new emphasis in the 2004 PSA on participation by people at risk of social exclusion. Gordon Brown has now set up the Russell Commission to develop a national youth volunteering strategy with elements of a US AmeriCorps programme for gap-year volunteering. However, these proposals are missing the point of volunteering, despite good intentions. It is questionable whether this type of 'mass' volunteering programme, if implemented, would represent genuine progress on volunteering. It is not clear, either, if it would help to close gaps in participation by less well-off people across age groups. An alternative would be to scale up provision in its current form – that is, a number of smaller programmes, administered locally – although this might be difficult and complex to implement.

## Changes to the quality of participation

The third possible reason why national statistics may not reflect New Labour progress on social participation is that a key area of action has concerned improvements to the quality of existing community work, and developing voluntary and community sector infrastructure. This does not deliver increased numbers of people (excluded or not) who participate, but contributes to the strengthening of the sector and its work. Indeed, capacity building has been a theme during New Labour's terms in office in response to the need for community development support, and the problems of coordination of support already described.

For example, the Community Development Learning Fund was set up by the Home Office in response to the need for learning and networking support for community groups identified in work on the National Strategy for Neighbourhood Renewal[5]. The Fund achieved take-up by socially excluded groups and groups doing risky work in areas of deprivation, before being merged with Community Champions (Duncan and Thomas, 2001).

The Public Administration Select Committee, among many others, has criticised the government for the confusing number of different policies and initiatives relating to public participation, and advocated the need for better single sources of information (House of Commons, 2001). Similar arguments have been raised by the voluntary and community sectors about funding streams for community activity. The government has taken these criticisms seriously, and has responded, for example, with a 'single portal' website for government funding for the sector (www.governmentfunding.org.uk). From 2001, the Home Office has funded a national web-based database of volunteering opportunities (www.do-it.org.uk), and the government has been involved in the merger of organisations into a new single national volunteering body, Volunteering England (www.volunteering.org.uk). Volunteering England is drafting "radical" plans to cohere volunteering infrastructure and bring together a "hopelessly fragmented" sector (Shifrin, 2003), linked to government funding. In response to feedback, the Neighbourhood Renewal Unit has merged three community participation funding programmes covering both community activity and community involvement in decision making into the Single Community programme from 2004.

## Assessment

New Labour has been criticised for their emphasis on involvement in groups and other semi-structured forms of participation (such as volunteering), which tend to have lower involvement among the less well off (Williams, 2002). People on lower incomes, in manual work or with fewer educational qualifications are not 'joiners' to the same extent as better-off people, but they are equally, if not more, likely to help out friends and neighbours on an informal basis (Coulthard et al, 2002; Attwood et al, 2003). Therefore, it is argued that New Labour could do more to encourage participation by disadvantaged people if they promoted mutual aid and informal helping rather than membership of groups.

While this is an initially attractive argument, it is mistaken on several counts. First, the government has backed mutual aid and informal volunteering schemes, such as Time Banks. Second, an obstacle to government promoting informal helping has not been ideological but practical; it is much more difficult and risky for government to support individuals than community organisations. New Labour did make an "unusual and challenging" foray (Duncan and Thomas, 2001, p 11) in 1999 into direct funding for individuals but the experience of Community Champions was that funding did not reach non-joiners (Johnston and Campbell-Jones, 2003, pp 2-3).

Third, three quarters of the population in lower-income areas already do favours for friends, acquaintances and relatives anyway, without any need for intervention (Coulthard et al, 2002; Attwood et al, 2003). Given this, it is not clear that this approach has the potential to significantly drive up participation by excluded groups. Fourth, there are other reasons to promote structured participation (for example, group members are more likely to get involved in other activities; it develops personal skills, and so on). Radical community practitioners, while recognising the value of informal helping, point out the additional value of collective organisation in mobilising people to tackle neighbourhood issues together (Gibson, 2004). Therefore, despite the cultural difficulties in closing participation gaps using conventional volunteering and community groups, the government's focus is arguably the right one.

We turn now to our third and final form of participation, involvement in decision making.

## Involvement in decision making

*New Labour's inheritance: pre-1997 levels of involvement in decision making*

There are many different measures of informal public involvement in decision making by public agencies. We do not focus here on activities such as writing to an MP, donating money or attending a political meeting. This is not the focus of New Labour policy, and there has been little change in these types of activity since 1984 (Whiteley, 2004). Despite the fall in voter turnouts, political participation more generally is alive and well in the UK, and data from 2000 shows the same is true around the world:

> Apathy schmapathy. People in post-industrial nations are more likely than ever to engage in forms of direct political action. (Institute for Social Research, 2003)

The main focus of New Labour's work has been citizen involvement in local government, regeneration and public services. Citizen involvement is not a new phenomenon. User involvement in UK health services extends from Community Health Councils from 1974 to the Patients Charter of 1991. A 1998 'stocktake' of tenant participation in council housing showed relatively high levels of activity (Cole et al, 2000), partly due to Compulsory Competitive Tendering in the 1980s. In contrast, New Labour inherited a low level of involvement in services like policing (Newburn and Jones, 2001).

Overall, user and public involvement was already well in train by 1997, as shown by Figure 5.2. For example, there had been significant growth in the use of traditional 'consumerist' approaches, such as complaints and suggestion schemes, initiated by local authorities as a response to the Conservative governments of the 1980s and 1990s (Lowndes et al, 2001).

However, other than social housing, public involvement was dominated by middle class, better-educated professionals (Bromley et al, 2000). Young people, people from ethnic minorities and 'traditionally excluded' groups were particularly unlikely to participate (Lowndes et al, 2001).

*Quality issues pre-1997*

Research consistently shows that ineffective user participation is worse than no participation at all (Policy Commission on Public Services, 2004).

Despite progress on levels of involvement pre-1997, there were recognised quality problems for both the consultees and the consulting organisations. Capacity building was needed on "both sides of the equation" (Gaventa, 2004, p 2). Issues included:

**Figure 5.2: The growth in different forms of participation**

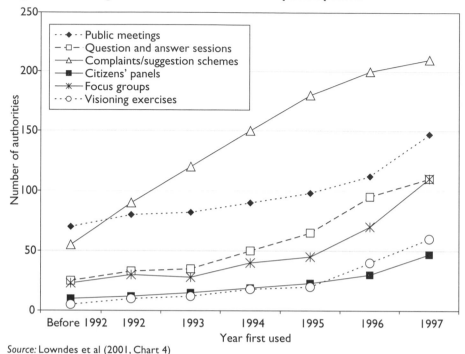

*Source:* Lowndes et al (2001, Chart 4)

- Citizens' lack of awareness of opportunities to participate, and lack of 'capacity' to be involved, such as confidence to articulate views to professionals (Taylor, 1995). Eighty per cent of the public said they had not been involved in local government consultation initiatives in 1999 (Bromley et al, 2000).
- Scepticism by agencies on the value of involvement, especially in relation to risks, costs and disbenefits (Taylor, 1995). Typical objections from councils were about resources, unrealistic expectations, the slowing of decisions and unrepresentativeness (Audit Commission, 1999).
- Lack of responsiveness of agencies, and failure to link public feedback to decision making (Burton 2003), for example, even three quarters of 'best practice' authorities failed to make these links (Audit Commission, 1999).

A big deterrent to participation is when people see local authorities not responding, or appearing not to respond. The institutional and policy context is a causal factor determining levels of participation (Lowndes and Wilson, 2001). New Labour in 1997 faced a difficult task to fully embed a genuine culture of involvement into public bodies and other agencies.

## Policy interventions from 1997

Support for extended public participation is at the heart of Labour's wider drive to modernise local government and public services. For example:

The government has a clear vision of successfully modernised local government. It will be characterised by councils which once again engage directly with their local communities. Such councils will actively promote public participation. (DETR, 1998)

As Table 5.2 illustrates, a defining feature of the New Labour administration is the extent to which their policies are comprehensively 'involvement-friendly' (Barnes et al, 2003; Burton, 2003; Gaventa, 2004). Most new approaches to service planning and delivery include ways that service users can be involved in decisions. Existing participation levers are maturing and being formalised.

Local government involvement is not a PSA but is monitored and reviewed as part of the performance indicators for Best Value. User satisfaction with council services and performance is measured via the local authority tri-annual user survey. Involvement in health services to 'enhance accountability to patients and public' is PSA 5. Other area-based initiatives or service improvement schemes, such as those listed in Table 5.2, have reporting requirements that include public involvement. There are no targets for the quality or effectiveness of involvement, but there is much guidance.

### Results post-1997: overall levels of involvement in decision making

It is difficult to collate a comprehensive picture but evidence suggests that levels of active involvement in decision making with local government and service providers have not increased significantly. Change between 1997 and 2001 in public involvement in local government showed no major leaps in the numbers of local authorities using different involvement techniques. There has been a rise since 1997 in the use of one technique – consultation – as shown by the sixfold increase in the number of consultation and survey exercises done by MORI between 1996 and 2002 for local government (personal communication with MORI). But this is a relatively passive form of involvement and does not mean an increase in active citizen involvement. There was growth in the use of more innovative and deliberative techniques for public involvement between 1997 and 2001, such as focus groups and citizen panels (18% to 71%), but these techniques do not involve large numbers of people. An estimated 14 million people were involved in local government decision making exercises in 2001 (Birch, 2002).

In public services such as social housing, already high levels of involvement have not substantially increased. The situation has also not improved in areas like policing/community safety where levels of involvement have traditionally been lower and more difficult to generate. The position in 2004 is that community engagement is still very patchy. Awareness of police consultative methods among the general public is small. In public health services, patient and public representation is very variable and there is a shortage of representatives. In regeneration, initial results in a few cases for election of community 'representatives'

**Table 5.2: Illustrative list of involvement policies**

| Policy area | Policy or initiative | Examples of community involvement guidance or requirements | Government department |
|---|---|---|---|
| **Liveability** | Public space policy | "Community involvement with public space schemes, large and small, is essential to getting a scheme that really works and is sustainable in the long-term."[1] The Liveability Fund supports significant local authority projects to improve parks and public spaces. This is part of a £201 million package of complementary initiatives aimed at improving liveability/the quality of local environments. Proposals to this fund must include community involvement. | ODPM |
| **Culture, sport and heritage** | Sport and physical activity strategy | "The Government has also introduced new legislation to require all state schools to seek approval from the Secretary of State for Education and Employment for the sale of playing fields, which includes consultation with community and other user groups. Approval is only given where funds raised are ploughed back into sport and education, and where remaining playing fields fully meet the needs of the school and community both now and in the future."[2] | DCMS |
| | Heritage policy | "This is the first statement of Government policy on the historic environment for a generation." "The historic environment has a long and valuable tradition of voluntary activity. The Government is firmly committed to promoting voluntary activity [in heritage]."[3] | |
| | Cultural strategy guidance | "We need to find ways that ensure that all sections of our communities are given the chance to express what is important to them and ensure that community views on cultural and quality of life issues are given the weight they deserve."[4] | |

**Table 5.2: contd.../**

| Policy area | Policy or initiative | Examples of community involvement guidance or requirements | Government department |
|---|---|---|---|
| **Community safety** | 1998 Crime and Disorder Act | The 1998 Crime and Disorder Act sets out requirements for statutory partnerships known as Crime and Disorder Reduction Partnerships, which "invite [the] co-operation of a range of local private, voluntary, other public and community groups including the community itself."[5] Partnerships "must make every effort to encourage local groups and communities to be actively involved in the audit and strategy process."[6] | Home Office |
| | Community cohesion policy | Recognises the voluntary sector as a partner and a valuable route to engagement with local communities. The guidance advises LA's to "establish a compact between themselves and the community sector and ensure that these groups have adequate funding and training to take part at a meaningful level."[7] | |
| | Police Consultative Committees | "Membership always includes representatives from the police, the police authority, constituent councils and voluntary, statutory and community groups. General meetings are open to the public."[8] | |
| **School education** | Extended schools | "Membership of groups and committees [to implement extended schools programmes] varies but they should all give community members and other groups the opportunity for representation." "In every school and community there will be key groups who need to be consulted about activities. They should be involved in the planning process…. Efforts should be made to consult as many parents as possible during the planning phase."[9] | DfES |
| **Planning** | Community Strategies and Local Development Frameworks | "The key to an effective community strategy will, therefore, be successful partnership working and community involvement throughout the process."[10] "[LDFs] will be subject to rigorous procedures of community engagement in accordance with the authority's statement of community involvement and can be material considerations of significant weight in the determination of planning applications."[11] "More effective community involvement is a key element of the Government's planning reforms."[12] | ODPM |

**Table 5.2: contd.../**

| Policy area | Policy or initiative | Examples of community involvement guidance or requirements | Government department |
|---|---|---|---|
| **Health** | 2001 Health and Social Care Act and Patient and Public Involvement (PPI) Forums | Section 11 of the 2001 Health and Social Care Act provides for a new statutory duty on the NHS to involve and consult patients and the public in service planning, operation and in the development of proposals for changes. "The NHS should put the patient at the centre of everything it does. To embed and sustain this approach within the NHS requires not just a change in attitude among staff but also a new approach to mechanisms for patient and public involvement. The new mechanisms for Patient and Public Involvement (PPI) Forums enable patients to be as involved as they want to be in decisions about their care and enable communities to be involved in their local health service. The PPI agenda overall supports this vision of a patient-centred NHS."[13] | DH |
| **Children, families and young people** | Children, families and young people policy | "There will be a duty placed on Local Authorities and others to co-operate to secure better outcomes for children. The key vehicle for doing this will be the Children's Trust. Children's Trusts will bring together a range of partners, including the voluntary and community sector, to integrate the planning and commissioning of children's services."[14] "The Government is committed to providing more opportunities for children and young people to get involved in the planning, delivery and evaluation of policies and services relevant to them."[15] | DfES |

*Sources:* [1] ODPM (2002); [2] DCMS (2000); [3] DCMS and DTLR (2001); [4] DCMS (2004); [5] www.crimereduction.gov.uk/regions00.htm; [6] Section 5 (3) of the Crime and Disorder Act 1998; [7] Home Office (2002); [8] www.police999.com/history/police15.html; [9] www.teachernet.gov.uk/wholeschool/extendedschools/detailedguidance/consultationandplanning; [10] DETR (2001); [11] ODPM (2004b); [12] ODPM (2004a); [13] DH (2003c); [14] DfES (2004); [15] www.cypu.gov.uk/youth/index.cfm

to New Deal for Communities Boards were promising (for example, turnouts of 42% by postal vote in Newcastle and 43% in Bradford). Unfortunately, later assessment of turnouts over 13 New Deal for Communities (NDCs) areas showed disappointing results overall, with some turnout figures dismally low (Rallings and Thrasher, 2002).

### Better targeting on social exclusion

There have been many additional efforts under New Labour to target participation more effectively on excluded groups and groups that traditionally do not get involved. There have been some successes in this area. New Labour's area-based initiatives targeting areas of exclusion have all had a strong emphasis on community involvement of some kind such as Neighbourhood Wardens, Neighbourhood Management Pathfinders, Housing Market Renewal Pathfinders, Healthy Living Centres, Market Towns Initiative, Home Zones and Education Action Zones. Table 5.3 illustrates five examples of targeted schemes to increase participation by excluded groups or in excluded areas under New Labour. While this is potentially positive, again, it does not involve large numbers of people and therefore is unlikely to have increased levels of involvement by a significant amount.

### Improving quality of involvement

In terms of the quality of participation, there have been moves to build the capacity of citizens to be involved, and parallel moves to change institutions to make them more responsive to involvement.

Lamentable practice in citizen involvement continues to be identified (Policy Commission on Public Services, 2004), and also witnessed in CASE research with tenants' and residents' groups. Some local authorities are still resistant to dialogue, and lack the political will or officer drive for involvement. Public services and local government continue to find it hard to engage people, particularly 'hard to reach groups'. Some remain to be convinced of the value of involvement, particularly in relation to the costs (Birch, 2002). Some agencies find it hard to listen and respond, and participants still feel intimidated. Chief executives of local authorities admit their organisations need new skills and cultural change.

However, while life is not yet perfect, the bigger picture is of a sea change under New Labour in the field of public involvement in local government and public services. Four things stand out:

1. Involvement policy is embedded in central government policy (see Table 5.2). The comprehensive cross-cutting nature of government policy of involvement also makes it much more difficult for public involvement to be marginalised or policy changed.

**Table 5.3: Examples of socially excluded groups involved in decision making under New Labour**

| Involvement | Government department and public service or policy area | Target for involvement | Area of involvement initiative | Numbers | Other comments/ successes |
|---|---|---|---|---|---|
| Sure Start | DfES – early years | Parents of under-4s in Sure Start areas | Planning and delivery of early years provision | Average 5 parents per local scheme management committee. Up to 550 schemes planned 1999-2006 | Local people involved in the delivery of services, eg local parents do research on local needs. All Sure Start programmes consulted parents on what services to offer. |
| Crime and Disorder Reduction Partnerships | Home Office – community safety | Community representatives | Planning and delivery of community safety strategies | – 86% of partnerships consulted minority ethnic groups<br>– 12% consulted unemployed people<br>– 26% consulted homeless people<br>– 16% consulted travellers | A Community Engagement Strategy is now being developed by the Police Standards Unit to get key delivery agencies such as Drug Action Teams actively consulting, and includes the introduction of a target. |
| Community Engagement Funding | Department of Health – public health | Black and minority ethnic communities | Development of local drugs strategies | 47 local BME community groups across England carried out 51 needs assessments for strategies. Over 12,000 community members (including 200 drugs users) were consulted. | A significant number of the groups now help design and develop local services.<br>22% of those trained to do research have secured employment in drug services or related fields. |

**Table 5.3: contd.../**

| Involvement | Government department and public service or policy area | Target for involvement | Area of involvement initiative | Numbers | Other comments/ successes |
|---|---|---|---|---|---|
| Healthy Communities Collaborative Pilot | Department of Health – public health | Community members including older people, local agencies and voluntary or charitable organisations | Reducing falls in older people | Three pilot sites each with five local teams made up of target groups. | Pilots involved older people with disabilities. Pilots now rolled out to a further eight areas. There is high-level buy-in with chief officers involved. |
| Neighbourhood Management Pathfinders | ODPM – neighbourhood renewal | Residents in the 10% most deprived wards ie the 88 renewal areas | Planning and delivery of neighbourhood management | Residents, and community and voluntary groups were 47% of all Board members across 20 Round 1 Pathfinders. | Four Boards had a clear resident majority.<br><br>Pathfinders also consulted wider groups of residents. |

*Sources:* Ball (2002); Newburn and Jones (2002); NRU (2004); unpublished research by the SQW Consortium

2. In the implementation of policy, Labour has tried to be simultaneously sympathetic to the roles of the public and local authorities; for example, emphasising local authorities' 'community leadership role' alongside roles for the public. This has allowed for easier acceptance of the principle of involvement by local government. The government has tried to keep cooperative relationships with local government over the introduction of changes, and, notwithstanding many areas of tension, it has been largely successful in winning backing for its change programme (Lowndes and Wilson, 2001). There is still continued wariness and even hostility of locally elected members towards citizen participation. But at an officer level, there is genuine commitment to informal participation (Stoker and Bottom, 2003). Local government feels that national policy is a positive spur to their work (Barnes et al, 2003). The other drivers for service providers to engage their users include 'market' competition in public services, as well as ongoing learning and development led by organisations themselves.

So, in contrast to 1997, by 2001 local authorities were more likely to believe that engaging the public improves service delivery. Twenty-six per cent of local authorities cited 'improving services' as the main benefit of public consultation. The majority of authorities (70%) believed that participation initiatives were 'often' or 'fairly' influential on final decision making (Birch, 2002), compared to the 56% of authorities that believed participation informed, or even merely confirmed, final decisions in the 1997 survey. And by 2001, only two local authorities felt involvement had no influence on decisions, compared to 20% in 1997 who thought it had "very little impact" (Lowndes et al, 2001, p 222). The results can also be seen in a public service like social housing where there was already a strong expressed commitment to user involvement in 1998 (Cole et al, 2000). Tenant Participation Compacts have been taken on in spirit as well as on paper, go beyond a begrudging approach and have reduced the marked variations between local authority areas in levels of tenant involvement (Aldbourne Associates and IRIS Consulting, 2003). Some local authorities have introduced strong involvement structures at a strategic local authority level, and are devolving decision making, for example Birmingham and Bradford City Councils. The introduction of Local Strategic Partnerships (LSPs) is supposed to facilitate public involvement in strategic work, although evaluation of LSPs to date has been critical.

3. Modernisation of local government and public services has led to better responsiveness by institutions to involvement, and better structures for involvement. Mayoral elections were a damp squib, but they were not the real point. The option of a mayor was part of wider local government modernisation. Modernisation has been shown to have positive effects on participation levels by people in deprived areas: for example, modernised local authorities have higher user involvement levels than un-modernised and less responsive authorities (such as John Prescott's constituency in Hull) with similar levels of deprivation (Barnes et al, 2003).

4. There has been extra provision of capacity building support for community representatives. Community Learning Chests provide £12 million each year in the 88 most deprived local authority areas for neighbourhood renewal skills development. It is likely that the recipients were already active in neighbourhood renewal so this does not increase numbers, but does build community 'capacity'. Research by CASE has shown that residents valued access to training and support to overcome skills and knowledge gaps for participation. More recently (and rather late in the day), the government has formally acknowledged what practitioners in the field have told them about the problems with coordination, coverage, quality and consistency in the capacity building field for all types of political and social participation. The government is currently working through proposals to deal with these issues (Civil Renewal Unit, 2003). The community work profession has welcomed moves such as better quality community development work standards.

## Summary and conclusion

Participation of all types – formal, social participation, and involvement in decision making – has been a priority for Labour, although target setting has been less developed. Progress is closely monitored in each specific service or policy area, and there have been many evaluations of particular initiatives. Despite poor results in closing gaps in participation rates on a grand scale, there have been successes: encouraging voting in local elections; targeting social participation programmes on socially excluded groups and areas (notably changes to National Lottery funding); starting to cohere the previously fragmented infrastructure for volunteering; and strengthening the institutional context for involvement in decision making. Therefore, New Labour can be judged well on its record on participation if we look at its work on quality, rather than quantity. The government has created an involvement-friendly environment across nearly all government departments that could mean participation is more difficult to marginalise in the future.

While our overall conclusions are optimistic, there are inevitably still gaps and tensions. There are still many political and practical challenges in making genuine participation a reality. There are policy gaps within central government, for example the Decent Homes Standard does not allow adequately for tenant priorities. There are some clearly self-inflicted policy gaps in the Sustainable Communities Plan which is notably quiet on the subject of community involvement, and there are policy contradictions in proposed changes to the planning system; for example, the Egan Review to speed up the planning process while simultaneously increasing involvement in decision making.

New Labour has failed to excite people about formal politics around a big idea: 'Third Way' compromise politics perhaps do not lend themselves to engaging political debate. One debate is whether New Labour is too closed, or too willing to listen. Some say the government is a clique with closed decision making procedures, citing for example the use of special advisers in policy making. It is criticised for being open to people on detail, but not over general policy direction. For example, tenants are given the right to debate and vote proposals to transfer their stock, but the stock transfer agenda is driven from the centre, although the controversial debate over a viable alternative for social housing stock is far from resolved. Others have derided moves to open up national policy formation to participation by citizens at the highest levels, for example through 'The Big Conversation' (www.bigconversation.org.uk), the now defunct People's Panel (1999-2002), the Community Forum (a grass-roots 'sounding board' on neighbourhood renewal policies) and other opinion research pejoratively portrayed in the media as 'focus group' politics. It is difficult not to see these criticisms – coming from both angles – as an attack on Labour's wider attempts to bring in non-elected bodies and other participatory structures to national policy formation. This is perhaps a predictable reaction: getting the balance right between representative and participatory democracy is never easy.

The tension between different forms of democracy has reverberated at local level too, as seen for example in resistance to change from grass-roots councillors (Wilson, 2002). This is a crucial area: if success in citizen participation undermines local government and local politicians this could cut across the overall goal of improving all forms of participation, local members included. Citizen involvement should complement not weaken local representative democracy. For example, residents' groups or Community Empowerment Networks could help to improve local authority services by challenging in ways that stimulate better practice. But, in order for this to work, local democracy must be healthy enough not to feel threatened, and the basis for the legitimacy of all parties must be credible.

Social participation as practised by middle class volunteers has yet to take hold in lower income areas but New Labour's 'capacity building' efforts to build up community organisations may take time to yield results. And any future results are likely to be hard won but yield relatively small numbers. There are many practical difficulties in implementing large-scale national programmes to get people to volunteer or to create community organisations. The government is still wrestling with this. Possibly a number of smaller programmes, administered locally, is the most appropriate solution, and this is what is happening, but slowly and not on a mass scale. Some have also pointed out that increased regulation in areas like childcare now work against voluntary efforts. There is an ongoing debate about the disincentives to doing unpaid work within the benefits system, run by the Department for Work and Pensions (DWP), creating contradictions in policy that are self-defeating for the government.

Involvement in decision making is now more rewarding for the minority of 'community representatives' who are involved on a regular basis with agencies, on committees, in forums or in any of the many other new structures that have sprung up. These active volunteers are more likely to be having an influence through their involvement than previously because agencies are more likely to listen and respond. This is not the case for the majority of people who remain outside these joint decision making structures, and are perhaps at best consulted by a MORI pollster from time to time. This point is well illustrated by the continued feelings of powerlessness of the families described in Chapter Thirteen of this volume. There is a way to go to help many ordinary people, especially in deprived areas, feel they have influence over local decisions. The neighbourhood issues discussed in Chapter Six of this volume are also critical; people are less likely to feel empowered when faced with neighbourhood disorganisation and residential segregation, although the government's neighbourhood management and wardens initiatives seem to be making a positive impact.

We know that people can feel more satisfied with local government or service provision when they have been consulted. However, another area of current debate is whether there are more effective routes to delivering actual service improvements. There is now the potential for a backlash against involvement in decision making if it cannot be proved to deliver results. Added to this is the fact that participation can be a slow, frustrating and complex process. Put together, these two issues mean that participation may not survive if it cannot be shown to add value, and if it conflicts with the urgent need to deliver neighbourhood and other improvements by slowing the process down. This debate has been taking place around several cases of badly implemented 'community-led' regeneration in the NDCs.

Tony Blair had the first word on participation in this chapter, so it would seem fitting to give the last word to some community participants on the value of participation at grass-roots level. The Centre for Analysis of Social Exclusion (CASE) visited and interviewed people involved in a tenants' and residents' association about their work on a council estate in the north east. Their experience is typical of many of over 60 community groups we have visited since 2001, and compares to the less positive welcome from agencies experienced by many of the 90 projects we visited between 1997 and 2000. Vera, the Chair of the group, told us:

> "When we first started we couldn't get past the desk in the municipal buildings but it's getting better and better, I have the direct numbers for everybody. We're really lucky because our council is quite good."

For the past five years, the group has had a member on the council's Customer Testing Panel:

> "There's about 30 tenants, [the council] brings the proposals to us and then we agree or disagree – change of rents, things like that, it's part of Best Value. [We work in partnership with] loads of people from every other agency, there isn't anything we won't do and no-one we won't work with ... there's all these agencies who are secretive, but we've all got to work together."

The group's building is also a base for an employment project. Vera and the rest of the women help the employment adviser with his work.

> "Not only do we target the hard to reach but they can then come downstairs for the social side. Everyone's welcome here, even the refugees who can't speak English, we just give them a cup of tea and work out what we can do!"

## Notes

[1] For example, see World Values Survey data (www.worldvaluessurvey.org), and European Values Survey. Also OECD (2001).

[2] Policy Action Team on Community Self Help (PAT 9).

[3] Funded by the Gatsby Charitable Foundation, part of the Sainsbury Family Charitable Trusts. The five-year pilot from 1996-2001 showed that community training plus small grants could create community self-help activity.

[4] There are now several surveys that will soon provide information about levels and variation between groups and over time on multiple measures of social and informal political participation. These include the European Social Survey, the Home Office Citizenship Survey, the Social Capital module in the General Household Survey, the longitudinal study of citizenship education in schools, the Families and Children Survey, and the Harmonised European Time Use Studies project (HETUS). For more information on data sources see ONS (2002a).

[5] See note 2.

# Part Two: Groups at risk

# SIX

# Disadvantaged by where you live? New Labour and neighbourhood renewal

*Ruth Lupton and Anne Power*

## Introduction

This chapter is about New Labour's efforts to reverse the long-running negative impact on urban conditions of concentrated poverty within deprived areas and to break the connection between poor social and physical conditions. It comprises three parts:

1. the situation New Labour inherited and the development of the National Strategy for Neighbourhood Renewal;
2. the measurable results of the strategy; and
3. the relationship between wider urban, regional and housing policies and the more focused neighbourhood renewal agenda.

We conclude by assessing the likelihood of future progress.

## Neighbourhood problems and the New Labour response

The multiple problems of poor neighbourhoods are nothing new and have been the focus of urban policy interventions in the UK since the turn of the 20th century (Atkinson and Moon, 1994; Hill, 2000). However, by 1997, there was evidence that some of these problems were getting worse. Divisions between declining cities and industrial areas and small towns and cities and rural areas had been widening for several decades, while the 1980s saw a particular increase in intra-urban polarisation, with growing contrasts between poorer and more affluent electoral wards within cities (Hills, 1995). There was increasing concern about so-called 'worst neighbourhoods', with concentrations of poverty and worklessness and the associated problems of high crime and disorder, diminishing and dysfunctional services, empty housing and environmental decay.

New Labour responded in 1997, asking its newly formed Social Exclusion Unit (SEU) to produce a report on neighbourhood problems. The report, *Bringing Britain together* (SEU, 1998c), identified approximately 3,000 neighbourhoods with common problems of poverty, unemployment, poor health and crime. Public services in these neighbourhoods tended to be less good, with a higher proportion of schools failing their OFSTED inspection and fewer general practitioners (GPs), many of them in substandard premises. Many neighbourhoods suffered from litter, vandalism and a lack of shops and other facilities. Neighbourhood-level data was limited, but the SEU's analysis revealed a wide gap between the most deprived local authority districts and others. The 44 most deprived districts had nearly two thirds more unemployment than average, one-and-a-half times more lone parents, mortality ratios 30% higher, a quarter more adults with poor literacy and numeracy and two to three times the levels of poor housing, vandalism and dereliction.

The policy response came in two phases. The first was initiated in 1997/98 while the SEU was still researching the problem, and comprised a range of area-based initiatives (ABIs), including Action Zones for education and health and the continuation of the Conservative government's Single Regeneration Budget (SRB) programme for comprehensive area regeneration. New Labour also announced its own area regeneration programme, the New Deal for Communities (NDC), funding 39 local partnerships to the tune of £20-50 million each over a ten-year period to tackle worklessness, crime, low skills, poor health and poor housing, with a strong focus on community ownership and leadership.

These initiatives are summarised in Table 6.1. They had some distinctive features: their proliferation, an emphasis on community involvement and leadership and on 'joining-up' services at the local level and, in the case of NDC, a longer time period than had previously been allowed (ten years compared with SRB's seven). However, this first phase of policy can essentially be seen as continuing the broad approach of preceding governments; that is, to tackle the additional problems of poor neighbourhoods primarily through additional, targeted, specific and time-limited programmes.

With the publication of *Bringing Britain together* came the start of a new and very different policy phase: the development of an overall strategy towards the problem. Whereas in the past, poor neighbourhoods had either been overlooked as a specific policy objective by departments whose welfare policies targeted individuals, or targeted by a series of separate ABIs, now the neighbourhood was to be seen as a key unit of policy delivery, with existing mainstream policies and ABIs being brought together in a single strategic approach. Following the report, the government set up 18 Policy Action Teams (PATs) to examine detailed aspects of the problem, and conducted a wide consultation exercise. In January 2000, it launched its National Strategy for Neighbourhood Renewal (NSNR).

The NSNR set out a new vision for neighbourhood renewal, that "within 10-20 years, no one should be seriously disadvantaged by where they live" (SEU, 2001, p 8). It also set out two long-term goals:

1. absolute improvement in economic and social conditions: "lower worklessness and crime; and better health, skills, housing and physical environment" in all the poorest neighbourhoods; and

**Table 6.1: New Labour's main area-based programmes**

| Programme | Start | Number | Size of areas | Description |
|---|---|---|---|---|
| Single Regeneration Budget (SRB) rounds 5 and 6 | 1997 | 65 districts (18%) | Whole district (thematic programme) or smaller area within | Area regeneration programmes involving physical renewal, employment and training and social welfare initiatives |
| Education Action Zones (EAZs) | 1998 | 73 | Clusters of schools | Partnerships between groups of schools, LEAs, businesses, parents and the community to raise educational standards |
| Health Action Zones (HAZs) | 1998 | 26 in 73 districts | Health authorities | New partnership approach to public health linking health, regeneration, employment, education, housing and anti-poverty initiatives to address health inequalities, identify health needs and modernise services |
| New Deal for Communities (NDC) | 1998 | 39 | Neighbourhoods of 1,000-4,000 households | Area regeneration programmes to tackle worklessness, poor health, crime, low educational achievement and improve housing and the environment |
| Sure Start | 1998 | 520 | Neighbourhoods with 400-800 children aged 0-4 | Work with parents and children to improve child health, social and emotional development and ability to learn, and strengthen families and communities |
| Excellence in Cities (EiC) | 1999 | 58 LEAs | Districts and district clusters | Raise educational standards for 11- to 16-year-olds through initiatives like mentoring, IT and City Learning Centres and opportunities for gifted and talented children |
| Employment Zones (EZs) | 2000 | 15 | Districts and district clusters. Up to 48,000 people | Help to long-term unemployed to get back into work, including personal job account to buy tailored help, guidance and counselling and in-work support |

*Sources:* ODPM, DoH, DfES, DWP

2. targets for relative improvement "to narrow the gap on these measures between the most deprived neighbourhoods and the rest of the country".

This was the first time that goals had been set for poor neighbourhoods as a group, and the first time that a UK government had set out how policy interventions by different departments and at different geographical levels would work together to impact on the poorest neighbourhoods. The NSNR incorporated some new neighbourhood-based initiatives, including pilot schemes for neighbourhood management and wardens and the development of neighbourhood learning centres, and the extension of some ABIs, such as Sure Start. However, its main contribution was to focus existing policies on the poorest neighbourhoods, so that mainstream national policies were not creating or perpetuating neighbourhood inequalities while area-based programmes were trying to redress them. With the NSNR in place, national policies would be expected to specifically target the poorest neighbourhoods. For example, welfare-to-work programmes would be expected to close the gap between unemployment rates in poor areas and others, boosted by the creation of additional Action Teams for Jobs, and there would be new incentives to recruit and retain primary health care staff in deprived areas.

Achieving a focus on neighbourhoods and coordinating the elements of the strategy was clearly going to be critical to its success. To do this, the government set up a Neighbourhood Renewal Unit (NRU) in the Department of the Environment, Transport and the Regions (DETR, later Office of the Deputy Prime Minister or OPDM), and Neighbourhood Renewal Teams in each region, charged with liaising with other departments, coordinating the delivery of the many different elements of the strategy, monitoring progress and building up a knowledge base on effective policy and practice in neighbourhood renewal. It also set up a new local delivery mechanism. Local Strategic Partnerships (LSPs) between local authorities, other public authorities and agencies, the private sector and local communities, were introduced in the 88 most deprived local authority areas, with a remit to develop local neighbourhood renewal strategies.

These were to be linked to the existing strategies of the partner organisations, and 'bend' mainstream activity, such as improvements in schools and health care, in favour of the most needy neighbourhoods rather than relying only on additional time-limited funding. The LSPs were the government's key local vehicle for making sure that poor neighbourhoods were supported in the long term by better public services: more responsive policing where it was needed most; better schools and additional educational inputs for children and families; better environmental services, lettings management and tenancy enforcement; better primary health care facilities and services, and so on. To support the delivery of the local renewal strategies, the government introduced a Neighbourhood Renewal Fund (NRF), available to the most deprived 88 authorities. It also emphasised the importance of involving local communities in the development and delivery of neighbourhood renewal, and set up a Community Empowerment Fund to support community involvement in LSPs, and Community Chests, to go directly to community groups in these areas (see Table 6.2).

The NSNR covers England. Different policies apply in Scotland and Wales (Box 6.1). In each of these two countries, the problems of deprived neighbourhoods have, as in England, been given a higher policy priority since 1997. In Scotland, 'building strong communities' is one of four planks of the country's Social Inclusion Strategy, while in Wales 'tackling social disadvantage' in the most deprived communities is one of three priorities in the Welsh Assembly's strategic plan. The Scottish Executive produced its own 'community regeneration

**Table 6.2: New funding to assist the implementation of the National Strategy for Neighbourhood Renewal**

| Fund | Purpose | Amount | |
|------|---------|--------|--|
| Neighbourhood Renewal Fund | Improve core services in deprived areas | £200m | 2001/02 |
| | | £300m | 2002/03 |
| | | £400m | 2003/04 |
| Community Empowerment Fund | Support community involvement in LSPs | £35m | 2001-04 |
| Community Chest | Support local initiatives | £50m | 2001-04 |

*Source:* Audit Commission (2002)

statement' in 2002, setting out its strategy for turning round disadvantaged communities and creating a better life for their residents. There are some notable differences between the Scottish and Welsh approaches and the English. For example, less money has been channelled into ABIs. Targets and performance monitoring have not been adopted to the same extent. There are differences in some of the policies that underpin neighbourhood renewal, such as transfer of local authority housing stock and social housing allocation systems. However, the key principles of the English approach have also been adopted in Scotland and Wales: a longer-term approach driven by changes in mainstream services rather than ABIs, coordinated local planning and delivery, and greater community involvement.

In this chapter, we concentrate on England and the NSNR. We do not attempt to evaluate each of the specific policies individually. Rather, we consider whether the many different interventions at local and national level have resulted in the achievement of the government's goals for the improvement of poor neighbourhoods, and whether they are likely to do so in the future.

## Measures of success

The government has commissioned its own evaluation of the NSNR, looking both at implementation and impact. This is currently in its early stages. On the implementation side, it remains to be seen whether the NRU can carry the influence within government to ensure that departmental policies are focused on neighbourhood inequalities; whether LSPs can effectively draw together the strategies and activities of agencies at local level when these agencies are also accountable on national performance targets; whether there will be the political support at local level to 'bend' mainstream budgets, such as education, health and policing, towards the poorest areas at the expense of others; and whether the neighbourhood focus can really be achieved in the absence of any devolution of budgets and decision making to the neighbourhood level. These answers will take time to emerge.

Meanwhile, policy impacts overall are being assessed through a set of targets relating to the long-term goals of the strategy: to reduce worklessness and crime,

## Box 6.1: The development of neighbourhood renewal policies in Scotland and Wales

**Scotland**

1999: *Social inclusion: Opening the door to a better Scotland.* Scottish Office document identifying "building stonger communities" as key objective. Launches Social Inclusion Partnerships (SIPs) (eventually 48, mainly area-based but some thematic) with £48 million funding, to develop coordinated local plans and bend mainstream services towards deprived neighbourhoods. Also, city-wide partnerships and two smaller programmes: 'Listening to Communities' to build local capacity and participation, and 'Working for Communities' to develop integration of local services and give communities more influence. These policies were implemented by the Scottish Executive as part of its 1999 Social Justice Strategy, which identified "reducing inequalities between communities" as a long-term target.

2002: *Better communities in Scotland: Closing the gap* (Community Regeneration Statement from the Scottish Executive). Sets priorities for change to close the gap on outcomes between the poorest neighbourhoods and the median. Introduces local service outcome agreements and launches specific initiatives on neighbourhood management, social economy, financial exclusion and others. Announces integration of SIPS under wider community planning partnerships.

**Wales**

1998: *People in communities* (pilot programme for eight communities, later extended to further eight). Funding to establish local partnership boards with coordinators to initiate interagency working and community involvement.

1999: Strategic agenda, *A better Wales*, establishes tackling social disadvantage as a main theme.

1999: *Sustainable communities* (grant aid programme for local regeneration projects).

2001: *Communities first* £80 million funding over three years to support development of local partnerships and action plans for three, five and ten years in 100 most deprived electoral divisions in Wales. Plans to be supported using mainstream funds. Emphasis on increased community participation and long-term integrated approaches.

*Sources:* Welsh National Assembly, Scottish Executive

improve skills, health, housing and environments, and to close the gap between poor areas and others on these measures. These targets were established in the Spending Review of 2000 and updated in 2002 (Table 6.3). The table shows the main deprivation-related targets, although clearly other government targets, such as the drive to improve adult basic skills, might also be expected to have a disproportionate impact in the poorest neighbourhoods. It shows that there are

**Table 6.3: National deprivation-related targets (updated 2002)**

| Goal | Target | Period | Type(s) of target | Unit |
|---|---|---|---|---|
| Increase employment rates | Increase the employment rate of disadvantaged areas and groups, taking account of the economic cycle – lone parents, ethnic minorities, people aged 50 and over, those with the lowest qualifications, and the 30 LAs with poorest initial labour market position – and reduce difference between their employment rates and overall rate | 2003-06 | Floor Convergence | LA level and aggregate of 30 worst LAs |
| Improve economic performance | Make sustainable improvements in the economic performance of all English regions and over the long term reduce the persistent gap in growth rates between the regions | Devise and report on measures by 2006 | Overall improvement Convergence | Region |
| Build an enterprise society | Increase the number of people going into business, improve the overall productivity of small firms, have more enterprise in disadvantaged areas (as measured by VAT registrations comparing the 20% most deprived wards with others) | Ongoing | Overall improvement | Ward |
| Reduce crime | Reduce crime and the fear of crime, including reducing the gap between the highest Crime and Disorder Partnership Areas and the best comparable areas and reduce: <br> – domestic burglary by 25% from 1998/99 to 2005 <br> – vehicle crime by 30% from 1998/99 to 2004 <br> – robbery in the ten Street Crime Initiative areas by 14% from 1999/2000 to 2005 | By 2004/05 | Overall improvement Convergence | CDRP/LA |
| Secondary education | 38% of pupils in every LEA to achieve 5 GCSEs at grades A*-C <br> 25% of pupils in every school to achieve 5 GCSEs at grades A*-C <br><br> 85% of pupils to attain level 5 or above in English, Maths and ICT at Key Stage 3 by 2007, with significant reduction in the number of schools where fewer than 60% achieve level 5 | By 2004 <br> By 2006 <br> (20% by 2004) <br><br> By 2007 <br> (75% by 2005) | Floor | LEA/school |

**Table 6.3: contd.../**

| Goal | Target | Period | Type(s) of target | Unit |
|------|--------|--------|-------------------|------|
| Primary education | 85% of 11-year-olds in every LEA to reach level 4 in English and maths. | 2004 | Floor | LEA/school |
| | Significant reduction in number of schools in which fewer than 65% achieve level 4 | 2006 | | |
| Improve life expectancy | Reduce by at least 10% the gap between the fifth of areas with lowest life expectancy at birth and the population as a whole | By 2010 | Convergence | Health authority |
| Reduce teenage pregnancy | Reduce U18 conception rate by 50% while reducing gap between worst fifth of wards and the average by a quarter | 2010 (15% by 2004) | Overall improvement/convergence | Health authority |
| Improve quality of social housing | Bring all social housing into decent condition | 2010 | Floor | LA |
| | Increase the proportion of private housing in decent condition occupied by vulnerable groups | | | |

*Note:* In addition in 2002 there was an additional target for the reduction of road accident injuries or deaths, tackling the higher incidence in deprived communities.
*Source:* ODPM

two main kinds of targets: *floor targets* (which refer to absolute improvements in the poorest areas to bring them up to a defined level) and *convergence targets* (which refer to closing the gap between the poorest areas and others). In some cases, there are also targets for overall improvement of the indicator in question, in all areas not just the poorest. Evidently, it would be possible for floor targets to be reached without any convergence taking place, and for convergence to take place without improvement in the poorest areas. Both definitions of progress are relevant to the NSNR's strategic aims.

At the time of writing, the government has not produced a report on progress against these indicators. We therefore present our own analysis of published data from the relevant departments for those targets where a time-series of more than one or two years' worth of data has been built up[1].

## Overall evidence of improvement

There is no doubt that, looking at the targets as a group, progress is being made, although not always quickly enough to reach the targets set, and still leaving a substantial gap between the poorest areas and others.

The social housing target shows the clearest sign of improvement. Up to 2000/ 01, there had been a reduction from 2.3 million to 1.6 million homes falling below the decency standard (that is, in good repair, safe with reasonable amenities and adequate thermal comfort) since 1995/96, a one third reduction that, if maintained, would see the target achieved by 2010. Since much social housing, and much the highest proportion of non-decent homes, is within disadvantaged areas, such improvements inevitably affect these areas most, although this does not necessarily result in convergence of housing standards, since private sector standards may be increasing more quickly. Nevertheless, progress towards the floor target is evident. Since the 2002 Spending Review, large amounts of additional money have been targeted at decent homes (ODPM, 2003a). Local authorities with a high proportion of social housing, particularly the 88 NRF areas, are working to hit the Decent Homes target and most expect to do so.

Progress towards the other targets has been less clear cut, although in all areas there is evidence of improvement. Employment rates have risen, on aggregate, in the 30 worst local authorities since 1998, and slightly faster than the national rate. In 1998, there was a gap of 12.5 percentage points between the national rate (73.4% of the working-age population in employment) and the aggregate for the 30 areas (60.9%). By 2003, the national rate had risen to 75% and the aggregate for the worst areas to 63.5%, closing the gap to 11.5 percentage points[2].

Progress in secondary education has been good (see Chapter Three of this volume), although some critics have been sceptical about the extent to which rising rates of examination passes reflect higher academic standards rather than lower examination standards. In 1997/98, 50 of the 148 LEAs (34%) (excluding the Isles of Scilly, which is a very small LEA) were below the 38% target for five A★-Cs at GCSE (see Figure 6.1). By 2002/03, this had fallen to just 12, as the performance of lower attaining LEAs had gradually improved, slightly converging with that of higher performing authorities. However, even this rate of improvement, if sustained, may not be sufficient to achieve the target. Individual LEA projections for the lowest performing LEAs, assuming continuing improvements at the same average rate as for the period 1997/98 to 2002/03, suggest that eight will still be below the target in 2003/04.

At primary level, the rate of progress between 1997/98 and 1999/2000 was exceptionally good, following the introduction of the national literacy and numeracy strategies. This exceeded many earlier expectations and, as a result, the government increased its target for 2004 from 78% to 85% of 11-year-olds reaching Level 4 in Maths and English in every LEA. However, the improvements came to a halt in 1999/2000, leaving virtually all authorities (all but three in English and all in Maths) still below the government's new target in 2002/03. There is certainly evidence of convergence, with the performance level of the lowest performing authority rising from 40% to 58% between 1997/98 and 2002/03 (in Maths), compared with a median rise from 58% to 72%, but not the continued overall increase for which the government had hoped.

Crime targets also seem likely to be missed. Rates of burglary and vehicle crime have fallen nationally, and on average in the 88 NRF areas[3], although not as much as the government had hoped. Against a targeted reduction of 25% by 2005, the burglary rate overall reduced by 3% by 2002/03, compared with 2% for England as a whole. Vehicle crime fell by 6% compared with 7% for England as a whole. These reductions were not sufficiently different to cause any convergence between NRF areas and others. On the other hand, rates of robbery increased by 21% in NRF areas, from 3.3 per 1,000 population per year to 4.0,

**Figure 6.1: Numbers of LEAs with fewer than 38% 5 A\*-C GCSE passes**

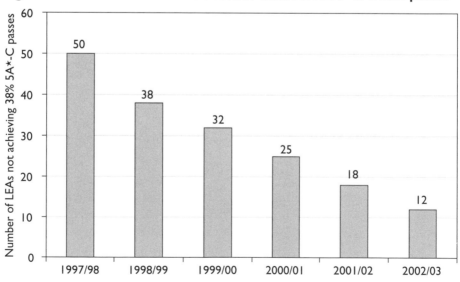

*Source:* DfES Performance Tables (1997/98 to 2002/03)

**Figure 6.2: Ratio of crime rates for NRF areas to national rate**

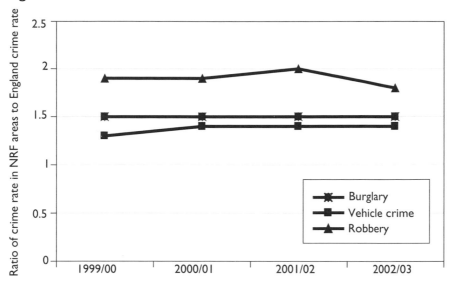

Source: Home Office *Statistical Bulletins, Crime in England and Wales* (1999/2000 to 2002/03)

but this was a smaller increase than in the country as a whole (29%), leading to slight convergence. As Figure 6.2 shows, convergence occurred particularly after 2001, possibly due to the government's Street Crime Initiative, launched in March 2002 and covering the ten police force areas with the highest rates of street crime. The Home Office reported a 17% decrease in robberies in these forces between 2001/02 and 2002/03, exceeding its target of 14%.

In health, there were overall improvements, but variable evidence on convergence. Life expectancy increased nationally, and in the fifth of authorities with the lowest life expectancy at birth (see Figure 6.3). (These are interim figures. Lowest quintile figures are subject to revision by the Office of National Statistics.) However, the lowest performing authorities failed to catch up at all with the rising national average and seem unlikely to catch up by the 10% that the government hopes for by 2010.

The government's other local health target is to reduce teenage pregnancy, lowering the under-18 conception rate by 15% by 2004 (50% by 2010) while reducing the gap between the worst fifth of local authority areas and the average by a quarter. By 2001, the national rate had already been reduced by 5.1 per 1,000 15- to 17-year-olds (11% of its starting point), from 47.6 to 42.5, compared with 1998. The average for the worst performing fifth of local authority areas had reduced by 7.1 per 1,000 (also 11% of its starting point), from 66.1 to 59.0 (Figure 6.4). The effect of this was to close the gap from 18.5 per 1,000 in 1998 to 16.5 by 2001, an 11% reduction, making it likely that the government might hit its target.

On this basis, we can conclude that on all the areas that the government has targeted, there have been improvements, in aggregate, in the poorest local authority

**Figure 6.3: Life expectancy at birth: worst performing fifth of LAs compared with England**

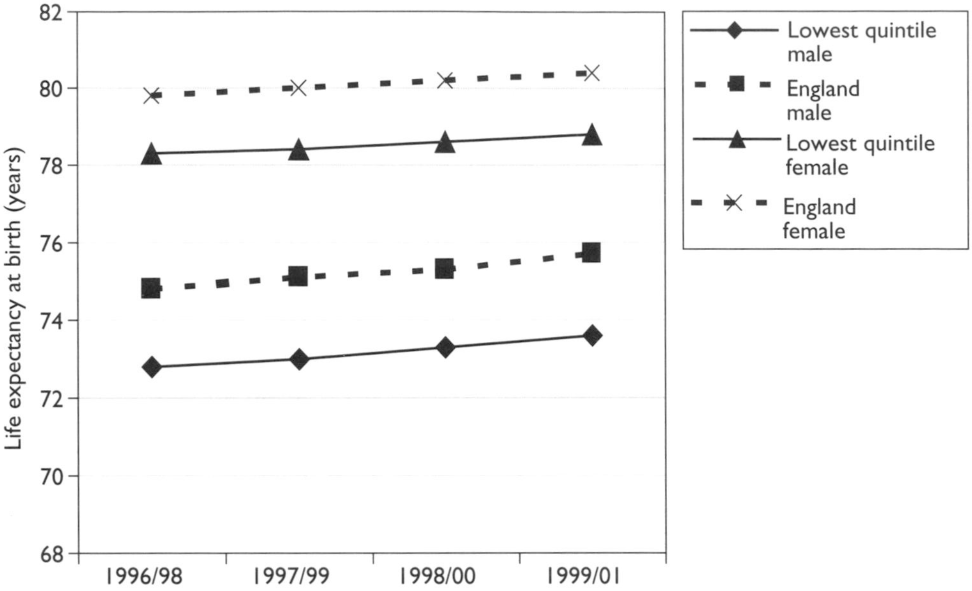

Source: ONS Statistical releases, Life expectancy at birth

areas. For employment, education and teenage pregnancy, there has also been some convergence between these authorities and the national average, while for crime and life expectancy there has not. In most cases, it seems likely that, despite the progress made, the government will not succeed in relation to its own targets, at least at the current level of intervention. Table 6.4 provides a summary.

## Progress at neighbourhood level

In broad terms, this is an encouraging picture of trends in poor areas, although perhaps not as dramatic as the government had hoped. As an indication of the success of the NSNR, however, it is, at best, inconclusive. First, we have to bear in mind that virtually all of the data presented here relates to the first period of the New Labour administration, not the second period when the NSNR was launched. The impact of this will not be seen until data for 2002/03 and beyond become available. What we are seeing in these indicators is probably the effect of the individual policies, as reported in the other chapters in this volume, not any additional effect of the better targeting, monitoring and coordination that the NSNR represented, nor its own local level interventions such as neighbourhood wardens.

Second, the indicators selected by the government give a limited picture of what is happening to poor neighbourhoods and the experience of living in them. The indicators relate directly to the goals of the strategy – lower worklessness,

**Figure 6.4: Teenage conception rates: worst performing fifth of LAs compared with England**

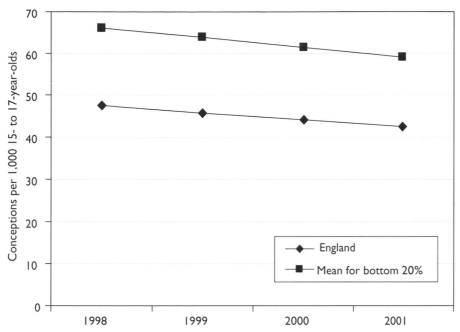

Source: DH Teenage Pregnancy Unit, *Conception statistics for local authorities* (1998-2001)

**Table 6.4: Summary of progress against targets**

| Target | Evidence of improvement in most deprived areas | Evidence of convergence | On target? |
|---|---|---|---|
| Employment rates | Yes | Yes | Yes |
| Secondary school performance | Yes | Yes | No |
| Primary school performance | Yes | Yes | No |
| Crime | Yes for burglary and vehicle crime, no for robbery | No for burglary and vehicle crime, yes for robbery | No |
| Health | Yes | No for life expectancy, yes for teenage pregnancy | No for life expectancy, yes for teenage pregnancy |
| Social housing | Yes | N/A | Yes |

less crime, better health, better skills and better housing and environment – but not necessarily to its vision that no one should be seriously disadvantaged by where they live. Clearly it would be possible for all of the chosen indicators to show improvement but for people still to be disadvantaged by where they live, for example because of declining environmental conditions, lack of transport, increasing racial tensions or neighbourhood stigma. Evidence from families living in low-income neighbourhoods (Chapter Thirteen of this volume) demonstrates the importance of these local 'liveability' factors, and lack of indicators about them makes it hard to translate progress on the strategic goals of the NSNR to the reality of living in the neighbourhoods concerned. Such evidence as there is suggests that there is still a very long way to go in addressing the day-to-day problems of poor neighbourhoods. The Survey of English Housing shows an increase in reported neighbourhood problems (on average) between 1999 and 2002 and that twice as many householders (23%) thought their area had got worse over the last two years than better (12%). (The survey shows that over a longer period, 1992-2002, neighbourhood conditions have improved.) The latest English House Condition Survey (ODPM, 2003c) shows a much higher level of environmental problems in poor neighbourhoods than others, with 24% of people in poor neighbourhoods reporting litter and rubbish problems, and 16% scruffy or neglected buildings, compared with none in other neighbourhoods (Figure 6.5).

Third, the data is reported at a highly aggregated level, often comparing the worst fifth of local authorities with the rest, and it is not clear whether the progress made has been experienced evenly at the neighbourhood level within these broad groupings. Aggregate data can obviously conceal wide variations.

The government has invested in the development of better local data, through its new Neighbourhood Statistics service, but at this stage is still not able to publish less aggregated data on its targets for any meaningful time-series. Here we draw on more localised data (at the neighbourhood level where possible and at the local authority level where not) from the 12 deprived areas that the Centre for Analysis of Social Exclusion (CASE) has been tracking since the second year of the New Labour administration in 1998 (reported in Lupton, 2003b), and which were selected to represent the distribution and characteristics of disadvantaged areas.

Data for these areas tracking progress against the government's targets are presented in Figures 6.6 to 6.10. The figures show three things:

1. *Significant variations in the level of problems in different areas.* For example, in the seven areas that CASE is following within the worst 30 employment areas, employment rates in 1998 ranged between 52.2% (Knowsley) and 67.0% (Caerphilly and Redcar and Cleveland). Robbery rates per 1,000 people ranged from 0.2 in Caerphilly to 12.5 in Hackney.
2. *General trends of improvement,* but also evidence of uneven progress, with considerable year-on-year variations.

**Figure 6.5: Neighbourhood problems reported by residents**

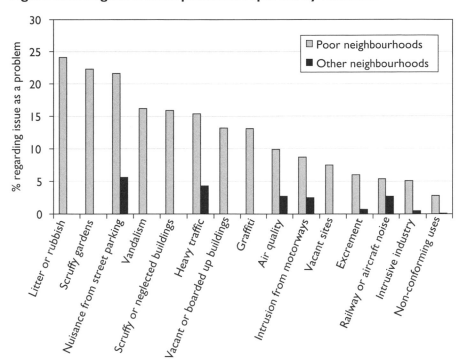

*Note:* Residents are asked to rate problems on a scale of 1 to 5, where 1 is 'no problems', and 5 is 'major problems'. The English House Condition Survey report defines dwellings with problems as only those rated either 4 or 5 on the scale, i.e. only significant problems are included. The graph demonstrates that for some issues no respondents gave a rating of 4 or 5 in 'other neighbourhoods'.
*Source:* English House Condition Survey 2001 (ODPM, 2003c, Table A5.5)

3. *Significant variations in trends between areas.* For example, Knowsley apparently saw a growth in employment rate over the period studied, while Newham saw a significant fall, even though it is well positioned to benefit from London's rapid economic growth. Robbery rates appear to have continued to rise in Nottingham while they have fallen in other areas since 2001/02. Teen conceptions, however, have fallen in Nottingham but apparently risen in Newcastle.

Considerable variation is evident at the local authority level, and even more so when smaller units of analysis are used. Figure 6.8 shows the progress of the lowest performing secondary schools in CASE's sample (the seven schools out of the 25 in CASE's study that were achieving 15% or fewer higher grade GCSE passes in 1997). The overall picture is one of progress, with greater improvements at the end of the period than the beginning. Four of the schools had reached the target of 25% five A*-Cs by 2002. However, the graph also demonstrates clearly the problems of uneven and patchy progress. Some schools, even those that were improving, had very variable performance, indicating that, while they might reach the target one year, they might not achieve it the next. Two schools (School 2 and School 7) showed virtually no improvement at all.

Other evidence also suggests that the fortunes of deprived areas relative to others may not have necessarily improved, even though there may have been improvements in absolute terms. Dorling and Simpson (2001) and Evans et al (2002) both found that benefit levels, while falling in all areas, have fallen less in areas with high claim rates than low, suggesting a widening gap between neighbourhoods. Dorling and Rees (2003, p 1288), drawing on Census Key Statistics for local authority areas, found that:

> Britain, which divided so dramatically and obviously in the 1980s, as the mines were closed and the yuppie houses built, divided even more rapidly but perhaps more surely in the 1990s.

**Figure 6.6: Employment rates in CASE's selected areas**

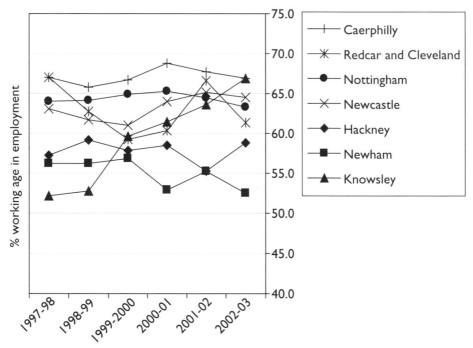

*Note:* 1997-98 shows average four quarters to Spring 1998, and so on for other years.
*Source:* Labour Force Survey from NOMIS. Includes data for 7 of CASE's 12 LAs included in worst 30 LAs on employment rates

**Figure 6.7: Robbery rates in CASE's selected areas**

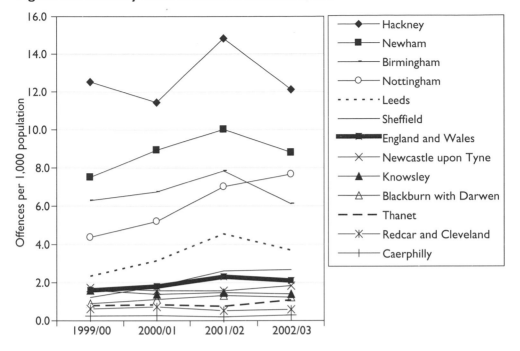

Source: Home Office *Statistical Bulletins, Crime in England and Wales* (1999/2000 to 2002/03)

They noted increasing segregation of white people, of council house tenants, of students, of unemployed people who have never worked, of the young unemployed and of those in full-time work, in professional occupations and with a degree. They argued (2003, p 1308) that:

> people who can choose are choosing to live further and further away from people who cannot choose.

If this is true, one would expect the same results to be manifest at the neighbourhood level.

## The wider context for neighbourhood change

What explains these localised differences in problems and trends and this evidence both of absolute improvement and possible polarisation? One obvious explanation is that broad indicators such as employment rates measure the outcomes of very different localised conditions and processes. For example, deprived neighbourhoods in London exist in a booming labour market but with many low-paid jobs, high housing costs that can be a disincentive to taking low-paid work and large minority ethnic populations which experience labour market discrimination and disadvantage. Deprived neighbourhoods in industrial areas

**Figure 6.8: Performance in the lowest attaining secondary schools in CASE's selected areas**

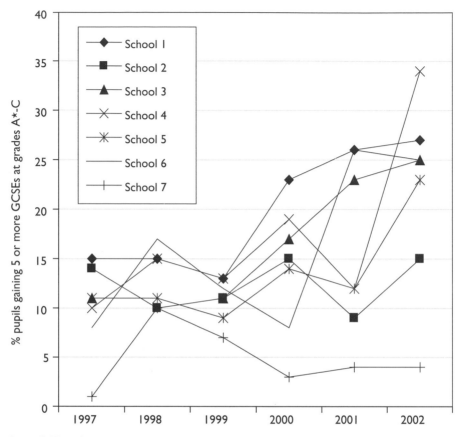

Source: DfES *Performance tables* (1997/98 to 2002/03)

in the north may be experiencing continued job loss and lack of labour demand. The benefits of economic growth are not distributed evenly and it cannot be assumed that all deprived neighbourhoods will respond to change in the same way. Similarly, there are localised factors that contribute to crime prevalence, such as the type of housing or the extent and character of illegal drug markets, which will inevitably make some neighbourhoods more resilient to change than others (Lupton, 2003b). This points to the need for much more detailed monitoring of neighbourhood trends if the government is really to identify variations between neighbourhoods and local authorities as well as aggregate trends, and for differentiated responses tailored to the specific circumstances of particular areas.

A second factor is that people move between neighbourhoods. Even within a local authority area, poor neighbourhoods as a whole may improve, but some poor neighbourhoods may become a lot worse, because of an exodus of more advantaged residents to improving neighbourhoods, and an increasing

**Figure 6.9: Progress in English at KS2 in CASE's selected areas**

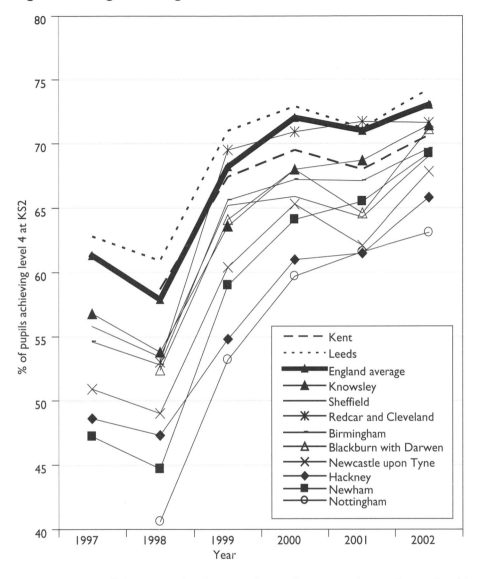

concentration of the most disadvantaged in others. We observed exactly this phenomenon in Knowsley between 1998/99 and 2001, where one neighbourhood stabilised due to housing improvements and community development activity, while a nearby estate suffered increasing numbers of empty properties, high levels of vandalism and environmental damage and youth nuisance (Lupton, 2003b). In the context of low housing demand, more advantaged people could choose to avoid the most troubled areas, leading to a rapid cycle of decline. The same effect can be observed in school markets, where an excess of school places and a high degree of differentiation between schools can mean that the lowest attaining pupils become increasingly concentrated in the least successful

**Figure 6.10: Teenage conception rates in CASE's selected areas**

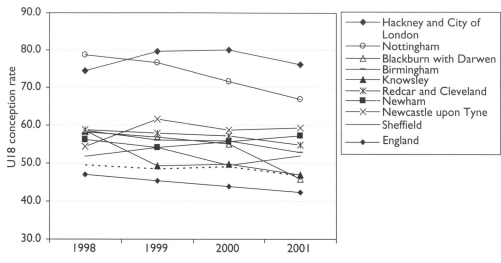

*Source:* DH Teenage Pregnancy Unit

schools, making it hard for them to improve, while the most popular schools go from strength to strength. Thus it is possible to observe increasing polarisation between neighbourhoods, even in the context of overall improvements in the poorest local authorities.

A third issue is that there are social and economic processes at work that may lead to greater polarisation, at the same time as the NSNR is attempting to combat neighbourhood problems. Principal among these are regional economic disparities and changes in housing preferences. Structural economic changes are continuing to have an uneven spatial impact, causing further decline in northern regions, Scotland and Wales, and intense growth pressures in the south. These shifts are reflected in high concentrations of poverty and intense neighbourhood decline in northern regions, and extreme pressure on housing and services in London (DETR, 1999). The Midlands, lying between the two, shares many of the problems of regional decline but is more closely connected to and benefits from the growth centres of the southern part of the country. These trends are compounded in urban areas by continuing counter-urbanisation trends and the growth of small towns and cities and rural settlements at the expense of cities, and in social housing areas by the increasing popularity and availability of home ownership as a tenure option. They create the conditions for increasing spatial segregation between rich and poor. Changes in the size and distribution of minority ethnic groups are also a factor, given the disadvantage suffered by many of these groups. Our own analysis of Census data (Lupton and Power, 2004: forthcoming) shows that, while minority ethnic populations are increasing in number in formerly white areas (suggesting a pattern of dispersal and integration), they are increasing most in numerical terms in areas of existing settlement (mainly inner-city areas) which, combined with falling white populations in these areas, is leading to their increasing segregation. There is a particular challenge in the increasing numbers of highly disadvantaged asylum seekers, who are concentrated in areas of low-cost housing in London and major cities (see Chapter Ten of this volume).

Given this context, it seems evident that success in neighbourhood renewal will depend not only on the neighbourhood-focused service improvements contained within the NSNR, but on the success of wider policies, not just those aimed at tackling disadvantage per se (such as reductions in child poverty) but those aimed at tackling spatial disparities. In the last part of the chapter, we look briefly at developments on these wider issues.

## Urban, regional and housing policies

Since 1997, New Labour has developed three interlinked urban and regional agendas, each with potential to link neighbourhood renewal into the wider structural problems we have identified:

* the 'urban renaissance';
* regional devolution; and
* the 'sustainable communities' plan.

### Urban renaissance

Early into office, John Prescott, as Deputy Prime Minister and an enthusiastic supporter of urban renewal, set up the Urban Task Force under the independent chairmanship of the architect Lord Richard Rogers. The force drew together planning, social, housing, transport, environmental, engineering and design experience to argue for a re-emphasis on 'brown-field' (that is, already used but redundant) land and buildings, largely urban; on the idea of the compact city, a closely woven, dense, integrated, mixed-use approach to cities and urban neighbourhoods; and protection of the countryside through the containment of 'sprawl' building, focusing on public transport, walking and cycling to reduce congestion and urban pollution while increasing densities. If successful, this approach could have a major impact on inner-city neighbourhoods, raising their value as the main source of brown-field land and buildings and encouraging better-off people with choice to stay or return to the city.

In the Urban White Paper (DETR, 2000) and the planning changes that followed (1999, 2003), the government reaffirmed its initial target of 60% of all new homes on brown-field land; it raised minimum densities to 30 homes per hectare (from an average of 23); and, through its ten-year transport plan, it underlined the importance of public transport and reduction in car congestion. These measures are slowly percolating out from city centres to inner urban neighbourhoods. The brown-field and density targets have been surpassed in many cities and almost every city now has a pro-urban agenda that reinforces neighbourhood renewal. Nevertheless, there is a long way to go before the barriers to urban renewal disappear and the incentives to move out diminish.

### Regions

Critically, the 'urban renaissance' did not have a focus on the economic renewal of cities and regions that would be necessary to revive their fortunes, demanding a regional as well as a purely urban agenda.

Regional policy under New Labour has principally focused on economic development through the creation of regional development agencies and devolving governance and decision making through a diluted form of regional government now being pursued in three northern regions. The government is actively discussing the redeployment of government services away from the south east. Its limited transport investment is also prioritising the national rail and road network over infrastructure in the south east where transport and congestion problems are arguably the most urgent. This should lead to faster access between regions and stronger connections beyond the south east, which would in turn aid regional development.

The connection between a rebalancing of regional economic success, decentralising government away from the centre, an urban renaissance and neighbourhood renewal is direct. It is clear from our discussion that there is a cascade effect from economic decline to regional or sub-regional decline, to job and population losses, to the harshest impacts on the most disadvantaged areas. Conversely regional progress should underpin neighbourhood recovery. Progress in neighbourhood renewal may stall unless linked into wider regional and urban development. However, whether this will happen is still unclear. The regional agenda is too fresh and unformed to make such an outcome inevitable. If the development of regional assemblies across the north leads to a serious devolution of decision making; if the fast speed rail links due to come in from September 2004 really happen; and if the urban regeneration now underway in northern city centres spreads into inner neighbourhoods, then regional inequalities may shrink.

### Sustainable communities

The third broad policy shift relates principally to housing. Housing was far down the SEU's priorities for neighbourhood renewal when it originally published the national strategy. However, ODPM, as the department responsible for delivering the programme, quickly recognised its centrality. The problems of low demand and housing market failure in the north, coupled with escalating house prices and real affordability problems for low-paid workers in London and other successful areas forced the government to act. First, it announced a plan to develop a housing market renewal programme, targeting the worst areas in the north and Midlands, with the core aim of restructuring housing markets to reverse the trend to abandonment in most acutely affected areas, and to balance housing supply and demand more closely. Then it re-ignited interest in the Thames Gateway, the declining ex-industrial eastern fringe of London, as a potential 'growth area'. At the same time, it announced a radical reform of planning. It pulled these different strands of action together into the most comprehensive set of proposals for housing renewal in decades: the 'Sustainable Communities' Plan (ODPM, 2003a; Power, 2004). If housing market renewal and the Thames Gateway work, many poor neighbourhoods stand to gain significantly – they will be upgraded, better connected, more mixed and more in demand. These changes have to work within the neighbourhood renewal framework so that existing communities benefit from the wider resources and wider regeneration the Communities Plan offers. However, many questions remain over funding, infrastructure, capacity and the sheer scale of the plan, and it is very early days to see how deliverable the plan is in practice.

## Conclusion

New Labour's strategic approach to neighbourhood renewal represents a significant policy advance, which has the potential to deliver improvements in the poorest areas. Some improvements do seem to be happening, although it is not clear that they are shared by all poor neighbourhoods; indeed, some may be getting worse. On the other hand, it is too early yet to see the real impact of the NSNR. Further improvements could be expected once the strategy has bedded down.

Perhaps the key point, however, is that we cannot expect neighbourhood policy on its own to deliver better neighbourhood outcomes. On the one hand, thriving neighbourhoods could make a vital contribution to city and regional recovery. Put simply, poor neighbourhoods, with their unattractive, poorly maintained, under-invested and cared for environments, deter investors, encourage abuse and drive families out (Power and Mumford, 1999; Mumford and Power, 2003). On the other hand, neighbourhood success is dependent on declining cities and regions becoming stronger economic engines, attracting major investment away from the overheated southern and eastern regions. There is an intimate connection between regional and urban revival and neighbourhood renewal. Equalising incentives for urban regrowth as opposed to outer sprawl and reducing the barriers to economic regrowth in the regions that were damaged by individual exploitation and collapse are needed if disadvantaged neighbourhoods are to bounce back. While there has been some progress at the regional level, it has been more limited, to date, than progress at the neighbourhood level, and transport, urban environments, services and skills all require investment on a scale not yet envisaged.

Possibly the biggest challenge is driving down to area or neighbourhood level the practical execution of policy – whether inward investment and skills training for jobs; brown-field remediation; integrated multi-tenure housing renewal and building; regional devolution; city government; neighbourhood management;

or social cohesion. All these issues cut across every level of government, but are eventually played out in specific local areas that require careful local organisation and management. The government, regeneration agencies and local partners need to adopt a locally focused, delivery oriented approach in order to bridge the gap between the need for neighbourhood renewal and its reliance on wider organisational and policy changes. Recovery may be possible if different policies from many directions are driven towards the same goal. Making links between bigger strategies – urban, regional and housing – and neighbourhood delivery is surely the key to delivering actual change.

**Notes**

[1] For some targets, there are not yet time-series of data that enable performance assessment. Measures of regional economic performance will not be reported on until 2006; VAT registrations data is only publicly available for 2000. Key Stage 3 performance data has only been published from 2002 onwards. School-level data for GCSE and Key Stage 2 are only publicly available by searching for individual schools, not as a complete dataset.

[2] These data are calculated from official labour market statistics. Population denominators have not been adjusted in line with the 2001 Census. Figures are for all people of working age and have not been weighted to reflect the different age profiles of different areas.

[3] Data at this level is only publicly available from 1999/2000. To measure progress, the government intends to compare the aggregate performance of the 67 NRF areas within the worst quartile of Crime and Disorder Reduction Partnerships (CDRPs) with that of all other CDRPs. This analysis is not yet available, so here we use all 88 NRF areas. All crime data must be treated with caution. Recorded crime numbers may fluctuate because of changes in reporting rates and police recording practices. The period in question is affected by the implementation of the national crime recording standard, effective nationally from April 2002 but in some police force areas from 1999 onwards, which resulted in significant changes in numbers of offences recorded in some forces. Burglary and vehicle crime were not seriously affected, but robbery figures may have been, particularly in relation to greater recording of business robberies. A further problem may arise from changes in population denominators. For 1999-2002, Office of National Statistics mid-year estimates were used. In 2002/03, these were revised (usually downwards) in the light of the 2001 Census, causing an apparent increase in crime rates in some areas disproportionate to the number of crimes.

# Towards an equal start? Addres childhood poverty and deprivation

*Kitty Stewart*

## Background and evidence

The number of children living in relative poverty in the UK increased dramatically over the two decades prior to 1997. As Table 7.1 shows, between one in three and one in four children lived in households with less than 60% of average income when Labour came to power, depending on whether income is measured before or after housing costs (BHC or AHC)[1]. This represented a much sharper rise in poverty among children than among the rest of the population. By the mid-1990s, child poverty in the UK was higher than in much of the rest of the industrialised world: UNICEF (2000) ranked the UK third bottom of 17 countries, ahead only of Italy and the US.

Table 7.1 also shows what happened to child poverty when measured against a fixed income poverty line (60% of average income in 1996/97). Measured AHC, nearly as high a share of children lived below the fixed line in 1997 as in

**Table 7.1:Trends in poverty (1979-97)**

| BHC measure | 1979 | 1987 | 1991/92 | 1996/97 |
|---|---|---|---|---|
| *Income below 60% of contemporary median* | | | | |
| All | 12 | 17 | 21 | 18 |
| Children | 12 | 21 | 27 | 25 |
| *Income below 60% of 1996/97 median in real terms* | | | | |
| All | 30 | 26 | 23 | 18 |
| Children | 34 | 31 | 30 | 25 |
| **AHC measure** | **1979** | **1987** | **1991/92** | **1996/97** |
| *Income below 60% of contemporary median* | | | | |
| All | 13 | 20 | 25 | 25 |
| Children | 14 | 25 | 32 | 34 |
| *Income below 60% of 1996/97 median in real terms* | | | | |
| All | 32 | 30 | 27 | 25 |
| Children | 37 | 36 | 35 | 34 |

*Notes:* Data for equivalent net income. From FES series up to and including 1991/92 (UK); from FRS for 1996/97 (GB).
*Source:* DWP (2004a)

1979: after housing costs, real incomes for the poorest families with children had barely changed, despite substantial improvements in average living standards.

The rising level of household worklessness was one important factor behind this trend. One in five children lived in a household with no member in work in 1997, compared to just 8% in 1979 (Gregg and Wadsworth, 2001). This in turn was partly due to the fact that more children were living with a single parent – 22% in 1995/96, up from 10% in 1979 (Gregg et al, 1999, Table 1). In addition, the 1980s and 1990s had seen polarisation of work among two-parent households, with rising numbers of dual worker families on the one hand and no-worker families on the other (Gregg and Wadsworth, 2001).

The incidence of poverty for children in households without work had also increased between 1979 and 1996, even against a constant real poverty line, as benefit levels had lagged behind rising incomes (Gregg et al, 1999a). But not all the poor were workless, and low pay and increasing wage inequality also contributed to rising poverty. While 54% of poor children in 1995/96 lived in a one-parent or a two-parent workless household, that left 46% living with self-employed workers or with low-paid and/or part-time employees (see Gregg et al, 1999a, Table 4). Even children in two-parent households with both parents employed experienced an increase in the risk of poverty between 1986 and 1991 (Bradshaw, 2000).

At the same time, a growing body of evidence pointed to the impact of poverty in childhood on outcomes in later life. Children growing up poor appeared to have lower self-esteem and expectations; they were less likely to be successful in education and in the labour market, and were at increased risk of early childbearing, low income, benefit dependency and homelessness (Hobcraft, 1998; Ermisch et al, 2001).

These findings did not escape the attention of a government that had declared itself committed to 'equal worth' and 'opportunity for all'. The conclusions of a Treasury workshop on the causes of persistent poverty and lifetime inequality in November 1998 underlined the central importance of childhood experiences:

> Childhood disadvantage frequently leads to low educational attainment … which in turn leads to low income and denial of opportunity for the next generation. (HM Treasury, 1999, p 27; see also CASE/HM Treasury, 1999)

Tackling childhood poverty therefore came to be seen as central to a long-term solution to adult disadvantage, as well as being a moral imperative in itself; Gordon Brown would describe the level of child poverty as "a scar on the soul of Britain" (_The Guardian_, 17 March 2000). In Blair's Beveridge speech in March 1999, in which he set out "our historic aim that ours is the first generation to end child poverty forever", this was clear:

We need to break the cycle of disadvantage so that children born into poverty are not condemned to social exclusion and deprivation. (Blair, 1999, p 16)

At the same time, the Treasury had been exploring a second strand of evidence about childhood experiences, this time relating to the services available to very young children. The Comprehensive Spending Review set up in 1997 included a review of young children's services, reflecting an interest in evidence from the US that Early Years programmes could make a long-term difference to children's lives. The statistic most often cited (see, for example, Blair, 2002) – that for every $1 invested by the state in pre-school programmes, $7 are saved to society because of reduced crime, higher educational attainment and lower teenage pregnancy – comes from the US Perry Pre-school/HighScope programme, a study of 123 children in the 1960s followed into adulthood. But there is further US evidence of the potential effectiveness of such programmes (Waldfogel, 1998, provides a review). Meanwhile, work on UK data had shown that social class inequalities in educational development showed up as early as 22 months, setting children from poorer backgrounds at a disadvantage long before they started school (Feinstein, 1998). In combination, this evidence pushed the Treasury to invest substantial funds into services for pre-school children for the first time.

 ## Policies

Tackling childhood poverty and disadvantage is not about providing either more money or better public services: it is of necessity about both. (Gordon Brown in HM Treasury, 2001, p iii)

This chapter looks at policies aimed at (1) providing more money for families with children, and (2) improving public services for children in the first few years. Other aspects of public services important to children's quality of life and opportunities are covered in other chapters of this volume, most obviously Chapter Three. A number of smaller initiatives for children are not considered in detail but are worthy of mention: in particular, the National School Fruit Scheme  which provides free fruit to all 4- to 6-year-olds in England every school day; the Children's Fund, which targets children aged 5 to 13 at risk of social exclusion, including travellers, asylum seekers and homeless children (Strategy Unit, 2002); and the Child Trust Fund, which provides a lump-sum payment plus top-ups for all new babies born from September 2002 (a higher sum for those in low-income families), to be drawn on when the child reaches adulthood.

## 'More money': tax–benefit reform and work promotion

Labour's strategy for tackling child poverty places strong emphasis on encouraging employment and making it pay. Some policies have affected all low-income workers:

- National Minimum Wage introduced at £3.50 in April 1999, rising to reach £4.85 in October 2004; and
- reforms to tax and national insurance contributions.

Many more have been targeted at working families with children:

- New Deal for Lone Parents;
- Working Families Tax Credit (WFTC) (October 1999 to March 2003);
- Children's Tax Credit (April 2001 to March 2003); and
- WFTC and Children's Tax Credit reformulated into the Working Tax Credit (WTC) and Child Tax Credit (CTC) from April 2003.

There have also been significant changes affecting all families with children, whether in or out of work:

- increases in Child Benefit for first children;
- increases in length and generosity of maternity allowance for mothers with some work record; and
- Sure Start Maternity Grant of £500 for low-income mothers.

Finally, and perhaps least publicised:

- increases in allowances for younger children (under 11 years of age) in non-working families claiming income support.

On the downside, in 1997 the government took the decision to implement Conservative plans to abolish One Parent Benefit and the lone parent premium in Income Support. For most families, the increased allowances for all children have since compensated for this.

Table 7.2 shows the increases in child benefit and income support and in net income AHC for families on average and half-average earnings (including all benefits and tax credits). In total, spending on child-contingent tax credits and benefits grew from £15 billion in 1999 to £22 billion in 2003 (2003 prices) (see Table 7.9 below).

**Table 7.2: Increases in Child Benefit, Income Support and net income AHC (April 1991 to April 2003) (£ per week, April 2003 prices)**

|  | April 1991 | April 1997 | April 2003 | Change 1991-97 (%) | Change 1997-2003 (%) |
|---|---|---|---|---|---|
| Child Benefit (first child) | 11.23 | 12.81 | 16.05 | 14.1 | 25.3 |
| Child Benefit (subsequent child) | 9.87 | 10.43 | 10.75 | 5.7 | 3.1 |
| Income Support (lone parent, 1 child under 11) | 87.70 | 91.18 | 108.90 | 4.0 | 19.4 |
| Income Support (couple, 1 child under 11) | 112.03 | 116.87 | 140.00 | 4.3 | 19.8 |
| Income Support (couple, 2 children under 11) | 129.93 | 135.71 | 178.50 | 4.4 | 31.5 |
| *Net income AHC* | | | | | |
| Couple, 2 children on average earnings | 297.18 | 311.73 | 352.00 | 4.9 | 12.9 |
| Lone parent, 1 child on average earnings | 217.64 | 229.33 | 266.22 | 5.4 | 16.1 |
| Couple, 2 children on 1/2 average earnings | 165.13 | 177.61 | 239.90 | 7.6 | 35.1 |
| Lone parent, 1 child on 1/2 average earnings | 146.01 | 156.95 | 193.55 | 7.5 | 23.3 |

*Source:* DWP (2003e)

### 'Better public services': the Early Years agenda

Unlike tax–benefit policy, which affects the whole of the UK, responsibility for early years education and childcare rests with the devolved administrations. Due to space constraints, this chapter concentrates on England (see Wincott, 2004, for discussion of early years policies in Scotland and Wales).

Service provision for under-fives in England has had three main aspects:

1. *The expansion of nursery school provision for three- and four-year-olds.* By April 2004, all three- and four-year-olds were guaranteed a free part-time nursery place, achieved through supply-side subsidies to providers.
2. *Sure Start local programmes for 0- to 4-year-olds in the most deprived 20% of wards.* Sure Start programmes were in place in 522 areas by 2004, reaching 400,000 children (including one third of all poor children under four years of age). Each programme is different, designed locally to meet local needs, but all offer five core services: outreach and home visiting; parenting support; support for good quality play, learning and childcare experiences; primary health care and advice; and support for children and parents with special needs. Each programme has roughly £1,000 to spend per child over the programme's 7 to 10 year lifetime.

3. *Investment in 'high quality childcare'*, intended to support parental employment while also offering children the benefits of early education.

The 1998 National Childcare Strategy aimed to deliver quality, affordable childcare in every neighbourhood: 900,000 new childcare places were pledged for 1.6 million children by March 2004, with a further 250,000 places by March 2006. The strategy for expanding provision is market-based. Money is available for partial funding of new nurseries for a three-year period in the most deprived wards through the Neighbourhood Nurseries Initiative and the New Opportunities Fund Out of School Programme; elsewhere the policy is to provide business support to private providers, for instance through the Small Firms Loan Guarantee Scheme for nurseries and the Childminder Start-up Grant. Support for lower-income families comes through a demand-side subsidy: families claiming the WFTC (later the WTC) are eligible for a childcare tax credit worth up to 70% of formal childcare costs.

At the same time, there have been limited attempts to improve the quality of childcare places. Day nurseries and childminders are now inspected by OFSTED, and childminder registration requirements are stricter. Funding has been made available for childminder networks and training. In 1997, the first Early Excellence Centre was established as a model of good practice in the provision of integrated care and early education. There are now 107 centres across England. The current vision is to provide a Children's Centre for every community, also built around a model of integrated education and care.

In total, funding for all early years programmes exceeded £3.5 billion in 2002/03, a real terms increase of over £1.5 billion from 1997/98 (Table 7.9).

The remainder of this chapter explores measurable outcomes of these two sets of policies. We examine first what has happened to child poverty, and then turn to the expansion of early years education and childcare.

## Outcomes: child poverty

Blair's pledge to eliminate child poverty led to a process of consultation about how child poverty should best be measured, and the eventual choice of a tiered measurement approach (see DWP, 2003c; and discussion later in this chapter). In the meantime, the first interim target was set in relative terms. The Treasury and the Department for Work and Pensions (DWP) were instructed to reduce by a quarter the proportion of children living in households with less than 60% of equivalised median income by 2004, against a baseline year of 1998/99. The question of whether income should be measured before or after housing costs was not explicitly addressed[2].

## A 25% fall in child poverty by 2004?

The latest available data (Table 7.3) show the share of children in poverty on this measure to have fallen to 28% in 2002/03 (AHC), from a peak of 34% in 1996/97; a drop of 700,000 out of 4.3 million poor children. This represents an 18% fall (15% from the official baseline year of 1998/99). Measured BHC, the proportionate fall has been similar. Rates of poverty have fallen for children living in almost all family situations, but most sharply for those in larger families, in one-earner couples and in families headed by a lone parent working part time. Much of the overall change will have been driven by families moving across categories (for example, from unemployment into work); we return to this later in this chapter. The only group of children for whom poverty has risen slightly are those living with two workless parents; this may reflect the lack of change in the adult element of income support.

Figure 7.1 shows these changes in the context of the rise in poverty during the 1980s: the impact appears small, but the figure clearly indicates the reversal of the long-run trend. The fact that this reduction in relative poverty has been achieved against a background of rapidly rising real average incomes (meaning a fast-moving poverty target) is also worth noting. However, are numbers falling fast enough to allow the government to meet the 2004/05 target?

Clearly, the rate of progress will need to have accelerated after 2002/03, bringing a further 550,000 children across the line between 2002/03 and 2004/05 AHC (450,000 children BHC). While this may seem hopeful, analyses of changes up to and including the April 2004 budget from both the Institute for Fiscal Studies and the Microsimulation Unit in Cambridge suggest that the government is on track. Brewer (2004, p 5) concludes that:

> the government should comfortably meet its target measuring incomes BHC, and is on course to just hit its target measuring incomes AHC.

### Table 7.3: Changes in child poverty by family type and employment status (1996/97 to 2002/03)

|  | BHC | | | AHC | | |
|  | 1996/97 | 2002/03 | % change | 1996/97 | 2002/03 | % change |
| --- | --- | --- | --- | --- | --- | --- |
| **All children** | 25 | 21 | −16 | 34 | 28 | −18 |
| Lone parent, FT work | 11 | 11 | 0 | 16 | 15 | −6 |
| Lone parent, PT work | 23 | 19 | −17 | 37 | 33 | −11 |
| Lone parent, no work | 50 | 48 | −4 | 82 | 76 | −7 |
| Couple: one FT, one no work | 21 | 15 | −29 | 27 | 21 | −22 |
| Couple: one or both PT | 54 | 51 | −6 | 61 | 58 | −5 |
| Couple: both no work | 68 | 70 | +3 | 77 | 80 | +4 |
| Households with 1-2 children | 17 | 16 | −6 | 26 | 24 | −8 |
| Households with 3+ children | 41 | 31 | -24 | 49 | 37 | −24 |

Source: DWP (2004a, Tables E3.1 and E4.1); and calculations based on the above and on Table B4

**Figure 7.1: Proportion of children in households with income below 50 and 60% of the equivalised median**

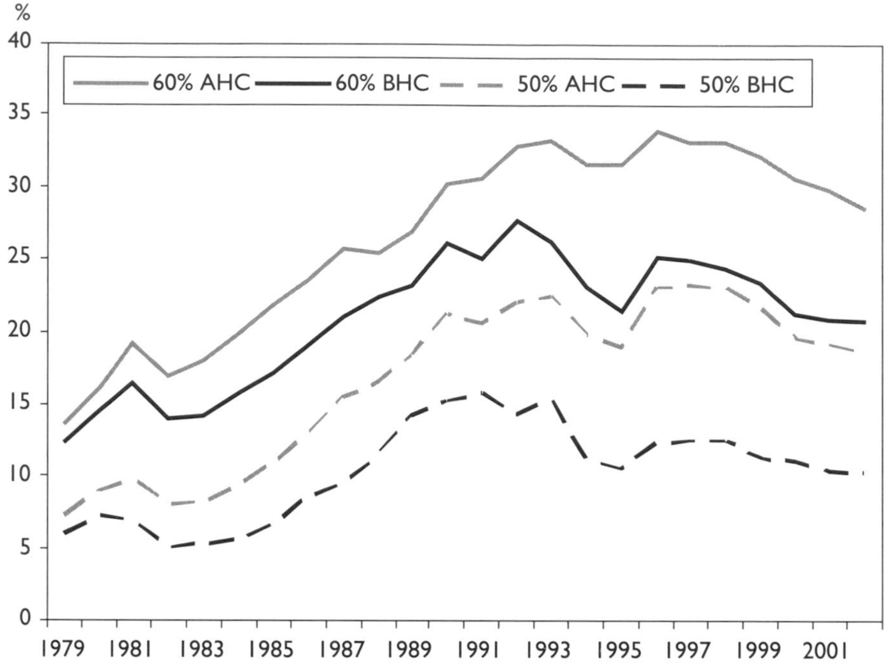

*Source:* Based on Brewer et al (2003, Figure 5); data kindly provided by the authors

Holly Sutherland (2004) reaches the same conclusion using a different simulation model, POLIMOD.

The problem with both estimates is that, while we know the details of tax–benefit policy affecting incomes in 2004/05, many other factors are impossible to predict for certain. For instance, if unemployment started to rise, poverty might rise too. A second key point is that, as poverty is measured relative to median income, changes in the median itself will affect outcomes. Most parts of the benefit system are price- rather than earnings-linked.

Predictions of government success must therefore be treated with care. On the other hand, the point about rising incomes reminds us that a relative income target was an ambitious choice. Median income rose in real terms by 17% between 1996/97 and 2002/03, taking the poverty line for a couple up from £166 a week to £194 (2002/03 prices; DWP, 2004a). If a fixed income threshold had been chosen for Blair's poverty pledge, the target of 25% out of poverty would have been met well ahead of time: the share living below the 1996/97 poverty line had *halved* by 2002/03 on both BHC and AHC measures (DWP, 2004a, pp 64-5). The impact of the moving poverty line is clearly illustrated in Figure 7.2, which shows the Sutherland simulations to 2004/05 (BHC). The income distribution moves to the right, taking all but 10% of children out of poverty against the 1997 line. However, the poverty line shifts right too: 15% of children are left below this higher (2004/05) line.

This is not to suggest that a fixed income line would have been a better choice. The idea that what a person needs to participate in society depends on what others have is widely accepted in the UK and across Europe. In the medium-run, a poverty line that does not shift with living standards is unlikely to reflect popular perception of poverty (see Hills, 2004a, ch 3 for references and discussion). However, a relative line can still obscure real changes in the living standards of children in low-income families. Chapter Twelve will explore in detail how the extra money families have received is being spent in practice; but Table 7.4 presents results from a survey which has tracked living standards in lone parent and low- to moderate-income families since 1999. The survey reveals quite striking improvements in the ability of households to afford everyday items, and in their sense of financial security.

### Children in severe poverty

One question arising from the 2004/05 target is whether it led the government to concentrate its efforts on pushing households just below 60% of the median

**Figure 7.2: Cumulative income distribution and relative poverty lines under 1997 and 2004/05 policies and incomes**

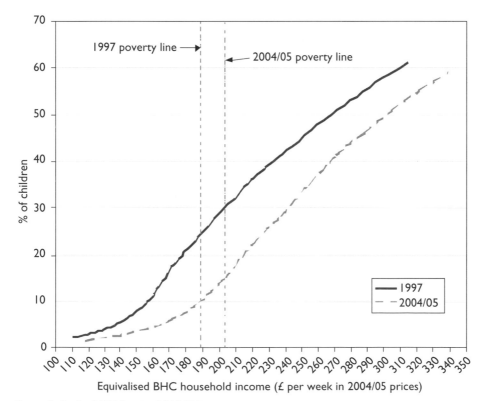

Equivalised BHC household income (£ per week in 2004/05 prices)

*Source:* Sutherland (2004), using POLIMOD

**Table 7.4: Material deprivation and financial stress among lone parents: evidence from the Families and Children Survey (FACS)**

|  | 1999 | 2000 | 2001 | 2002 |
|---|---|---|---|---|
| *Proportion unable to afford selected items* |  |  |  |  |
| Cooked main meal every day | 8 | 6 | 5 | 3 |
| Fresh fruit on most days | 17 | 13 | 11 | 9 |
| New, not second-hand, clothes when needed | 41 | 35 | 28 | 25 |
| Best outfit for children | 20 | 19 | 15 | 13 |
| Celebration with presents at special occasions | 27 | 23 | 17 | 14 |
| Money for outings, trips or gifts for parties | 59 | 52 | 46 | 41 |
| One week holiday away from home | 74 | 69 | 62 | 58 |
| *Indicators of financial stress* |  |  |  |  |
| Problems with debts almost all the time | 15 | 13 | 10 | 12 |
| Always runs out of money before end of week | 27 | 24 | 21 | 19 |
| Worries about money almost always | 45 | 38 | 33 | 30 |
| Never has money left over | 48 | 40 | 34 | 17 |

*Source:* McKay and Collard (2003, Table 7.1)

to just above it, ignoring those in more severe poverty. In fact, there is considerable evidence that real incomes are rising for many families who are still not making it across the line. Figure 7.1 showed that the poverty headcount using 50% of the median follows broadly the same pattern as the 60% line, and Figure 7.2 that the whole length of the income distribution has moved to the right. Hills and Sutherland (2004) find that the median child poverty gap ratio – the share of the poverty line by which the median poor child fell short – fell between 1996/97 and 2004/05 (modelled results) by two percentage points on a BHC basis and by eight points AHC. This is evidence that children from the poorest half of the poor are moving up towards the poverty line. Brewer et al (2004) also point to a falling median poverty gap ratio for children to 2002/03 (but a rising ratio for the whole population).

On the other hand, Sutherland et al (2003) suggest that there has been a slight increase in the number of children in households on the very lowest incomes. This may in part be due to measurement problems, but may also reflect the fact that not all families claim the benefits to which they are entitled. As benefits rise, this will leave them relatively worse off, even compared to other poor families. The DWP estimate that in 2001/02 up to 15% of eligible couples with children and 6% of lone parents were not taking up the Income Support to which they were entitled. This represents a slight increase in the take-up problem since 1997/99, when the corresponding figures were 13% and 4% (DWP, 2004b, and earlier equivalents).

## On track for 2010 and beyond?

Whether or not the government hits its 2004/05 target, what are the prospects of child poverty being halved by 2010 and eradicated by 2020? The precise goals have changed a little as a result of the consultation on child poverty measurement, which finished with the government's choice of a 'tiered approach' to measurement based on three indicators:

(1) the relative low income indicator used earlier, but measured BHC only;
(2) absolute low income (children living in households below 60% of the 1998/99 median); and
(3) an indicator combining relative low income with material deprivation (children living in households with income below 70% of the contemporary median and unable to afford certain goods and services) (DWP, 2003c).

The goal for 2010 was confirmed in July 2004: between 1998/99 and 2010/11, to halve both the number of children in poverty under measure (1) and the number in poverty under measure (3) (HM Treasury, 2004c). The goal for eradication, under current thinking, is to ensure by 2020 that no children are poor under measure (3) and that the UK is ranked "among the best in Europe" on measure (1) (DWP, 2003c, p 20).

While the use of the material deprivation target will ensure the government gains credit for real income changes that might otherwise be overlooked, as pointed to earlier in this chapter, concern has been expressed at the relative measure being downplayed, and also at the switch to BHC indicators (for example, see Brewer et al, 2004; Work and Pensions Committee, 2004). There is no space to consider these issues here, but it may be noted that enormous progress still needs to be made under the new definitions. For instance, the consultation suggested that 'best in Europe' might mean the average of the best four countries in Europe – just over 8% in 2001, compared to 24% on a comparable basis for the UK (European Commission, 2003a; see also Chapter Fourteen of this volume).

What will it take to achieve this sort of change? For more children to move out of relative poverty, benefits, credits or the wages of the low paid need to rise in relation to median income, and/or more adults from low-income families need to move into employment or increase their hours of work. The outlook for increased employment looks promising on the surface. Household worklessness fell between 1996 and 2003, as Table 7.5 shows, but it remains high by international standards, and there is still a long way to go to reach the government's target of

**Table 7.5: Worklessness and children**

|  | Children under 16 in workless households | | Children under 16 in workless households by family type | |
|  | 1000s | % | Lone parent (%) | Dual parent (%) |
|---|---|---|---|---|
| 1993 | 2,300 | 19.9 | 53.8 | 9.5 |
| 1996 | 2,300 | 19.6 | 53.9 | 8.8 |
| 1998 | 2,200 | 18.5 | 51.2 | 7.4 |
| 2001 | 1,900 | 16.2 | 46.9 | 6.2 |
| 2003 | 1,900 | 16.2 | 45.7 | 5.8 |

*Source:* Provided by Paul Gregg from household Labour Force Survey

70% of lone parents in work: in 2002, only 51% of lone parents were in work (Gregg and Wadsworth, 2003, Table 2.4).

On the other hand, the UK unemployment rate has fallen steadily for a decade and may be unlikely to fall further at a time when unemployment has started to rise in many other OECD countries (see Chapter Fourteen, Figure 14.6 in this volume). On the supply side, results from the Families and Children Survey (FACS) show that 22% of workless lone parents and 45% of respondents in workless couples were not looking for work in 2001 due to illness or disability (their own or that of a partner or child), while in both groups more than one third were not looking because they preferred to remain home with their children (Kasparova et al, 2003). The FACS results do suggest that the expansion of childcare availability and affordability (discussed later in this chapter) would make a difference to between one fifth and one third of non-working lone parents. But any further reductions in worklessness may be difficult to achieve, barring the introduction of greater compulsion in labour market policy.

This points to the importance of pay and of benefits. Continuing increases in minimum wages and in the generosity of government support for families with children, over and above average income growth, will be needed to lift more children in both working poor households and non-working households across the poverty line. Table 7.3 showed that relative poverty rates have fallen only slightly for children living with workless lone parents, and have risen slightly in workless couple households, where they are between 70% and 80%. Sustained falls in the overall rate of child poverty depend on the needs of these households being addressed. In the longer run, looking ahead to 2020, it must be hoped that the health and education strategies discussed in previous chapters of this volume – and the Early Years agenda which is the subject of the next section – will have been successful in addressing the underlying causes of worklessness and low pay.

## Outcomes: the Early Years agenda

Investment in childcare is seen by the government as providing a 'double dividend' (Strategy Unit, 2002, p 29), helping to bring down child poverty rates by enabling more parents to work, while also supporting child development objectives. At its best, childcare can contribute to both goals, but it should not be assumed that they automatically go together.

The story about what is best for early child development is complicated. Recent evidence from Bristol suggests that children's cognitive development suffers if both parents work full time within 18 months of a birth, leaving the child with an unpaid relative or friend, but that children left in a formal nursery do at least as well as those whose mothers remain at home (Gregg and Washbrook, 2003). After 18 months, mothers' return to work has little apparent impact. A separate UK study which looks at a wider set of outcomes supports the finding that nursery attendance can be good for cognitive attainment, but points to higher levels of anti-social behaviour for children who spend long hours in nurseries before the age of three, and especially before the age of two (Sylva et al, 2003).

One problem with both studies is that neither is able to take account of variations in the quality of centre-based care in these critical first few years. Sylva et al (2003) – part of the Effective Provision of Pre-School Education Project (EPPE) – primarily focus on nursery attendance among slightly older children, age three and four, and here different settings can be distinguished. In general, attendance is found to make a big difference to school-readiness, with disadvantaged children benefiting most. But quality emerges as very important, with staff qualification levels making the biggest difference to both intellectual and social outcomes. State nursery schools and classes, as well as 'integrated centres' – those that fully combine education with care – are found to provide the best quality, with playgroups and day nurseries doing less well. A review of 48 studies in seven other countries suggests that staff qualifications and training are also very important for childcare quality and developmental outcomes in the earlier years (Thomas Coram Research Unit, 2002).

With this evidence in mind, this section begins by examining the provision of affordable formal childcare places, essential to family finances and preferable (for some outcomes) to informal care options. It goes on to look at what has been done to improve the quality of these places. The section then discusses the expansion of pre-school education, and considers the impact of Sure Start in the most deprived wards.

First, however, the increased generosity of the maternity allowance should be mentioned – up over 50% in real terms to £100 a week and paid for 26 rather than 18 weeks. This will certainly have enabled more low-income children to spend more time with their mothers in the first six months of life.

## Availability of formal childcare places

Figure 7.3 shows a substantial increase in the total number of formal childcare places, with a particularly sharp change since 2001. Day nursery places have doubled since 1997 and after-school places have tripled. Yet the net increase to 2003 is just 350,000, a long way from the 2004 target of 900,000 new places. Oddly enough, this is a target the government claims to have met (speech by Minister for Work Jane Kennedy to the One Parent Families Annual Conference, 13 May 2004). The discrepancy is explained by two factors. First, government numbers include part-time places provided for three- and four-year-olds, although 2.5 hours a day is clearly inadequate childcare cover. Second, they are not adjusted for childcare places that have been lost over this period – some 301,000 between 1998 and 2003, compared to 626,000 places created (National Audit Office, 2004). This is partly due to nursery closures but mostly to the fall in childminder numbers reflected in Figure 7.3, itself explained by a combination of tighter regulation and better opportunities elsewhere in a strong economy.

The combination of the childcare tax credit and the Neighbourhood Nurseries

**Figure 7.3: Childcare places**

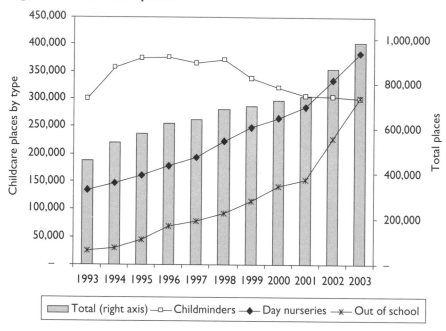

*Source:* Provided by the Daycare Trust

Initiative in the poorest 20% of wards should have ensured that lower-income families benefited more than proportionately from the extra places that have been provided. At local authority level, this does not seem to have happened. Overall, the childcare gap between the 20% of Local Authorities (LAs) with the highest and lowest levels of child poverty narrowed slightly between 1999 and 2003, but this turns out to be entirely due to childminder places, which rose slightly in the poorer areas, while falling elsewhere. Nursery places increased by 63% in the 30 most deprived LAs and across the country, and by 95% in the best-off 30.

At ward level, the use of formal childcare services increased overall in 2001, but not in the most deprived 20% of wards, where we see a small drop in the use of formal services (Woodland et al, 2002). Evidence from FACS suggests low-income families and lone parents remain heavily reliant on informal childcare (Kasparova et al, 2003). In 2001, in the bottom income fifth, only 19% of pre-school children and 3% of school-age children with working parents were looked after in formal childcare settings eligible for the childcare tax credit, compared to 68% and 18% in the top fifth. Table 7.7 below shows that, between 1997 and 2002, the share of older pre-schoolers (three- and four-year-olds) in day nurseries doubled from 2% to 4% among social classes IV and V, but remained a long way behind attendance among classes I and II, up from 11% to 16%.

These data reflect the story to 2001 or 2002, but the big changes in provision only really began in 2001. The most recent data on the childcare tax credit suggest that things may now be changing more quickly. Just 11-13% of WFTC recipients claimed the childcare credit between 2000 and 2002, but numbers subsequently jumped: by April 2004, 20% of WTC recipients with children were receiving an average childcare award of £50 a week (Inland Revenue, 2004). This remains a small share of the potential caseload but indicates that the use of formal childcare is responding to the availability of places. For those eligible for the full credit, the policy will have made a big difference to the weekly childcare bill, bringing the cost of an average nursery place for an under-two down from £128 to £38 (Daycare Trust, 2003).

Five years after the introduction of the National Childcare Strategy, then, the supply of formal (and affordable) childcare places is still far from sufficient, but the sharp rise in places since 2001 suggests that the government may simply need more time. The indirect method of stimulating private supply rather than providing bricks-and-mortar nurseries may be working, but slowly.

However, a number of concerns remain. First, there are issues surrounding the sustainability of nurseries and clubs that benefited from funding in their first three years: only half of new providers have a plan for when their start-up funding ends (National Audit Office, 2004, p 7). There are also questions about whether the current system will benefit all low-income families, even if sufficient places are created. Those receiving maximum childcare credit must still find 30% of childcare costs: for some families, especially those with more than one child, this may be prohibitive. Furthermore, payment of the credit is dependent on family circumstances: if these change (for example, if a parent cuts his/her working hours to less than 16), the family loses eligibility and (very likely) also the childcare place. Other systems of childcare support are in place to assist with job search or retraining, but a family would be lucky to keep a child in the same nursery throughout job transition. Perhaps it is not surprising that many families with precarious work arrangements choose to stick with the relative stability of informal options.

## Childcare quality: ages 0 to 3

The government has made a number of changes with a view to improving the quality of formal childcare settings (see earlier in this chapter). The shift in responsibility for the sector from the Department of Health to the Department for Education and Employment (DfEE) and the start of OFSTED regulation of childcare providers are particularly significant. Interested childminders have benefited from funding and opportunities for training. However, no serious attempt has been made to address the major challenge to quality childcare provision in the UK – poorly qualified and low-paid staff.

The 1998 childcare Green Paper stated that:

> there is no sensible distinction between good early education and care. (DfEE, 1998, para 1.4)

Yet policies for early years provision are currently based on precisely such a distinction, with the education, pay and career opportunities of childcare staff vastly different from those of teachers. A nursery schoolteacher has a four-year degree; a day nursery supervisor or nursery nurse has two years of post-16 training (NVQ Level 3), and many childcare staff are less qualified or hold no qualifications at all. A childcare worker's wage is less than half that of a teacher, and also substantially lower than the average for similarly qualified women (Cameron et al, 2003; Rolfe et al, 2003). Low pay and poor conditions, including sick pay and pension rights, have a cost in morale and recruitment difficulties: in a survey for the DfEE, four in five childcare providers mentioned recruitment as a barrier to the delivery of high quality care (Callender, 2000). Staff turnover rates in day nurseries approach 30% a year (Rolfe et al, 2003).

The sector has been affected by increases in the minimum wage: research by the Low Pay Commission suggests one tenth of childcare workers are paid close to the minimum wage, while 90% of childcare firms claim that increases in the minimum have resulted in increases for higher grades too to retain pay differentials (LPC, 2003). But the New Earnings Survey shows that median hourly pay for qualified nursery nurses was still £7.38 in April 2003, compared to £17.55 for nursery/primary schoolteachers. Furthermore, the LPC found that 17% of childcare firms (the highest of any sector) had responded to rises in the minimum wage by increasing the use of unqualified labour to keep the overall wage bill down.

The UK is by no means unique in having such a sharp divide between the requirements made of staff in charge of children aged 0 to 5 in one setting and those in charge of children aged 3+ in another, although there are countries (largely in Scandinavia) which offer an alternative, integrated model. The OECD (2001b, p 132) points to "serious consequences for the quality of provision for children" in split systems. Yet although the Interdepartmental Childcare Review of 2002 concludes that "the opportunity to use childcare to further educational and wider objectives is being missed" (Strategy Unit, 2002, p 6), radical changes in training and pay do not appear to be on the agenda. Children's Centres, one pledged for each of 1,700 of the 8,000 English wards by 2007/08, are advised to employ a qualified teacher, at least part time, to ensure early learning goals are met. This may be seen as a start, but it also reinforces the distinction between 'teachers' and 'carers', and does nothing to benefit the vast majority of children who will remain in other childcare centres.

## Nursery places: ages 3 to 4

Table 7.6 shows recent increases in participation in early years education among three- and four-year-olds, all of whom were guaranteed a part-time place in an early years setting in 2004. By January 2003, 88% of three-year-olds and 98% of four-year-olds were benefiting from a funded place, representing a dramatic increase in support for three-year-olds in particular. This looks to have been a

**Table 7.6: Participation in early years education: evidence from the Annual Schools Census and Early Years Census**

| | 1997 | 1998 | 1999 | 2000 | 2001 | 2002 | 2003 |
|---|---|---|---|---|---|---|---|
| *Threes in early years ed (%)* | | | | 86 | 90 | 90 | 99 |
| State nursery school/class | 34 | 35 | 37 | 38 | 38 | 38 | 38 |
| Independent school | 4 | 4 | 4 | 4 | 5 | 5 | 5 |
| Private or voluntary providers | | | | 44 | 47 | 48 | 56 |
| *Fours in early years ed (%)* | | | 99 | 100 | 101 | 101 | 104 |
| State nursery/primary schools | 77 | 78 | 79 | 79 | 79 | 80 | 79 |
| (including reception class) | 53 | 55 | 56 | 57 | | 60 | 60 |
| Independent schools | 4 | 4 | 5 | 5 | 5 | 5 | 5 |
| Private or voluntary providers | | | 15 | 16 | 17 | 16 | 19 |
| *Threes with a funded place (%)* | | | | 44 | 59 | 71 | 88 |
| State nursery school/class | | | | 38 | 38 | 38 | 38 |
| Private or voluntary providers | | | | 6 | 20 | 33 | 50 |
| *Fours with a funded place (%)* | | | | 93 | 94 | 95 | 98 |
| State nursery/primary school | 77 | 78 | 79 | 79 | 79 | 80 | 79 |
| Private or voluntary provider | | | | 14 | 15 | 15 | 19 |

*Notes:* (i) The Early Years Census started in 1999 for four-year-olds and 2000 for three-year-olds. The Annual Schools Census provides earlier information but only for nursery and primary schools. (ii) 2003 figures provisional. (iii) Figures are for January each year. (iv) Numbers of three-year-olds in schools may include some two-year-olds, while any child attending more than one provider in the census week may have been counted twice. Hence percentages can sum to more than 100. (v) 'Private and voluntary providers' only includes providers registered to receive the nursery education grant.
*Source:* DfES (2003c)

highly successful (if expensive) intervention, illustrating both the cost and effectiveness of a universal policy: it is clear that many (perhaps better-off) children are now being funded for places they already enjoyed, but the policy has also managed to reach almost the whole age group, including children who would otherwise have received no pre-school education. (The big jump in four-year-old participation is likely to have come between 1997 and 1999, when data are incomplete.)

However, not all early years places are of equal quality, and it is interesting that there has been very limited expansion in the provision of places found by Sylva et al (2003) to provide the highest quality education – those in maintained nursery schools and nursery classes. The share of children in these settings has remained steady since 2000, despite falling total numbers of children in this cohort and a rising share of four-year-olds in reception classes rather than nursery; that is, this is not simply a question of capacity constraint. The expansion is largely taking place among 'private and voluntary providers', which includes private nursery schools, many of which were found in the EPPE study to offer a high standard of pre-school education, but also private and local authority day nurseries and playgroups (usually run by parents or volunteers), which were found, in general, to be weaker. Playgroup attendance may cover children attending for just one or two sessions a week.

Table 7.7 provides greater detail on providers, along with a social class

**Table 7.7: Types of nursery education provider used in the last week, by social class (% of all 3- and 4-year-olds) (1997 and 2002)**

|  | I and II | | III Non-Manual | | III Manual | | IV and V | | Total | |
| --- | --- | --- | --- | --- | --- | --- | --- | --- | --- | --- |
|  | 1997 | **2002** | 1997 | **2002** | 1997 | **2002** | 1997 | **2002** | 1997 | **2002** |
| Nursery school or class | 36 | **32** | 36 | **31** | 38 | **38** | 35 | **42** | 36 | **35** |
| Reception class | 21 | **29** | 22 | **33** | 19 | **30** | 22 | **30** | 21 | **30** |
| Day nursery | 11 | **16** | 7 | **14** | 4 | **7** | 2 | **4** | 7 | **11** |
| Playgroup/ pre-school | 26 | **24** | 22 | **19** | 21 | **20** | 20 | **15** | 22 | **21** |
| Other | 7 | **4** | 6 | **4** | 6 | **4** | 4 | **5** | 7 | **4** |
| None | 7 | **3** | 11 | **4** | 15 | **5** | 17 | **7** | 11 | **4** |

*Note:* Total exceeds 100 in some columns as children can attend more than one provider a week.
*Source:* Stratford et al (1997, Table 1.2E) and Bell and Finch (2004, Table 2.2); from an annual survey of parents

breakdown. Total figures show no change in the share of children in nursery schools and classes or the share in playgroups between 1997 and 2002; growth has instead come from significantly higher shares of children attending reception classes and from the expansion of day nurseries. However, the overall picture masks very different trends by social class. In 1997, attendance patterns were broadly similar across classes with the exception of day nurseries, which were used more heavily by classes I, II and IIINM. But by 2002, nursery school/class attendance had risen sharply for social classes IV and V and fallen for classes I, II and IIINM. Use of playgroups had meanwhile fallen among classes IV and V. The result is that, in 2002, children from manual class backgrounds were considerably more likely to be attending higher quality settings than other children, perhaps a result of the priority given to nursery school expansion in deprived areas. It remains the case that more of these children were not attending at all (7% in classes IV/V, compared to 3% in classes I/II) but this is a big improvement from 1997 (17% compared to 7%).

 ## Sure Start

Sure Start local programmes for under four-year-olds have received widespread approval from parents (see Chapter Thirteen of this volume, for example) and were declared Britain's "best kept secret" by Gordon Brown in his 2003 Labour Party Conference speech. Their popularity recently led to the rebranding of the whole early years strategy under the Sure Start label. But how successful has the programme really been at meeting its (short-term) objectives? (Many of the desired impacts are not expected to emerge for many years.)

Table 7.8 shows progress towards Public Service Agreement (PSA) targets, as measured by the DfES. Results are mixed. The early programmes did well at providing parenting support and play and learning opportunities (hence their high recognition among parents). Whether these opportunities have been associated with improvements in educational and social development cannot yet be assessed, but their provision should be seen as an achievement in itself. Sure Start areas have also witnessed a remarkable reduction in re-registrations on the child protection register. However, progress towards other child health goals –

**Table 7.8: Public Service Agreements for Sure Start programme areas (DfES assessment)**

| TARGETS FOR 2001/02: 59 Sure Start programmes | MET? |
|---|---|
| *Objective 1: Improving children's social and emotional development* | |
| • Parenting support and information available for all parents | Yes |
| • 10% reduction in children re-registered on child protection register | Yes |
| • Agreed and implemented culturally sensitive support for mothers with post-natal depression | Yes |
| *Objective 2: Improving children's health* | |
| • 5% reduction in low birth weight babies | No |
| • 10% reduction in emergency hospital admissions in first year (gastroenteritis, respiratory infection or severe injury) | No |
| *Objective 3: Improving children's ability to learn* | |
| • 90% of children with normal speech and language development at 18 months and 3 years | Not assessed |
| • All children to have access to good quality play and early learning opportunities | Yes |
| *Objective 4: Strengthening families and communities* | |
| • 75% of families to report personal evidence of improvement in quality of family support services | Yes |
| • Parent representation on all local Sure Start programme boards | Yes |
| *Objective 5: Increasing productivity* | |
| • 250 local programmes in England | Yes |
| • All families to be contacted by local Sure Start within 2 months of birth | No |
| • Evaluation strategy in place by 2000/01 | Yes |
| **TARGETS FOR 2004: 522 Sure Start programmes** | **ON COURSE?** |
| *Objective 1: Improving children's social and emotional development* | |
| • 20% reduction in re-registrations with child protection within a year (1) | Yes |
| *Objective 2: Improving children's health* | |
| • 10% reduction in mothers who smoke during pregnancy (2) | No |
| *Objective 3: Improving children's ability to learn* | |
| • Reduction of 5 percentage points in number of children with speech and language problems requiring specialist interventions by the age of four (3) | Not assessed |
| *Objective 4: Strengthening families and communities* | |
| • 12% reduction in number of children 0 to 3 living in workless households (4) | Yes |

*Notes:* (1) Progress: those programmes reporting saw a 37% reduction in re-registrations between 2001/02, but on very small numbers of children. (2) No progress: programmes reported an increase in mothers smoking, from 40% to 42% 2001/02. (3) Absence of data means progress will be assessed from 2003 onwards. (4) Progress: reduction of 5 percentage points between 2001/02. (For 2001/02, DfES has not published details of the margin by which targets were missed or overachieved.)
*Source:* DfES (2003d)

reducing smoking during pregnancy, low birth weight and emergency hospital admissions – looks less impressive.

There are two reasons for caution in interpreting these findings. First, we do not know what would have happened to indicators in the absence of Sure Start. For instance, Chapter Four of this volume noted that the social class gap for low birth weight has widened nationally in recent years. Hence Sure Start may have failed to meet its target but still managed to reduce low birth weight relative to similar areas. Second, Sure Start local programmes by definition vary across areas, with each programme offering a different combination of services. Outcomes might therefore also be expected to vary widely, with some more effective than others at reaching one target rather than another.

The formal evaluation of Sure Start is able to avoid these problems: it compares outcomes in Sure Start areas with those in very similar areas without Sure Start ('Sure-Start-to-be communities'); and it is able to consider outcomes for individual programmes as well as for the initiative as a whole. Only preliminary results were available at the time of writing, and these again show mixed results (NESS, 2004). Of 24 child development and parenting outcomes examined, only one (albeit a very important indicator) showed a Sure Start effect that was significant by itself: mothers/main carers in Sure Start areas were observed to treat their children in a warmer and more accepting manner than in comparison areas. However, when 20 indicators were combined into a single score, Sure Start areas appeared more than twice as likely as comparison communities to achieve a better result than expected given population characteristics. This suggests that different Sure Start programmes may indeed be having some impact on different indicators; it is also likely to be the case that some local programmes are generally more effective than others.

On balance these preliminary results indicate that Sure Start is doing something right, even if many of the PSA targets are still far out of sight. Some of the targets may simply have been too ambitious. However, the lack of improvement in several of the health indicators is cause for concern, even if it reflects a similar (or worse) situation in the country as a whole. It may be that too much has been expected of this relatively low-budget programme, allowing reduced mainstream focus on young children. For instance, children were conspicuously absent from the priorities for Primary Care Trusts for 2002/03, despite the emphasis in the Acheson Report on the importance of promoting child health (see Chapter Four of this volume), and although Sure Start programmes cover only one third of poor children.

## Conclusion

In 1997, few could have predicted the central role that would be given by this government to children. Child poverty and early child development have been placed high up on the agenda, and substantial additional sums spent – particularly in addressing child poverty, but also in developing services for young children.

Table 7.9 shows that government expenditure on child-contingent support is up by nearly 70% in real terms since 1997/98, and on early years by nearly 80%. Together, the share of GDP this represented was up by 0.8 percentage points by 2002/03 (before the Child Tax Credit was implemented). Real progress has been made on child poverty: the government is on track to meet its target of reducing child poverty by one quarter by 2004/05. A role for central government in supporting childcare provision has been acknowledged for the first time in the UK, and places have increased steadily from a low base. The government has also extended the state's responsibility to include part-time education for all three- and four-year-olds. Early indications suggest Sure Start local programmes have had mixed success at meeting their objectives but have done well at providing parenting support and play and learning opportunities for disadvantaged children, and have proved widely popular with parents.

However, if the government is to leave a lasting legacy, progress to date will need to be only the first step. Continuing falls in child poverty will require ever greater investment in tax credits and benefits for families in and out of work, greater support for childcare and, in the longer-run, the success of health and education policies in improving poor children's chances of becoming skilled workers and non-poor parents in the future.

With regard to childcare provision and the Early Years strategy, issues remain about both quantity and quality, particularly for children aged under three. Table 7.9 shows an increase in annual expenditure of over £1.5 billion since 1997/98; most has gone to fund nursery places for three- and four-year-olds but some £700 million is now spent on childcare and Sure Start. While this is an enormous leap forward from 1997, government spending on the early years as a share of GDP still looks very low next to that in many other European countries (see Chapter Fourteen of this volume). Further context is provided by a recent report that estimated the cost of universal childcare provision at £7.4 billion a year (0.7% GDP); £9.2 billion if 20% extra was spent per place to improve quality (Ambler, 2004). (Net costs, adjusted for increased tax revenues and lower benefits arising from greater maternal employment, are likely to be much lower.) The government does seem committed to a steady increase in early years spending: the 2004 Budget announced a further £669 million for childcare and services for disadvantaged children by 2007/08 compared to 2004/05, to be directed at Children's Centres and at early education for disadvantaged two-year-olds. If they continue, these incremental increases will eventually change the landscape, but there remains a long way to go.

## Table 7.9: Government spending on child-contingent benefits and tax credits and on services for under-5s (£million, 2002/03 prices)

| | 1997/98 | 1998/99 | 1999/00 | 2000/01 | 2001/02 | 2002/03 |
|---|---|---|---|---|---|---|
| *Spending on child-contingent support* | *13,261* | *13,222* | *15,051* | *18,220* | *21,310* | *22,179* |
| of which Child Benefit | 7,954 | 7,968 | 8,884 | 9,130 | 9,042 | 8,971 |
| Working Families Tax Credit/Family Credit (1) | 1,256 | 1,269 | 1,993 | 4,360 | 5,148 | 5,628 |
| Children's Tax Credit | | | | | 2,049 | 2,170 |
| Income Support/Jobseeker's Allowance | 2,783 | 2,692 | 2,863 | 3,295 | 3,579 | 3,814 |
| Other | 1,268 | 1,294 | 1,310 | 1,435 | 1,492 | 1,596 |
| *Spending on early years and childcare* | *1,996* | *1,988* | *2,298* | *2,730* | *3,352* | *3,568* |
| of which Sure Start local programmes | | | 8 | 59 | 139 | 211 |
| Childcare tax credit | | | 54 | 197 | 265 | 319 |
| Other DfES childcare spending (2) | | 49 | 60 | 69 | 113 | 94 |
| Nursery education and local gov't childcare (3) | 1,996 | 1,939 | 2,160 | 2,369 | 2,789 | 2,878 |
| National lottery (New Opportunities Fund) | | | 16 | 35 | 46 | 66 |
| Child-contingent support (% GDP) | 1.38 | 1.34 | 1.47 | 1.74 | 2.00 | 2.04 |
| Early years and childcare (% GDP) | 0.21 | 0.20 | 0.23 | 0.26 | 0.31 | 0.33 |

*Notes:* (1) Excluding childcare tax credit. (2) Includes funding for Neighbourhood Nurseries, childminder start-up grants, childminder training and networks. (3) Includes inheritance of local authority funded day nurseries and spending on under-5s in state primary and nursery schools. Increases across the period are largely due to financing of extra nursery places for 3- and 4-year-olds.

*Source:* DWP Benefit Expenditure Tables; Inland Revenue (2003) and earlier equivalents; DfES (2003b); NAO (2004). Thanks to Sandy Gordon and Tom Sefton for assistance

## Notes

[1] Neither before nor after housing costs measures provide a perfect guide to differences and changes in living standards: a full picture needs to take account of both. See Hills (2004a, ch 3) for discussion of further issues surrounding the measurement of poverty.

[2] An additional question concerns the equivalence scale. The calculations in HBAI (and those in this chapter) have traditionally used the McClements equivalence scale, which gives a very low weighting to young children. The government will be using the modified OECD scale in future analysis (DWP, 2003). This is likely to increase BHC poverty measures by about 1 percentage point (DWP, 2004a, p 294).

# EIGHT

# A secure retirement for all? Older people and New Labour

*Maria Evandrou and Jane Falkingham*

## Introduction

Labour's 1979 Election Manifesto reiterated the party's long-standing objective of achieving a state pension of one third adult average earnings for single people and half average earnings for couples. However, in 1981 the Conservative government broke the link between pensions and earnings, and the basic state pension (BSP) became indexed to prices. Restoring the link to earnings became a central plank of Labour policy in opposition. Both the 1987 and 1992 Manifestos promised to increase the pension by an extra £5.00 per week for a single person and £8.00 per week for a married couple as a first step. The 1997 Manifesto, however, marked a paradigm shift, with the restoration of the BSP's level noticeable by its absence. The Manifesto still argued that "all pensioners should share fairly in the increasing prosperity of the nation" but proposed "a partnership between public and private provision, and a balance between income sourced from tax and invested savings" (Labour Party, 1997, pp 26-7). Beyond a statement that they would "examine means of delivering more automatic help to the poorest pensioners", there was no explicit target to reduce pensioner poverty, although there was a promise to "set up a review of the central areas of insecurity for elderly" (Labour Party, 1997, p 27).

Fulfilling this promise, within a year systematic reviews of both pensions and long-term care provision had been established, leading to the Green Paper *Partnership in pensions* (DSS, 1998) and the report of the Royal Commission on Long Term Care (Sutherland, 1999). These were followed by the publication of *Opportunity for all* (OFA) (DSS, 1999), the blueprint of the government's approach to poverty and social exclusion (see Chapter One of this volume). In this, New Labour's three key priorities for older people are:

- tackling the problems of low income and social exclusion among *today's* pensioners;
- improving opportunities for older people to live secure, fulfilling and active lives; and
- ensuring that more of *tomorrow's* pensioners can retire on a decent income.

Taking each of these in turn, this chapter examines the policy changes introduced to achieve these goals and assesses the success of these policies in terms of measurable outcomes, using both the government's own monitoring data and other sources.

## Tackling problems of low income and exclusion among today's pensioners

Between 1979 and 1996/97, the position of pensioners improved relative to the rest of society. Average gross incomes of all pensioner households increased in real terms by 62%, from £142 a week in 1979 to £230 in 1996/97 (2002/03 prices) (DWP, 2004c, Table A1). Over the same period real average earnings grew by just 38%. However, not all pensioners benefited equally – incomes increased three times faster for pensioners in the richest fifth of the whole population than for those in the poorest fifth. For those in the poorest fifth, the 31% increase over 1979 to 1996/97 was less than the growth in real earnings. Thus, the poorest pensioners fell behind relative to others, and the gap between rich and poor pensioners widened substantially. When New Labour came to power in 1997, over a quarter of pensioners were living in relative poverty, with a household income of below 60% of contemporary median household income (after housing costs).

The first two years of the New Labour Government saw few explicit policy measures aimed at pensioners, with the exception of the introduction of annual Winter Fuel Payments of £100 in November 1997. Since April 1999, however, there has been a raft of reforms designed to improve the living standards of the poorest pensioners. The 1999 budget rebranded income support for pensioners as the Minimum Income Guarantee (MIG) (renamed again in 2003 as the guarantee element of the Pension Credit). It also included above inflation increases, and a commitment to increase MIG in line with earnings rather than prices from 2000 onwards. This was reaffirmed in the 2001 Manifesto, which pledged to uprate MIG in line with earnings throughout the next parliament. There have also been smaller real increases in non-means-tested benefits, including the BSP, and the introduction of new benefits-in-kind (free eye tests for people age 60+, and free TV licences for people aged 75+). In addition, there were above inflation increases in pensioners' personal tax allowances.

The government has chosen to target increases in state provision to older people via a means-tested guarantee rather than through increasing the 'universal' BSP. This extends means testing in later life. In April 2004, the guarantee element of the new Pension Credit for a single person was £105.45 per week. This is equivalent to around 25% of average earnings – that is, the level the BSP would have been if the link with earnings had not been broken. If the guarantee element remains linked to earnings, it will remain just above the relative poverty line of 60% median household income (after housing costs). If everyone entitled claimed, pensioner poverty (as defined by the government) could be effectively abolished.

However, in 2001/02 between 17% and 37% of entitled pensioners failed to claim the means-tested payments they were entitled to, compared with 2% to 14% of the population as a whole[1] (DWP, 2004b). Some non-claimants may miss out on relatively little, and so may have thought it not worthwhile claiming, but the average amounts unclaimed were non-trivial at £25 per week. In total, £730-£1,260 million was unclaimed in 2001/02, up from £470-£820 million in 2000/01. Family Resources Survey data suggest that 56% of the entitled non-claimants were aged 75+, and two thirds were living in households in the bottom fifth of the income distribution (DWP, 2004b). An additional £25 per week would make a big difference to their living standards.

There are also concerns that more generous means-tested benefits may undermine future incentives to save. People who accumulate only relatively small pension entitlements may end up with an income in retirement only just above the means-tested guarantee – the so-called 'pensions poverty trap'. If the minimum guarantee continues to rise in line with earnings but BSP with prices, the gap between them will widen over time, increasing the width of the poverty trap. As a response to this, in October 2003, MIG was replaced by the Pension Credit (PC), which added a Savings Credit element to the guarantee element. In effect, the PC introduces a less sharp taper to MIG, ensuring that those who have saved a little are better off than those who have not saved at all. Although in principle a welcome move, this adds a further layer of complexity to an already complex pension system.

The introduction of the PC has been accompanied by a drive to improve benefit awareness. Indeed, increasing the number of households receiving PC to at least three million by 2006 is one of the Department for Work and Pensions' (DWP) Public Service Agreement (PSA) targets. Whether these new initiatives will overcome the problems of take-up and incentives has yet to be determined, but it is likely that significant numbers of older people will remain on low incomes into the foreseeable future. Research exploring barriers to pensioner take-up of MIG found that 57% of entitled non-recipients were unaware of any benefits payable to people on low income. Three quarters of these agreed that they would be more likely to apply if *most* pensioners were entitled to claim, highlighting the preference for universal benefits. The strongest reasons for resistance to claiming MIG were related to fears of appearing in need, losing independence and the belief that respondents could manage on their own (DWP, 2004a).

Table 8.1 shows the additional cost of New Labour's reforms, giving each element's full effect in the financial year they came into force. The high spending in 2001/02 reflects the above inflation uprating in MIG for pensioners, and in 2003/04 the introduction of the PC.

How has this impacted upon pensioner poverty? As discussed in other chapters, there is no consensus around a single definition of poverty. The closest to an officially accepted definition of poverty are the relative measures of low income published in the Households Below Average Income (HBAI) series. In 2002/03,

**Table 8.1: Increased spending due to policies affecting pensioners (1998/99 to 2003/04)**

|  | £ millions |
|---|---|
| 1998/99 | — |
| 1999/00 | 1,070 |
| 2000/01 | 1,120 |
| 2001/02 | 3,330 |
| 2002/03 | 300 |
| 2003/04 | 2,700 |

*Note:* The table shows the estimated cost of new policies, with the full effect estimated in the financial year in which they were introduced.
*Source:* Brewer et al (2004, Table 3.5)

the proportion of pensioners with an income below 60% of contemporary median income stood at 21%, that is, around 2.2 million pensioners were living in relative poverty (DWP, 2004a). As Table 8.2 shows, this represents a substantial improvement on the position in 1996/97 when measured after housing costs (AHC), but no real change when measured before housing costs (BHC). The difference between the two series is primarily because pensioners as a group have relatively low housing costs, with more owning their property outright, while these costs have fallen relative to those of non-pensioners (Brewer et al, 2004).

Given the increased spending identified in Table 8.1, one might have expected an even greater improvement in pensioner poverty. However, as the median income for the whole population has increased, the relative poverty line has shifted upwards, so relative pensioner poverty (BHC) has not improved significantly. If pensioners' incomes are compared against the 1996/97 threshold held constant in real terms, a different picture emerges, also shown in Table 8.2. The proportion of pensioners living in households with *absolute* low incomes fell from 27% to 9% on the after housing costs measure, and 21% to 12% before housing costs.

The data in Table 8.2 do not reflect the impact of policy changes made or announced after March 2003, and thus exclude the important impact of PC. Sutherland (2004), updating previous work in Sutherland et al (2003), uses policy simulation to estimate the effect of recent policy, allowing an assessment of the impact of policy changes over the whole period 1997 to 2004/05. Table 8.3 presents projected relative poverty rates in 2004/05 compared with rates in 1997. The figures take account of changes in taxes and benefits as well as earnings growth. The difference in poverty reduction on the two income measures remains. The relative poverty rate falls from 27% to 17% with 2004/05 policies and incomes on an AHC basis, but by only two percentage points on a BHC basis.

Policy simulation also gives a measure of the impact of policy change by itself. Line (c) in Table 8.3 shows what *would have* happened if the tax and benefit system of 1997 (uprated by prices) had still applied in 2004/05. Comparing lines (a) and (c) shows that if there had been no policy changes, relative poverty

**Table 8.2: Percentage of pensioners below thresholds of contemporary and 1996/97 real terms mean and median income**

| | Below 50% mean | Below 60% median | Below 70% median |
|---|---|---|---|
| **Contemporary income thresholds** | | | |
| *Before housing costs* | | | |
| 1996/97 | 21 | 21 | 35 |
| 1998/99 | 25 | 23 | 36 |
| 2000/01 | 23 | 21 | 34 |
| 2002/03 | 23 | 21 | 34 |
| *After housing costs* | | | |
| 1996/97 | 28 | 27 | 39 |
| 1998/99 | 30 | 27 | 38 |
| 2000/01 | 27 | 24 | 36 |
| 2002/03 | 23 | 21 | 36 |
| **1996/97 income thresholds held constant in real terms** | | | |
| *Before housing costs* | | | |
| 1996/97 | 21 | 21 | 35 |
| 1998/99 | 21 | 20 | 33 |
| 2000/01 | 16 | 15 | 26 |
| 2002/03 | 12 | 12 | 21 |
| *After housing costs* | | | |
| 1996/97 | 28 | 27 | 39 |
| 1998/99 | 24 | 24 | 35 |
| 2000/01 | 16 | 15 | 27 |
| 2002/03 | 10 | 9 | 18 |

*Source:* DWP (2004a)

rates would have been *higher* in 2004/05 than they were in 1997. It could be argued that the impact of policy in reducing pensioner poverty has been greater than that observed by simply comparing 1997 and 2004/05, and that between 810,000 and 1.5 million fewer pensioners are in poverty than would have been without the reforms. On these measures, New Labour's policies to tackle pensioner poverty have met with considerable success. However, whether this is an appropriate measure depends on accepting that a 'neutral' policy would have been to index benefits and pensions in line with prices. An alternative baseline would be indexation with a measure of earnings or income, which would substantially reduce the impact of policy change (Hills, 2004a, ch 9).

Alternative definitions of poverty compare incomes to an absolute amount estimated as being required to attain a particular standard of living. Two such measures have been calculated by the Family Budget Unit: the Low Cost but Acceptable (LCA) living standard, below which health and social integration are thought to be at risk (Parker, 2001), and the Modest but Adequate (MBA) living standard, which is slightly higher and takes into account the resources necessary to participate in society. In 2002, the MBA threshold for a single person aged 65 to 74 ranged from £157 for a male homeowner to £204 for a female local authority tenant (Parker, 2002). In April 2003, a single pensioner aged 65 to 74

**Table 8.3: Simulated estimates of pensioner poverty in Britain (1997 to 2004/05)**

| | % in relative poverty (60% median income) | Numbers (000s) |
|---|---|---|
| *Before housing costs (BHC)* | | |
| (a) 1997 policies and incomes | 21 | 2,160 |
| (b) 2004/05 policies and incomes | 19 | 1,950 |
| (c) 1997 policies and 2004/05 incomes | 27 | 2,760 |
| (a) – (b) | 2 | 210 |
| (c) – (b) | 8 | 810 |
| *After housing costs (AHC)* | | |
| (a) 1997 policies and incomes | 27 | 2,750 |
| (b) 2004/05 policies and incomes | 17 | 1,760 |
| (c) 1997 policies and 2004/05 | 33 | 3,360 |
| (a) – (b) | 10 | 990 |
| (c) – (b) | 16 | 1,590 |

*Source:* Sutherland (2004, Tables 1, 2)

needed £105-£110 to reach the LCA threshold (Family Budget Unit, 2003); slightly more than the value of MIG (£100 per week). The shortfall between the means-tested guarantee and the MBA threshold was even higher. Thus, although recent above inflation increases may have lifted the value of the pension guarantee above LCA, it is fair to say that the 1.8 million pensioners reliant on the guarantee element of the PC are still living on low incomes, and that the 600,000-900,000 entitled non-claimants are living on very low incomes indeed.

Moreover, significant differences remain within the pensioner population. Pensioner poverty remains particularly concentrated among women, who tend to have low personal incomes. In 2001/02, two fifths of single female pensioners and four fifths of married female pensioners had individual gross incomes of less than £100 per week (DTI, 2003). At the end of 2003, nearly twice as many women as men were reliant on means-tested benefits in retirement, with 1.2 million women aged 60+ receiving MIG compared to 615,000 men (DWP, 2004d). Persistent poverty is also concentrated among older women, with the proportion experiencing such poverty being three times that of the whole population (DWP, 2004a). This reflects both the lower wages of women while in work, 'the wage gap', and the fact that they are much more likely to have experienced interruptions to their earnings histories – 'the pay gap'. As discussed later in this chapter, changes in the pension mix, particularly increasing reliance on personal pensions based on contributions made during working life, which often result in the purchase of a 'single life' annuity (and hence no survivors' benefits for widows), do not bode well for future trends in women's pension income.

Black and minority ethnic pensioners also experience an elevated risk of poverty, with 31% of ethnic elders living in households with incomes below 60% of the contemporary median compared to 21% of their white counterparts (DWP, 2004a, Table 6.5). In part, this reflects the fact that many of the current generation of ethnic elders entered the UK part-way through their working lives and so have not had an opportunity to accumulate a full pension (Evandrou, 2000). This disadvantage will reduce as younger cohorts of UK-born minority ethnic groups enter retirement. Minority ethnic groups, however, are more likely to experience unemployment and are disproportionately found in low-skill, low-income employment (ONS, 2004a), so differences in employment-based pensions are likely to remain.

In summary, New Labour has made significant progress in tackling pensioners' poverty in the seven years since 1997. Aggregate pensioner incomes in 2003/04 are £9 billion higher in real terms than in 1997 (Brewer et al, 2004) and PC has made a real difference to some of the poorest pensioners. However, a fifth of pensioners were living in poverty in 2002/03 and a further 15% were just above this level and below 70% of the median (Table 8.2). Significant numbers of older people fail to claim their entitlements. Unlike child poverty, there remains no explicit target for reducing pensioner poverty. There is, however, a target for increasing take-up of benefits within the PSA agreed target of delivering PC to three million households by 2006. This implies a take-up rate of just 72% (House of Commons, 2003), and begs the question whether New Labour are content to leave 1.2 million low-income pensioner households without the benefits they need and are entitled to.

## Improving opportunities for older people to live secure, fulfilling and active lives

The stated OFA goal of "improving opportunities for older people to live secure, fulfilling and active lives" (DSS, 1999, p 10) is much more amorphous than the other two goals that relate to older people. Quality of life is multidimensional and for older people health, access to services and the ability to live independently in one's own home are central. A range of policies have addressed these dimensions of quality of life. This section focuses on New Labour's policy agenda within health and social care. Other initiatives aimed at improving older people's housing conditions include the Home Energy Efficiency Scheme and the Healthy Homes Initiative, as well as policies to reduce crime.

### Health and health care

One of the most significant achievements of the 20th century was the improvement in mortality. In 1901, life expectancy at birth was 51 years for men and 58 years for women. By 2001, these were 76 and 80 years respectively (ONS, 2004b). However, it is not just length of life that matters, but also the state of health in which that life is lived. *Opportunities for all* therefore includes healthy life expectancy (HLE) at age 65 as a key indicator of progress in the quality of life and independence of older people. Table 8.4 shows that both life expectancy and HLE at age 65 have risen. However, the *proportion* of remaining life that older people can expect to live in good health actually fell between 1997 and 1999, from 78% to 75% for men and 71% to 70% for women. Moreover, significant differences in life expectancy at age 65 by previous occupation remain: 17.5 years for men from social class I ('professionals', such as doctors, chartered accountants), compared to 13.4 years for men from social class V ('manual unskilled', such as labourers, cleaners and messengers). The figures for women are 20.8 and 16.3 years respectively (Donkin et al, 2002).

New Labour's health reforms started with the 1997 White Paper, *The new NHS: Modern and dependable: A national framework for assessing performance* (DH, 1997a). This replaced the internal market with a system of integrated care, based on partnership and driven by performance (see Chapter Four of this volume). For older people, the most significant changes in the NHS were closer integration between health and social services and establishment of Primary Care Trusts as a result of the *Better services for vulnerable people initiative* (DH, 1997b).

*The new NHS* also set out the idea of National Service Frameworks (NSF) for different client groups. The first NSF for mental health services was developed in 1998. Notably, however, the NSF for Older People was not published until 2001 (DH, 2001c). This outlines standards of care, effective interventions and models of good practice for older people living at home, in residential care or in hospital. It is backed by £1.4 billion to be invested each year, starting from 2004. There are eight NSF Standards: rooting out age discrimination, person-centred care, intermediate care, general hospital care, stroke prevention, falls prevention, mental health in older people and promoting an active healthy life in old age.

Various initiatives and projects have been set up within the NSF to drive up the quality, availability and consistency of services available to older people: for example, changes in long-term care funding, including the availability of NHS

**Table 8.4: Life expectancy at 65 and healthy life expectancy at 65 for men and women, GB**

|  | Men | | | Women | | |
|---|---|---|---|---|---|---|
|  | LE at 65 (years) | HLE at 65 (years) | % of life remaining in healthy state | LE at 65 (years) | HLE at 65 (years) | % of life remaining in healthy state |
| 1981 | 13.0 | 9.9 | 76.2 | 16.9 | 11.9 | 70.4 |
| 1985 | 13.4 | 10.2 | 76.7 | 17.3 | 12.1 | 69.9 |
| 1990 | 14.0 | 10.9 | 77.9 | 17.8 | 12.7 | 71.8 |
| 1995 | 14.7 | 11.3 | 76.9 | 18.3 | 13.0 | 71.0 |
| 1996 | 14.8 |  |  | 18.4 |  |  |
| 1997 | 15.1 | 11.7 | 78.0 | 18.5 | 13.2 | 71.4 |
| 1998 | 15.2 |  |  | 18.6 |  |  |
| 1999 | 15.4 | 11.6 | 75.3 | 18.7 | 13.1 | 70.1 |
| 2000 | 15.7 |  |  | 18.8 |  |  |
| 2001 | 15.9 |  |  | 19.0 |  |  |

*Note:* LE = life expectancy; HLE = healthy life expectancy; % of life remaining in healthy state is calculated as HLE/LE x 100.
*Source:* ONS (2002b)

nursing care in all settings; the expansion of intermediate care services across health and social care; Care Direct to provide comprehensive information; and initiatives to help older people stay healthy, such as flu immunisation and retirement health checks. Progress will be measured against agreed milestones (DH, 2001c, ch 4) and will be overseen by the Modernisation Board and the Older People's Taskforce. It is too early to tell if the NSF for Older People will deliver the better quality services promised. However, some indicators of New Labour's progress in assisting older people to live independently are presented in the section below.

### Social care

In 1996/97, local authorities in England spent £3.6 billion on personal social services for older people, of which 52% was on residential and nursing care. An explicit aim of the 1990 Health Community Care Act (implemented in 1993) had been to shift responsibility for financing the costs of long-term care in residential and nursing homes from central government, via social security payments, to local authorities. In 1992, 29% of residents in the independent sector were paying wholly for themselves without any public subsidy. The majority received income support (66%), and local authorities funded only 4%. By 1995, the proportion of residents funded by local authorities had risen to 32% (Evandrou and Falkingham, 1998). By the time New Labour came to power in 1997, the Special Transitional Grant, which had provided additional financial support to assist local authorities in meeting their new responsibilities towards older people, had been phased out and many local authorities were struggling to meet the rising costs of residential care.

Soon after taking office, New Labour established a Royal Commission to consider the funding of long-term care for older people, chaired by Sir Stewart Sutherland. Its terms of reference were:

> to examine the short and long term options for a sustainable system of funding of long term care for elderly people, both in their homes and in other settings and ... to recommend how, and in what circumstances, the cost of such care should be apportioned between public funds and individuals. (Sutherland, 1999, p ix)

The commission reported in March 1999, concluding that "the costs of long term care should be split between living costs, housing costs and personal care. Personal care should be available after assessment, according to need and paid for from general taxation: the rest should be subject to a co-payment according to means" (Sutherland, 1999, p xvii). However, a dissenting minority of the commission argued that personal care should also be subject to a means-test. The government, setting policy for England and Wales, agreed with the minority view and extended the principle of means-testing to both personal care and

## Free personal and nursing care for older people in Scotland

In January 2001, the Scottish Executive established the Care Development Group (CDG), to investigate the issues surrounding long-term care for older people in Scotland. The CDG commissioned a series of research papers examining the case for and against free personal and nursing care. Its recommendation mirrored the majority view of the Royal Commission, that local social services departments should meet all long-term care costs (CDG, 2001). In contrast to the experience in England and Wales, the Scottish Executive accepted in full the CDG's report and recommendations. The 2002 Community and Care (Scotland) Act introduced free personal and nursing care for all older people in Scotland, which also meant that local authorities no longer charge for personal care provided to those aged 65+ living in their own homes. Older people aged 65+ living in care homes in Scotland currently receive £145 per week towards personal care and a further £65 if nursing care is also needed.

living costs. Interestingly, following devolution, Scotland has followed a different path.

Although the key recommendations of the Royal Commission were not adopted in England and Wales, other proposals, such as the establishment of a National Care Commission, have been. New Labour's plans for reform of social services were set out in the 1998 White Paper, *Modernising social services*, which aimed to "promote independence, improve prevention and rehabilitation and improve quality" and highlighted the need to make the system more centred on service users and their families (DH, 1998c, p 9). The language of 'efficiency and effectiveness', which dominated policy discourse throughout the 1990s, has been replaced with a less 'managerial vocabulary'. In the early 2000s, 'needs-led' care interventions have been replaced with 'person-centred' packages of care.

A key innovation of the 1998 White Paper was the introduction of direct payments to give people greater control over the choice of services and how their own care is delivered. Since February 2000, older people who have been formally assessed as having a need for services have been able to apply to their local authority for a direct payment with which to buy non-residential independent sector services for themselves (rather than leaving social services to arrange this on their behalf). Early evaluation confirms that direct payments are a positive option for older people, improving their quality of life. However, continuing assistance from local authority support services were found to be crucial in enabling older people to use such payments, particularly in meeting audit and administrative demands (Clark et al, 2004).

The 1998 White Paper continued the emphasis on supporting older people to live independently in their own homes. The PSA for the Department of Health includes the target of increasing those supported intensively to live at home to 30% of the overall total being supported by social services (either at home or in residential care) by March 2006.

What has happened to the balance between residential and community care under New Labour? Figure 8.1 shows trends in the number of residents aged 65+ supported by councils with social services responsibilities (CSSR). There was a significant increase over the period 1994-98, reflecting the shift in responsibility for financial support from social security to local authorities. Between 1998 and 2002, the number of older people supported by CSSR in residential care was relatively stable at just over 200,000, but in 2003 there was an increase of 12,000 (6%) on the previous year.

There has been a marked change in the *type* of provider across time, with a rapid growth in the number of supported residents living in the private and independent sector. In 2003, CSSR homes accounted for just 13% of all supported residents compared with 25% in 1997 and 52% in 1994. Although CSSR supported residents have increased over the last decade, there has been no significant change in the overall number of residential care places for older people in England (Figure 8.2). This is despite the increase in the total number of people aged 75+ in England from 3.4 to 3.8 million.

In contrast, the volume of home help hours purchased or provided by councils has increased by 14% since New Labour came to power in 1997. Again there is evidence of a growing split between finance and provision. In 2002, direct

**Figure 8.1: Council supported residents by type of accommodation, people aged 65 and over, England (1994-2003)**

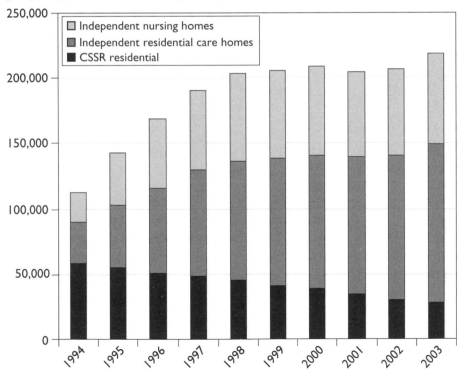

*Source:* DH, *Community care statistics 2003: Supported residents* and selected previous years

**Figure 8.2: Places in residential care homes for people aged 65 and over, England (1994-2001)**

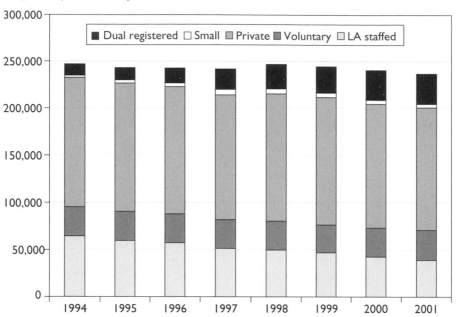

Source: DH, *Community care statistics 2001: Residential personal social services for adults, England* and selected previous years

provision accounted for just over a third (36%) of all contact hours, compared to two thirds in 1996 (64%) (Figure 8.3).

These figures do not take into account changes in the volume of people in need of care. Figure 8.4 shows both the total number of households receiving CSSR-funded home care and the number of households receiving home care services per 1,000 population aged 75 and over. Although the overall number of hours supplied has increased, the number of households receiving CSSR funded home care services has fallen consistently since 1994. The fall per 1,000 population aged 75+ has been even sharper. This suggests that councils are providing more intensive services for a smaller number of service users. This is confirmed by the trends in the intensity of home help/home care provision since 1992, shown in Figure 8.5. The proportion of households receiving more than five hours of contact and six or more visits has increased steadily from 11% in 1992 to 42% in 2002. Interestingly, the White Paper, *Modernising social services*, highlighted the problem of falling levels of support among those requiring *less* intensive support, arguing that people who would benefit from the occasional visit from a home help or other forms of support but who do not get it, were being put at risk. The increased targeting of resources has done little to address this.

Tables 8.5 and 8.6 supplement the administrative data with analysis of the General Household Survey (GHS). Table 8.5 confirms the fall in the proportion of older people receiving local authority home help. There has been no change

**Figure 8.3: Number of contact hours of home care by sector (000s), England (1992-2002)**

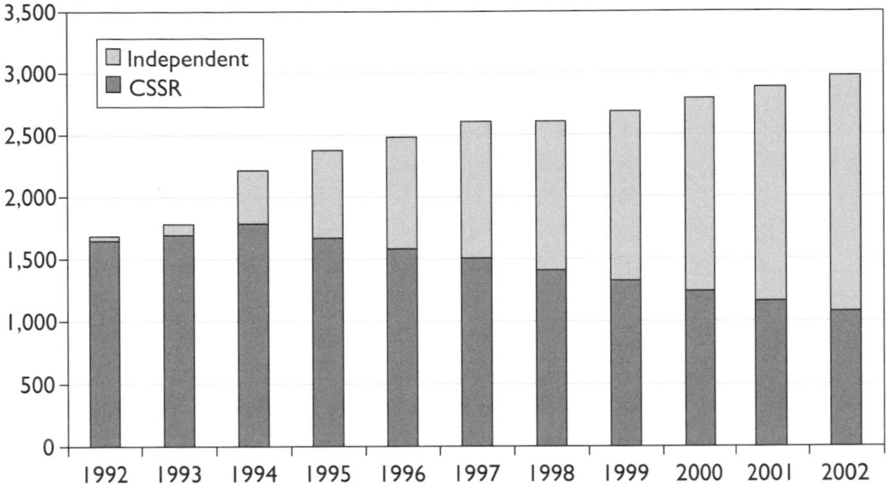

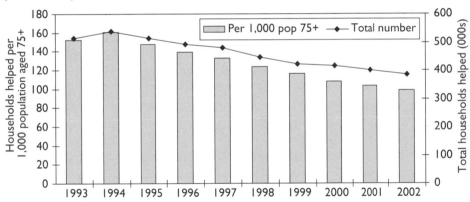

Source: DH, *Community care statistics 2002: Home care services for adults, England* and selected previous years

**Figure 8.4: Households receiving CSSR-funded home care/help, England (1993-2002)**

Source: DH, *Community care statistics 2002: Home care services for adults, England* and selected previous years

in the proportion receiving a visit from a district nurse or health visitor or receiving meals on wheels. This is despite the change in the composition of the population aged 65+, with an increase in the very old who are likely to be in greatest need of services.

Taking need into account, a different picture emerges. Table 8.6 shows the proportion of older people who used a personal social service in the last month *among* those who were unable to walk out of doors unaided, by their household composition. Comparing Tables 8.5 and 8.6, receipt of services is higher among dependent older people, indicating that services are targeted to those in need.

**Figure 8.5: Intensity of home help/home care, England (1992-2002)**

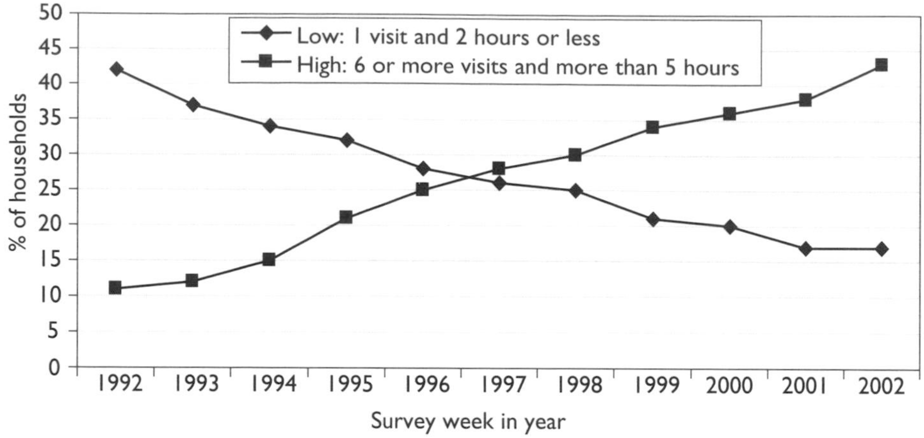
50
45
40
35
30
25
20
15
10
5
0
% of households
Low: 1 visit and 2 hours or less
High: 6 or more visits and more than 5 hours
1992
1993
1994
1995
1996
1997
1998
1999
2000
2001
2002
Survey week in year

*Source:* DH, *Community care statistics 2002: Home care services for adults, England* and selected previous years

Service receipt is also higher among older people unable to walk out of doors unaided and living alone compared to others, although there has been a significant fall over time in public services. For example, receipt of local authority home care services by this group fell from 45% in 1994/95 to 28% in 2001, and meals on wheels fell from 17% to 12% over the same period.

Looking at the performance of councils, the Audit Commission reports evidence of overall steady improvement in the provision of social care services since 1996 (Audit Commission, 2004). Nevertheless, there remains a significant and

**Table 8.5: Use of Personal Social Services in the previous month among persons aged 65 and over, Britain (1980 to 2001/02)**

| | 1980 | 1985 | 1990/91 | 1994/95 | 2001/02 |
|---|---|---|---|---|---|
| *(a) Home help (local authority)* | | | | | |
| Men | 4 | 6 | 6 | 5 | 3 |
| Women | 12 | 12 | 11 | 10 | 5 |
| All | 9 | 9 | 9 | 8 | 4 |
| *(b) Home help (private)* | | | | | |
| Men | | | 4 | 5 | 9 |
| Women | | | 4 | 8 | 12 |
| All | | | 4 | 7 | 10 |
| *(c) Meals on Wheels* | | | | | |
| Men | 2 | 2 | 2 | 2 | 1 |
| Women | 3 | 3 | 3 | 3 | 2 |
| All | 2 | 2 | 3 | 3 | 2 |
| *(d) District nurse/health visitor* | | | | | |
| Men | 4 | 4 | 4 | 4 | 4 |
| Women | 8 | 8 | 7 | 7 | 6 |
| All | 6 | 6 | 6 | 6 | 5 |

*Note:* Table uses unweighted data. Analysis using weighted data for 2001/02 showed little difference in the results and overall trends.

*Source:* Evandrou and Falkingham (1998, Table 6.17), updated using authors' own additional analysis of 2001/02 GHS

**Table 8.6: Use of Personal Social Services in the previous month among persons aged 65 and over by functional capacity and living arrangements, Britain (1980 to 2001/02)**

|  | 1980 | 1985 | 1994/95 | 2001/02 |
|---|---|---|---|---|
| Percentage of people aged 65 and over unable to walk out of doors unaided | 12 | 12 | 13 | 14 |
| Of whom percentage in receipt of Personal Social Services: | | | | |
| *(a) Home help (local authority)* | | | | |
| Lives alone | 62 | 55 | 45 | 28 |
| Lives with others | 15 | 17 | 15 | 8 |
| *(b) Home help (private)* | | | | |
| Lives alone | | | 19 | 32 |
| Lives with others | | | 6 | 10 |
| *(c) Meals on Wheels* | | | | |
| Lives alone | 18 | 18 | 17 | 12 |
| Lives with others | 4 | 3 | 4 | 2 |
| *(d) District nurse/health visitor* | | | | |
| Lives alone | 33 | 30 | 30 | 27 |
| Lives with others | 24 | 18 | 18 | 19 |

*Note:* Table uses unweighted data. Analysis using weighted data for 2001/02 showed little difference in the results and overall trends.
*Source:* Evandrou and Falkingham (1998, Table 6.18), updated using authors' own additional analysis of 2001/02 GHS

unacceptable gap between the best and the worst councils in providing high quality care. Moreover, the report notes that there is a gap between providers' aspirations and the experiences of users on the ground. Culturally appropriate services, which served the needs of black and minority ethnic communities were generally undeveloped in 1996. By 2003, the provision of culturally competent services remained mixed, and progress has been largely limited to better access to translation and interpretation services.

It is too early to assess the impact of the new Care Trusts on either the quantity or quality of health and social care for older people, but it is clear that there were improvements in New Labour's first five to six years. The expansion of residential care has been halted and more older people in residential care are receiving financial support from councils. The overall volume of home care provision in terms of total number of hours supplied has increased. There is greater consultation with older people concerning appropriate packages of care, and more older people are being empowered through direct payments. However, the number of households supported has fallen. Fewer older people who live alone and who are dependent in terms of mobility are receiving support. Concentration of scarce resources on fewer older people means that others with lesser or more occasional needs may be being put at risk, and may be more likely to need a higher level of support in the future due to, say, preventable falls and other accidents in the home.

## Ensuring that more of tomorrow's pensioners can retire on a decent income

New Labour's approach to future pension provision represents a significant break with the past. The 1998 Green Paper, *A new contract for welfare: Partnership in pensions* (DSS, 1998) set out a 'New Insurance Contract for Pensioners'. A central tenet of the reforms is that where individuals can save for their own old age they should be encouraged to do so, but for those who were unable to save enough either because of low income or interrupted working lives, the state should provide an adequate safety net. The aim of 'ensuring that more of tomorrow's pensioners can retire on a decent income' has involved a two-pronged approach: active labour market policies aimed getting more people into work, reversing the trend towards early retirement (and increasing the time people are able to 'save' for their retirement); and increasing the number of people able to build up good (non-state) second pensions through reform of the pension system itself.

### Older people and the labour market

Encouraging older workers to stay in the labour market has been an explicit objective of New Labour, both as an end in itself and to improve future pension entitlements. Both the 1998 and 2002 Pensions Green Papers included proposals to tackle 'distortionary incentives' in the tax and benefit system that might encourage people to leave work before retirement age, including changes to disability benefits and Inland Revenue tax rules for occupational pension schemes (DSS, 1998; DWP, 2002b). A key policy initiative has been the New Deal 50 plus (ND50plus). Launched in 1998, it provides a subsidy for six months for employers who recruit people aged 50+, and offers opportunities to undertake full-time education and training while on benefits.

Since 1997, the employment rate for men aged between 50 and the state pension age has risen from 67% to 72% (January-March 2004). Participation rates for older women have also increased, from 61% to 67% (Figure 8.6). However it is not possible to attribute this solely to the success of the New Deal and other specific Labour policies, as the trend towards higher pre-retirement employment began in 1993, coinciding with the fall in overall unemployment (see Chapter Two of this volume for more detailed discussion).

### Improving second tier pensions

Improving second tier pension provision lies at the heart of New Labour's pensions reforms. The 1998 Green Paper aimed to introduce "a public-private partnership in pensions". Rather than returning to the Old Labour vision of an assured income in retirement provided almost entirely by the state sector, the 1998 Green Paper reaffirmed the Conservative emphasis of increasing the private sector's role in pension provision. Indeed, for the first time the shift in the balance of

**Figure 8.6: Employment rates, men aged 50 to 64, women aged 50 to 59, GB**

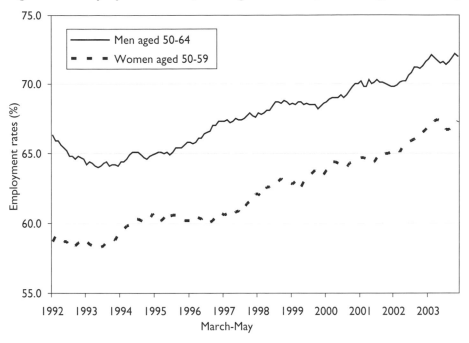

*Source:* Quarterly Labour Force Survey March-May 1992 to January-March 2004

pension provision was explicitly included in a policy document; with the stated expectation being a change from the ratio of 60:40 state to private provision towards 40:60 (DSS, 1998, ch 4, para 18).

The Green Paper highlighted occupational pensions as "one of the great welfare success stories of the century" (DSS, 1998, ch 2, para 19), and an aspiration of the reforms was to share this success story more broadly across the population. The vehicle chosen to do this was the new Stakeholder Pension (SHP), which became available in April 2001. Recognising that private provision through earnings-related second tier pensions is not necessarily suitable for individuals with low lifetime earnings or high levels of absence from the labour market, the 1998 Green Paper also introduced a new State Second Pension (S2P) to replace SERPS (DSS, 1998).

The jury is still out on whether New Labour's pension reforms will deliver decent incomes for all of tomorrow's pensioners (see for example, Brooks et al, 2002; Curry and O'Connell, 2003). It is far from clear that reforms will lead to better pension outcomes, particularly for those with low incomes. The vehicle chosen to deliver adequate incomes in later life to those currently on low pay, primarily women, is the S2P. Previous work investigating the effectiveness of the government's proposals in protecting individuals from a means-tested old age (Rake et al, 2000) estimated that S2P in combination with BSP would provide an income equivalent to just £1.00 above the MIG. Since then, the MIG has been increased by more than earnings growth and now has been replaced by the 'guarantee credit' of the new PC. As discussed earlier in this chapter, these increases in means-tested benefits are to be welcomed in terms of alleviating poverty among today's pensioners. However, the government's aspirations (but not long-term commitment) to index the PC to earnings growth while leaving BSP and S2P indexed to prices, mean that by 2050 anyone with income from BSP and S2P alone will automatically fall into means-testing on retirement. Projections by the Government Actuary's Department suggest that BSP will be worth 7.5% of average male earnings in 2050 and that the average S2P will be worth around 10.4%. This implies that together, BSP and S2P will be worth just 17.9% of average male earnings – that is, below the current value of the guarantee element of PC (20% of average male earnings). This raises real questions about the purpose of S2P and its relationship with other tiers of the pension system. Hills (2004b) concludes that the combined effect of the pensions reforms will be to restore something akin to a flat rate pension from the support people get from these, but with significantly more complexity and more means-testing.

Furthermore, the reforms do nothing to solve the issue of providing better coverage to the self-employed (not compelled to contribute) and the unemployed, or of providing coverage to those not covered by National Insurance because of very low/seasonal earnings. In 2003, an estimated 1.4 million women were excluded from making National Insurance contributions towards their state pension because they earned less than the lower earnings limit of £77 per week. Although the introduction of the minimum wage has had some impact[2], someone working 16 hours a week at the minimum wage still does not earn enough to begin to build up entitlement to a state pension. In 2002/03, an estimated five million people were not accruing rights to *any* state pension (including BSP) and a further seven million were accruing rights to BSP but not S2P (O'Connell, 2004). This means that a third of all working-age adults are not accruing any second tier pension – state or private.

There are also questions around the vehicle chosen to extend the 'success' of occupational pensions – Stakeholder Pensions (SHPs). These differ from a traditional occupational pension in a number of important ways. Occupational pensions have worked, in part, by limiting the individuals across whom they pool risk; for example, by excluding part-time employees or workers in particular parts of the company or by adopting long vesting periods. Furthermore, the level of contributions is generally decided not by the employee but by the company and is set at a reasonably high level. By contrast, membership of SHP is open. On the one hand, this can be seen as a positive attribute, but there is also the risk that some individuals may mis-purchase SHPs that are not appropriate to their circumstances. Furthermore, as there are no set levels of contribution to SHPs, some individuals may under-invest in their pension. Finally, they are defined contribution schemes (mirroring the shift within the occupational sector itself) and have no mechanism for pooling risk.

New Labour's aspiration to shift the pensions mix from 60:40 in favour of state provision to 40:60 was predicated on a constant level of public expenditure and a rising level of private savings. As more people took out private second pensions, public spending would be concentrated on the less well off. Implicit in this was the optimistic assumption that contributions into private pensions would increase both from employees and employers. In reality, many employers are replacing final salary schemes with defined contribution (DC) plans, with the net effect being a transfer of risk back to employees on modest incomes (TUC, 2002). A key problem is that employers generally pay less into a DC pension than they do into a defined benefit (DB) pension. Employers are also cutting back on contributions overall (NAPF, 2001). The combination of lower employer and employee contributions means that younger cohorts will enter retirement with lower accumulated rights and at greater risk.

The problem of people 'under-saving' for retirement was highlighted in the 2002 Green Paper, *Simplicity, security and choice* (DWP, 2002b). However, the proposals recently proposed in the 2004 Pension Bill, concentrate almost exclusively on simplifying the taxation systems and financial products rather than the system as a whole. While this is to be welcomed, the primary beneficiaries of these changes may be financial advisers and pension scheme administrators, and the changes are unlikely to provide a substantial stimulus to individual saving. It is widely acknowledged that the current system is too complex. Indeed, the head of the government's own pension advisory service has recently commented, "You've got to be Einstein to understand pensions" (Jolliffe, 2003, p 29).

Looking at the immediate past, it is debateable whether the reforms and the introduction of SHPs have extended the proportion of working-age people contributing to a non-state pension. Data from the Family Resources Survey shown in Figure 8.7 show that, between 1999/2000 and 2002/03, the proportion contributing remained broadly constant, falling slightly among men (51% to 49%) and rising slightly among women (38% to 39%). There remain significant inequalities in membership of such schemes. For example, just 3% of women of Pakistani origin have a company pension (Ginn and Arber, 2001).

In summary, New Labour's pension reforms have contributed to reducing current pensioner poverty. However this success has been achieved by an extension of means-tested benefits. New Labour's strategy to ensure that more of tomorrow's pensioners can retire on a decent income has largely focussed on extending private pension saving. Whether this is compatible with the extension of means-testing remains to be seen. It has been estimated that the introduction of the PC will extend means-testing to an estimated 70% of pensioners by 2050 (Hawksworth, 2002), resulting in unclear incentives to save. Further disincentives are provided by the sheer complexity of the system. Moreover, it is clear many people do not trust the private sector. In an ICM Survey for Age Concern/ Fawcett Society (2003), 64% of women stated that they would rather put their money into other types of savings than a pension. Given growing fears over future under-provisioning, further reform of the system clearly remains on the agenda.

**Figure 8.7: Proportion of working-age people contributing to non-state pensions, GB**

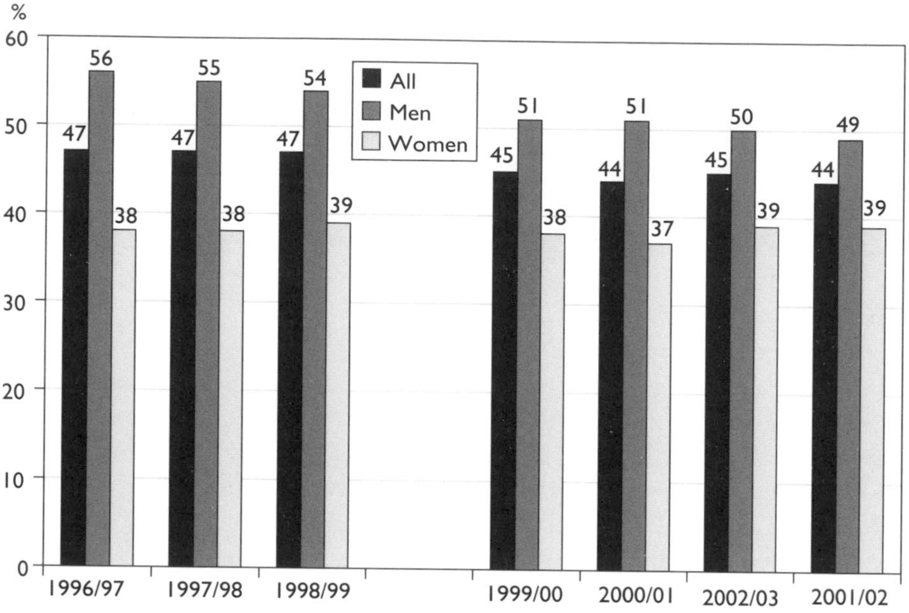

*Source:* DWP (2003d)

## Conclusion

Since coming into office, New Labour has developed a wide range of policy reforms and initiatives affecting the lives of older people. To what extent have they resulted in tangible benefits for older people? How has New Labour performed in relation to the three OFA priorities for older people identified at the start of this chapter? There has been significant progress in tackling poverty among *today's* pensioners in the seven years since 1997. However, this has been achieved through the extension of means-testing, and significant numbers of older people continue to fail to claim their entitlements and so live in poverty. New Labour's strategy to ensure that more of *tomorrow's* pensioners can retire on a decent income has largely focussed on extending private pension saving while concentrating state help on poorer pensioners via (softer) means-testing. As a consequence, there is a real tension between what is good for today and what is good for tomorrow. Contributions to private pensions have clearly not increased to the extent envisaged and the most notable outcome has been the 'seismic shift' from final salary to money purchase schemes. The growing individualisation of risk means that incomes in later life are likely to become more unequal in the future.

There is also a mixed picture with respect to the outcomes of policies in health and social care. More hours of home care are being delivered but these are being received by fewer households, with an intensification of care among those who receive such support. Personal social service provision appears not to have kept pace with need. More older people in residential care are being supported by councils but again there has been an extension of means-testing, with the government rejecting the Royal Commission's majority recommendation of free personal care. Overall, the picture for older people under New Labour has been one of a world where targeting is playing an increasingly important role. This is necessarily accompanied by the risk that some older people who need support, either in terms of income or health and social care, are falling outside the net. Despite some success on pensioner poverty, New Labour's record has proved not to be the inclusive agenda for older people hoped for by many.

## Notes

[1] Take-up among pensioners for the Minimum Income Guarantee was estimated between 63% and 72% by caseload or between 73% and 83% by expenditure, compared to take-up among non-pensioners for Income Support of 86-95% by caseload and 91-98% by expenditure (DWP, 2004b).

[2] Over two million women were below the LEL in 1998 (McKnight et al, 1998).

# NINE

# Ethnic inequalities under New Labour: progress or entrenchment?

*Coretta Phillips*

## Historical and contemporary policy landscapes

The New Labour party elected to government in 1997 came to power inheriting a legacy of ethnic inequalities in housing, education, employment, health and criminal justice outcomes. The early research evidence from the First Survey of Ethnic Minorities carried out in the mid-1960s documented racialised disadvantage and discrimination in the lives of all minority ethnic groups, most of whom had arrived from Britain's colonial territories to fill job vacancies in the post-war period (Daniel, 1968). Since the mid-1970s, however, while the broad pattern of ethnic inequalities has persisted, there has also been considerable differentiation, with those of Pakistani and Bangladeshi origin, and to a lesser extent those of black origin, generally faring worse than those of Indian and Chinese origin (see, for example, Smith, 1977; Jones, 1993; Modood et al, 1997)[1]. While the earlier period provided unequivocal evidence of both direct and indirect racial discrimination, the empirical research has additionally, over the intervening years, accumulated to reveal a complex interplay of socioeconomic, demographic, institutional, structural and cultural factors as contributing to the less favourable outcomes for minority ethnic groups.

In its first period of office, New Labour's policy response to ethnic inequalities was framed by the public inquiry into the Metropolitan Police Service's investigation of the racist murder of black teenager Stephen Lawrence in 1993. The government is to be applauded for fully endorsing the inquiry team's findings that 'institutional racism' had played a part in the flawed police investigation, and that it was endemic to public organisations such as the police, schools and government departments[2]. It was defined by Macpherson (1999, para 34) as:

> The collective failure of an organization to provide an appropriate and professional service to people because of their colour, culture, or ethnic origin. It can be seen or detected in processes, attitudes and behaviour which amount to discrimination through unwitting prejudice, ignorance, thoughtlessness and racist stereotyping which disadvantage minority ethnic people.

Despite the conceptual imprecision of the term (Mason, 1982; Miles and Brown, 2003) and some resistance to accepting its pervasiveness (Dennis et al, 2000), eliminating institutional racism was a central plank of the government's policy rhetoric, at least during New Labour's first term of office. Academic and policy commentators alike saw this as a 'watershed' and 'benchmark' in British race relations (Bourne, 2001).

In practice, New Labour policy has ultimately settled for promoting race equality, a more liberal and less politically controversial policy goal. The flagship element of this approach was the 2000 Race Relations (Amendment) Act, a recommendation of the Macpherson Report, representing the first race relations legislation for 25 years. It is now possible for the police and government departments to be found guilty of racial discrimination. The act also places a statutory duty on all public authorities to promote equality of opportunity, to proactively promote good relations between people of different racial groups, and to publish a race equality scheme. Public authorities are also required to audit, consult and monitor existing policies and services to assess whether these impact differently on different ethnic groups.

As Tony Blair has espoused in numerous speeches, New Labour's aim is to achieve "true equality: equal worth, an equal chance of fulfilment, equal access to knowledge and opportunity", and "not equality of income or outcome" (see, for example, his 1999 Labour Party Conference Speech). The social exclusion agenda is central to this, providing both an ethical and business case for a level playing field through which individuals can compete equally for social rewards. A range of initiatives has been mounted which have the broad aim of reducing multiple disadvantage for all groups, with fewer measures specifically targeted at minority ethnic groups. The chapter will consider the impact of these policies on long-standing ethnic inequalities in education, employment and policing. The last section of this chapter will attempt an overall assessment of New Labour strategies to reduce ethnic inequalities, as well as providing some thoughts on where further policy developments are required.

## Neighbourhood contexts

After the Second World War, migrants came to Britain, acting as a replacement population in urban areas that had suffered significant war casualties or population losses following upward white mobility (Peach, 1996). South Asian groups tended to settle in areas where manufacturing and textiles industries were the key employers, with Black Caribbeans (and later Black Africans) concentrated in urban centres where public sector employment (for example, hospitals, transport) was readily available. Patterns of residence were significantly constrained by limited financial resources, experiences of racial harassment and discrimination in obtaining private property and residency restrictions that prevented access to council housing. Ethnic clustering also resulted from a desire to maintain cultural, linguistic and religious ties, and to provide social support (Karn and Phillips,

1998). These factors together have set the context for contemporary patterns with minority ethnic groups experiencing relatively static geographical concentration and disadvantage.

Making up only 8% of the UK population according to the 2001 Census, minority ethnic groups are residentially concentrated in metropolitan areas in England and Wales. They are more likely than their white counterparts to live in areas where unemployment and social deprivation is higher, to be housed in poor living conditions and to experience high levels of overcrowding, and this is particularly the case for Pakistani/Bangladeshi ethnic groups (Lakey, 1997; Harrison and Phillips, 2003). These adverse conditions at the neighbourhood level provide the backdrop for minority ethnic groups' experiences in other areas, and it is these which are now considered.

## Education

It is difficult to overestimate the influence of education on life chances, with qualifications increasingly seen as the key to future study, employment, social position and income. The role of education in social reform is similarly important, with education in the 1960s viewed as a key means of integrating minority ethnic groups into the labour market and civil society, and as a tool for reducing prejudice and discrimination.

### Educational attainment

However, the attainment levels of black pupils have long been lower than those of their white counterparts, while their rates of exclusion from school have been higher. In the 1970s and 1980s, these features of black educational experience were assumed to be the result of these pupils possessing a negative self-image reinforced by a culturally irrelevant curriculum and poor linguistic skills (Swann Report, 1985). By the 1980s and into the mid-1990s, the statistical picture showed considerable differentiation in minority ethnic educational attainment. As Table 9.1 shows, based on attainment at age 16 (5+ higher grade GCSE passes), there is a higher-attaining cluster of ethnic groups (Indian, white, and findings from other research include those of Chinese origin in this group), and a lower-attaining cluster (black, Pakistani and Bangladeshi). The empirical research evidence has pointed to a range of explanations for these disadvantageous outcomes including socioeconomic disadvantage, racist teacher attitudes and expectations, a culturally biased and alienating National Curriculum, anti-school black masculinities, poor family–school links and parental support and large concentrations of minority ethnic pupils in unpopular and poorly resourced schools (Sewell, 1997; Gillborn, 1998; Tomlinson, 2001; Abbas, 2002).

**Table 9.1: Changes in GCSE attainment by ethnicity, England and Wales: 1988, 1995 and 1997 compared**

| Ethnic group | Five or more higher grade passes | | | Improvement (+/-) | | Attainment inequality relative to white performance |
|---|---|---|---|---|---|---|
| | 1988 (%) | 1995 (%) | 1997 (%) | 1995-97 | 1988-97 | |
| White | 26 | 42 | 44 | +2 | +18 | |
| Black | 17 | 21 | 28 | +7 | +11 | Gap narrowed in latest figures (from 21 to 16 points) but grew overall (from 9 to 16 points) |
| Indian | 23 | 44 | 49 | +5 | +26 | Inequality eliminated by 1995 and white level exceeded by 5 points in latest figures |
| Pakistani | 20 | 22 | 28 | +6 | +8 | Gap narrowed in latest figures (from 20 to 16 points) but grew overall (from 6 to 16 points) |
| Bangladeshi | 13 | 23 | 32 | +9 | +19 | Gap narrowed in latest figures (from 19 to 12 points) and fell narrowly overall (from 13 to 12 points) |

*Note:* Improvement and gap relative to white attainment is measured in percentage points between the relevant cohorts.
*Source:* Gillborn and Mirza (2000, Figure 2)

## Government policies

New Labour expressed its early commitment to reducing educational disadvantage in its pre-election manifesto and in Blair's mantra of 'Education, education, education'. The Excellence in Cities policy initiative has a core aim of raising educational standards in areas suffering socioeconomic disadvantage, which means that over 70% of minority ethnic pupils are included in a range of schemes to tackle educational disaffection, truancy and behavioural problems (see Chapter Three of this volume).

A key element of the government strategy to improve educational attainment among minority ethnic groups is the Ethnic Minority Achievement Grant (EMAG), introduced in 2001/02. Funding of £154 million has been allocated to local education authorities with high concentrations of minority ethnic pupils for language development training, peer mentoring and mediation schemes, targeted literacy and numeracy sessions, behaviour management programmes and summer schools. In response to the Macpherson Report recommendation, the National Curriculum for secondary schools now incorporates a citizenship element that teaches about the history of Britain's diverse ethnic communities.

Government initiatives have also focused on improving initial teacher training and increasing the recruitment of minority ethnic teacher trainees.

## Outcomes

It appears that New Labour's early commitment to reducing educational disadvantage has produced some positive results. Figure 9.1 shows that the proportion of pupils in all ethnic groups obtaining 5+ GCSEs at grades A*-C has increased considerably (see Chapter Three of this volume). It is also significant that the highest achieving groups in 2003 were of minority ethnic origin: 79% of Chinese girls and 71% of Chinese boys achieved 5+ GCSE grades A*-C in England, followed by 70% of Indian girls and 60% of Indian boys (DfES, 2004d). Interim evaluation findings on the Excellence in Cities programme also indicate higher levels of progress for Asian and black/black British pupils at Key Stage 4, although the opposite was found for the latter group at Key Stage 3 (Kendall et al, 2002).

However, it is disappointing that ethnic inequalities in educational attainment are still observable. The evidence points to a widening gap between the higher and lower attaining cluster of ethnic groups (see Demack et al, 2000). A more comprehensive categorisation of pupils by ethnic origin for 2003 indicates further differentiation between the high-attaining cluster (Chinese, Indian and Irish), a mid-range cluster (White British, Mixed, Bangladeshi, Travellers [Irish], Pakistani and Black African), and the performance of the lowest attaining cluster (Black Caribbean and Gypsy/Roma) (DfES, 2004d).

**Figure 9.1: Proportion of pupils obtaining five or more GCSEs, grades A*-C (1992-2002)**

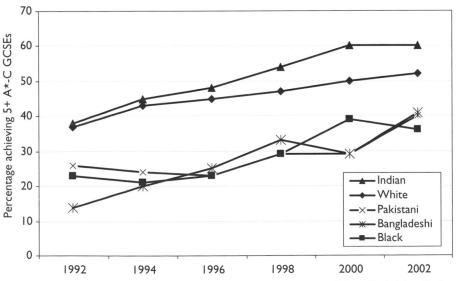

*Source:* Based on Bhattacharya et al (2003, Figure 4); data from *Statistical First Release, Youth Cohort Study: The activities and experiences of 16 year olds: England and Wales 2002*

Figure 9.2 takes into account socioeconomic status (using the proxy of free school meals). It is evident that pupils of Black Caribbean and Black Other origin have lower attainment, and Chinese pupils higher attainment, regardless of their eligibility for free school meals. The only exception to the pattern is the majority ethnic group of white pupils. One fifth of White British pupils eligible for free school meals achieved 5+ higher grade GCSEs, an attainment level similar to that of the poorer-performing minority ethnic groups (see Table 3.8 and related discussion in Chapter Three of this volume for a breakdown by gender as well as ethnicity). These findings point to the need for further exploration of ethnicity and socioeconomic status in attainment outcomes.

### School exclusions

The most recent data on permanent exclusions is also discouraging, showing that Black Caribbean pupils are over three times as likely as white pupils to be permanently excluded, with only slightly lower exclusion rates for those of Black Other origin. Indian, Pakistani, Bangladeshi and Chinese pupils are either proportionately or under-represented among those excluded (DfES, 2004e). While this represents a significant improvement over previous years (see Figure 9.3), undoubtedly in response to the government target of reducing exclusions by one third (SEU, 2000, Table 2), there is still disproportionality in the use of this sanction. The 16% reduction in permanent school exclusions between 1996/97 and 1998/99 (24% for those of Black Caribbean origin), predated the introduction of the government target (SEU, 2000, Table 2).

**Figure 9.2: Proportion achieving five or more A\*-C GCSEs, by eligibility for Free School Meals (FSM) (2003)**

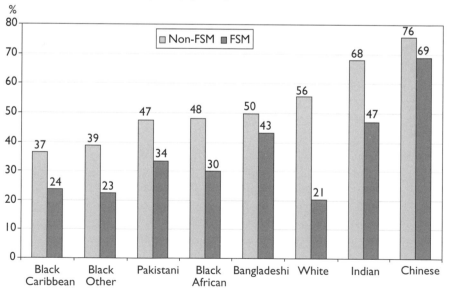

*Source:* Based on Bhattacharya et al (2003, Figure 5); updated using DfES (2004d)

**Figure 9.3: Permanent Exclusions from School in England (1997/98 to 2002/03)**

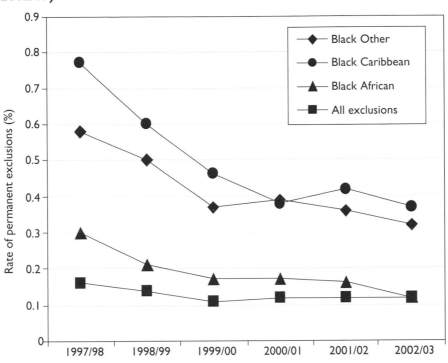

*Note:* 2002/03 data are provisional.
*Source:* DfES (2004e) and earlier equivalents

Promising approaches to raising educational achievement and reducing school exclusions include mentoring programmes, structured learning and support programmes with assessment and target setting, an inclusive curriculum which shows respect for the cultural background of all pupils, parent–school initiatives and support for supplementary schools (DfES, 2002; see also OFSTED, 2002; Tikly et al, 2002).

In October 2003, the government announced the 'Aiming Higher' strategy, targeting resources on raising African Caribbean attainment in 30 secondary schools. Schools will receive a package of support, resources and expert consultancy. It remains to be seen whether these approaches will alter the pattern of persistent ethnic inequalities in attainment and exclusion. Still inadequately addressed is the issue of teacher racism and conflict in teacher–black pupil interactions. Both Gillborn (2001) and Osler and Starkey (2001) have also questioned the role of citizenship education in bringing about significant anti-racist change in schools, promoting 'understanding' and 'tolerance' rather than challenging racism.

## Employment and poverty

Like education, employment represents a critical experience in our society, affecting social status, quality of housing, health and enjoyment of leisure. At the beginning of New Labour's first term, the Fourth National Survey of Ethnic Minorities demonstrated that, at each level of qualification (none, O-level or equivalent, A-level or higher), unemployment levels for Black Caribbean and Pakistani/Bangladeshi men and women were higher than for white men and women (Modood et al, 1997; see also Wadsworth, 2003). This differential was reduced for those of Indian and African Asian origin. A similar pattern was observed for male occupational attainment and average earnings, broadly mirroring the higher and lower attaining ethnic clusters found in educational outcomes.

Analysis of the Family Resources Survey by Berthoud (1998) also included samples of Chinese and African populations. This found higher average earnings for working Chinese, but also a larger proportion of poor Chinese (28%) compared with poor white households (16%). The African subsample was found to fare worse than Caribbeans and was significantly poorer than white households. Findings for other ethnic groups were generally similar to those of the Fourth National Survey of Ethnic Minorities. Of particular concern were very high levels of worklessness among Pakistani and Bangladeshi households, and their much lower levels of average earnings even in work.

Patterns for minority ethnic women were similar, although the differences were smaller. Exceptions included higher average weekly earnings among minority ethnic compared with white women, although this parity did not extend to women of Pakistani/Bangladeshi origin.

While men of Indian (and Chinese) origin perform better than other minority ethnic groups in terms of unemployment, earnings and occupational attainment, multivariate analyses which examine the effect of ethnicity on occupational outcomes after allowing for factors such as qualifications reveal an ethnic penalty for *all* minority ethnic groups (Cabinet Office, 2001, Table 4.11). Controlling for education, training, experience, marital and parental status and region, for example, the average Indian man was 1.64 times as likely to be unemployed as the average white man, with black men 2.51 times and Pakistani/Bangladeshi men 2.85 times as likely. Indian men received average weekly earnings £23 less than their white counterparts, rising to £81 for Caribbean men, £132 for African men and £129 for Pakistani/Bangladeshi men. Similarly, the average Indian man was 0.61 times as likely to be in a professional or managerial position as the average white man, and the figure was even lower for Pakistani/Bangladeshi men (0.56) and black men (0.36). The trend is broadly similar for women, although only the foreign-born face an ethnic earnings penalty (Cabinet Office, 2001, Table 4.12).

## Government policies

Labour market policy is an area in which New Labour has placed enormous stock, seeing increased participation as a means for reducing poverty and social exclusion. Labour market underachievement also has implications for national economic performance. As minority ethnic groups will make up more than half the growth of the working-age population in the next decade (Cabinet Office, 2003), increasing their employment rates is an issue which requires policy attention, and has indeed been one of the government's key objectives: initially, this was a Public Service Agreement (PSA) target for 2001-04, but it has now been extended to 2006.

The various general initiatives established to meet this aim are scrutinised in Chapter Two of this volume. Policy developments specifically targeted at minority ethnic groups have centred on promoting the business case for equal opportunities, improving ethnic monitoring of programmes such as the New Deal and enhanced partnership working with local minority ethnic providers of employment training and support. Early evidence on the impact of the New Deal for Young People on minority ethnic groups in Oldham indicates that personal advisers tended to be viewed positively, although dropout rates at the Gateway stage are higher nationally for minority ethnic groups than for young white people. Fewer individuals from minority ethnic groups entered subsidised or unsubsidised employment, with more going into education and training or the voluntary sector options. It is unclear whether this reflects a greater degree of commitment to training, lack of choice or lower expectations by clients or advisers (Fieldhouse et al, 2002).

## Outcomes

The data presented in Figure 9.4 show that all minority ethnic groups have lower economic activity rates than the white majority. For both men and women this trend is as much in evidence in summer 2002 as in summer 1997, with the exception of Chinese men whose rates of economic activity increased significantly over the time period. For women, the pattern was similar, but economic activity rates also increased for Mixed and Asian women, while declining for black women. These data are somewhat hard to interpret given the aggregation of Indians, Pakistanis and Bangladeshis into the Asian subcategory.

The 1990s saw a significant drop in unemployment, as well as an increase in average earnings and the proportion of people in professional jobs, and these improvements benefited most minority ethnic groups. However, relatively poor labour market outcomes have continued, although there is variation in the degree of inequality. Table 9.2 reveals the extent of ethnic inequalities in employment outcomes among both men and women in 2003[3]. Economic activity rates remained lower for minority ethnic groups compared with the white majority ethnic group, although this gap was small for men of Black Caribbean, Indian

**Figure 9.4: Economic activity rates by ethnic group and sex (1997-2002)**

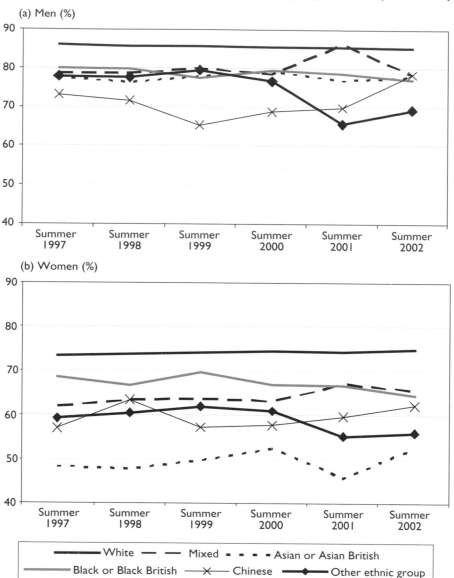

(a) Men (%)

(b) Women (%)

White — Mixed ▪ ▪ ▪ ▪ Asian or Asian British
Black or Black British —✕— Chinese ◆ Other ethnic group

*Note:* Economic activity rates for people of working age (men aged 16 to 64, women aged 16 to 59).
Data for the period 1997 to 2000 are backcast.
*Source:* ONS (p 663) *Labour Market Trends*, December 2002

and Mixed ethnic origins, and non-existent for Black Caribbean women.
Disparities in unemployment were generally sharper: with the exception of Indian
men, unemployment rates were between two and four times those of the white
majority. The pattern is slightly less marked for women, but unemployment
among Black Caribbean, Black African and Indian women is still double that

**Table 9.2: Male and female economic activity and unemployment rates, by ethnic group (Autumn 2003)**

| Ethnic group | Economic activity | Unemployment |
|---|---|---|
| *Men* | | |
| White | 85.0 | 4.8 |
| Black Caribbean | 83.4 | 16.1 |
| Black African | 77.5 | 10.5 |
| Chinese | 71.4 | – |
| Indian | 82.1 | 7.7 |
| Pakistani | 72.3 | 10.9 |
| Bangladeshi | 76.4 | 21.5 |
| Mixed | 83.1 | 18.4 |
| *Women* | | |
| White | 74.7 | 4.1 |
| Black Caribbean | 75.0 | 9.7 |
| Black African | 60.0 | 9.2 |
| Chinese | 58.7 | – |
| Indian | 68.7 | 10.4 |
| Pakistani | 34.2 | 13.2 |
| Bangladeshi | 26.6 | – |
| Mixed | 68.4 | 13.6 |

*Source:* ONS (2004c)

among white women, while for those of Mixed and Pakistani ethnic origins the rate is three times as high.

This goes some way to explaining why minority ethnic groups' position in the income distribution is generally lower than that of their white counterparts, and this too is a long-standing pattern. If all ethnic groups were equally positioned in the income distribution we would expect to see 20% of each group in the bottom income fifth, but as Table 9.3 illustrates, this is not the case. Almost two thirds of those of Pakistani/Bangladeshi origin were in the bottom fifth before or after housing costs in 2002/03. While all minority ethnic groups are consistently over-represented at the bottom of the income distribution, those of Indian and Caribbean origin are closest to the white ethnic group. The proportion of the latter group in the bottom fifth departs more clearly from those of Indian origin once the self-employed are included, suggesting that this form of employment is less successful for Caribbeans.

Comparable data on child poverty among ethnic groups are only available since 2000/01 (and for 1999/2000 excluding the self-employed). The recent picture appears similar to that already discussed in relation to income distribution, but with very significant progress for Indian children: 37% of Indian children lived in households below 60% median income after housing costs in 2000/01, reduced to 22% in 2002/03. This compares to a fall from 28% to 26% for children in the white ethnic group. On an after housing costs measure, Indian children are now less likely to live in relative poverty than white children; before housing costs, 19% of Indian children are poor compared to 18% of white children (DWP, 2004a).

**Table 9.3: Share of each ethnic group in the bottom income fifth**

**BHC**

| Ethnic group | 1996/ 97 | Excluding the self-employed | | | | Including the self-employed | |
| | | 1997/ 98 | 1998/ 99 | 1999/ 2000 | 2000/ 01 | 2001/ 02 | 2002/ 03 |
|---|---|---|---|---|---|---|---|
| White | 19 | 19 | 19 | 19 | 19 | 19 | 19 |
| Black[a] | 29 | 34 | 31 | 27 | 29 | 30 | 31 |
|    Caribbean | | | | 22 | 25 | 29 | 28 |
|    Non-Caribbean | | | | 34 | 34 | 31 | 35 |
| Indian | 31 | 28 | 27 | 32 | 31 | 24 | 21 |
| Pakistani/Bangladeshi | 73 | 58 | 61 | 64 | 64 | 60 | 66 |
| Other[b] | 31 | 33 | 31 | 29 | 32 | 29 | 25 |
| All | 20 | 20 | 20 | 20 | 20 | 20 | 20 |

**AHC**

| Ethnic group | 1996/ 97 | Excluding the self-employed | | | | Including the self-employed | |
| | | 1997/ 98 | 1998/ 99 | 1999/ 2000 | 2000/ 01 | 2001/ 02 | 2002/ 03 |
|---|---|---|---|---|---|---|---|
| White | 18 | 18 | 19 | 18 | 18 | 18 | 18 |
| Black[a] | 39 | 42 | 40 | 35 | 37 | 38 | 36 |
|    Caribbean | | | | 26 | 29 | 34 | 31 |
|    Non-Caribbean | | | | 49 | 47 | 43 | 42 |
| Indian | 29 | 25 | 26 | 32 | 27 | 26 | 22 |
| Pakistani/Bangladeshi | 67 | 57 | 60 | 61 | 62 | 61 | 65 |
| Other[b] | 42 | 42 | 39 | 37 | 36 | 37 | 31 |
| All | 20 | 20 | 20 | 20 | 20 | 20 | 20 |

Notes: [a] For 1999/2000, 2000/01 and 2001/02, calculated as a weighted average of Black Caribbean and Black Non-Caribbean; [b] For 2002/03, calculated as a weighted average of Mixed, Asian (but not Indian, Pakistani/Bangladeshi) and Chinese and Other.
The presentation of these data in HBAI statistics changed in 2001/02 to include the self-employed.
Source: DWP (2004a) and earlier equivalents

In contrast, there is no evidence of any movement out of poverty for children of Pakistani/Bangladeshi origin, 75% of whom were poor after housing costs in 2002/03, or for children of Black/Black British origin, 46% of whom were poor in 2002/03. Thus, government policies on child poverty discussed in Chapter Seven of this volume appear to have been less than effective for most minority ethnic groups. The very high levels of child poverty concentrated among Pakistani/Bangladeshi children are of particular concern.

Analytical research undertaken by the Cabinet Office (2001) has highlighted the complex explanations for labour market underachievement, relating to, on the demand side, fewer business opportunities in areas with high minority ethnic concentrations, with cultural and religious factors seeming to play a part. On the supply side, lower skills and qualifications among some minority ethnic groups, poorer language fluency, poorer health and the quality and location of childcare and transport facilities may all contribute to less advantageous outcomes. There is official acknowledgement that racial discrimination still has an impact, although its extent is very difficult to quantify.

A 'new' intellectual and policy framework was launched in early 2003 with a ten-year vision of eliminating disproportionate barriers to employment for minority ethnic groups (Cabinet Office, 2003, p 7). The report stridently sets out policy measures to increase employability by raising educational and skills attainment, connecting people with work through the tailoring of programmes, increasing housing mobility and improving access to childcare and transport, and promoting equal opportunities in the workplace. These are clearly important elements of increasing labour market participation among minority ethnic groups. Equally essential, however, are the sometimes subtle processes of direct and indirect discrimination which operate to limit minority ethnic individuals from reaching their potential according to their qualifications and levels of employment experience, and to perpetuating employment segregation as some employment opportunities are viewed as exclusively 'white' (Cabinet Office, 2001).

## Policing[4]

As the introduction to this chapter noted, the Macpherson Report provided New Labour with the framework for achieving racial equality in society. The Home Secretary's Action Plan which followed the report mainly addressed itself to extensive reform within the police service. Foremost in its programme of work was the establishment of a Ministerial Priority "to increase trust and confidence in policing among minority ethnic communities" (Home Office, 1997, 1998a). This was to be measured using performance indicators relating to public satisfaction, family liaison, racism awareness training, racist complaints, the recruitment, retention and progression of minority ethnic police officers, the policing of racist incidents and the use of stop and search powers. Given their importance in understanding the historical and contemporary relationship between the police and different minority ethnic communities, it is the latter two that are considered in detail in this chapter[5].

### Racist incidents

Historical and recent research have shown the heightened risk that minority ethnic groups have faced from racially motivated victimisation, with police recorded racist incidents increasing 200% between 1988 and 1996/97 (Home Office, 1997, 1998a), although such data are subject to under-reporting and under-recording (Maynard and Read, 1997). Moreover, the historical evidence on the poor response that victims have received from the police in this area was reinforced by the police investigation of Stephen Lawrence's racist murder (Macpherson, 1999; see also Bowling, 1999; Clancy et al, 2001).

Following the Macpherson Report, the Home Office produced the *Code of practice on reporting and recording racist incidents* in April 2000, which applied to all statutory, voluntary and community groups, and the Association of Chief Police Officers drafted its own guidance, *Identifying and combating hate crimes* (2000), which is now used by all police forces. These accepted the Macpherson definition of a racist incident as "any incident which is perceived to be racist by the victim or any other person". Additionally, many police forces have created specialist units with officers specially trained to investigate racist and other hate crimes.

These policies have had some impact on police practice. It is clear, for example, that there has been an increase in victims' reporting racist incidents to the police and their willingness and ability to record them as racist incidents, with a doubling of recorded incidents between 1998/99 and 1999/2000 (Clancy et al, 2001; Home Office, 2003a). Burney and Rose's (2002) study has highlighted the more intensive and closely supervised investigation of racist incidents by the police following the Macpherson Report. Nonetheless, while the BCS has estimated that racist victimisation rates dropped in 1999 compared with 1995, it is probably too soon to attribute any of this decline to post-Macpherson policing reforms.

### Stop and search

The use of stop and search powers by the police has long been the most controversial issue in debates about the policing of minority ethnic communities (see Bowling and Phillips, 2002). In 1997/98, the rates of stop and search were 19 per 1,000 for the white population, but seven times higher (139 per 1,000) for black people and two times higher for Asians (45 per 1,000) (Home Office, 1998a). Academic debates have centred on the extent to which these patterns of disproportionality can be legitimately explained by minority ethnic groups' younger age structure, their greater 'availability' on the street because of higher levels of school exclusions and unemployment, their residential concentration in higher crime areas where more stop and searches take place and their elevated rates of offending according to victim reports, particularly for 'street crime' offences (see Phillips and Bowling, 2003, for a review).

The disproportionate use of police stop and search powers is also consistent with patterns of selective enforcement based on negative stereotyping and the heightened suspicion that police officers have of black people, which has been well-documented in research studies and police inspections (for example, FitzGerald and Sibbitt, 1997; Her Majesty's Inspectorate of Constabulary, 2000; Bowling and Phillips, 2002). Even the Macpherson Report (1999, para 45.10) acknowledged that "the majority of police officers who testified before us accepted that an element of the disparity was the result of discrimination".

The government's response to the problem of disproportionality was to attempt to tighten the regulation of powers with a revised 1984 Police and Criminal Evidence Act Code of Practice A[6]. This included providing those stopped with a record containing reasons for the stop, improving the supervision and monitoring of stop and searches by senior officers and more clearly specifying what is meant by the concept of 'reasonable suspicion' which must exist before a stop is conducted.

Figure 9.5 shows that the pattern of ethnic disproportionality in stop and search remains largely unchanged since these policy developments were introduced. However, levels of recorded stop and search fell from one million at the time of the Macpherson Inquiry (late 1998-early 1999), to around three quarters of a million in 1999/2000, with sharper falls for those of minority ethnic origin. This reduction was probably at least partly attributable to the criticism that the use of the power was frequently unlawful and unjustified (FitzGerald, 1999), but probably also reflected officers' concerns about being accused of racism.

Despite the absolute drop in the numbers of all ethnic groups stopped and searched by the police between 1997/98 and 2001/02, the fall was lower for black (-23%) and Asian people (-21%) than for white people (-31%). The black:white ratio fell from 7:1 in 1997/98 to 5-6:1 between 1998/99 and 2000/01. However, the 'Macpherson effect' subsequently waned: ethnic disproportionality reached its highest levels in 2001/02 with a black:white ratio of 8:1. While it is difficult to be sure about the reasons for the increase, the target to reduce robbery imposed on Crime and Disorder Reduction Partnerships in the government's crime reduction strategy is probably a contributory factor.

**Figure 9.5: Stop and search rates per 1,000 population (1997/98 to 2001/02)**

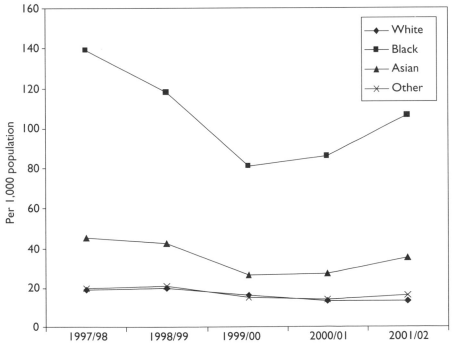

*Source:* Home Office (various) Section 95 statistics *Race and the criminal justice system*

There also remains evidence of the use of 'racial profiling', as described by the minority ethnic police officers interviewed by Cashmore (2001, p 652), who reported being advised to stop "black kids with baseball caps, wearing all the jewellery", in order to enhance their performance levels: "if you see four black youths in a car, it's worth giving them a pull, as at least one of them is going to be guilty of something or other". Evidently, further work is necessary with senior officers giving unequivocal guidance that stop and search is not a measure of productivity, and with individual officers being made fully aware that the misuse of stop and search powers could lead to disciplinary action. Moreover, since in 2001/02 only 13% of stop and searches resulted in an arrest, a reconsideration of the value of stop and search as a crime control technique is urgently required, particularly given the adverse impact it has on police–community relations (Home Office, 2003a; Phillips and Bowling, 2003).

## Community cohesion

The structural inequalities and racial discrimination already discussed in relation to education, employment and policing appear to have coalesced and erupted into racialised confrontations between young Pakistani/Bangladeshi and white men, amidst serious clashes with the police in the northern towns of Bradford, Burnley and Oldham in spring/summer 2001. In the aftermath, the official reports into the disturbances focused on communities experiencing 'parallel lives', inhabiting segregated residential, educational, occupational and leisure spaces, with much negative stereotyping of 'the Other'. While there was recognition of extreme levels of socioeconomic deprivation in these communities, alongside problems of political leadership, disengagement, weak policing and the presence of extremist groups, much attention focused on communities lacking shared values and a shared vision (Cantle, 2001; Denham, 2001).

Critical commentators have challenged the emphasis the government placed in these reports on cultural difference, 'Asian criminality' and self-segregation among Asian communities as the key factors in the disturbances, arguing that this played down the role of wider socioeconomic inequalities and institutionalised discrimination (Kundnani, 2001; Kalra, 2002; Alexander, 2004: forthcoming; Burnett, 2004). For Amin (2002, p 963):

> rather too much has been made of Asian retreat into inner-urban wards to preserve diaspora traditions and Muslim values, while not enough has been said about White flight into the outer estates, which has been decisively ethno-cultural in character – in escaping Asian ethnic contamination and wanting to preserve White Englishness.

Self-segregation undoubtedly poses significant policy problems for a government committed to integration and a communitarian model of citizenship. However, while educational and residential segregation along ethnic lines is pronounced in some parts of the country (Burgess et al, 2004), the role of choice and external constraints in explaining these spatial inequalities remains unclear.

The policy response has included the setting up of the Community Cohesion Unit and the establishment of 14 Community Cohesion Pathfinder projects in April 2003, to assist in the development and dissemination of best practice. Local programmes include initiatives such as funding a voluntary sector worker to establish an interfaith council, including a political champion in strategy groups and producing a video and feedback event to illustrate the perspectives of young people, parents and professionals. The progress report for the first six months points to the need for the concept of community cohesion to be well understood locally and for all government initiatives to be joined up at a local level (Home Office, 2003b).

Further policy direction could be provided to indicate the mechanisms for assisting safe geographical integration at the neighbourhood level. Suggestions for Bradford include developing local neighbourhood compacts with residents' groups who are willing to help with welcoming Asian families into housing areas, rewarding those that actively encourage and achieve cross-racial involvement in neighbourhood activities, and integrating educational and leisure activities (Anne Power in Ratcliffe et al, 2001; see also Haddock, 2003). Such efforts will probably only succeed if they additionally address the more deep-rooted problems which affect divided communities. These are inextricably linked to poverty, exclusion, marginalisation and to processes of discrimination in education, housing and employment. A political call for a re-imagining of Britishness and belonging which can incorporate the diverse, hybrid and diasporic identities of those whose ancestry lies outside Britain is also of paramount importance in fostering a common investment in local communities (Parekh, 2000).

## Assessing the impact of New Labour policies on ethnic inequalities

During their first two terms in office, New Labour presided over some significant improvements in the life of socially disadvantaged groups, which have also benefited minority ethnic groups, albeit that some of these trends (in education and unemployment particularly) were already evident under the previous government. Turning to look specifically at ethnic *inequalities* reveals a less flattering picture. In education, employment and policing, New Labour policies have had little discernible impact on reducing differences between ethnic groups, even if, overall, all ethnic groups have experienced some positive change. It seems likely that there are a number of reasons for this disappointing assessment.

A bureaucratic limitation of New Labour policy measures relates to their timing. Many initiatives which specifically address the needs of minority ethnic groups have been launched only during New Labour's second term in office. This may well be precisely because ethnic inequalities have shown no sign of abating; it is testimony to the complexity of the barriers to more equal outcomes for all ethnic groups, and may reflect a recognition that a policy focus on social exclusion is insufficient to improve the experiences of the most disadvantaged minority ethnic groups (see SEU, 2004). This clearly indicates the need for a policy response that more directly addresses direct and indirect forms of discrimination as alluded to in the substantive sections of this chapter.

A further criticism relates to the emerging evidence of a tension between New Labour's public managerialist policies, quasi-market reforms and the 'targets culture' on the one hand, and equal opportunities and cultural diversity initiatives on the other. Carter's (2000) research on equal opportunities in the NHS found that the devolved local management of staff has allowed discriminatory practices in recruitment and selection as individual staff members are given power to recruit staff directly, largely through informal and non-regulated mechanisms. Similarly, as discussed earlier in this chapter, Cashmore's (2001) research with minority ethnic officers has also highlighted the implicit pressures on officers to stop and search 'easy targets' in order to boost performance profiles. 'Racially informed' choosing of schools by white parents using basic league tables may be a further example of the ways in which elements of quasi-market reforms have adverse consequences for minority ethnic groups (Tomlinson, 1998; Gillborn, 2001).

Research such as that by Carter (2001) and Cashmore (2001) also highlights the internal resistance to reform amidst perceptions of preferential treatment for minority ethnic groups. Such pockets of resistance will necessarily militate against change at both an individual and institutional level. Further research and development work is required to uncover effective processes of change within public and private sector organisations that carefully but rigorously challenge assumptions of preferential treatment. Moreover, while it would be a brave politician who promoted the radical goal of equality of outcome rather than opportunity, New Labour can be criticised for not devoting more resources, particularly through education and neighbourhood policies, for perhaps the most promising element of the new statutory duty contained in the 2000 Race Relations (Amendment) Act – the "promotion ... of good relations between persons of different racial groups". This requires public authorities, and not just those affected by the Northern disorders, to proactively encourage positive relationships and reduce the segregation of communities along ethnic lines.

A further conceptual criticism of New Labour policies relates to Doreen Lawrence's (the mother of murdered black teenager Stephen Lawrence) claim that race is no longer a central pillar of the government's equalities agenda (Dodd and Hopkins, 2003). It is certainly true that recent policy statements rarely refer to institutional racism[7], instead preferring the more politically innocuous term, 'race equality'. It is not clear whether this political sleight of hand is meant to dodge the more difficult task of changing the culture of organisations or whether the promotion of race equality is simply a more pragmatic strategy for bringing about change in the short term.

It is hard not to concur with the chorus of critical commentators who favour the former conclusion, and have variously referred to New Labour's approach to dealing with racism as "naïve multiculturalism" (Gillborn, 2001, p 19), "facing both ways" (Bourne, 2001, p 14) and "the new assimilationism' (Back et al, 2002, p 452). With the exception of Gillborn, all castigate New Labour for promoting social inclusion while at the same time introducing restrictive and exclusionary immigration and asylum policies which contribute to the demonisation of asylum seekers and refugees amidst the global movement of peoples (discussed further in Chapter Ten of this volume). For all, continuities between Conservative government policies of earlier periods and New Labour policy approaches are evident, with both failing to address structural forms of inequality and racism.

## Conclusion

The challenge for New Labour is to reduce the deeply entrenched ethnic inequalities seen in these key areas of social and criminal justice policy. It seems likely that success will rest upon specifically targeted initiatives which address socioeconomic disadvantage more generally, in addition to 'tough measures' to eradicate racism and discrimination. Promoting minority-influenced organisations such as black and minority ethnic housing associations, supplementary schools and culturally sensitive services, at the same time as improving mainstream provision, must also form part of this strategy. It will be some time yet before it will be possible to assess how well New Labour has performed against its recently expressed policy objectives in the areas of education, employment, policing and community cohesion.

## Notes

[1] It is acknowledged that the concepts of 'race' and ethnicity are socially constructed and contested. This chapter relies on the categorisation of ethnic groups according to the research and statistical material it reviews, recognising the pitfalls of designations sometimes far removed from self-perceptions of ethnicity and ethnic identity. See, for example, Fenton (1996) and Anthias et al (1993).

[2] Both Jack Straw, then Home Secretary, and David Calvert-Smith, Director of Public Prosecutions, publicly announced that the organisations for which they had responsibility (the Home Office and the Crown Prosecution Service) were 'institutionally racist' (Straw, 1999; *The Guardian*, 26 July 2001).

[3] Figures comparing economic activity and unemployment rates by ethnic origin for 1997 and 2003 are not available, because the Labour Force Survey changed ethnicity classifications in 2001 to be in line with the Census.

[4] This section of the chapter draws heavily on the author's co-authored work with Ben Bowling (Bowling and Phillips, 2003; Phillips and Bowling, 2003).

[5] For a discussion of the experiences of minority ethnic communities in relation to these other areas of policing, see Phillips and Bowling (2003).

[6] It also commissioned a programme of research on the issues of 'availability', public perspectives, the impact of stop and searches on deterrence, detection and intelligence gathering, and police decision making. Findings are summarised in Miller et al (2000).

[7] Recall also Home Secretary David Blunkett's comment that he was worried about the term 'institutional racism' deflecting attention from responsibility for eradicating racism at the individual level (speech to the Home Office Ethnic Network AGM, 14 January 2003).

# TEN

# Selective inclusion: asylum seekers and other marginalised groups

*Tania Burchardt*

## Introduction

Establishing the Social Exclusion Unit (SEU) in 1997 as part of the Cabinet Office was an early initiative of the Labour government. The brief of the SEU fell into two parts: neighbourhood renewal (considered in Chapter Six of this volume); and countering the exclusion of marginalised groups (considered in this chapter). Up to early 2004, the groups about whom the SEU has produced reports have been as follows:

- pupils excluded from school or truanting (published in 1998);
- rough sleepers (1998);
- teenage parents (1999);
- 16- to 18-year-olds not in education, employment or training (NEET) (1999);
- young runaways (2002);
- ex-prisoners (2002); and
- children in care (2004).

Although the rationale for selecting these particular groups is not immediately obvious, some inferences can be drawn from the characteristics that the groups have in common. Five out of the seven are groups of children or young people. A process of exclusion which begins early in life is likely to have long-term consequences for both individuals and for the services which are required to support them. Correspondingly, successful policy interventions for these groups have the potential to reduce significantly social exclusion over a lifetime.

Many of the groups identified are ones whose exclusion is perceived to impose costs on the rest of society; for example, children not in school are associated with petty crime; people sleeping rough may be intimidating or offend the sensibilities of the better off; and teenage parents and their children often need considerable support through social security and social services. This may have contributed to the selection of these groups as targets for the SEU.

A third feature that the groups have in common is that responsibility for each is spread between a number of different government departments and agencies.

Providing 'joined up solutions to joined up problems' was seen as a key task for the SEU, and indeed, since the SEU did not have an implementation budget of its own, it was entirely dependent on other departments and organisations to pursue the policies it recommended.

This chapter examines New Labour's record on the first three groups listed earlier. For each in turn (the following three sections), the chapter considers the policy context and trends prior to 1997, the targets set and the policies recommended by the SEU and the outcomes. The other listed groups are no less important but for most it is too early to assess whether the SEU initiatives have had any effect. For the 16- to 18-year-old NEET group, the SEU report identified only preliminary policy recommendations; they are given some consideration in Chapter Two of this volume.

The penultimate section of this chapter turns to one of the marginalised groups that the SEU did not consider; namely, asylum seekers. The SEU could have focussed its attention on any number of disadvantaged groups – disabled children, Pakistani and Bangladeshi women, the over-80s, to name but a few – so the selection of just one omitted group is inevitably somewhat arbitrary. However, asylum seekers provide a particularly interesting case study because they are among the most vulnerable of vulnerable groups: often they arrive traumatised, penniless, alone and unable to speak the language. Furthermore, asylum has been an active area of government policy, with four major parliamentary acts in the last decade and another currently making its way through parliament, but one where policy has had the effect of generating social exclusion, rather than preventing or ameliorating it.

The chapter concludes with an assessment of the extent to which the government's efforts to reduce the exclusion of marginalised groups has been successful. It applauds the evidence-based approach adopted by the SEU but notes the gap that has often emerged between structural analysis of the problems and the 'supply-side' nature of proposed solutions. The gap may have arisen in part because of the SEU's reluctance to confront actual or perceived conflicts of interest between the marginalised and the included majority. This, and the fact that some policies that fell outside the SEU's remit have been actively generating social exclusion, points towards the need for mainstreaming social inclusion policy for the future.

## Pupils excluded from school or truanting

### Inheritance

Since 1994, when statistics on truanting were first collected systematically, the numbers have been relatively stable. In contrast, the number of pupils excluded from school rose rapidly during the 1990s. A range of possible causes have been suggested, including increases in inequality, mental illness among children, competition between schools and integration of Special Educational Needs pupils

(Hallam and Castle, 2001). Some groups were of particular concern: children from some black ethnic minority backgrounds had disproportionately high exclusion rates, as did children in care and children of traveller families (Commission for Racial Equality, 1997; West and Pennell, 2003).

One of the most immediate impacts of truanting or of being excluded from school is on the education that the pupil receives. However, research suggests that the impact of truancy on later life chances is not restricted to the effects of low qualifications: even after controlling for qualifications and other background characteristics, young people who played truant were found to be more likely than others to have low-status occupations at age 23, or to be unemployed (Hibbert et al, 1990). The SEU was also concerned about the link with youth offending. According to the Home Office, 78% of boys and 53% of girls who truanted once a week or more committed offences (quoted in SEU, 1998a).

In 1998, the Department for Education and Employment (DfEE) was already supporting school attendance and behaviour projects through the Standards Fund. Other projects were run through the Single Regeneration Budget, the Home Office, the Department of Health, individual Local Education Authorities (LEAs), schools and local police forces. The time was ripe for an overview of 'what works'.

## Policies adopted

The SEU set a headline target of reducing the number of pupils excluded from school by one third by 2002 (SEU, 1998a). The rate of exclusions by ethnicity was to be monitored but no separate targets were set. All pupils excluded for more than three weeks were to receive full-time education in an alternative setting.

The targets were to be achieved through a combination of exhortation, monitoring and alteration of incentives. Existing guidance for schools on exclusions was to be rewritten and high-excluding schools would be subject to special OFSTED inspections. If schools did not succeed in reducing the number of exclusions, funding through the DfEE Standards Fund grant would be reduced (West and Pennell, 2003)[1].

The initial target on truancy was to reduce by one third the days lost to truancy, by 2002. Subsequently, a second target of a reduction of 10% from 2002 to 2004 was added. Parents of truants would face stiffer penalties, including fines, parenting orders to require the parent(s) to accompany the child to school and, in extreme cases, imprisonment. The police were also given an explicit power to pick up truants during school hours.

In 2002, elements of the truancy and exclusions policies were drawn together into the Behaviour Improvement Project, funded in a selection of LEAs with the highest rates of truancy and street crime (DfES, 2003b). The Behaviour Improvement Project aimed to spread good practice especially in preventative work with pupils at risk of truancy or exclusion, for example through providing key workers, in-school learning support and police officers with links to schools.

### Outcomes

Permanent exclusions rose from 2,910 in 1990/91 to a peak of 12,668 in 1996/97. They then fell slightly (Figure 10.1), so the SEU intervention came at a time when the numbers were already beginning to decrease somewhat. A sharp decline followed in 1999/2000, so much so that the target of reducing exclusions by one third (taking 1997/98 as the base year) was met ahead of schedule. However, since then the numbers have begun to creep up again. In 2002/03, 9,290 pupils were permanently excluded, 24% fewer than in 1997/98. This is a significant reduction, but a downwards trend is not clearly established.

A breakdown by ethnic group indicates that drawing attention to the disproportionate exclusion of Black pupils has been successful in altering schools' behaviour. There is no room for complacency, however, since exclusion rates of Black Caribbean pupils are still three times as high as for white pupils. Chapter Nine of this volume considers New Labour's impact on the educational experience of different ethnic groups in more detail.

**Figure 10.1: Permanent Exclusions from School (maintained schools in England)**

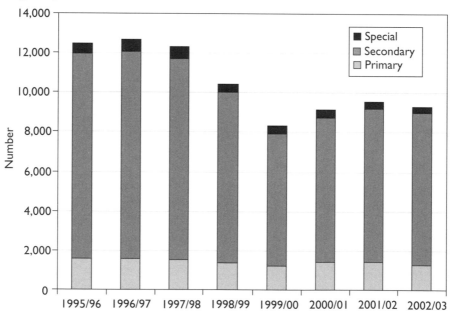

*Notes:* 2000/01 and 2001/02 figures are estimates, due to incomplete school returns; 2002/03 figures are provisional.
*Source:* DfES (2004e) and previous editions

A number of caveats must be made in interpreting these statistics. In some cases, consecutive fixed-term exclusions (not included in the figures) amount almost to permanent exclusions (Vulliamy and Webb, 2001). In other cases, pupils may be obliged or put under pressure to change schools without this being recorded as exclusion (Osler et al, 2001). These alternatives to permanent exclusion are not necessarily used cynically, but do highlight problems both of target setting and of monitoring policy success, especially in the context of schools competing for position in league tables.

A further problem is the balance between the needs of pupils at risk of exclusion and the needs of pupils remaining in class. Arguably, the initial emphasis on reducing rates of exclusion did not take sufficient account of the impact on other pupils (and teachers) of retaining disruptive pupils in class, without additional resources to provide in-school support. After protests from head teachers' organisations and others, the Department for Education and Skills (DfES) announced that the exclusions targets would not be extended (DfES, 2001). New guidance to schools, issued in March 2004, shifted the emphasis towards ensuring that appropriate alternative arrangements were made for excluded pupils.

Turning to truancy, estimates of truancy derived from sample surveys are much higher than official rates, which are calculated on the basis of entries in twice-daily school registers. Post-registration truancy is part of the explanation. However, even according to the official series, rates of truancy in 2001/02 were only slightly lower than in 1997/98, and there has been considerable fluctuation in-between (Table 10.1).

The target of reducing truancy by one third has clearly not been met. On current trends, even the more modest later target, a reduction of 10% between 2002 and 2004, seems out of reach[2]. The difference between the rapid changes that have occurred in rates of exclusions and the very slow changes in truancy may be explained by the fact that the former is at the discretion of teachers and governors – over whom the government has considerable influence – while the latter depends on decisions made by individual pupils and parents.

**Table 10.1: Truancy: percentage of half-days missed through unauthorised absence (all schools in England)**

| Year | Maintained primary | Maintained secondary | All (including special and non-maintained) |
|---|---|---|---|
| 1996/97 | 0.48 | 1.01 | 0.70 |
| 1997/98 | 0.50 | 1.10 | 0.74 |
| 1998/99 | 0.49 | 1.07 | 0.73 |
| 1999/2000 | 0.47 | 1.04 | 0.71 |
| 2000/01 | 0.49 | 1.07 | 0.73 |
| 2001/02 | 0.45 | 1.09 | 0.72 |
| 2002/03 | 0.43 | 1.07 | 0.70 |
| % change 1997/98 to 2002/03 | −14% | −3% | −5% |

*Source:* DfES (2003e)

# Teenage parents

*Inheritance*

Following a recognition that the UK had the highest rate of births to teenage mothers in Western Europe, the White Paper, *Health of the nation* (DH, 1991), set a target of halving the conception rate of women under age 16. However, the trend in the mid-1990s was not encouraging (Wellings and Kane, 1999).

International comparisons suggested that age at first sexual activity was not unusually young in the UK, but contraceptive use was low. Widening income inequality, and especially educational inequality, giving young women from disadvantaged backgrounds little to look forward to in the way of rewarding occupations, were also thought to be contributory factors (SEU, 1999).

Teenage pregnancy is a matter of concern for a number of reasons. First, there is the welfare of the baby: although not biologically problematic, pregnancies of teenage mothers tend not to be 'well-managed'; for example, teenage mothers are much less likely than older mothers to receive timely antenatal advice. Babies of teenage mothers have lower birth weights and higher mortality, on average.

Second, there is the immediate welfare of the mother. Teenage mothers experience high rates of post-natal depression and of relationship breakdown, and they often leave education before gaining any qualifications. They may be obliged to subsist on a very limited income: a mother under 16 has no Income Support entitlement in her own right, while rates for 16- and 17-year-olds are low.

Third, there may be long-term consequences for the mother. Women who were teenage mothers are found in adult life to have low educational qualifications, low employment rates, low rates of partnership stability, low incomes and a high probability of depression (Hobcraft and Kiernan, 2001), but the evidence on whether these associations are causal is mixed. Chevalier and Viitanen (2003) find negative outcomes for teenage mothers over and above those predicted by pre-existing characteristics, using the 1958 birth cohort (National Child Development Study) and a methodology based on propensity score matching. On the other hand, Ermisch and Pevalin (2003), using the 1970 birth cohort and comparing women who had a miscarriage as a teenager (and who were intending to have the baby) to those who gave birth as a teenager, find little difference in terms of qualifications, employment or earnings at age 30. The difference in results between the two studies could be explained by the different methodologies or by the fact that the first study is based on an earlier cohort.

*Policies adopted*

The key target set by the SEU in 1999 was to halve conceptions to under-18s in England by 2010. In 2001, an additional interim target was included in the NHS plan, to reduce conceptions to under-18s by 15% by 2004. Despite the identification of deep-seated causes for high teenage pregnancy rates, the reduction was to be achieved principally by improving access to information and advice, including:

- a national media campaign using 'teen' magazines and local radio (one element aimed at boys, another reassuring teenagers that advice was confidential);
- a national helpline (Sexwise);
- new guidance on sex education in schools, encouraging primary schools to begin the process, secondary schools to include boys, to talk about relationships and to give advice about local contraception and advice services;
- teaching sex education to be covered as a core part of teacher training; and
- clearer guidance for health professionals about the legality of providing contraception for under-16s.

The SEU was also concerned to reduce the impact of teenage pregnancy. In 2002, a target was set that, by 2010, 60% of teenage mothers should be participating in education, employment or training in some way. To this end, Reintegration Officers were funded in 89 LEAs and personal advisers for pregnant teenagers were made available through Sure Start Plus in 20 pilot areas.

### Outcomes

Figure 10.2 shows that conception rates have fallen since 1999 among all three categories of young women. However, the downward trends were established

**Figure 10.2: Trends in conception rates among young women, by age group**

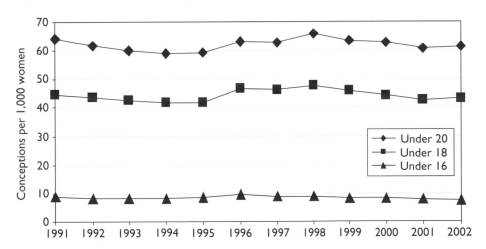

*Notes:* Conceptions are estimates derived from birth registrations and abortion notifications.
Rates for women of under 16, under 18, and under 20 are based on the population of women aged 13 to 15, 15 to 17 and 15 to 19 respectively. 2001 and 2002 data are provisional. Rates for 2001 and 2002 are based on population estimates released by ONS 26 September 2003.
*Source:* ONS (2003a, Table 4.1) and previous editions

before the SEU's intervention, and were partly the result of an unusually high rate of conceptions in 1996, following a pill scare in 1995. This means that there is a 'numbers game' in assessing progress against targets: the selection of a baseline year influences both the denominator and the annual rate of change that can be used for projections. Using the year of the SEU's report, 1999, as the baseline, the average annual fall up to 2002 for the under 18 age group is 2.0%. Projecting this forward to 2004 suggests a total fall of 10% (compared to the 15% DH target) and a fall of 20% by 2010 (compared to the 50% SEU target).

However, using the most favourable possible combination of dates – 1998 as the baseline, and the average annual fall between that year and 2001 – the DH is exactly on target to achieve its 15% reduction by 2004. A cynical observer would conclude that this was not a coincidence, especially since there is no mention of a 15% target in earlier policy documents. Nevertheless, even on this optimistic basis, the 2010 target will not be met unless there is a significant change in the trend: the fall, if this trend continues, will be 25%, only half the SEU target.

Outputs from various parts of the policy seem promising: 79% of 13- to 17-year-olds recognise campaign materials and the Sexwise helpline has received 1.4 million calls from young people (Teenage Pregnancy Unit, 2003). However this does not yet seem to be feeding through into a step change in the trend in conception rates.

The responsive arm of policy on teenage parenthood has arguably been more successful. An evaluation of the early phases of 'reintegration' programmes found that it was not so much a case of reintegration as integration for the first time in many cases. Reintegration officers were very successful in overcoming the barriers to continuing (or recommencing) education, and provided support to the young mothers in a number of other ways (Selman et al, 2001; Hosie, 2003). According to the Teenage Pregnancy Unit (2003), 27% of teenage mothers were in education, training or work in 2003, compared to 16% in 1997. The target of 60% by 2010 does not seem out of reach.

## Rough sleepers

### Inheritance

Street homelessness was a very visible problem in London and other major cities in the 1990s. The increases in the numbers sleeping rough in the 1980s and 1990s may have been due to restrictions on benefits for young people, tightening definitions of 'vulnerable' single people whom local authorities had a duty to house and a reduction in the supply of social housing (Pleace, 2000). However, by 1997, the numbers had already begun to fall, as a result of the Rough Sleepers Initiative and other programmes (Randall and Brown, 1999).

The consequences of rough sleeping are extreme: rough sleepers aged 45 to 64 have mortality rates 25 times higher than the general population, death by unnatural causes is four times more common than average and suicide is 35 times more likely (SEU, 1998b).

The SEU found there were insufficient hostel places free on any one night, funding streams were fragmented, and there was an almost total lack of preventative work. Statutory services were often difficult for homeless people to access, especially general practitioners and social security benefits.

## Policies adopted

As with many of the SEU reports, there appears to be a disjunction between the evidence-based analysis of the problems and the policies that are proposed to address them. In the SEU's publication, *Rough sleeping* (1998b, p 20), "the explicit intention of the policy is to deliver clear streets", and, "the public will feel they have a right to expect hostel places to be taken up as more become available". This is odd, given that a few pages earlier, the report identifies significant problems with hostel provision: often unsafe, unsuitable for couples, those with addictions or mental health problems or those with dogs. The report also quotes evidence suggesting that only about 5% of street homeless sleep rough by choice.

Similarly, the report states that service providers must ensure that their services are "not so attractive that they draw in more clients" (SEU, 1998b, p 24), yet analysis presented earlier shows that the immediate triggers for homelessness are relationship breakdown, de-institutionalisation and unemployment – not people seeking services available to them only if they are homeless. Overall, the government stopped short of further criminalising rough sleeping but there was explicitly a 'tough' element to the policy.

Following the report, the Rough Sleepers Unit (RSU) was established to coordinate policy, with a key target of reducing the number of people sleeping rough to one third of the 1998 level by 2002. Its total budget, drawn mainly from existing schemes, was £200 million over three years.

One of the key innovations was establishing Contact and Assessment Teams (CATs) for 'assertive' street outreach work. The CATs allocated individuals unique numbers, thus providing for the first time the possibility of tracking individuals through different placements and services. The RSU also supported Tenancy Sustainment Teams for ex-street homeless, in an attempt to reduce the speed of the revolving door between unsupported tenancies and street homelessness.

Other strands of the policy were aimed at those at highest risk of becoming street homeless. The Department of Health was asked to investigate the provision of ongoing care for care leavers beyond the age of 16, the Prison and Probation Services were given a new performance indicator on preventing homelessness, the Ministry of Defence was to improve education and training for current service personnel to aid transition to civilian life, and the DfEE was to spread good practice about alerting young people to the realities of homelessness. In addition, housing authorities were to be given clearer guidance about who to include under statutory homelessness provisions, so that 'vulnerable' groups included care leavers and 16- to 17-year-olds with no parental support.

Commentators argued that New Labour policy represented "more continuity than change" (Crane and Warnes, 2000, p 26). However, the higher profile given to the issue and the renewed efforts to coordinate policy more effectively across departments was broadly welcomed.

### Outcomes

Table 10.2 shows the estimated number of people sleeping rough, in London and in England as a whole, at various dates. It is difficult to obtain accurate estimates, because the population is a widely distributed and mobile one. All the figures in the table are based on street counts of the number of people found by enumerators on a single night. This approach is likely to lead to an underestimate, first, because counts take place only in areas known to have a relatively high density of street homelessness; second, because people sleeping in hidden places such as car parks and vacant buildings may be missed; and third, because rough sleepers who know that a count is to take place may seek to avoid being enumerated, through fear of being moved on, arrested or harassed. This last reason could have become more of a problem over the period if rough sleepers perceived the approach of the RSU to be more coercive than previous programmes. In general, however, the trend is more reliable than the point estimates.

A count on a single night can only provide a snapshot; the flow over a year is much greater. In 2000/01, 3,031 different individuals were contacted by CATs in London, compared to a single night street count of 319 in May 2001 (Randall and Brown, 2002).

**Table 10.2: Estimated number of people sleeping rough**

| Date | 'Street count' of number of people sleeping rough on a single night | |
| | England | London |
|---|---|---|
| 1983 | – | 486 |
| 1991 (census) | 2,674 | – |
| June 1998 | 1,850 | 650 |
| June 1999 | 1,633 | – |
| June 2000 | 1,180 | – |
| May 2001 | – | 319 |
| June 2001 | 703 | – |
| November 2001 | 550 | – |
| June 2002 | 596 | – |
| June 2003 | 504 | 267 |
| % change | 1998 to 2002: –68% | 1998 to 2003: –59% |

*Note:* There is seasonal variation in rough sleeping, so the counts in November are not directly comparable with those carried out in May or June.
*Sources:* Randall and Brown (2002); ODPM (2003b); Shelter (2001)

Notwithstanding these caveats, the estimates in the table indicate that the target of reducing street homelessness to one third of its 1998 level by 2002 was met for England as a whole.

The RSU was evaluated by Randall and Brown (2002). The work of the CATs and the Tenancy Sustainment Teams were largely deemed a success. The free direct access shelters funded by RSU were found to be an important piece of the jigsaw of provision and one that was previously missing. The evaluation highlighted some remaining problems:

- These are continuing high rates of return to the streets. Of the individuals contacted by CATs in London in 2000/01, 55% were helped into some sort of accommodation. About two fifths of these were known to have returned to the streets subsequently.
- Evictions and bans from hostels and shelters still affect a large number of rough sleepers. There are also continuing difficulties for those with pets or partners, drug users and individuals with behavioural problems.
- Those now on the streets have higher average levels of need. An increasing proportion use hard drugs, and a high proportion have unmet mental health needs.

The evaluation also drew attention to the need to address the flow of new arrivals. In 2000/01, over 1,000 CAT contacts were first contacts, indicative of the rate of new arrivals. In addition, the current prioritisation of hostel beds for rough sleepers can mean that others who need access to hostels, for example when a tenancy has broken down, can be excluded and hence, paradoxically, lead to rough sleeping (Shelter, 2001). It remains to be seen whether the 2000 Homelessness Act, which required local authorities to develop a strategy to *prevent* homelessness in a broader sense than just rough sleeping, will have a significant impact on the flows onto the streets.

## Omissions: asylum seekers

As noted in this chapter's introduction, the SEU's approach of targeting specific groups has much to commend it but a drawback is the inevitable omission of many vulnerable groups. One such group for whom the risks of exclusion are acute and about whom there have been several major policy interventions since 1997 is asylum seekers.

There are some important dimensions of the asylum debate that this section will not address. The most fundamental is whether immigration controls can be philosophically justified at all, given the moral arbitrariness of where an individual happens to be born (see, for example, Jordan and Düvell, 2002). Another question is whether the restriction of the number of asylum seekers coming to the UK is defensible on a pragmatic basis, given the small number of applicants relative to the population and the high skill levels of new arrivals, in a context of low unemployment and a worsening 'dependency ratio'. Important as these questions are, this is not the place to consider them. Rather, in common with the rest of this chapter, this section concentrates on how a vulnerable group have fared under New Labour; that is, the impact of government policy on those who succeed in overcoming the legal, financial, practical and psychological barriers of gaining entry to the country.

The focus here is on asylum seekers, as distinct from immigrants. Moreover, the analysis concentrates on asylum seekers (that is, those whose refugee status has yet to be determined) rather than on refugees. In principle, once an asylum seeker is accepted as a refugee, he or she is entitled to benefits and services on the same basis as a UK-born citizen. In practice, integration and resettlement support is very limited.

*Inheritance*

Figure 10.3 shows the trend in asylum applications to the UK since 1990. The increase since 1997 is large by comparison with the 1990s, but by no means unprecedented: a bigger rise in proportionate terms took place at the end of the 1980s, due to a large increase in the volume of claims by Kurds, Somalians and Ugandans.

It is useful to put these figures in international context. Within the EU, the UK has been the largest recipient of asylum applications for the years 2000-2003 (Home Office, 2004). As discussed later in this chapter, the number of asylum applications *to* a particular country is largely determined by which countries are generating asylum seekers at the time. For this reason, comparing host countries

**Figure 10.3: Total number of asylum applications to the UK**

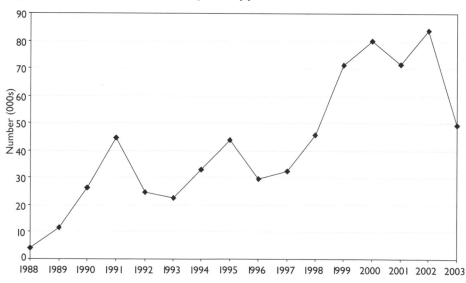

*Source:* Home Office (2004) and previous editions

over a short period can be misleading. Since 1990, the UK has received fewer asylum seekers than its European neighbours, both in absolute terms and proportionately to its population (Table 10.3). Ranked according to the number of asylum seekers per head of population in the EU between 1990 and 2003, the UK comes ninth, with its rate almost identical to the EU average.

Globally, it is the poorer countries of the world that bear the greatest burden of providing for refugees. There were over 20.5 million 'people of concern' to UNHCR in 2003, three quarters of whom were being hosted by developing countries (people of concern are refugees not yet settled or integrated asylum seekers, internally displaced people and stateless individuals) (UNHCR, 2003).

Asylum flows are the result of a combination of push and pull factors. Push factors are determined by the conditions of war, civil unrest and oppression in the countries of origin. Analysis by Castles et al (2003) confirms that the shifting balance between countries of origin of asylum seekers in the EU is correlated with the timing of conflicts. The patterns are not consistent with the hypothesis that asylum seekers are economic migrants by another name.

Pull factors are important in determining to which country asylum seekers apply. They depend on perceived or actual cultural links, through language, existing community or family, past colonial tie, and former labour recruitment (Stalker, 2002). Research suggests that the availability of welfare benefits is not an important influence on asylum seekers' choice of destination, since most have no knowledge of what their entitlements would be (Robinson and Segrott, 2002).

The combination of factors is apparent in the list of countries that were the most common countries of origin for asylum seekers in the UK in 2001-2003: Iraq, Afghanistan, Somalia, Zimbabwe and China. The UK is directly involved in continuing conflicts in the first two of these countries, and has colonial links

**Table 10.3: Asylum claims submitted in the EU (1990-2003)**

| Country | Number of claims | Percentage of total claims | Per 1,000 population |
|---|---|---|---|
| Sweden | 349,700 | 6.6 | 39.4 |
| Austria | 249,800 | 4.7 | 30.8 |
| Belgium | 283,400 | 5.3 | 27.5 |
| Netherlands | 433,500 | 8.1 | 27.0 |
| Germany | 2,168,000 | 40.7 | 26.3 |
| Denmark | 117,900 | 2.2 | 22.0 |
| Luxembourg | 9,700 | 0.2 | 21.7 |
| Ireland | 59,300 | 1.1 | 15.2 |
| **UK** | **851,930** | **16.0** | **14.4** |
| France | 485,700 | 9.1 | 8.1 |
| Finland | 29,600 | 0.6 | 5.7 |
| Greece | 47,000 | 0.9 | 4.3 |
| Spain | 113,100 | 2.1 | 2.8 |
| Italy | 118,800 | 2.2 | 2.1 |
| Portugal | 6,400 | 0.1 | 0.6 |
| Total | 5,323,830 | 100.0 | 14.0 |

*Source:* UNHCR (2004)

with the other three. (Britain occupied parts of present-day Somalia from the 1880s to independence in 1960.)

The first two columns of Table 10.4 summarise the entitlements of asylum seekers in 1993, when the first asylum legislation in the UK (except in relation to specific resettlement programmes) was passed, and under the 1996 Asylum and Immigration Act. The latter introduced a distinction between applicants who applied when already in the UK ('in-country' applicants) and those who applied immediately on arrival ('at port' applicants), presumably as a proxy for those respectively less and more likely to have a well-grounded fear of persecution[3]. All benefit entitlement was removed for in-country applicants. This measure was challenged in the courts and effectively overturned by a series of rulings that

**Table 10.4: Changing entitlements of asylum seekers**

| | Acts of Parliament | | | |
| | 1993 | 1996 | 1999 | 2002 |
|---|---|---|---|---|
| **Benefits** | | | | |
| *claim made 'at port'* | 90% IS + all other | 90% IS + HB + CTB only | No benefits. Excluded from 1948 and 1989 Acts. Vouchers (value 70% IS) | NASS cash support if applied asap and would otherwise be destitute (value 70% IS) |
| *claim made 'in-country'* | 90% IS + all other | No benefits. LA support through 1948 National Assistance Act and 1989 Children Act if otherwise destitute | As above | No benefits. NASS support only if denial would constitute human rights abuse ("section 55") |
| **Housing** | Housing Benefit. LA housing. Restricted access to homelessness assistance | Excluded from waiting lists for LA housing | All rights to social housing removed. NASS accommodation arranged through compulsory dispersal | 'At port' applicants: induction centres followed by NASS dispersal. 'In-country': NASS only if denial would constitute human rights abuse |
| **Right to work** | No restrictions | Not for first six months | Not for first six months | Not for duration of asylum claim |

*Notes:* The table shows the effects of the Acts as eventually implemented. IS = Income Support; HB = Housing Benefit; CTB = Council Tax Benefit; LA = local authority; NASS = National Asylum Support Service

  1948 National Assistance Act
  1989 Children Act
  1993 Immigration and Asylum Appeals Act
  1996 Asylum and Immigration Act; also 1996 Housing Act
  1999 Immigration and Asylum Act
  2002 Nationality, Asylum and Immigration Act
*Sources:* Various

found that legislation dating back to 1948 required local authorities to provide for the basic needs of those who would otherwise be destitute. Local authorities, especially those who hosted larger numbers of asylum seekers, resisted this additional demand on their resources (Cohen, 2002).

The 1997 Labour government, therefore, inherited a conflict between local and central government, and between parliament and the courts, over the treatment of asylum seekers. One straightforward solution, advocated vociferously by Labour in opposition, was to restore benefit entitlement; this was not, however, the route the new government took.

## Policies adopted

In contrast to the reports produced by the SEU on other groups, the government's 1998 White Paper on asylum did not begin with an overview of research but simply asserted:

> There is no doubt that the asylum system is being abused by those seeking to migrate for purely economic reasons. Many claims are simply a tissue of lies. (Home Office, 1998b, para 1.14)

Asylum policy under New Labour was clearly not to be an area of evidence-based policy making.

The right-hand columns of Table 10.4 continue the story. (For simplicity, the special rules applying to asylum seekers who are appealing or who have exhausted their rights of appeal are not included.) The 1999 Act removed benefit entitlement from *all* asylum seekers and explicitly excluded them from the coverage of the 1989 Children Act and 1948 National Assistance Act. It created the National Asylum Support Service (NASS) to deliver two main services: the distribution of vouchers to asylum seekers to purchase food and essential items, and the compulsory dispersal of asylum seekers to accommodation around the country, provided under contract by local authorities, voluntary organisations and private landlords. The objectives were to relieve pressure on local authorities in areas of the country in which asylum seekers were concentrated and to deter economic migrants (and, de facto, anyone else) from using the asylum system.

The 2002 act provided for the phasing out of vouchers in favour of support through accommodation centres. Since accommodation centres were expected to take time to build and make operational, the act allowed for cash support through NASS in the interim, but on a more restricted basis. From January 2003, NASS support has been available only to applicants who apply for asylum 'as soon as reasonably practicable' on reaching the country and who can show that they have no other means of support. (Asylum seekers who have, or are, children under 18 are exempt from this restriction.) Those denied support have become known as 'Section 55' cases, after the part of the act which describes the exclusions. The 2002 act also extended the period in which asylum seekers are forbidden to take paid employment to encompass the entire duration of the claim process.

Successful legal challenges were made to the implementation of Section 55 in early 2003 and again in March 2004 on behalf of individuals denied support, on the grounds that it breached their rights under the European Convention on Human Rights (ECHR). This has led to two reviews of decision making procedures, ensuring fewer people are denied basic support, but no substantive change in policy.

At the time of writing, another Asylum and Immigration Bill is making its way through parliament – the third since 1997. The government's original proposals for 'simplifying' the appeals process, described by the Lord Chief Justice as "fundamentally in conflict with the rule of law" (quoted in a Refugee Council press release, 16 March 2004), have been dropped. The proposed ending of NASS support and the imposition of 'workfare' for asylum seekers whose claims have been refused still stands. It has also been announced that free health care will be withdrawn from asylum seekers in this situation (DH, 2003b). It appears that a further tightening of the screws is intended, and that healthcare is being drawn into the range of services to which access is limited.

The summary shows a progressive reduction in the financial and material support available to asylum seekers, halted only temporarily by 'ping-pong' between the government and the courts about the minimum level of assistance the state is legally required to provide. It also shows the marginalisation of asylum seekers from mainstream services and society – from Income Support to vouchers, from local authority housing to segregated accommodation centres and from the opportunity to support themselves through paid work to exclusion from employment. The policies pursued are consistent with the 'less eligibility' principle of the Poor Law era[4]. Without any evidence that the disincentives are effective in deterring those the government wishes to deter, and without any mechanism to identify them except through their response to the reduction and stigmatisation of support available, the policies inevitably punish the deserving and undeserving alike.

## Outcomes

### Dispersal

The choice of locations to which asylum seekers were dispersed generated considerable tensions. All the areas were areas of low housing demand and high levels of deprivation; some were already experiencing racial tension before the arrival of asylum seekers (Cohen, 2002). In Manchester, those asylum seekers placed by the local authority were housed in wards that were already ethnically diverse, but asylum seekers placed through private landlords were sometimes located in wards without significant ethnic minorities (Neuburger, 2001).

The combination of dispersal and restrictions on travel meant that asylum seekers were cut off from important sources of support. There are an estimated 500 refugee community organisations in London but very few elsewhere (Sales, 2002); specialist lawyers and health professionals are also concentrated in the capital. Difficulty in accessing services in dispersal areas was found in several studies, including GPs (Johnson, 2003), schools (Cohen, 2002) and community care assessments (Roberts and Harris, 2002).

### *Vouchers*

Vouchers proved to be a costly and cruel mistake. The unit cost for supporting a single asylum seeker on Department of Social Security benefits was £425 per month in 1999/2000; under the voucher scheme in the following year it was £700 (Oxfam, 2000). Advice agencies described a catalogue of delays, misinformation and errors in the administration of the scheme (NACAB, 2002a, 2002b). Asylum seekers were often left without means of subsistence for days or weeks at a time.

Even in the absence of administrative errors, the voucher system was problematic. Vouchers could only be exchanged at specific outlets, sometimes several miles from the accommodation to which the asylum seeker had been dispersed (Oxfam, 2000). No change was given for vouchers, which effectively reduced their value. Many basic goods and services were inaccessible because they were too expensive or unavailable in the designated outlets, including, for example, religious dietary requirements and nappies (Eagle et al, 2002). Being excluded from the cash economy was widely perceived to be stigmatising and asylum seekers reported experiencing hostility and racist abuse from other shoppers and sales staff (Sales, 2002).

### *Section 55*

Early experience of the stipulation in the 2002 act that applicants must apply for asylum 'as soon as reasonably practicable' in order to be eligible for support, showed that it was being interpreted extremely strictly. Forty-nine per cent of clients who were refused Section 55 support in a survey period (November 2003) had applied for asylum the same day or the day after they arrived in the UK (IAP, 2004)[5].

Moreover, a very high threshold was placed on what constituted a breach of human rights, and therefore legitimate grounds for appeal against denial of support: destitution itself was deemed insufficient; rather, it had to be shown that there had been a significant deterioration in physical or mental health *as a result of* destitution. Successful legal challenges have produced a marginally more lenient regime, but for those refused support the situation remains grave.

Unsurprisingly, 70% of those refused support under Section 55 in the Inter-Agency Partnership survey had difficulty getting food (IAP, 2004). Sixty-one per cent were on the streets, adding an estimated 140-150 people to the total of rough sleepers in London on any one night (Mayor of London, 2004). The conflict between current asylum policy, and the policies on rough sleeping considered earlier in this chapter, is stark.

### Overall outcomes

When the number of asylum applications fell in 2003 (see Figure 10.3), the government was quick to claim success for its new regime. However, the drop in 2003 was part of a wider picture of falling applications across the EU as a whole, by an average of 22%. More careful analysis suggests that, as in previous years, the fluctuation in asylum numbers has more to do with the state of conflict and oppression in countries of origin and the cultural and historical links between them and host countries, than it does to do with changes in entitlements for asylum seekers (UNHCR, 2004).

This analysis is backed by research commissioned by the Home Office itself. Zetter et al (2003) concluded that withdrawal of benefits and other entitlements in the 1990s had had limited impact on reducing numbers of asylum seekers. Another Home Office study (Robinson and Segrott, 2002), found that asylum seekers had very little idea before they arrived in the UK about what benefits or accommodation they would be entitled to, or to what procedures they would be subject[6]. They certainly had not carried out a comparison of the advantages and disadvantages of the UK's provision relative to other European countries.

In short, the attempt to deter 'undeserving' asylum applications through restricting welfare entitlements was misguided. At the same time, the withdrawal of benefits and associated measures has a devastating impact on 'deserving' and 'undeserving' cases alike. Under current rules, even those fortunate enough to be deemed eligible for support are entitled to a weekly income which is *one third* of that required to be on the poverty line[7]. Other dimensions of social inclusion for asylum seekers are similarly circumscribed: they are denied the right to seek employment, have only limited and problematic access to health services and are dispersed to highly deprived areas without social networks, where they are vulnerable to harassment and physical attacks. In future, their children are to be educated in segregated institutions. It would be hard to concoct a better recipe for social exclusion.

Asylum policy is not an example of joined-up government. In 1997, Robin Cook announced that the new government would be pursuing an 'ethical foreign policy', but since then UK arms sales have continued to represent a higher proportion of GDP than for any other country in the world. Many of these sales are to countries currently engaged in conflict and which generate flows of asylum seekers. The combined efforts of the Foreign Office, Department of Trade and Industry and the Ministry of Defence directly counteract the determination of the Home Office to reduce the number of asylum applications. The response of the Home Office, withdrawing all legal means of subsistence from some asylum seekers, is in turn contrary to policies being advocated by the SEU, the Department for Work and Pensions and, indeed, the Home Office itself – to reduce rough sleeping, encourage productive employment and to create a tolerant, inclusive society.

## Assessment

The government's own assessment of the success of its social exclusion strategy is currently in progress (SEU, 2004). At time of writing, the political future of the Social Exclusion Unit itself hangs in the balance: being moved from the Cabinet Office to the Office of the Deputy Prime Minister gives a distinct impression that policy to counter marginalisation of vulnerable groups is itself being marginalised.

In terms of the groups initially identified as a priority by the SEU, the degree of joining up across government and beyond initiated by the SEU has been innovative and largely successful. The genuinely evidence-based approach adopted by the SEU was also refreshing. However, although the analysis of the problems was often excellent – identifying structural causes of disadvantage and the short- and long-term impacts on individuals – the policy recommendations did not always match. Offering advice and exhortation to the group in question to manage their lives better feature more prominently in the policy solutions than the analysis of the roots of the problem would lead one to expect.

One of the difficulties may have been a certain timidity in confronting actual or perceived conflicts of interest; for example, between pupils at risk of exclusion and their less disruptive classmates, between rough sleepers and the general public, or between asylum seekers and 'home-grown' deprived populations. Is the reason for tackling social exclusion because it is bad for individuals or because it is bad for society? In some cases, the government's approach seems to have been weighted in favour of the interests of the included majority.

The SEU made extensive use of targets. To be useful, targets need to avoid perverse incentives and to be non-manipulable. The target on teenage conception rates scores well in this respect, although it seems unlikely that it will be met. Truancy targets have shifted from 'unauthorised absence' to attendance – a tougher standard that will require pupils to change their behaviour, and which has, as yet, shown little improvement. By contrast, the targets on rough sleeping and school exclusions were less robust – and these were both met.

The selective approach of the SEU was perhaps necessary, but it was also limiting. Other parts of government have been creating social exclusion as fast (or faster) than the SEU has been tackling it. Policy towards asylum seekers has had disastrous consequences in this respect: failing to achieve its own objectives, while creating acute suffering and isolation among an already vulnerable group, and storing up problems of race relations for the longer term. Perhaps we should worry less about whether the government is doing enough to promote inclusion than whether the government is doing too much in creating exclusion. Monitoring the impact on social inclusion and exclusion of a wide range of policies needs to be brought into the mainstream. All major policy proposals could, for example, be subject to a social exclusion audit, much like the regulatory impact audits and environmental impact assessments that are currently undertaken. This might avoid, or at least mitigate, the worst excesses of exclusionary policy.

## Acknowledgement

I am grateful to the editors of this volume, and to Ruth Lupton, Jenny Neuburger and Philip Noden for very helpful comments on earlier drafts. Responsibility for errors of fact or judgement is mine alone.

## Notes

[1] Since the Standards Fund was designed, in part, to help improve pupil attendance and behaviour, this seems likely to have been counterproductive.

[2] For truancy, departmental targets and the series given in *Opportunity for all*, the government's annual assessment of progress, have been switched from unauthorised absence to 'school attendance'. School attendance is 100% minus unauthorised and authorised absences. This series shows a 0.4 percentage point improvement since 1996/ 97 (DWP, 2003d). School attendance is a more robust measure, because the distinction between authorised and unauthorised absence is applied inconsistently across schools.

[3] A poor proxy, it might be said, given that in the latest available data (third quarter 2003), 79% of those eventually granted refugee status had applied when already in the country.

[4] The 'less eligibility' principle is that public welfare provision should be so unattractive that anyone who has an alternative means of supporting him or herself will not choose to rely on the state.

[5] The survey was carried out by the Inter-Agency Partnership (IAP). This is made up of the six main refugee organisations contracted to NASS to provide advice and emergency accommodation to newly arrived asylum seekers. The proportion of new arrivals with whom they have contact is unknown, but is probably around 80%.

[6] Similarly, 152 of 154 clients in a Refugee Council survey (IAP, 2004) did not have prior information on the UK asylum system and 8% did not even know they were coming to the UK until they arrived.

[7] Comparing entitlement of a couple without children to the poverty line for them, using a poverty line of 60% of median equivalised income after housing costs for the whole population (DWP, 2004a).

# Part Three:
# Overall impact

# ELEVEN

# Inequality and poverty under New Labour

*Tom Sefton and Holly Sutherland*

## Introduction

One of the legacies of the Thatcher years was the marked shift towards greater inequality. While average incomes grew rapidly during the 1980s, the benefits were spread very unevenly. Between 1979 and 1996/97, the median income of the richest 10% increased by over 60% in real terms, but that of the poorest 10% rose by just 11% (or fell by 13% if incomes are measured after housing costs). Although inequality did stop rising during the recession of the early 1990s, it started to rise again in the mid-1990s. When Labour came to power in 1997, the distribution of incomes in Britain was more unequal than at any time in recent history. The increase in inequality over the preceding twenty years was also exceptional in international terms.

Previous research suggests a number of factors contributed to rising inequality (Hills, 2004a, ch 4):

- a dramatic rise in the dispersion of earnings between low- and high-skilled workers, which is widely attributed to technological changes favouring those with greater skills;
- a large increase in the proportion of workless households, even after individual employment rates returned to the levels they were at in the late 1970s;
- the increasing importance of other sources of income, such as occupational pensions and income from savings and self-employment, which are even more unequally distributed than earnings; and
- tax and benefits policies that did not dampen the rising inequality in market incomes: uprating benefits in line with prices, rather than earnings, meant that a growing minority fell gradually further behind the rest of the population, while discretionary changes in taxes during the 1980s favoured the rich.

This chapter assesses New Labour's approach to income inequality:

- What has New Labour said on this subject prior to being elected and since coming into power?
- How has the level of inequality changed since 1997?
- What policies have they introduced that may have had an impact on the distribution of incomes, including policies designed to address the long-term drivers of inequality, as well as more conventional redistribution through the tax and benefit system and spending on public services?
- Have these policies been successful in halting and reversing the trend rise in inequality?

There is an important distinction between inequality and poverty, although the two are clearly related. The most common way of measuring poverty is to compare the incomes of the poorest households against the median income. (The poverty line is typically defined as 60% of contemporary median household income, after adjusting for differences in household size.) This is effectively a measure of inequality, although only a partial one that is determined by what is going on in the bottom half of the income distribution. Chapters Seven and Eight examined poverty among two specific subgroups – children and pensioners, respectively. This chapter fills a gap by looking at changes in overall poverty, including the working-age population. However, the main focus is on inequality and what has happened to incomes across the whole distribution, including the top end.

## New Labour's approach

The Labour Party's stance on inequality has changed considerably since the 1970s when Dennis Healey threatened to "tax the rich until the pips squeak". Ministerial statements about inequality and about redistribution, in particular, have been cautious, almost embarrassed at times. According to Leonard (2000), 'Third Way' politics is undecided on whether inequality in itself is axiomatically bad, whether the gap in itself matters, or whether an increasing gap is acceptable within an increasingly fluid social order that is becoming more prosperous.

New Labour's emphasis to date has been on raising the living standards of the poorest, rather than on curbing those of the richest. So, on the one hand, it set itself an ambitious target in 1999 to eliminate child poverty within a generation. The new approach to measuring child poverty would require the UK to reduce the proportion of children living in households with incomes below a relative poverty line to a level that is 'among the best in Europe'. If this is to be achieved, it will entail a very significant reduction in inequality between the incomes of many of those at the bottom and those in the middle of the distribution.

On the other hand, it has made a very conscious effort not to be seen to be trying to penalise those at the top end of the income distribution, starting with its electoral commitment in 1997 not to raise either the basic or higher rates of income tax. Although subsequent tax changes have been progressive – benefiting poorer households proportionately more than richer ones – the top rate of income tax remains untouched. In a Newsnight television interview about the gap between rich and poor, Tony Blair said this:

> The issue isn't in fact whether the very richest person ends up becoming richer. The issue is whether the poorest person is given the chance that they don't otherwise have ... the justice for me is concentrated on lifting incomes of those that don't have a decent income. It's not a burning ambition of mine to make sure that David Beckham earns less money. (Quoted in Bromley, 2003, p 74)

There was an influential body of opinion in the 1970s and 1980s that greater inequality was necessary to restore Britain's economic vitality; lower rates of tax, for example, would reward success and promote innovation, the benefits of which would eventually trickle down to everyone. While these arguments have since lost much of their potency, something of them lives on in New Labour's hands-off approach to top earners.

Yet, there is inevitably a tension between New Labour's commitment to social justice and tackling social exclusion, on the one hand, and its concerns about the economic and political consequences of pursuing a more overtly egalitarian agenda, on the other. One way that New Labour has attempted to resolve this tension is by seeking to redefine the problem in terms of equality of opportunities, as opposed to incomes. 'Third Way' philosophy gives less weight to income redistribution and more weight to other policies designed to improve the life chances of the poorest, such as Early Years initiatives, raising the educational attainment of disadvantaged pupils, widening access to higher education and welfare-to-work programmes. This is summarised in a statement made by Gordon Brown in 1996:

> For too long, we have used the tax and benefit system to compensate people for their poverty rather than doing something more fundamental – tackling the root causes of poverty and inequality ... the road to equality of opportunity starts not with tax rates, but with jobs, education, and the reform of the welfare state. (Cited in Powell, 1999, p 17)

Arguably, this is an issue about the means rather than the end. If successful, improving the opportunities of those who are disadvantaged presumably ought eventually to feed into reduced income inequality, although, like other long-term objectives, this makes it harder to assess the impact of government policies in the short term.

New Labour's approach to inequality can be contested on at least two grounds. First, the choice between redistributing incomes and redistributing opportunities need not be as stark as has sometimes been implied. Critics have pointed out that there was "a subtle shift from arguing that tackling poverty cannot simply be about extra money for those on benefit, which no one disputes, to arguing that better benefits can play no role at all" (Lister, 1998, p 15). Indeed, many would argue that genuine equality of opportunity is not possible in such an unequal society (Lister, 2001). Subsequent redistributive government budgets have stolen some of their thunder, but these critics would still argue that New Labour policies have placed too much emphasis on 'work for those who can' and neglected the 'security for those who cannot'.

Second, there is evidence from public attitudes surveys of concern about incomes that are seen as too high. When asked how much they think people in particular jobs are paid and how much they should be paid, the gap between the highest- and low-paid occupations is around twice as large as is felt appropriate (even though people generally underestimate the extent of earnings inequality). Furthermore, the 'problem' of inequality is seen to lie at least as much at the upper end of the income distribution. It is not so much that those on low incomes are seen to be underpaid; rather, those on higher incomes are seen as being very much overpaid (Bromley, 2003; Hills, 2004a). If this evidence is taken at face value, then it is much harder to justify the government's passive stance to rising inequality at the top end of the income distribution. However, New Labour has apparently taken the view that such attitudes are not sufficiently strongly held to support a much more progressive tax system. Even on the issue of large pay increases for senior executives, where there is greatest public disquiet, the government has said very little and done even less to try to limit 'excessive' pay increases.

## Changes in income inequality and poverty since 1997

The analysis presented in this section is based on the official Households Below Average Income dataset, which covers a representative sample of UK households (DWP, 2004a). This measures household income from all the main sources, including benefits, and net of direct taxes, adjusted for differences in household size and composition. For ease of presentation, we mainly focus on one measure of income, before deducting housing costs (BHC), although the broad conclusions are the same if the after housing costs (AHC) measure is used.

The level of income inequality was relatively stable throughout the 1960s and 1970s, rose sharply in the 1980s and has been relatively stable again since the early 1990s (Figure 11.1). The Gini coefficient shows a slight increase between 1996/97 and 2002/03, which is statistically significant at the 5% level (Brewer et al, 2004). Since the Gini coefficient is the most frequently cited indicator of inequality, this has led to the general perception that inequality had risen under Labour, in spite of all its policies to tackle poverty and social exclusion (for example, Bunting, 2003; Robinson, 2003). However, this increase is very small by comparison with the rise that occurred in the preceding period, and even smaller if incomes are measured after housing costs.

A particular feature of the Gini coefficient is that it gives a relatively high

**Figure 11.1: Measures of overall income inequality (1961 to 2002/03)**

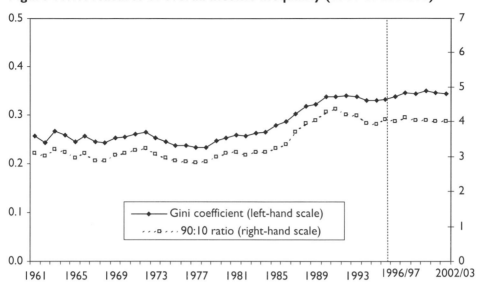

Note: Based on equivalised household incomes before housing costs.
Source: Using data from an updated version of the Institute for Fiscal Studies Inequality Spreadsheet, which is available on the IFS website (www.ifs.org.uk/inequalityindex.shtml). Based on HBAI dataset

weight to the distribution of incomes at the top end (Clark and Taylor, 1999). Figure 11.1 also shows changes in an alternative indicator of inequality, the 90:10 ratio, which is the ratio of the incomes of households at the 90th and 10th percentiles. According to this indicator, inequality has actually fallen very marginally over the same period (more so for AHC incomes). Incomes at the very top end of the income distribution (above the 90th percentile) have continued to rise at a faster rate than average; this pushes the Gini coefficient up, but does not affect the 90:10 ratio. However, throughout most of the income distribution, incomes have become slightly less unequally distributed (see later in this chapter). Overall, considering both these indicators and the historical context, it seems more reasonable to conclude that inequality has been broadly unchanged since 1996/97.

On either indicator, inequality has fallen in the two most recent years (between 2000/01 and 2002/03), which may mark the beginning of a downward trend, although it is too early to tell.

As well as putting recent changes into context, this graph also shows that inequality has generally risen during periods of economic growth (in the early 1970s and 1980s), and fallen (or stopped rising) during recessions (in the late 1970s and early 1990s). Even if earnings growth is evenly distributed across the earnings distribution, inequality will tend to rise during an upswing, because a proportion of poorer households are economically inactive and will, therefore, fall further behind the rest (unless benefits are raised at least in line with average incomes). Seen in this light, the fact that inequality has not risen significantly in recent years could be seen as a positive achievement and contrary to what we might otherwise have expected during a period of fairly rapid economic growth.

Figure 11.2 shows how incomes have changed at different points across the whole distribution. Between 1996/97 and 2002/03, average incomes grew at a relatively fast rate: around 3% per annum in real terms. Across most of the distribution – between about the 15th and 85th percentile – it is generally poorer individuals who have gained most over this period, which would explain the fall in certain indicators of inequality, such as the 90:10 ratio. This also accounts for the slight decline in relative poverty over this period (see later in this chapter), as the gap between the incomes of some households near the bottom of the income distribution and those in the middle has narrowed. This contrasts with what happened over the 1980s (also shown in Figure 11.2) when average incomes grew at about the same rate, but the benefits were concentrated among the rich.

However, it is what is happening at the two extremes of the income distribution that explains the small rise in overall inequality, as measured by the Gini coefficient. Individuals in the bottom 15 percentiles have experienced slower income growth than average, particularly those at the very bottom. This may in part be due to measurement error: incomes at the very bottom of the income distribution, which include many self-employed, are notoriously unreliable. However, this is unlikely to be purely a measurement issue. Other factors are also likely to have played a role, including the non take-up of benefits, the selective nature of benefit increases and temporarily low incomes during transitions to and from being in work and on benefits (Brewer et al, 2004). There is some evidence, therefore, that

**Figure 11.2: Annual growth in real incomes (1996/97 to 2002/03)**

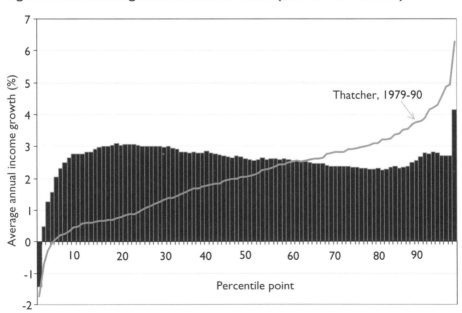

*Source:* Adapted from Brewer at al (2004), based on HBAI dataset

certain groups near the bottom of the distribution have not benefited from recent reforms or at least not enough to keep up with the rest of the population. We return to this later in assessing the impact of the government's tax and benefit reforms.

At the same time, incomes at the very top of the income distribution have been growing at a faster rate than average. Above the 85th percentile, income growth rises with income, with a large 'spike' at the 99th percentile – higher than at any other percentile point. This is a continuation of an existing trend, whereby income growth during the 1980s and 1990s have been concentrated in the top part of the income distribution (Table 11.1). The share of total income received by the top decile group rose from 20.4% in 1979, to 26.1% in 1996/97, and 27.7% in 2002/03, while the shares received by each of the bottom eight decile groups either fell (up to 1996/97) or remained roughly constant (between 1996/97 and 2002/03). An analysis of individual incomes using tax records – rather than household incomes using survey data – tells a similar story of growth being concentrated among the very richest 0.5% or so of individuals (Atkinson, 2002). Thus, rising inequality has been driven by what has been happening at the very top of the income distribution as much as, if not more than, by what has been happening at the bottom end.

As discussed earlier in this chapter, New Labour's policies to reduce inequality have tended to focus on the bottom half of the income distribution and on the reduction of poverty rates among children and pensioners in particular (see Chapters Seven and Eight of this volume for details on progress in reducing child and pensioner poverty). Table 11.2 shows the change in relative poverty rates (below 60% of median incomes measured before housing costs) in the period between 1979 and 2002/03. During Labour's period of office, overall poverty rates have been falling in absolute terms (that is, relative to a fixed poverty line) as real incomes have grown to some extent for all groups. However, relative

**Table 11.1: Share of total income received by income group (1979 to 2002/03[a]) (%)**

| Decile group (tenth of individuals) | 1979 | 1996/97 | 2002/03 |
|---|---|---|---|
| Bottom | 4.2 | 3.1 | 2.8 |
| 2nd | 5.7 | 4.7 | 4.7 |
| 3rd | 6.7 | 5.6 | 5.6 |
| 4th | 7.6 | 6.6 | 6.6 |
| 5th | 8.6 | 7.7 | 7.6 |
| 6th | 9.6 | 8.9 | 8.8 |
| 7th | 10.8 | 10.3 | 10.1 |
| 8th | 12.2 | 12.1 | 11.7 |
| 9th | 14.2 | 14.9 | 14.4 |
| Top | 20.4 | 26.1 | 27.7 |

*Note:* [a]Based on net equivalised household incomes before housing costs.
*Source:* Using data from an updated version of the Institute of Fiscal Studies Inequality Spreadsheet, which is available on the IFS website (www.ifs.org.uk/inequalityindex.shtml). Based on HBAI dataset

**Table 11.2: Trends in relative and absolute income poverty[a]**

|  | 1979 | 1996/97[b] | 2002/03 |
|---|---|---|---|
| **Relative poverty: income below 60% of contemporary median (%)** | | | |
| All | 12 | 18 | 17 |
| Children | 12 | 25 | 21 |
| Pensioners | 28 | 21 | 21 |
| Working-age adults | 7 | 15 | 14 |
| – of which those with children | n/a | 19 | 16 |
| – of which those without children | n/a | 12 | 13 |
| **Absolute poverty: income below 60% of 1996-97 median in real terms (%)** | | | |
| All | 30 | 18 | 10 |
| Children | 34 | 25 | 12 |
| Pensioners | 62 | 21 | 12 |
| Working-age adults | 19 | 15 | 10 |
| – of which those with children | n/a | 19 | 10 |
| – of which those without children | n/a | 12 | 9 |

*Notes:* [a] Based on net equivalised household incomes before housing costs;
[b] Financial year. This and later figures for GB (earlier figures for UK).
*Sources:* DWP (2004a, Tables F3.1 H1, H2, H4, H5, H6, H7, H8)

to contemporary median incomes the overall poverty rate only fell by one percentage point. Relative poverty among children and working-age adults with children fell significantly, while among pensioners it remained at the same level, reflecting the later timing of major benefit increases for low-income pensioners. Working-age adults *without* children actually saw a small increase in their risk of relative poverty over this period (from 12% to 13%), because most of their benefits have been uprated by no more than prices.

Thus, policies aimed at reducing poverty among children had made some progress, but had not contributed much in terms of overall relative poverty reduction, at least up to 2002/03. Even if the government's policies are successful on their own terms, they may be limited in their impact on overall inequality, because they have been selective in whom they have helped at the bottom end of the income distribution and have not addressed rising inequality at the top end.

In summary, income inequality has been relatively stable since the early 1990s, including the period since 1997. There has been a small increase on the most commonly cited indicator, but a small fall on an alternative indicator that gives less weight to incomes at the extremes of the distribution. This is unusual compared with previous upswings when inequality has risen significantly. In contrast to what happened during the 1980s, individuals in the lower-middle section of the income distribution have experienced above-average income growth and have been catching up with those in the middle. However, there is also evidence that those at the very top are continuing to pull away from the rest, while many of those at the very bottom are not doing so well. On the latest figures, relative poverty rates have fallen for children, but have stayed constant for pensioners and risen slightly for working-age adults without children.

## Assessing the impact of New Labour policies

There are two ways of looking at what has happened in recent years. On the one hand, critics point out that income inequality in the UK has not fallen and, at least until recently, has been worsening on the most common measure of inequality. Inequality is still at, or close to, its highest level since consistent data on incomes have been collected at the beginning of the 1960s – and this, after seven years of a Labour government. Government policies have been variously criticised for being on the right lines but not going far enough; for placing too much emphasis on paid work as a route out of poverty; and for being too selective, giving plenty of help to families with children, for example, but ignoring the plight of single people and couples without children (see, for example, Lister, 2001).

On the other hand, a more optimistic interpretation is that the trend rise in inequality under previous Conservative governments has at least been stemmed, even if it has not yet been reversed. While inequality did start to stabilise, and even fell slightly, in the early 1990s, this was during an economic recession when inequality often falls in any case. By the mid-1990s, inequality appeared to be rising again prior to the election in 1997. It could, therefore, be regarded as a positive achievement that inequality has not risen further during a period of fairly rapid economic growth. Other things being equal, we might have expected rising earnings to have pushed up the incomes of the richest households relative to the poorest. If this is the case, then government policies may have prevented the situation from getting worse and may even have started to reduce inequality in the two most recent years.

Furthermore, the level of relative poverty, which this government has always emphasised rather than the overall level of income inequality, has fallen among the group that it is most concerned about – *children*. It is a significant achievement that relative poverty has fallen and that the gap between those at the bottom of the income distribution and those in the middle has narrowed, at least for some types of households, during a period when median incomes have themselves been rising fast. Some would argue that it is of less concern that a relatively small proportion of individuals at the very top of the income distribution may have done even better. This is certainly the stated view of the Prime Minister. Against their own target for reducing child poverty (and this is an ambitious target), New Labour have made significant progress to date and seem to be on track to meet their 2004/05 target to reduce the numbers of children in relative poverty by a quarter (see Chapter Seven of this volume).

Proponents of either view would recognise that reducing inequality is not something that can easily be achieved in the short term. Many of the factors that have contributed to rising inequality over the last two decades are structural phenomena that may take a long time to shift. It has been argued that a particular feature of the UK, which has made it vulnerable to the decline in the market for unskilled labour, is the much higher proportion of low-skilled individuals compared to other developed countries, except perhaps the US. Illiteracy rates are much higher in the UK than in other north European countries – around 20%, compared to between 5% and 10% (based on figures for the mid-1990s) – and there is no sign of any improvement among younger age groups (Nickell, 2003; see also Chapter Three of this volume). This suggests that any substantial improvement, if there is to be any, is likely to be gradual and largely the consequence of long-term policies aimed at tackling the root causes of inequality.

The next section looks at recent trends in two of the main driving forces of the rise in income inequality during the 1980s: rising pay differentials between high- and low-skill workers and the increasing number of workless households. In particular, we look at whether there is any evidence of change in either of these trends and, if so, how far this might be attributable to government policies, such as the National Minimum Wage (NMW) and the various New Deal programmes. The subsequent sections focus on the impact of changes in the tax and benefit system (the government's most direct instrument for tackling inequality) as well as public spending on in-kind benefits, such as health care and education.

## Changes in long-term drivers of income inequality

### Earnings dispersion

Earnings inequality is the largest single contributor to overall inequality, reflecting its overall importance in total household incomes (Goodman et al, 1997). The gap between the lowest- and highest-paid workers has widened considerably since the late 1970s and continues to widen. For full-time male earnings, the ratio between the 90th and 10th percentiles – the 90:10 ratio – rose from just under 2.5 to just over 3.5 between 1979 and 2003 (Figure 11.3). A similar trend is evident in full-time female earnings (not shown here), although the differential between low and high earners has not risen quite as sharply as for men.

Figure 11.3 shows that, up until the mid-1990s, the earnings of the lowest paid were falling behind those in the middle of the earnings distribution, who in turn were falling behind the highest earners. In other words, earnings were becoming more dispersed across the whole distribution. Over this period, the average hourly wage of those in the bottom decile group of earners grew by around 24% in real terms, compared with 36% for the median earner, and 68% for those in the top decile group.

Since the mid-1990s, the picture is slightly different. Those at the top of the distribution are still pulling further ahead of those in the middle – the 90:50 ratio in Figure 11.3. However, low earners appear to be keeping up with or even catching up with middle earners – the 50:10 ratio. Again, the same trend is evident in the earnings distribution for full-time female employees.

An important feature of the rise in wage inequality during the 1980s was the increasing wage differential between workers with high and low levels of education. A leading explanation is that technological change has increased the

**Figure 11.3: Changes in the distribution of male earnings (1971-2003)**

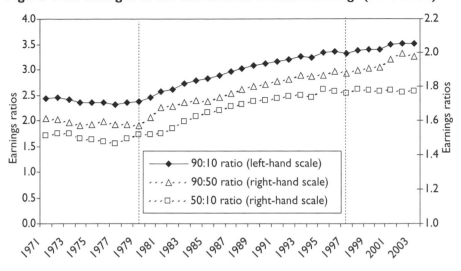

*Note:* Gross weekly earnings for full-time male employees.
*Source:* New Earnings Survey

returns to higher levels of skill – 'skill-biased technological change'. Controlling for age, men with a degree (or higher) in 1980 had a wage premium of 48%, compared with men with no qualifications. By 1995, this wage differential had risen to 72%, despite the rapid rise in the education levels of the workforce (Machin, 2003).

There is some preliminary evidence that wage differentials by education levels may have stopped rising at the end of the 1990s and at the start of the 2000s (Machin, 2003). One explanation is that this is due to the very rapid expansion of the higher education system having a moderating influence on wage inequality, by reducing or tempering the wage premium for more educated workers. If this is indeed the case, then it could continue in the future as the higher education system expands further with the government seeking to increase to 50% by 2010 the proportion of young people staying on to higher education. However, this does not explain the changes that have occurred in the earnings distribution in recent years. The 50:10 earnings ratio stabilised and started to fall well before the wage premiums for educated workers appear to have stopped rising.

A particular Labour policy that might help to explain what has happened at the bottom end of the earnings distribution is the introduction of the NMW. However, there are several reasons for being sceptical about its likely impact on the trends noted above. First, the timing is not right: the NMW was introduced in April 1999; but Figure 11.3 shows that the 50:10 ratio stopped rising several years before this. Second, analysis by Dickens and Manning (2003) suggests that, at most, it is likely that only 3.7% of adult workers are likely to have benefited directly from the NMW; that is, too few to have had a significant effect on this measure of earnings inequality.

The impact on poverty and income inequality is even less clear-cut, because some of those who have benefited are second earners in middle-income households. The biggest gainers from the NMW are households in decile groups three to six, while the very poorest households have relatively few beneficiaries because they tend to be out of work or retired. As such, NMW will always have a limited role in reducing poverty and income inequality; the overall effect is likely to be positive, but small. So, although the earnings of low-paid workers are no longer falling behind median earnings (and may even be catching up somewhat), it is difficult to attribute very much of this improvement to this government's policies.

The NMW should instead be seen as part of a package of measures designed to make work pay and increase work incentives, possibly contributing towards the increase in employment rates in recent years, especially among lone parents (see later in this chapter). More specifically, the NMW made it possible for the government to offer a more generous system of tax credits to low earners without employers taking as much advantage as they otherwise could by cutting gross wages below the minimum level.

### Worklessness

Worklessness has been another major contributor to growing inequality. Between 1981 and 1996, the proportion of households with no one in work increased from around 11% to nearly 20%, even though the individual non-employment rate was around the same level in both years (Table 11.3). Households with no one in work were, and still are, much more likely to be on relatively low incomes. Three quarters of workless households are poor and this is a particularly important driver of child poverty. Furthermore, the gap between them and the rest of the population grew rapidly during the 1980s. Benefit increases were generally tied to prices rather than earnings, so these households, who depend on benefits for most of their income, have gradually fallen further behind the rest of the population.

So what explains the increase in household worklessness? Changes in the demographic composition of households are part of the explanation, in particular the growing proportion of single person and lone parent households. Lone parent

**Table 11.3: Household worklessness, Britain (1975-2002) (%)**

|  | Employment rate | Workless (households of working age) | Households where all adults work |
|---|---|---|---|
| 1975 | 76.6 | 6.5 | 56.2 |
| 1981 | 72.9 | 10.9 | 51.8 |
| 1985 | 71.6 | 16.5 | 51.8 |
| 1990 | 76.9 | 14.6 | 60.9 |
| 1996 | 74.6 | 19.3 | 60.7 |
| 2002 | 77.3 | 16.8 | 65.7 |

*Source:* Gregg et al (1999) and Gregg and Wadsworth (2003), based on data from the Labour Force Survey

households have very low employment rates, compared with other types of households and compared with lone parent households in other EU countries (see Chapter Fourteen, Figure 14.8, of this volume). In 1996, 60% of lone-parent households were workless, compared with 9% of couples with children. However, even among two-adult households, work has become more polarised between households: a greater proportion of these households had two or more earners, but also a greater proportion had no earners (Gregg and Wadsworth, 2003).

The New Labour government has introduced a series of policies designed to encourage people in these households to enter work, by increasing the returns to work, encouraging people to look for work and tackling other barriers to moving into work. This package of measures includes tax credits for low-paid workers, the NMW, New Deal programmes and an increase in childcare provision.

Since 1996, the proportion of workless households has fallen from 19.3% to 16.8% (Table 11.3). The improvement has been most marked among families with children, with nearly 500,000 fewer children in workless households than in 1996. The greatest increase in employment rates was among lone parents – from 47% in 1996 to 53% in 2002. This rise began before Labour were elected, but the rate of increase in employment was notably faster after 1998 when government policies aimed at raising the employment rates of lone parents, the New Deal for Lone Parents and the Working Families Tax Credit, came into effect. Research found that these policies raised the proportion of lone parents in work by at least five percentage points, compared with a matched control group of single people with otherwise similar characteristics (Gregg and Harkness, 2003). This was achieved despite increases in welfare payments to lone parents who are not in paid work.

While the employment situation of lone parents has improved substantially in recent years, this effect has been counteracted by the increase in the proportion of lone parents and single people, both of whom are more likely to be workless than other types of household. Meanwhile, inactivity rates among low-skilled workers and those with a long-standing limiting illness or disability – other groups that have relatively high inactivity rates – have not fallen in spite of policies targeted at these groups (Faggio and Nickell, 2003).

Overall, Gregg and Wadsworth (2003) find that, although the distribution of employment between households became less 'polarised' between 1996 and 2002, the improvement was no greater than would be expected given the growth of the economy over this period. However, things have stopped getting worse – and they probably would have got worse without the government's policies to increase employment rates among lone parents.

## Impact of tax and benefit policies

Most of those on low incomes are dependent in whole or in part on income from the state. In order to understand what is happening at the bottom end of the income distribution, it is important, therefore, to examine the distributional impact of changes in the tax and benefit system. Tax and benefit policy is also the most direct and immediate instrument the government has to influence the income distribution.

Since Labour came to power, it has increased out-of-work benefits to selected groups, in particular families with children and, more recently, pensioners. It has also introduced a number of new or extended measures to make work pay, including tax credits for low-earning families. We would expect these policies to have had an equalising impact on the income distribution. In order to estimate the size of this, a micro-simulation model is used to estimate the impact of changes in the tax and benefit system since 1997. The advantage of this approach is that we can hold other factors constant, such as the demographic composition and employment patterns of the population, in order to isolate the net impact of tax and benefit changes over this period. This is done by using a single representative sample of the British population and recalculating incomes according to the tax–benefit systems in place in 1997 and in 2004/05. Incomes are uprated to 2004/05 levels, based on forecasts of earnings growth and growth in other sources of income (see Sutherland et al, 2003, for details of the methodology).

The results presented in this chapter are based on a comparison between estimated incomes in 2004/05 under the 2004/05 tax–benefit regime and estimated incomes in 2004/05 if the tax–benefit regime had remained as it was in 1997. All benefit levels and tax thresholds are uprated to 2004/05 prices, so the 1997 policy scenario assumes, for example, that the basic state pension rises in line with prices over the period 1997 to 2004/05. The 2004/05 policy scenario will, therefore, pick up any increases in benefit levels over and above the rate of inflation.

Taken as a whole, the impact of tax and benefit policies introduced since 1997 imply a significant redistribution of income towards those with low incomes, compared with what would have happened if the old system had simply been adjusted for inflation (Figure 11.4). The results are broken down by individuals' family type, distinguishing between pensioners, families with children (which includes children and working-age adults with children), and working-age adults without children. All income groups up to and including the eighth decile gain, on average, from changes under the projected impact of the 2004/05 tax–benefit system. These gains are substantially greater as a proportion of incomes (and in absolute terms) for individuals in lower income groups – up to a quarter of average incomes for individuals in the bottom decile group. Overall, and within each income group, the gains are substantially greater for pensioners, children and working-age adults with children than for working-age adults without children.

Table 11.4 shows the estimated impact of changes in the tax–benefit system on two different indicators of income inequality. The policy impact under a price-indexed system is equivalent to a fall of around three percentage points in

**Figure 11.4: Distributional impact of changes in tax–benefit system (1997 to 2004/05) (projected)**

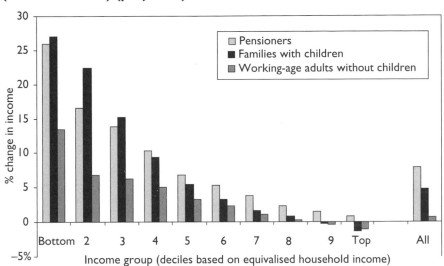

*Note:* Policy-induced change in incomes as a percentage of household incomes before housing costs.
*Source:* Authors' estimates using POLIMOD

the Gini coefficient (from 33.8% to 31.0%). This effect is smaller than the rise in inequality that took place between 1979 and 1996/97, but significant. The reduction in the Gini coefficient is around one third of the size of the increase over the previous 20 years and the impact on the 90:10 income ratio is even larger by comparison – over half the size of the increase over the preceding period.

This result is sensitive to the benchmark against which current (that is, 2004/05) policies are compared. In a price-indexed system, relative benefit levels would fall over time (assuming earnings grow at a faster rate than inflation) and so

**Table 11.4: Impact of policy on income inequality (1997 to 2004/05)**

|  | Gini coefficient[a] | 90/10 ratio[a] |
|---|---|---|
| (1) 1997 policies (price-indexed system)[b] | 0.338 | 4.346 |
| (2) 1997 policies (earnings-indexed system)[b] | 0.325 | 3.971 |
| (3) 2004/05 policies[b] | 0.310 | 3.660 |
| Policy impact on inequality: | | |
| – price-indexed system (3)-(1): | –0.028 | –0.686 |
| – earnings-indexed system (3)-(2): | –0.015 | –0.311 |
| Net change in inequality, 1979-1996/97[c] | +0.084 | +1.058 |
| Net change in inequality, 1996/97-2002/03[c] | +0.013 | –0.047 |

*Notes:* [a] Based on net equivalised household incomes before housing costs;
[b] Simulation results, rather than actual income data;
[c] IFS figures, based on HBIA dataset.
*Source:* Authors' estimates using POLIMOD

inequality and relative poverty would rise; current policies are thus being compared above with a benchmark that assumes growing inequality. An alternative benchmark would be the 1997 tax and benefit system indexed by some measure of average income growth. Other things being equal, inequality and relative poverty rates would be stable under this scenario. When compared with this more generous version of the 1997 system, the projected 2004/05 tax and benefit system is still more egalitarian, but the impact on both measures of inequality is reduced by about a half.

Thus, if other factors had not changed over this period, then policy changes would have made a significant indent on the rise in inequality over the preceding period. However, other factors have inevitably changed. Over the period 1996/97 to 2002/03, it appears that offsetting effects, such as the continuing rise in earnings inequality, have more or less cancelled out any beneficial effects on inequality from changes in the tax and benefit system. Unless there are more fundamental changes in some of the underlying drivers of inequality discussed in the previous section of this chapter, progressive changes to the tax and benefit system are always likely to be working against the tide of pre-tax and benefit growth in inequality.

One specific criticism of this government's redistributive policies is that its carefully targeted strategy for alleviating relative poverty has been too carefully targeted (Robinson, 2003). Some groups have benefited significantly from redistributive policies, notably families with children and, more recently, pensioners. However, those whose incomes have remained tied to prices may be falling further behind in the income distribution. Table 11.5 provides some evidence to support this case. Calculating changes in the Gini coefficient within subgroups of the population shows that the reductions in inequality have been greater among pensioners and children than among working-age adults without

**Table 11.5: Impact of policy on income inequality and poverty by family type and individual status (1997 to 2004/05)**

|  | 1997 policies[b] (price-indexed system) | 2004/05 policies | % change |
|---|---|---|---|
| **Impact on Gini coefficient[a]** | | | |
| Children | 0.328 | 0.288 | −12 |
| Pensioners | 0.277 | 0.248 | −10 |
| Working-age adults without children | 0.334 | 0.322 | −4 |
| **All** | **0.338** | **0.310** | **−8** |
| **Impact on relative poverty rates (%)** | | | |
| Children | 27 | 15 | −44 |
| Pensioners | 27 | 19 | −30 |
| Working-age adults without children | 13 | 13 | 0 |
| **All** | **20** | **14** | **−30** |

Note: [a] Based on net equivalised household incomes before housing costs;
[b] Simulation results, rather than actual income data.
Source: Authors' estimates using POLIMOD

children. Also shown are changes in relative poverty rates due to the policy changes alone. While child and pensioner poverty rates under 2004/05 policies are 44% and 30% lower than they would be if 1997 policies had remained on a price uprated basis, poverty rates for working-age adults without children remain unaltered by policy changes.

## Impact of the social wage on inequality

So far, the analysis of inequality has been based solely on cash incomes. The income measure used is net of direct taxes, but ignores some of the benefits of government spending that those taxes are used to fund. The value of spending on services such as the NHS, state education, social housing and social services can be thought of as income in-kind – a 'social wage' – that represents a substantial addition to cash incomes, and has a distributional effect of its own. The government has put a strong emphasis on improving public services and has begun to translate this into higher spending on health and education, in particular. Although standard indicators of income inequality generally ignore the social wage, its inclusion is necessary if we are to capture the overall distributional impact of the government's social policies.

Recent research estimates that the social wage is worth over £2,000 per annum for individuals in the bottom two fifths of the income distribution around twice as much as for individuals in the top fifth (Sefton, 2002). Furthermore, this 'pro-poor' bias has been rising gradually over the long term. Since 1996/97, spending on these services has been growing at a faster rate than over the previous twenty years and there has been a further incremental shift in favour of lower-income groups across all the major services. The overall impact of changes in the social wage is smaller than the impact of changes in the tax and benefit system (around half the size) and less progressive, but the effect is significant and reinforces the distributional effects of fiscal reforms over the same period.

A measure of 'final' income can be calculated by adding the monetary value of the social wage to cash incomes. On average, the social wage makes up around a sixth of household's final income, but this is much higher for individuals lower down the income distribution – up to 40% for those in the bottom fifth. As expected, inequality is significantly lower when the social wage is included. (To have no effect, the social wage would need to be as unequally distributed as cash incomes.) However, the equalising impact of the social wage was roughly constant between 1996/97 and 2000/01. On the one hand, the social wage has become more pro-poor since 1996/7, which, other things being equal, would have reduced the inequality in final incomes. On the other hand, the social wage grew more slowly than cash incomes over this period, so its share in final incomes has fallen; other things being equal, this would lead to increased inequality in final incomes. These two factors virtually cancel each other out (Table 11.6), hence the impact of the social wage on inequality has been neutral up to this point, although

**Table 11.6: Impact of the social wage on inequality (1996/97 to 2000/01)**

| | Impact on Gini coefficient[a] | | |
| | 1996/97 | 2000/01 | Change: 1996/97–2000/01 |
| --- | --- | --- | --- |
| Cash incomes | 0.337 | 0.353 | +0.016 |
| Final incomes | 0.276 | 0.291 | +0.015 |
| **Social wage effect** | **–0.061** | **–0.061** | **–0.001** |

Note: [a] Based on net equivalised household incomes before housing costs.
Source: Author's estimates based on analysis of data presented in Sefton (2002)

substantial increases in public spending since 2000/01 may have had a small equalising impact.

## Conclusion

Income inequality has neither risen nor fallen significantly since 1997. One indicator of inequality shows a small rise over this period, while a different indicator shows a small fall. The discrepancy is accounted for by changes that have occurred at different points in the income distribution. The gap between incomes at the very bottom and top has increased a little, but the gap between those *near* the bottom and those in the middle or *near* the top has fallen a little. The net effect on inequality depends on the weight attached to changes at the very extremes of the income distribution. These changes are, in any case, small compared with the rise in inequality that took place over the preceding 20 years.

There are two ways of looking at what has happened in recent years. On the one hand, income inequality in the UK has not fallen after seven years of a Labour government, despite all the resources that have been channelled to low-income households. While the poorest households have benefited most from recent changes in the tax–benefit system, some households, notably working-age adults without children, have benefited much less than others, if at all. Some of the underlying problems that have led to rising inequality in the past, such as the high proportion of individuals with very low skills, will not be resolved quickly. While household worklessness has fallen in recent years, the distribution of work remains polarised between households. The gap between low earners and middle earners may have narrowed slightly, but it is difficult to attribute very much of this improvement to government policies. Meanwhile, incomes at the very top end of the income distribution have continued to grow at a faster rate than the average and Labour has said little and done even less to address public concerns on this issue. This is in spite of evidence which shows that rising inequality has been driven by what has been happening at the very top of the income distribution as much as, if not more than, by what has been happening at the bottom end.

On the other hand, the trend rise in inequality under previous Conservative governments has at least been stemmed, even if it has not yet been reversed and this has been achieved during a period of rapid economic growth when inequality has tended to rise in previous economic cycles. The level of poverty, which this government has focused on rather than overall income inequality, has fallen or is predicted to fall among those groups that it is most concerned about – children and pensioners. Much of this improvement in the position of low-income households can be attributed to government policies. Changes in the tax–benefit system have strongly favoured the poorest households; we estimate that these have reduced the Gini coefficient by up to a third of the rise experienced over the preceding two decades, compared with what would have happened if 1997 policies had remained in place. Other policies that address the root causes of inequality may also be starting to take effect: improved childcare, and making-work-pay policies have increased the living standards of families with children, especially lone parents. Some would argue that it is of less concern that the incomes of a small minority of individuals at the very top of the income distribution have continued to grow at an even faster rate.

The choice between these two perspectives depends in part on prior expectations: those with a strong belief in a much more egalitarian society are likely to be disappointed by the lack of progress towards this objective. Those who had fewer expectations, or whose expectations were dampened during Labour's first two years in office, may be quietly reassured that things have not continued to get worse and that some progress is now being made. Poverty is back on the political agenda even if explicit redistribution is not yet there. In the short term, tax–benefit policies have had a positive impact on poverty and have prevented inequality rising further. In the longer term, the emphasis on tackling the root causes of inequality should start to pay dividends, while recognising that these policies may take many years to make a real difference and that the growth of very high incomes may need to be addressed. In the end, it is probably too early to judge whether the small progress made under New Labour is 'scratching the surface' of the problem or whether it does indeed represent the beginning of a new trend towards greater equality.

# TWELVE

# That's the way the money goes: expenditure patterns as real incomes rise for the poorest families with children

*Paul Gregg, Jane Waldfogel and Elizabeth Washbrook*

## Introduction

As prior chapters of this volume have documented, there has been a raft of new initiatives in UK labour market and welfare policies (see Chapters Two, Three and Seven in this volume), many of which will have had a particular bearing on mothers' labour market status and child poverty. These include the National Minimum Wage (NMW), Child and Working Families Tax Credits, National Childcare Strategy, improved maternity and family leave provision and New Deals for Lone Parents and Partners of the Unemployed. There have also been benefit increases for families with children (through increases in Child Benefit and Income Support).

The rapid pace of reform means that there have been sharp increases in household income among poor families with children, whose incomes have risen somewhat faster than incomes on average. As a result, the number of children in relative poverty has started to fall. This change is particularly dramatic given the trends prior to 1997.

Over the 20 years prior to 1997, children replaced pensioners as the group with the highest incidence of relative income poverty in UK society. While average incomes of the elderly rose in real terms and this held even among the poorest fifth, the poorest fifth of children in 1996/97 were in households with real incomes no different in absolute terms from those reported for the corresponding group in 1979 (Gregg et al, 1999b; Dickens and Ellwood, 2003; Chapter Seven of this volume). A number of studies, such as Breadline Britain, highlighted the material deprivation experienced by Britain's poor (see, most recently, Gordon et al, 2000, which documents the extent of poverty and social exclusion in Britain in 1999). Gregg et al (1999b) documented how the poorest families with children had fallen further behind other families in spending on children's clothing, shoes, toys and fresh fruit and vegetables, even though low-income families spend proportionately more of their household income on these goods, foregoing spending on other items.

After such a long period of broadly stable real incomes, the sudden burst of rising living standards since 1997 engendered in part by real increases in in-work and out-of-work benefits offers a unique opportunity to assess how household spending patterns among the poorest families with children react to increases in incomes and specifically benefits. Hence, in this chapter, we explore changes in expenditure patterns and access to specific goods and services over the four-year period 1997-2001, as incomes rise in response to benefit changes as well as employment shocks. The data used come from the Family Expenditure Survey (FES) (1996/97 to 2000/01).

Our overall aim is to show where increased income goes in terms of patterns of household consumption and ownership of goods. We pay particular attention to spending on specific items that are directly used or consumed by children (clothing, footwear, fruit and vegetables) or that are likely to promote their learning and development (toys, books, games, computers, and so on). We know from prior research that low-income families lag behind others in their spending on these items; we would like to know whether, as incomes rise, low-income families increase their spending and narrow the gaps.

The methodological approach is to compare spending patterns for low-income families with children to spending patterns of higher-income families with children before and after the policy reforms. Then comparisons between families with children who are more or less likely to be affected by the reforms are undertaken. That is, families can be divided by the age of their children, taking advantage of the fact that families with younger children have seen larger benefit increases.

The chapter also throws some light on how measures of material deprivation move as incomes rise. Specifically, we look at the share of low-income families owning durable goods such as a car, telephone, washing machine, tumble dryer or computer. Understanding how measures of material deprivation move is important in light of the government's decision to include an indicator of consistent poverty, akin to the Irish measure, in its new official poverty measurement. Although the government ruled out using an indicator of consistent poverty as the sole measure of poverty, it will be included in a tiered approach, along with a measure of absolute poverty and relative poverty (DWP, 2003c)[1].

Our results clearly show how low-income families are spending this extra money to produce spending patterns that are rather similar to those of more affluent families. However, they have a number of slightly different emphases in their spending: they clearly are spending less of the extra income on housing and alcohol and tobacco and placing more emphasis on clothing and transport. Further, there is clear evidence of how spending is focused on child-related goods such as children's clothing, toys and books. In these spheres, spending among low-income families is converging to that of more affluent families. Car ownership, central heating, telephones and washing machines are also showing patterns of marked convergence of low-income families and more affluent families. However, there are areas where low-income families are not catching up, most markedly in holidays and the presence of computers within the household. So, the picture that emerges is one of low-income families seeing rising material circumstances and spending the extra money much like more affluent families. Yet they are maintaining spending on goods for children as a priority, more than affluent families. This must be extremely reassuring to policy makers and campaigners arguing for resources to tackle child poverty.

## Background

As other chapters in this volume document, there have been extensive reforms to welfare and labour market policies since New Labour came to office in 1997, and the real incomes of low-income families with children have risen sharply since the reforms (see, in particular, Chapters Seven and Eleven). Recent evidence indicates that low-income families have experienced important declines in financial hardship (Vegeris and Perry, 2003). Yet, we know surprisingly little about what these income gains and declines in hardship have meant in terms of children's well-being. As incomes have risen for the lowest-income families with children, are these families purchasing more goods that contribute to children's well-being? Are the children better-off? And do low-income families spend any extra income differently from better-off families?

Prior research sheds little light on these kinds of questions, because few studies have been able to look at how increases in income affect changes in expenditures or consumption. For the most part, studies have only been able to compare the expenditures of low-income versus higher-income families at a point in time, or over a period of time when low-income families have been losing ground. Gregg et al (1999b) examine family expenditure patterns over the period 1968 to 1995/96, using FES data and dividing families into fifths of the income distribution, and show that low-income families spend less overall, and fewer pounds on child-related items such as children's clothing, shoes and toys as well as fresh fruit and vegetables than more affluent families. Moreover, these expenditure gaps between the lowest-income and more affluent families with children grew over the period, such that they were larger in 1995/96 than they had been in 1968, as spending on children in higher-income families grew while remaining constant or rising just slightly in lower-income families.

Studies by Sue Middleton and colleagues (Middleton et al, 1997; Shropshire and Middleton, 1999) provide more detailed information on what low-income families spend on children and the extent to which children are deprived of basic necessities – items that the majority of parents consider to be essential for children – because their families cannot afford them. Middleton's work also indicates the extent to which parents, especially mothers, sacrifice consumption for themselves in order to protect their children from deprivation.

Two Breadline Britain Surveys, conducted in 1983 and 1990, and the Poverty and Social Exclusion Survey of Britain, conducted in 1999, have allowed researchers to document how the concept of necessities has evolved over the past 20 years and how the share of children deprived of necessities has changed over the same period (Gordon et al, 2000). This work shows that items such as a car and a telephone have increasingly come to be viewed as a necessity (the share viewing these as necessities rose from 22% to 36% from 1983 to 1999 for a car, and from 43% to 72% for a telephone). However, the share of children deprived of necessities because their parents cannot afford them for the most part changed relatively little or, in some instances, increased over the 1990s. There were only a few items that families were substantially less likely to be deprived of in 1999 than in 1990; these included a car (share deprived fell from 18% to 11%), telephone (7% to 2%), videocassette recorder (11% to 2%) and dishwasher (18% to 11%). The increasing share of families owning these items probably reflects their increasingly becoming seen as necessities, as well as their falling prices over the 1990s.

As informative as these cross-sectional studies are, they leave open the question of how increases in income would affect the observed differences in expenditures or deprivation. Cross-sectional studies cannot tell us whether and how additional income would alter the spending patterns and consumption of low-income families. If the incomes of low-income families did rise, how would they spend the money? Would they spend the additional pounds in the same way as the income they had already, or differently? For instance, given prior evidence that adults (in particular, mothers) cut back their own expenditures to shield children from the effects of poverty, would adults use some of the money to make up for the past shortfall in goods for themselves? Or would adults continue to prioritise children and target the extra income mainly on expenditures for them?

Few studies have addressed these types of questions. In a study of child benefit reforms in the 1970s, Lundberg et al (1997) found that shifting benefits from the man's wallet to the woman's purse led to increases in expenditures on both women's and children's clothing[2]. More recently, a qualitative study of 37 low-income families who had moved from benefits to work between 2000 and 2001 found that as incomes rose, families' expenditures changed in a number of ways (for example, more money spent on food, resulting in higher quantity and quality of food purchased, and more money spent on clothing), but mothers continued to prioritise spending on their children (Farrell and O'Connor, 2003). As one lone mother commented:

> No, [your priorities don't change], because you're still buying for your kids.... It's generally them if they want anything. I think even when you're on a small amount of money or a large amount of money you still prioritise them. (Farrell and O'Connor, 2003, p 44)

However, this study also found that, if incomes increased enough, adults began spending more money on themselves, once children's needs began to be met.

Thus, when it came to clothing purchases, parents reported spending additional income first on their children, and then, once their children were well dressed, on themselves. These results suggest, as a working hypothesis, that low-income parents may react to income increases of the type that occurred in our period by continuing to prioritise spending on their children but also by spending some of the additional income to catch up on goods and services for themselves.

As a first step in answering these kinds of questions, in this chapter we look at changes in families' expenditures on children over the period 1996/97 to 2000/01. The 1996/97 data provide information on the living conditions of children immediately prior to New Labour coming to office, while the 2000/01 data (which are the most recent expenditure data available at the time of writing) provide a perspective on the situation of families four years later, after the initial phase of tax credit and benefit reforms (but prior to the April 2003 reforms). We consider the amount that families spend on essential items such as food and clothing for their family, as well as the share of their income that they devote to these items. We consider in detail expenditures on items that the whole family uses, such as food, housing and motoring, and items that are *assignable* to individual family members or categories of family members, such as children's, women's and men's clothing, and children's toys, books, and games. We are particularly interested in the children's items since they are used or consumed by children, or are likely to directly affect their learning and development. We also look at families' ownership of durable goods, such as a car, telephone, washing machine, tumble dryer or computer. We use data from the FES and a method that compares changes for different groups over time, which we describe in the following section. The succeeding sections then present our results, and draw conclusions.

## Data and methods

Our data come from the UK FES, a continuous survey of household expenditure and income which has been in existence since 1957. Annual samples of around 6,000 households provide information about household and personal incomes and certain payments that recur regularly (such as rent, gas, electricity and telephone bills and hire purchase payments) and also maintain a detailed expenditure record for 14 consecutive days. As discussed earlier in this chapter, we analyse data from the 1996/97 and 2000/01 samples.

We restrict our working samples by excluding households in which the head or spouse is over retirement age or in full-time education and also households in which the main source of household income is recorded as self-employment income. (Throughout, the term 'spouse' refers to cohabitees as well as married partners.) Consumption patterns in these households are likely to differ substantially from those of households of childbearing age, which is our population of interest, and, for students and the self-employed, the relationship between income and expenditure is notoriously noisy. This selection results in sample sizes of 4,042 households for 1996/97 (of which 1,826 have a child aged under 16 years of age) and 4,219 households for 2000/01 (1,782 with children).

We classify households according to the presence of a child aged under 16 and, for households with children, according to whether the youngest child is aged 0 to 4, 5 to 10, or 11 to 15 years. In our supplemental analyses, we also distinguish between 'working' and 'workless' households (according to whether at least one of the head or spouse is employed for any hours).

Throughout our analysis, we categorise households as falling into one of three thirds (tertile groups) of the income distribution. Our construction of these income groups gives us confidence that we have separated those most likely affected by the reforms from those least likely to be affected, while still leaving samples large enough to be analysed. Our low-income group, made up of the bottom third of the income distribution, probably captures quite well those families most likely to be affected by the reforms, while our middle-income and especially higher-income tertiles capture those least likely to be affected.

The measure of household income used to define these groups is normal weekly disposable household income, that is, gross income from all sources net of National Insurance contributions, income tax and council tax payments. Housing benefit payments are included in our measure of income (and housing expenditure) regardless of whether they are paid directly to the household. To take account of differences in household size and composition, we deflate the income and expenditure figures for each household by the relevant modified OECD equivalence scale rate to give its equivalent for a childless couple (that is, this scale assigns a weight of 0.67 to the first adult, 0.33 to all other people in the household aged 14+, and 0.2 to children aged under 14; hence a couple without children has a scale rating of 1). (We use the modified OECD scale because it is the one now used in official UK and EU statistics and will be used in monitoring future progress towards eradicating child poverty.) The month in which the household is sampled can vary between January and December, and so, to take account of within-year inflation, all income and expenditure figures are expressed in terms of the same price level – the All Items Retail Price Index (RPI) for September 2003. The upper bounds to the low- and middle-income groups defined on this measure of real equivalised household income are £260 and £431 per week respectively for 1996/97, and £289 and £474 per week for 2000/01.

The FES breaks down total expenditure into 14 categories of goods and services. To simplify our analysis, we combine a number of these categories and comment on nine broad types of expenditure. (Specifically, we group housing with fuel, light and power; alcoholic drink with tobacco; household goods with household services; leisure goods with leisure services; and motoring with fares and other travel costs. Food, clothing and footwear, personal goods and services and miscellaneous expenditure stand alone.) Weekly household expenditure on each of the broad groups is equivalised in the same way as disposable income and expressed in September 2003 prices.

We also present results relating to a number of more narrowly defined goods and services that can be assigned to individual members of the household, or that are of particular relevance for child well-being. The analysis of separate expenditures on children's, women's and men's clothing gives us the rare opportunity to see how spending on a broad category of goods is distributed between different household members. For these expenditures, we do not equivalise using the modified OECD scale, but rather by the number of household members of each type (that is, under 16, female aged 15+ and male aged 15+). Expenditure on toys, hobbies and games is similarly deflated by the number of under-16s in the household. Other narrow groups of expenditure that we examine are books, newspapers, magazines and periodicals, fruit and vegetables and holidays (these three categories are equivalised in the standard way). As before, we present results that express expenditures in terms of the September 2003 All Items RPI. However, we also explored the sensitivity of our results to deflating by price indices more specific to each type of expenditure (for example, we used the Total Food Price Index to deflate spending on fruit and vegetables). Doing so changed the numbers for specific items but did not change the overall pattern of results across income groups[3].

In addition to examining family spending patterns, we also explore the ownership of 'lumpy' consumer durables that make an important contribution to quality of life but that are purchased infrequently and will not show up in weekly expenditure data. We document the proportion of houses possessing a range of ten items such as a car or van, telephone, washing machine and computer.

The FES data allow us to track expenditures of similar types of families over time and to document how expenditures have changed over time. Thus, we can easily track, for instance, the growth in expenditures for families with children since New Labour came into office in 1997. However, we cannot infer that the pattern of spending only reflects the impact of rising incomes after 1996/97, as changing trends and relative prices could have meant changes in spending patterns in the absence of rising incomes. Without a counterfactual, we do not know how much expenditures would have risen without the reforms.

To provide the counterfactual, we use an approach inspired by the difference-in-difference methodology used by economists. We begin by comparing the change in expenditures for our focus group, say low-income families with children (defined as families with incomes in the bottom third of the income distribution), to changes in expenditures for a comparison group, say middle- or high-income families with children (defined respectively as families with incomes in the middle or top third of the income distribution). This can be contrasted with differences in expenditures between the groups at the beginning of the period. This enables us to see whether spending associated with the increased incomes of low-income groups looks more similar to spending patterns of high-income groups than the initial levels.

However, we should still be concerned that expenditures might have been changing differentially for low-income families with children from higher-income families with children for reasons other than the reforms. Perhaps there was increased awareness among lower-income families of the importance of learning or nutrition-related items for children and this awareness, not benefit reforms, boosted the child-related expenditures of lower-income families relative to higher-income families. Further we may wish to explore comparisons among low-income groups where incomes rose faster or slower because of the specifics of the reforms introduced under Labour during the period 1996/97 to 2000/01. For instance, families with younger children saw the largest benefit increases over those four years. Thus, we compare the expenditure patterns for low-income families with young children (children under the age of five) to those for families with older children (children age 5 to 10, or age 11+) over this period. In supplemental analyses, we also contrast working and workless households with children of different ages, since these groups were differentially affected by tax and benefit changes over the four years. However, we place less weight on these latter analyses since we are unable to control for the fact that the composition of the two groups is likely to have changed over time (as workless families moved into work in response to the tax and benefit reforms and the stronger labour market).

## Results

### Changes in income and expenditure

Table 12.1 summarises changes in real equivalised mean disposable income and expenditure levels, in pounds (£s) per week, over the period 1996/97 to 2000/01 for low-, middle- and high-income groupings of households[4]. Looking first at all households, and all households with children under the age of 16, it is clear that all income groups experienced gains in real income and expenditures over the period, with low-income groups tending to have experienced the largest gains as a percentage of their prior levels but less in absolute numbers of pounds. Patterns of increases in income and expenditure broadly match.

When we break out families by age of youngest child (in the bottom part of Table 12.1), we can see that this pattern of stronger relative income and expenditure growth for the low-income families is being driven by the gains made by the families with the youngest children. Low-income families with a child under five years of age saw their incomes rise by 13% and their expenditures by 11%, as compared to increases of only 5% for both income and expenditures for high-income families with a child under five – thus, the difference in the change across the two groups is eight percentage points for income (13%-5%) and six percentage points for expenditures (11%-5%).

The pattern for families with older children is quite different: among families whose youngest child is aged 10+, low-income families saw smaller percentage increases relative to high-income families, their income rising 3% versus 6% for the high-income families, and their expenditures rising 3% versus 7% for the

**Table 12.1: Changes in total income and expenditure levels by household type (1996/97 to 2000/01)**

| | Real equivalised disposable income (£ per week, Sept 2003 prices) | | | | Real equivalised total expenditure (£ per week, Sept 2003 prices) | | | |
|---|---|---|---|---|---|---|---|---|
| | 1996/97 Mean | 2000/01 Mean | Change in £ | % change | 1996/97 Mean | 2000/01 Mean | Change in £ | % change |
| *All households* | | | | | | | | |
| Low income | 177 | 197 | 19 | 11 | 225 | 252 | 27 | 12 |
| Middle income | 342 | 378 | 36 | 10 | 338 | 373 | 34 | 10 |
| High income | 637 | 705 | 68 | 11 | 531 | 581 | 50 | 9 |
| *Households with a child <16* | | | | | | | | |
| Low income | 177 | 199 | 21 | 12 | 220 | 241 | 21 | 9 |
| Middle income | 337 | 371 | 34 | 10 | 334 | 365 | 31 | 9 |
| High income | 614 | 658 | 44 | 7 | 547 | 580 | 33 | 6 |
| *Households with youngest child aged:* | | | | | | | | |
| **0 to 4** | | | | | | | | |
| Low income | 172 | 194 | 22 | 13 | 213 | 235 | 23 | 11 |
| Middle income | 333 | 370 | 38 | 11 | 321 | 357 | 36 | 11 |
| High income | 640 | 674 | 34 | 5 | 539 | 567 | 28 | 5 |
| **5 to 10** | | | | | | | | |
| Low income | 177 | 203 | 26 | 15 | 222 | 244 | 22 | 10 |
| Middle income | 336 | 369 | 33 | 10 | 337 | 366 | 28 | 8 |
| High income | 575 | 648 | 72 | 13 | 550 | 581 | 31 | 6 |
| **11 to 15** | | | | | | | | |
| Low income | 195 | 202 | 7 | 3 | 242 | 248 | 7 | 3 |
| Middle income | 348 | 375 | 28 | 8 | 351 | 377 | 26 | 8 |
| High income | 607 | 644 | 37 | 6 | 558 | 597 | 40 | 7 |

*Notes:*
1) Households in which the head or spouse is over state retirement age or a student are excluded from the sample. Also excluded are households whose main source of income is self-employment income.
2) Income and expenditure are equivalised for household size using the modified OECD scale (with weights 0.67 for the first adult; 0.33 for all other household members aged 14 and over; and 0.2 for all under-14s).
3) Figures are expressed in Sept 2003 prices using the RPI All Items series.
4) Income groups are defined as the three thirds (tertiles) of real equivalised disposable income for the sample as a whole.
5) Income and expenditure include Housing Benefit, whether paid directly or indirectly to households.

high-income families. If we compare the differences for the families with children under five to those for the families with children over ten, the larger gains for families with young children would be sizable. These comparisons for families with children aged 5 to 10 would also be positive, although smaller in magnitude. In this way, the extra welfare spending on families with young children produces an age variation in the reform package that allows us to focus on the impact of the package itself rather than other trends occurring over this time period.

## Patterns of expenditure

Having established that low-income families did experience relatively large income and expenditure gains over our period, we now turn to patterns of expenditures. In our discussion of these results, and the ones that follow, we continue to focus on differences between the changes over time for low- and high-income families with children of different ages.

Table 12.2 shows levels of expenditure on the nine major categories of goods and services recorded in the FES, while Figure 12.1 shows shares of expenditure on these categories in 1996/97 and the changes between 1996/97 and 2000/01. Looking first at Panel A of Table 12.2, for all families with children under age 16 broken down by income group, we can see that low-income families with children did spend their money differently in 1996/97 from more affluent families. Figure 12.1a shows that there was a markedly larger share of expenditure going on essential items, in particular, housing and food. In 1996/97, low-income families allocated 52.8% of their expenditures to housing, fuel, heat and lighting (29.4%) and food (22.4%), whereas this was 40.8% and 36.3% for middle- and high-income groups. In contrast, a far smaller share of income was spent on leisure goods and services and motoring and fares.

The share spent on these two categories of essentials fell to 48.5% in 2000/01 among the lowest-income group, and there was also a marked shift away from alcohol and tobacco, while the shares spent on clothing and footwear, household goods and services, leisure and motoring all increased. Thus, as low-income families' incomes and expenditures increased over the period, their expenditure patterns by 2000/01 had moved towards those seen among middle-income groups at the beginning of the period[5]. Figure 12.1b highlights how changes in expenditure among low-income groups were far more focused on clothing and footwear, household goods and services and motoring and away from housing and alcohol and tobacco. Hence, in these areas low-income groups are closing gaps in the share of expenditure quite rapidly, and for clothing and footwear and household goods and services they actually narrow the absolute spending gap in pounds. Nevertheless, large differences in spending levels remain, even in 2000/01 (see Table 12.2, Column 2). Although low-income families with children did increase their spending on items such as clothing and footwear, household goods and services, leisure, and motoring, their consumption of these items still lags behind that of more affluent families. Furthermore, for motoring, while low-income families narrowed differences in the share of expenditure relative to more affluent families, the absolute spending gap widened. However, the clear overall impression is that, as incomes have risen, spending patterns of low-income families have converged with their more affluent counterparts.

Panel B of Table 12.2 shows levels of expenditure on the nine major categories, for families with a pre-school age child. Here, as noted earlier in this chapter, the increases in income for low-income families have been especially rapid due to sharp increases in welfare payments. In 1996/97, low-income families with young

## Table 12.2: Changes in expenditure on broad categories of goods and services, by household income group

A. All households with a child <16

| | Levels of real equivalised total expenditure (£ per week, Sept 2003 prices) 1996/97 2000/01 | | | | Shares of total expenditure 1996/97 2000/01 | | |
|---|---|---|---|---|---|---|---|
| | Mean | Mean | Change in £ | % change | Mean | Mean | Change in share (% points) |
| *Low-income households* | | | | | | | |
| Housing, fuel, heat and lighting | 60.0 | 58.7 | −1.3 | −2.2 | 29.4 | 26.9 | −2.5 |
| Food | 47.4 | 49.2 | 1.8 | 3.9 | 22.4 | 21.6 | −0.7 |
| Alcohol and tobacco | 14.2 | 13.0 | −1.2 | −8.4 | 6.6 | 5.6 | −1.0 |
| Clothing and footwear | 14.2 | 18.2 | 4.1 | 28.6 | 6.0 | 7.0 | 1.0 |
| Household goods and services | 25.8 | 31.1 | 5.3 | 20.4 | 10.9 | 12.2 | 1.3 |
| Leisure goods and services | 23.6 | 30.9 | 7.4 | 31.3 | 9.8 | 11.7 | 1.9 |
| Motoring and travel | 23.4 | 30.4 | 7.0 | 30.1 | 9.7 | 11.3 | 1.6 |
| Personal goods and services | 8.1 | 8.4 | 0.4 | 4.6 | 3.6 | 3.4 | −0.2 |
| Miscellaneous | 3.7 | 0.8 | −2.9 | −79.0 | 1.6 | 0.4 | −1.3 |
| Total | 220.2 | 240.8 | 20.5 | 9.3 | 100.0 | 100.0 | 0.0 |
| *Middle-income households* | | | | | | | |
| Housing, fuel, heat and lighting | 64.5 | 66.7 | 2.2 | 3.4 | 20.4 | 19.5 | −1.0 |
| Food | 64.5 | 64.5 | 0.1 | 0.1 | 20.4 | 18.8 | −1.5 |
| Alcohol and tobacco | 17.5 | 16.7 | −0.8 | −4.3 | 5.5 | 4.9 | −0.6 |
| Clothing and footwear | 23.7 | 26.2 | 2.5 | 10.6 | 6.8 | 7.0 | 0.1 |
| Household goods and services | 46.6 | 50.9 | 4.3 | 9.2 | 13.2 | 13.4 | 0.2 |
| Leisure goods and services | 48.5 | 64.7 | 16.2 | 33.3 | 13.8 | 16.6 | 2.8 |
| Motoring and travel | 51.3 | 60.6 | 9.3 | 18.2 | 14.8 | 15.8 | 1.0 |
| Personal goods and services | 13.0 | 13.6 | 0.6 | 4.7 | 3.9 | 3.8 | −0.1 |
| Miscellaneous | 4.1 | 1.2 | -2.9 | -71.1 | 1.3 | 0.3 | −1.0 |
| Total | 333.6 | 365.0 | 31.5 | 9.4 | 100.0 | 100.0 | 0.0 |
| *High-income households* | | | | | | | |
| Housing, fuel, heat and lighting | 99.3 | 106.0 | 6.6 | 6.7 | 19.3 | 19.4 | 0.1 |
| Food | 83.1 | 79.0 | −4.0 | −4.8 | 17.0 | 15.5 | −1.5 |
| Alcohol and tobacco | 19.8 | 19.0 | −0.8 | −4.2 | 4.1 | 3.5 | −0.6 |
| Clothing and footwear | 36.1 | 33.6 | −2.5 | −6.9 | 6.7 | 5.8 | −0.9 |
| Household goods and services | 92.3 | 94.7 | 2.3 | 2.5 | 14.3 | 15.3 | 1.0 |
| Leisure goods and services | 99.0 | 119.9 | 20.9 | 21.2 | 17.4 | 19.1 | 1.7 |
| Motoring and travel | 91.2 | 105.2 | 14.0 | 15.4 | 16.4 | 17.3 | 0.9 |
| Personal goods and services | 19.7 | 21.8 | 2.1 | 10.5 | 3.7 | 3.9 | 0.2 |
| Miscellaneous | 6.7 | 1.1 | −5.6 | −83.6 | 1.2 | 0.2 | −1.0 |
| Total | 547.1 | 580.2 | 33.1 | 6.1 | 100.0 | 100.0 | 0.0 |

## Table 12.2: contd.../

B. Households with a youngest child age 0 to 4

| | Levels of real equivalised total expenditure (£ per week, Sept 2003 prices) 1996/97 2000/01 | | | | Shares of total expenditure 1996/97 2000/01 | | |
|---|---|---|---|---|---|---|---|
| | Mean | Mean | Change in £ | % change | Mean | Mean | Change in share (% points) |
| *Low-income households* | | | | | | | |
| Housing, fuel, heat and lighting | 62.4 | 61.5 | −0.9 | −1.4 | 31.3 | 28.8 | −2.6 |
| Food | 43.6 | 46.4 | 2.8 | 6.4 | 21.4 | 21.0 | −0.4 |
| Alcohol and tobacco | 13.1 | 12.8 | −0.3 | −2.2 | 6.4 | 5.6 | −0.8 |
| Clothing and footwear | 12.5 | 18.5 | 6.0 | 47.7 | 5.6 | 7.2 | 1.6 |
| Household goods and services | 26.9 | 30.0 | 3.1 | 11.4 | 11.4 | 12.0 | 0.5 |
| Leisure goods and services | 21.0 | 28.0 | 7.1 | 33.6 | 9.1 | 10.6 | 1.5 |
| Motoring and travel | 22.4 | 27.8 | 5.4 | 24.1 | 9.8 | 10.5 | 0.7 |
| Personal goods and services | 8.7 | 9.5 | 0.9 | 10.0 | 4.1 | 4.1 | 0.0 |
| Miscellaneous | 1.8 | 0.6 | −1.2 | −67.4 | 0.9 | 0.3 | −0.6 |
| Total | 212.5 | 235.3 | 22.8 | 10.7 | 100.0 | 100.0 | 0.0 |
| *Middle-income households* | | | | | | | |
| Housing, fuel, heat and lighting | 67.3 | 72.2 | 4.9 | 7.2 | 22.0 | 21.7 | −0.3 |
| Food | 59.5 | 59.3 | −0.2 | −0.3 | 19.6 | 17.9 | −1.7 |
| Alcohol and tobacco | 15.1 | 16.5 | 1.4 | 9.0 | 5.0 | 4.8 | −0.2 |
| Clothing and footwear | 21.4 | 22.8 | 1.4 | 6.5 | 6.5 | 6.3 | −0.2 |
| Household goods and services | 50.2 | 54.4 | 4.2 | 8.4 | 14.7 | 14.3 | −0.4 |
| Leisure goods and services | 40.7 | 52.0 | 11.4 | 28.0 | 12.1 | 14.1 | 2.0 |
| Motoring and travel | 51.3 | 64.5 | 13.2 | 25.7 | 15.3 | 16.7 | 1.3 |
| Personal goods and services | 13.7 | 13.8 | 0.1 | 0.8 | 4.1 | 4.0 | −0.1 |
| Miscellaneous | 1.8 | 1.2 | −0.6 | −32.6 | 0.6 | 0.3 | −0.3 |
| Total | 321.0 | 356.7 | 35.7 | 11.1 | 100.0 | 100.0 | 0.0 |
| *High-income households* | | | | | | | |
| Housing, fuel, heat and lighting | 109.8 | 109.9 | 0.1 | 0.1 | 21.4 | 21.0 | −0.4 |
| Food | 76.8 | 72.7 | −4.2 | −5.4 | 15.7 | 14.3 | −1.4 |
| Alcohol and tobacco | 16.1 | 16.8 | 0.7 | 4.3 | 3.4 | 3.2 | −0.1 |
| Clothing and footwear | 34.4 | 28.7 | −5.7 | −16.7 | 6.3 | 5.0 | −1.2 |
| Household goods and services | 93.7 | 103.5 | 9.8 | 10.4 | 15.9 | 17.7 | 1.8 |
| Leisure goods and services | 95.1 | 106.9 | 11.8 | 12.4 | 16.3 | 17.3 | 0.9 |
| Motoring and travel | 89.0 | 107.8 | 18.7 | 21.0 | 16.5 | 17.8 | 1.3 |
| Personal goods and services | 21.9 | 20.6 | −1.4 | −6.2 | 4.1 | 3.6 | −0.5 |
| Miscellaneous | 2.3 | 0.8 | −1.5 | -66.7 | 0.5 | 0.1 | −0.3 |
| Total | 539.2 | 567.5 | 28.3 | 5.2 | 100.0 | 100.0 | 0.0 |

*Notes:* See notes to Table 12.1.

**Figure 12.1: Patterns in broad categories of expenditure, by income group, households with children only**

a) Shares of total expenditure allocated to each category in 1996/97

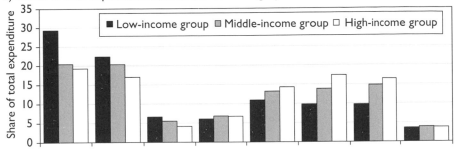

b) Percentage change in expenditure on each category (1996/97 to 2000/01)

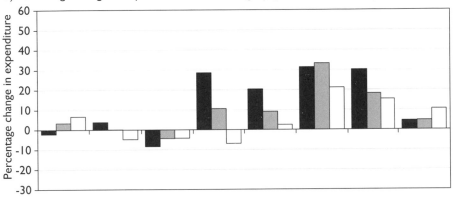

c) Expenditure levels for each category in 2000/01 (equivalised, September 2003 prices)

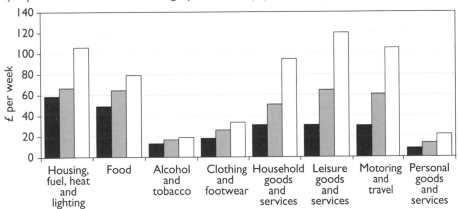

children spent 31% of their income on housing and power and underspent heavily on motoring and leisure goods and services, compared with other families with young children. Low-income families also spent less on clothing and footwear. However, over the period, we can see that low-income families increased their expenditure on this category by £6.00 per week, nearly a 50% increase over their 1996/97 level. In contrast, results for middle-income and higher-income families show that these families increased their expenditure on this category by a much smaller amount, or actually decreased it. As a result, the share of spending that low-income families devoted to clothing and footwear rose, while falling for middle- and high-income families. Low-income families with young children sharply reduced the share of total income spent on housing and alcohol and tobacco. They increased their expenditures on food, although these fell slightly as a share of total expenditures (in contrast to higher-income groups, who decreased their expenditures on food over the period). Since relative food prices were falling over the period, this means that low-income families increased their spending on food in real terms, while middle- and higher-income families cut it[6].

This section suggests that patterns of spending among low-income families have moved towards those of higher-income families, especially in the switch away from housing and alcohol and tobacco and towards clothing and footwear, leisure and motoring. The increases in incomes among poorer families have enhanced this rebalancing in particular with the move towards spending on clothing and footwear and motoring. In addition, the increase in spending on food by low-income families with children, while higher-income families were spending less, suggests that some poor families were initially constrained in spending on essentials.

### Changes in expenditures on children's items, and other items

Within these large expenditure categories, we are particularly interested in items that are used by children or that potentially are related to children's health and development. Prior research has documented the adverse effects of low income, particularly for young children, and also the importance of aspects of the home environment in promoting children's health and development (Duncan and Brooks-Gunn, 1997; Burgess et al, 2004). Accordingly, we examined detailed expenditure patterns on specific items such as children's clothing and footwear, toys, books, games, and so on. We also examined families' expenditures on adult clothing and footwear, to see whether low-income families who had been constrained in their purchases would start to catch up as their incomes rose. The results shown in Tables 12.3 and 12.4 (and Figures 12.2 and 12.3) indicate that as incomes and expenditures were rising for the lowest-income families with children, parents increased their spending on child-related items and on their own clothing and footwear. These shifts are so strong that low-income families are closing the deficit with spending in more affluent families in pounds spent per week.

Table 12.3 (and Figure 12.2) show that expenditure on children's clothing and footwear, per child, grew faster for low-income families than for higher-income families. Among families with children under five years of age, expenditures rose by more than a third for the low-income families as compared to a 17% fall for the most affluent. However, among families with older children this catch-up by low-income groups was not apparent. Expenditures for women's clothing increased for all low-income families with children and more so than they did for higher-income families with children, but to a larger extent (and from a smaller base) for families with children under age five, where expenditures in low-income families rose by more than half. Expenditures on men's clothing increased more rapidly (or fell less) for low-income families with a man in the household than for higher-income families with a man in the household, with particularly large increases for low-income families with children under five or children aged 11 to 15, where expenditures on men's clothing more than doubled. Taken together, these results indicate that low-income families used their additional income in 2000/01 to catch up on clothing and footwear for both the children and the adults in the home, lending some support to the hypothesis that, as incomes rise, parents will continue to prioritise children but will also start making up for some of the shortfall in their own goods.

The FES data also allow us to track families' expenditures on toys, hobbies and games (including computer games). Table 12.4 (and Figure 12.3) show that here as well we see the pattern of low-income families increasing spending on toys and games while spending actually fell among higher-income families. Again, this pattern was much stronger for families with the youngest children (under age five), who made the largest gains relative to high-income families. A similar pattern is found for changes in expenditures on books and other reading material and to a lesser degree fruit and vegetables (although here the small relative gains by low-income families with young children are driven by reductions in expenditures by high-income families with young children, which are likely due to falling relative prices for fruit and vegetables over the period we consider)[7].

There is, then, very striking evidence that low-income families are using their additional income in ways that are likely to benefit children. Toys, books, children's clothing and, to a lesser extent, fruit and vegetables all see convergence in spending towards that of higher-income families, and this is usually more clearly marked in families with younger children where families have enjoyed large increases in benefits and tax credits. Given evidence as to the importance of resources in the home, these gains for low-income children are likely to be important to their health and development. At the same time, parents are also spending some of the additional income on clothing for themselves. This may be because as incomes rise, parents are under less pressure to sacrifice their own consumption and thus begin to catch up on items, such as their own clothing.

The picture for another specific item, spending on holidays, is not so bright. Although low-income families with young children increased their expenditures on holidays by a larger percentage than higher-income families, these increases were from a small base and were dwarfed by much larger increases in absolute terms by higher-income families, so that, by 2000/01, the absolute gaps between low- and high-income families were larger than they had been in 1996/97 (see Table 12.4, and Figure 12.3)[8]. These results suggest that, even with the increases

**Table 12.3: Changes in expenditure on children's, women's and men's clothing and footwear, by household type and income group (September 2003 prices)**

| | Children's clothing and footwear[a] | | | | | Women's clothing and footwear[b] | | | | | Men's clothing and footwear[c] | | | | |
|---|---|---|---|---|---|---|---|---|---|---|---|---|---|---|---|
| | Expenditure in £ | | % change | Expenditure as % of high-income group | | Expenditure in £ | | % change | Expenditure as % of high-income group | | Expenditure in £ | | % change | Expenditure as % of high-income group | |
| | 1996/97 | 2000/01 | | 1996/97 | 2000/01 | 1996/97 | 2000/01 | | 1996/97 | 2000/01 | 1996/97 | 2000/01 | | 1996/97 | 2000/01 |
| *Households with a child <16* | | | | | | | | | | | | | | | |
| Low income | 5.3 | 6.3 | 17.7 | 0.49 | 0.58 | 6.5 | 9.3 | 41.9 | 0.32 | 0.49 | 4.5 | 7.3 | 62.2 | 0.31 | 0.64 |
| Middle income | 8.0 | 9.3 | 16.3 | 0.73 | 0.86 | 11.8 | 13.9 | 17.6 | 0.58 | 0.74 | 9.0 | 9.3 | 2.8 | 0.63 | 0.81 |
| High income | 11.0 | 10.8 | −1.9 | 1.00 | 1.00 | 20.4 | 18.7 | −8.1 | 1.00 | 1.00 | 14.3 | 11.4 | −19.9 | 1.00 | 1.00 |
| *Households with youngest child aged:* | | | | | | | | | | | | | | | |
| **0 to 4** | | | | | | | | | | | | | | | |
| Low income | 4.1 | 5.6 | 35.5 | 0.42 | 0.69 | 5.8 | 9.0 | 55.4 | 0.31 | 0.62 | 3.7 | 8.3 | 122.0 | 0.30 | 0.76 |
| Middle income | 6.7 | 7.7 | 14.3 | 0.70 | 0.96 | 10.6 | 11.1 | 5.5 | 0.56 | 0.76 | 6.7 | 7.3 | 9.7 | 0.53 | 0.68 |
| High income | 9.7 | 8.1 | −16.9 | 1.00 | 1.00 | 18.8 | 14.6 | −22.2 | 1.00 | 1.00 | 12.5 | 10.8 | −13.5 | 1.00 | 1.00 |
| **5 to 10** | | | | | | | | | | | | | | | |
| Low income | 5.8 | 6.2 | 6.7 | 0.51 | 0.51 | 6.3 | 8.4 | 33.1 | 0.34 | 0.43 | 5.6 | 4.0 | −28.1 | 0.52 | 0.68 |
| Middle income | 7.6 | 7.9 | 4.4 | 0.66 | 0.64 | 10.9 | 11.2 | 2.6 | 0.58 | 0.58 | 10.8 | 9.1 | −16.0 | 1.00 | 1.54 |
| High income | 11.5 | 12.3 | 7.1 | 1.00 | 1.00 | 18.8 | 19.5 | 3.5 | 1.00 | 1.00 | 10.8 | 5.9 | −45.2 | 1.00 | 1.00 |
| **11 to 15** | | | | | | | | | | | | | | | |
| Low income | 8.4 | 8.1 | −3.1 | 0.66 | 0.62 | 9.3 | 11.2 | 20.1 | 0.38 | 0.47 | 5.1 | 10.3 | 102.0 | 0.24 | 0.58 |
| Middle income | 10.8 | 13.6 | 26.2 | 0.85 | 1.04 | 15.4 | 21.9 | 41.9 | 0.62 | 0.91 | 10.9 | 13.0 | 19.2 | 0.53 | 0.73 |
| High income | 12.6 | 13.1 | 3.4 | 1.00 | 1.00 | 24.7 | 23.9 | −3.4 | 1.00 | 1.00 | 20.8 | 17.8 | −14.5 | 1.00 | 1.00 |

*Notes:* [a] Expenditures per child under 16 in household;
[b] Expenditures per female over 15 in household. Averages taken over households containing a female over 15 only;
[c] Expenditures per male over 15 in household. Averages taken over households containing a male over 15 only.

# Table 12.4: Changes in expenditure on selected specific child-related items, by household type and income group (September 2003 prices)

| | Toys, hobbies and games (including computer games)[a] | | | | | Books, newspapers, magazines and periodicals[b] | | | | | Fruit and vegetables[b] | | | | | Holidays[b] | | | | |
|---|---|---|---|---|---|---|---|---|---|---|---|---|---|---|---|---|---|---|---|---|
| | Expenditure in £ | | % change | Expenditure as % of high-income group | | Expenditure in £ | | % change | Expenditure as % of high-income group | | Expenditure in £ | | % change | Expenditure as % of high-income group | | Expenditure in £ | | % change | Expenditure as % of high-income group | |
| | 1996/97 | 2000/01 | | 1996/97 | 2000/01 | 1996/97 | 2000/01 | | 1996/97 | 2000/01 | 1996/97 | 2000/01 | | 1996/97 | 2000/01 | 1996/97 | 2000/01 | | 1996/97 | 2000/01 |
| *Households with a child <16* | | | | | | | | | | | | | | | | | | | | |
| Low income | 1.9 | 2.8 | 46.7 | 0.29 | 0.50 | 2.3 | 2.4 | 5.4 | 0.37 | 0.43 | 3.8 | 3.6 | −4.2 | 0.49 | 0.50 | 2.2 | 3.8 | 74.6 | 0.12 | 0.15 |
| Middle income | 3.4 | 4.7 | 36.1 | 0.52 | 0.84 | 3.7 | 3.9 | 4.2 | 0.60 | 0.70 | 5.0 | 5.3 | 5.8 | 0.65 | 0.73 | 8.4 | 13.1 | 55.9 | 0.45 | 0.50 |
| High income | 6.6 | 5.5 | −15.4 | 1.00 | 1.00 | 6.2 | 5.5 | −11.0 | 1.00 | 1.00 | 7.8 | 7.3 | −6.5 | 1.00 | 1.00 | 18.6 | 26.1 | 40.4 | 1.00 | 1.00 |
| *Households with youngest child aged:* | | | | | | | | | | | | | | | | | | | | |
| **0 to 4** | | | | | | | | | | | | | | | | | | | | |
| Low income | 1.7 | 2.8 | 62.8 | 0.20 | 0.54 | 1.8 | 2.0 | 9.6 | 0.31 | 0.44 | 3.6 | 3.6 | 0.1 | 0.46 | 0.50 | 2.0 | 3.4 | 72.9 | 0.11 | 0.16 |
| Middle income | 3.6 | 4.5 | 27.2 | 0.42 | 0.90 | 2.9 | 3.6 | 24.4 | 0.49 | 0.79 | 4.8 | 5.0 | 4.3 | 0.62 | 0.70 | 5.6 | 8.6 | 53.3 | 0.32 | 0.40 |
| High income | 8.5 | 5.1 | −40.2 | 1.00 | 1.00 | 6.0 | 4.6 | −23.3 | 1.00 | 1.00 | 7.7 | 7.1 | −7.7 | 1.00 | 1.00 | 17.8 | 21.3 | 19.9 | 1.00 | 1.00 |
| **5 to 10** | | | | | | | | | | | | | | | | | | | | |
| Low income | 2.1 | 3.1 | 50.7 | 0.43 | 0.39 | 2.6 | 2.5 | −2.7 | 0.41 | 0.38 | 3.8 | 3.7 | −1.0 | 0.47 | 0.53 | 2.1 | 4.4 | 106.6 | 0.11 | 0.20 |
| Middle income | 3.1 | 5.5 | 80.0 | 0.64 | 0.68 | 4.1 | 3.9 | −5.6 | 0.65 | 0.59 | 5.2 | 5.6 | 7.9 | 0.64 | 0.80 | 11.2 | 14.9 | 33.1 | 0.60 | 0.68 |
| High income | 4.8 | 8.1 | 68.8 | 1.00 | 1.00 | 6.4 | 6.6 | 4.0 | 1.00 | 1.00 | 8.1 | 7.0 | −13.3 | 1.00 | 1.00 | 18.6 | 21.8 | 17.2 | 1.00 | 1.00 |
| **11 to 15** | | | | | | | | | | | | | | | | | | | | |
| Low income | 2.2 | 2.2 | 1.4 | 0.44 | 0.63 | 3.1 | 3.1 | 0.9 | 0.49 | 0.55 | 4.5 | 3.6 | −21.0 | 0.60 | 0.46 | 3.0 | 3.8 | 28.2 | 0.15 | 0.10 |
| Middle income | 3.7 | 3.6 | −0.6 | 0.73 | 1.03 | 4.6 | 4.2 | −7.8 | 0.71 | 0.74 | 5.3 | 5.5 | 3.7 | 0.70 | 0.71 | 9.4 | 17.4 | 85.0 | 0.47 | 0.46 |
| High income | 5.0 | 3.5 | −29.2 | 1.00 | 1.00 | 6.4 | 5.7 | −10.7 | 1.00 | 1.00 | 7.6 | 7.7 | 2.5 | 1.00 | 1.00 | 20.0 | 37.5 | 87.7 | 1.00 | 1.00 |

*Notes:* [a] Expenditures per child under 16;
[b] Total expenditure equivalised for household size using Modified OECD scale.

**Figure 12.2: Weekly expenditure on clothing and footwear, by type of clothing and income group, households with a child under 16 only**

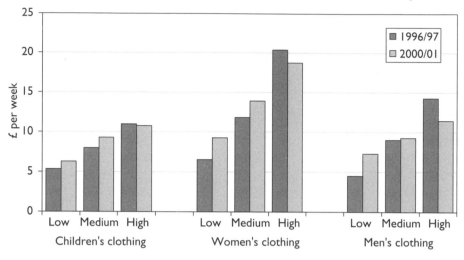

**Figure 12.3: Weekly equivalised[a] expenditure on selected specific child-related items, by income group, households with a child under 16 only (September 2003 prices)**

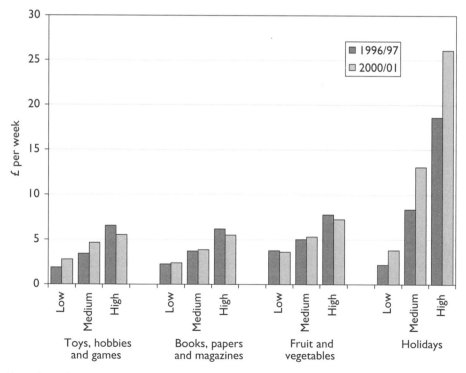

*Note:* [a] Expenditure on toys, hobbies and games is given per child under 16 in the household, rather than equivalised for family size as a whole.

in income, spending on holidays remains an item that low-income families have trouble affording.

## Changes in possession of durable goods

As families' incomes rise, they may also be more likely to possess durable goods such as a car or van, telephone, washing machine, tumble dryer, computer, and so on. Some of these goods may make a direct contribution to a child's health and development, while others may make an indirect contribution by helping the family connect with employment or leisure activities or by reducing parental stress and isolation. The spread of some of these goods within society will reflect falling relative prices rather than changing incomes.

In Table 12.5, we show results for a broad set of durables, again separating families by income level (Panel A) and then extending the analysis to include variations by the age of the youngest child (Panel B). The results shown in Panel A, for all families with children, indicate a good deal of catch-up over the period in the ownership of durables by low-income families with children, but with some mixed patterns. For cars, telephones, central heating, microwaves and CD players, the less affluent are narrowing the gap in having these goods by at least five percentage points. For a middle range of goods, there are modest advances (washing machines, freezers and VCRs). However, for others, there is no trend towards convergence. While for tumble dryers this may reflect that they are a low priority, it is perhaps more worrying that for computers the income-related gap across households with children is still widening[9]. Possession of a computer showed a very strong income gradient in 1996/97, and this gradient was even stronger in 2000/01. Even though low-income families with children nearly doubled their rate of computer ownership, from 22% to 42%, rates of ownership increased even more in percentage point terms among middle- and high-income families, rising from 44% to 69% among the middle-income and from 63% to 85% among the high-income families.

We extend our analysis to consider variation by the age of the youngest child, as shown in Panel B. For some items, we find the largest amount of catch-up among the low-income families with young children (youngest child aged 0 to 4). This is the case for telephones, where the share of families with young children possessing this item rose by 14 percentage points more among the low-income than the high-income families. Low-income families with older children also made gains in terms of the ownership of a telephone, but less markedly than for the families with younger children. Ownership of a car, however, follows a different pattern: low-income families with older children make larger gains relative to high-income families than low-income families with younger children. It may be that, as children move into the school years and especially the teenage years, a car becomes more essential; it may also be that low-income families with younger children have less income free to spend on a car, given other needs.

**Table 12.5: Changes in possession of durable goods, by income group (1996/97 to 2000/01)**

A. All households with children <16

| | Car or van | | | Telephone (any type) | | | Central heating | | | Washing machine | | | Freezer | | |
|---|---|---|---|---|---|---|---|---|---|---|---|---|---|---|---|
| | Proportion possessing item 1996/97 | 2000/01 | Change in % points | Proportion possessing item 1996/97 | 2000/01 | Change in % points | Proportion possessing item 1996/97 | 2000/01 | Change in % points | Proportion possessing item 1996/97 | 2000/01 | Change in % points | Proportion possessing item 1996/97 | 2000/01 | Change in % points |
| Low income | 0.53 | 0.62 | 0.08 | 0.95 | 0.98 | 0.03 | 0.85 | 0.90 | 0.05 | 0.95 | 0.98 | 0.03 | 0.94 | 0.98 | 0.03 |
| Middle income | 0.90 | 0.92 | 0.02 | 0.99 | 0.99 | 0.00 | 0.92 | 0.94 | 0.02 | 0.99 | 0.99 | 0.00 | 0.98 | 0.99 | 0.01 |
| High income | 0.99 | 0.99 | 0.00 | 1.00 | 1.00 | 0.00 | 0.98 | 0.98 | 0.00 | 1.00 | 1.00 | 0.00 | 0.99 | 0.99 | 0.00 |

| | Microwave | | | Tumble dryer | | | Computer | | | Video | | | CD player | | |
|---|---|---|---|---|---|---|---|---|---|---|---|---|---|---|---|
| | Proportion possessing item 1996/97 | 2000/01 | Change in % points | Proportion possessing item 1996/97 | 2000/01 | Change in % points | Proportion possessing item 1996/97 | 2000/01 | Change in % points | Proportion possessing item 1996/97 | 2000/01 | Change in % points | Proportion possessing item 1996/97 | 2000/01 | Change in % points |
| Low income | 0.79 | 0.91 | 0.12 | 0.58 | 0.59 | 0.01 | 0.22 | 0.42 | 0.19 | 0.90 | 0.95 | 0.05 | 0.66 | 0.88 | 0.21 |
| Middle income | 0.87 | 0.93 | 0.05 | 0.68 | 0.67 | -0.01 | 0.44 | 0.69 | 0.25 | 0.97 | 0.99 | 0.02 | 0.82 | 0.96 | 0.14 |
| High income | 0.90 | 0.95 | 0.04 | 0.77 | 0.78 | 0.01 | 0.63 | 0.85 | 0.22 | 0.97 | 0.99 | 0.02 | 0.92 | 0.97 | 0.06 |

## Table 12.5: Contd.../

*B. Households with children <16, by age of youngest child*

| | Car or van | | | Telephone (any type) | | | Central heating | | | Washing machine | | | Freezer | | |
|---|---|---|---|---|---|---|---|---|---|---|---|---|---|---|---|
| | Proportion possessing item 1996/97 | 2000/01 | Change in % points | Proportion possessing item 1996/97 | 2000/01 | Change in % points | Proportion possessing item 1996/97 | 2000/01 | Change in % points | Proportion possessing item 1996/97 | 2000/01 | Change in % points | Proportion possessing item 1996/97 | 2000/01 | Change in % points |
| **0 to 4 years** | | | | | | | | | | | | | | | |
| Low income | 0.53 | 0.56 | 0.03 | 0.82 | 0.95 | 0.14 | 0.85 | 0.89 | 0.04 | 0.94 | 0.97 | 0.03 | 0.93 | 0.98 | 0.05 |
| Middle income | 0.91 | 0.93 | 0.02 | 0.99 | 1.00 | 0.01 | 0.93 | 0.93 | 0.01 | 0.98 | 0.99 | 0.01 | 0.98 | 0.98 | 0.00 |
| High income | 0.99 | 0.97 | -0.01 | 1.00 | 1.00 | 0.00 | 0.99 | 0.99 | 0.01 | 1.00 | 0.99 | -0.01 | 0.98 | 0.99 | 0.01 |
| **5 to 10 years** | | | | | | | | | | | | | | | |
| Low income | 0.56 | 0.66 | 0.11 | 0.90 | 0.95 | 0.04 | 0.85 | 0.90 | 0.05 | 0.94 | 0.98 | 0.04 | 0.94 | 0.97 | 0.02 |
| Middle income | 0.87 | 0.91 | 0.04 | 0.96 | 1.00 | 0.04 | 0.91 | 0.93 | 0.02 | 1.00 | 0.98 | -0.02 | 0.97 | 0.99 | 0.02 |
| High income | 0.97 | 1.00 | 0.03 | 1.00 | 1.00 | 0.00 | 0.97 | 0.97 | 0.00 | 1.00 | 1.00 | 0.00 | 1.00 | 0.98 | -0.02 |
| **11 to 15 years** | | | | | | | | | | | | | | | |
| Low income | 0.51 | 0.67 | 0.16 | 0.87 | 0.97 | 0.09 | 0.82 | 0.90 | 0.08 | 0.98 | 0.99 | 0.01 | 0.96 | 0.97 | 0.01 |
| Middle income | 0.90 | 0.90 | 0.00 | 0.98 | 1.00 | 0.02 | 0.90 | 0.96 | 0.06 | 0.99 | 0.99 | 0.00 | 0.98 | 0.98 | 0.00 |
| High income | 1.00 | 0.99 | -0.01 | 1.00 | 1.00 | 0.00 | 0.99 | 0.98 | -0.01 | 1.00 | 1.00 | 0.00 | 1.00 | 1.00 | 0.00 |

| | Microwave | | | Tumble dryer | | | Computer | | | Video | | | CD player | | |
|---|---|---|---|---|---|---|---|---|---|---|---|---|---|---|---|
| | Proportion possessing item 1996/97 | 2000/01 | Change in % points | Proportion possessing item 1996/97 | 2000/01 | Change in % points | Proportion possessing item 1996/97 | 2000/01 | Change in % points | Proportion possessing item 1996/97 | 2000/01 | Change in % points | Proportion possessing item 1996/97 | 2000/01 | Change in % points |
| **0 to 4 years** | | | | | | | | | | | | | | | |
| Low income | 0.78 | 0.91 | 0.13 | 0.54 | 0.57 | 0.02 | 0.17 | 0.30 | 0.13 | 0.87 | 0.94 | 0.07 | 0.67 | 0.86 | 0.19 |
| Middle income | 0.87 | 0.91 | 0.04 | 0.66 | 0.67 | 0.01 | 0.33 | 0.56 | 0.23 | 0.97 | 0.99 | 0.02 | 0.81 | 0.95 | 0.14 |
| High income | 0.88 | 0.95 | 0.08 | 0.69 | 0.75 | 0.06 | 0.52 | 0.75 | 0.23 | 0.97 | 1.00 | 0.03 | 0.92 | 0.98 | 0.06 |
| **5 to 10 years** | | | | | | | | | | | | | | | |
| Low income | 0.81 | 0.88 | 0.07 | 0.63 | 0.59 | -0.04 | 0.28 | 0.51 | 0.23 | 0.95 | 0.96 | 0.01 | 0.64 | 0.87 | 0.24 |
| Middle income | 0.86 | 0.94 | 0.07 | 0.70 | 0.62 | -0.08 | 0.43 | 0.73 | 0.30 | 0.98 | 0.99 | 0.01 | 0.78 | 0.96 | 0.18 |
| High income | 0.92 | 0.94 | 0.02 | 0.88 | 0.76 | -0.12 | 0.71 | 0.90 | 0.19 | 0.97 | 0.98 | 0.01 | 0.92 | 0.95 | 0.03 |
| **11 to 15 years** | | | | | | | | | | | | | | | |
| Low income | 0.77 | 0.95 | 0.19 | 0.59 | 0.65 | 0.06 | 0.29 | 0.54 | 0.24 | 0.93 | 0.97 | 0.03 | 0.68 | 0.91 | 0.23 |
| Middle income | 0.88 | 0.94 | 0.06 | 0.68 | 0.71 | 0.04 | 0.64 | 0.82 | 0.18 | 0.95 | 0.98 | 0.02 | 0.91 | 0.97 | 0.06 |
| High income | 0.93 | 0.95 | 0.02 | 0.79 | 0.83 | 0.04 | 0.74 | 0.95 | 0.21 | 0.97 | 1.00 | 0.03 | 0.91 | 0.98 | 0.07 |

The pattern for the spread of household appliances across families by ages of children is more mixed. In some instances (for example, possession of a freezer, or washing machine), low-income families with the youngest children have made the largest relative gains; in others (for example, central heating, or a microwave), gains have been more even or have favoured families with older children. These results suggest that, as incomes and expenditures rise, families make choices as to which durables to invest in, taking into account the cost of the item, and its importance for their family relative to other items. Thus, for a family with a young child, investing in a washing machine would be more of a priority (and more affordable) than investing in a dryer; so too would be owning a freezer for storing inexpensive frozen foods, rather than having a microwave for heating prepared meals.

Perhaps reassuringly, when we divide families by age of children, we can see that lower-income families with school-age children did close some of the gap relative to high-income families in access to computers in the home. Low-income families with children under age five lost ground, however, as computer ownership soared among the higher-income, from 52% in 1996/97 to 75% in 2000/01. If access to a computer at home confers advantages in terms of school readiness and school performance, these continuing differentials are worrisome, but at least for school-age children the digital divide is not worsening. The picture for entertainment items is quite different. As we have seen, low-income families made gains, relative to high-income families, in the rates at which they owned a video or CD player. Possession of a video player increased most among families with young children (aged 0 to 4). Low-income families with youngest children aged 5 to 10, or 11 to 15, made the largest gains, relative to high-income families, in ownership of a CD player.

## Results by household work status

Although a full consideration of issues concerning working as compared to workless households is beyond the scope of this chapter, we did examine whether and how the broad patterns of income and expenditure changes documented here differed for families that did or did not have a working adult. As shown in Table 12.6, when we examined low-income households separately by working status and age of the children, we found that working status did make an important difference to the pattern of results. Among all low-income families with children under 16 years of age, those where an adult was in work made somewhat larger income gains, and notably larger expenditure gains, than those where no adult was in work. In line with changes in generosity of Income Support payments and tax credits, income and expenditure gains are more marked for those with younger children for both working and workless families. Interestingly, generally larger gains, relative to working families, are found among workless families with young children than for workless families with older children. Among families with a youngest child under age five, workless families increased their income by

**Table 12.6: Changes in total income and expenditure among low-income households, by work status of household (1996/97 to 2000/01)**

| Low income households | Real equivalised disposable income (£ per week, Sept 2003 prices) | | | | Real equivalised total expenditure (£ per week, Sept 2003 prices) | | | |
|---|---|---|---|---|---|---|---|---|
| | 1996/97 Mean | 2000/01 Mean | Change in £ | % change | 1996/97 Mean | 2000/01 Mean | Change in £ | % change |
| *Households with a child < 16* | | | | | | | | |
| Working | 187 | 211 | 24 | 13 | 234 | 261 | 27 | 11 |
| Workless | 158 | 175 | 17 | 11 | 193 | 204 | 11 | 6 |
| *Households with youngest child aged:* | | | | | | | | |
| **0 to 4** | | | | | | | | |
| Working | 183 | 206 | 24 | 13 | 228 | 257 | 29 | 13 |
| Workless | 155 | 176 | 21 | 13 | 187 | 200 | 14 | 7 |
| **5 to 10** | | | | | | | | |
| Working | 185 | 215 | 30 | 16 | 233 | 260 | 27 | 12 |
| Workless | 160 | 178 | 18 | 11 | 199 | 211 | 12 | 6 |
| **11 to 15** | | | | | | | | |
| Working | 206 | 217 | 12 | 6 | 254 | 269 | 15 | 6 |
| Workless | 168 | 168 | 0 | 0 | 211 | 204 | −7 | −3 |

*Notes:* See notes to Table 12.1; Households are defined as 'working' if the head or spouse is employed and 'workless' if neither is employed.

13% and their expenditures by 7%, compared to working families who increased both their income and expenditures by 13%. In contrast, among families with a youngest child aged 11 to 15, workless families saw no increase in income and their expenditures fell by 3%, compared to working families whose income and expenditures increased by 6%. Of course, without taking into account selection into employment, which may have changed over the period in response to tax and benefit changes, we can not be sure that we are comparing like with like over the period, but nevertheless these results are broadly consistent with our prior assumption that the benefit changes over the period (in particular, increases in child benefit and Income Support) did serve to help workless families with young children more than workless families with older children.

## Conclusion

When policy makers seek to raise income transfers for the support of children, there is a concern that the money may not be spent with the interests of the child in mind. Over the last few years, the Labour government has put substantial resources into income transfers to working and non-working low-income families. The evidence presented here suggests that low-income families have made good use of the additional income available to them over the period 1996/97 to 2000/01.

Low-income families have always prioritised spending on necessities such as housing and food, but our results indicate that as incomes have risen the extra income has also been spent disproportionately on items for their children, in particular, clothing, footwear and toys and games. Families have also spent some more money on clothing for the adults in the household, an area where their spending had lagged. Families have not spent more money on alcohol or tobacco or housing. As incomes have risen, low-income families have become increasingly likely to own learning and entertainment items such as a computer, video or CD player. However, their possession of these items still lags behind more affluent families, with a particularly notable gap in computer ownership among families with young children. There is also a notable gap in spending on holidays, an area where low-income families lost ground over the period.

What do these changes in expenditures mean in terms of family hardship and child well-being? The overall pattern of our results suggests that low-income families with children should be experiencing less hardship and improved well-being, and this is indeed what the recent Families and Children Survey (FACS) found (see Chapter Seven, Table 7.4, of this volume). Analyses of cross-sections of low-income families in 1999, 2000 and 2001 indicated that as family incomes rose, there were substantial drops in hardship (as measured by items such as problems with heat or accommodation, money worries or shortfalls in food, clothing, consumer durables or leisure items), leading the authors of the survey to conclude that "families are using their extra finances to improve living conditions for their children" (Vegeris and Perry, 2003, p 140).

How important are these gains in income, and reductions in hardship, for children living in low-income families? Although parents try hard to protect their children from the effects of low income and hardship, even young children are aware of their parents' financial situation and the constraints that it places on their families (Middleton et al, 1997; Shropshire and Middleton, 1999). And, many of the items that money can buy (items such as books, or outings) matter a good deal for child health and development. As incomes rise and those constraints are eased, and parents are able to purchase more items for their children, we would expect to see improvements in child health and development. How large those improvements are, and in what areas of health and development, is a topic we hope to tackle in further research.

## Notes

[1] Material deprivation data on both adults and children will be gathered in the Family Resources Survey. The questions relating to child deprivation will identify families who would like to have but can not afford the following items for their children: a holiday away from home at least once a year; swimming at least once a month; a hobby or leisure activity; friends round for tea or snack once a fortnight; a separate bedroom for each child over age ten of different sex; leisure equipment (such as a bicycle); celebrations on special occasions (such as birthdays); playgroup or nursery at least once

a week for pre-schoolers; and school trips at least once a term for school-age children. See DWP (2003c) for further details.

[2] The reforms in our period temporarily shifted benefits in the opposite direction for a small number of families who had previously received Family Credit paid to the mother but now receive in-work benefits through the man's paycheck. Future reforms will shift benefits back towards the mother, in a larger number of cases. We do not examine this aspect of the reforms here but intend to do so in future work.

[3] The annual price index for all items rose by 13% from 1996 to 2001. Changes over the period in price indices for specific expenditure categories varied (for instance, food prices increased only 5% from 1996 to 2001), and we carried out additional analyses to test the sensitivity of our results to using these different price indices. We do not report the results of those additional analyses here, but they did not change the overall pattern of results.

[4] We focus on means, rather than medians, because some expenditures even within these broad categories may be lumpy or sporadic and here averaging over a number of households will give a more accurate picture than concentrating on only a single household at the median position.

[5] There is also a notable drop in expenditures on the miscellaneous category across all groups, but from a very small base. This category includes credit card interest payments, and the drop may reflect falling interest rates over the period.

[6] As mentioned in note 3, food prices rose only 5% over the period as compared to 13% for all goods on average. Thus, relative food prices were falling and so reduced expenditure need not reflect reduced consumption.

[7] See notes 3 and 6 about falling relative food prices over the period.

[8] We also looked at the share of families with any spending at all on holidays but found that this increased somewhat faster among high-income families than among low- or middle-income families, although this varied by the age of the youngest child. For instance, among families with a youngest child aged 11 to 15, by far the greatest gain was made by high-income families, whereas among families with younger children, larger gains were made by low- or middle-income families.

[9] For recent evidence on the so-called 'digital divide' in computer ownership and its consequences for educational attainment, see Schmitt and Wadsworth (2002).

# THIRTEEN

# Bringing up families in poor neighbourhoods under New Labour

*Anne Power and Helen Willmot*

## Introduction

For five years, we have been tracking the lives of 200 families in four of the most disadvantaged urban areas in the country; two in East London (West City and East Docks) and two in Yorkshire (Kirkside East and The Valley)[1]. We visit the same families every year and record their changing views and experiences about bringing up their children in difficult and unpopular neighbourhoods. We almost invariably speak with mothers, only very occasionally with partners or other relatives.

The four areas were chosen from the 12 representative deprived areas that we are studying more broadly in an attempt to understand the changing fortunes of such places (see Chapter Six of this volume). Three of the four neighbourhoods are rapidly changing, and becoming ethnically far more diverse (half of our families are from a minority ethnic background). The other area is an almost entirely white large council estate in Leeds. The families offer very new and different insights into life in deprived areas. We ask mothers about their children, relatives, friends, work, local services and conditions, community life, race relations, the changes under way and embedded problems. Our questions evolve as the families express interest in explaining particular problems or ideas, hopes or fears. (For further detail about the study and its methodology, see Mumford and Power, 2003.)

As discussed earlier in this volume, shortly after the new government took office in 1997, the Prime Minister announced a new approach to what he called "joined up problems" requiring "joined up solutions" (Blair, 1997b). The government set up a unit directly under the Prime Minister to tackle a relatively new phenomenon, social exclusion (see Chapter Ten). The Social Exclusion Unit (SEU) recognised the centrality of area conditions in holding back families and particularly children and young people from opportunities; it advocated a broad set of targets to reduce deprivation within disadvantaged areas and most importantly it recognised the complexities and interlocking problems of the worst areas.

As the range of area initiatives multiplied and hit the ground, there were complaints from local authorities and within Whitehall that 'initiativitis' had got out of control, which has led to a scaling back in area-specific programmes. This makes it crucial for us to understand what is really happening within areas, whether programmes and interventions really matter and whether mothers and their children – arguably the most vulnerable to any failures – benefit or not. This is the focus of our chapter.

The chapter begins by examining two areas of government action targeted at the population at large, but with potentially greater impact in the most disadvantaged areas where the problems are most severe (see also Chapter Six of this volume): employment and education (see also Chapters Two and Three of this volume). We then look at three initiatives that are targeted at deprived areas, although sometimes they can also apply more generally: New Deal for Communities and Sure Start (see also Chapter Seven); community policing and neighbourhood wardens; and community participation and empowerment (see also Chapter Five). There are many problems we have not discussed, such as social exclusion as a process in and of itself. We chose areas of government action with directly visible outcomes to see whether the families recognised and valued these interventions.

## Employment

At Round One of the interviews in Kirkside East and The Valley (2000), 65% of the interviewees were receiving state benefits (not including the universal child benefit) and the problem of worklessness (with no-one in the household employed, studying or training) was intense in both neighbourhoods. Fifty-seven per cent of all the adults in the Yorkshire families were not working, studying or training, compared to 25% nationally. Nearly half of the families were entirely dependent on state benefits for all their income – more than double the national average. The situation was less acute in the two London neighbourhoods but still far above the national and London average. The first round of London interviews was conducted in 1999: in West City, 44% of the families were receiving out-of-work benefits and in East Docks, 38%; similar percentages of adults within the families were not working, studying or training (see Bowman, 2001; Mumford, 2001; Lupton, 2003b, pp 28-9; Mumford and Power, 2003, p 94).

What happened to the 200 families after the first round of interviews? By 2001/02, the numbers of interviewees receiving state benefits (excluding child benefit) had decreased in all four neighbourhoods. In Kirkside East, just 25% of the interviewees were receiving state benefits, a decrease of 40%, while The Valley had seen a decrease of 31%. In both West City and East Docks, the number still receiving state benefits had halved. This decrease across all four neighbourhoods resulted from growing access to jobs, with interviewees gaining paid employment throughout the study.

The fifth round of interviews in Kirkside East and The Valley in 2003 continued to reflect this positive shift: 58% of interviewees in Kirkside East and 50% in The

Valley were now in paid work (one third full time and two thirds part time). The employment figures for interviewees' partners were similarly rising, with 50% in Kirkside East and 48% in The Valley in work. In both of these neighbourhoods, nearly half of interviewees' partners were working full time, much higher than for the mothers. Given the acute employment problems in low-income areas in the North, even in the late 1990s, this change is significant.

In London, only 27% of interviewees were working in Round One, but by Round Five 63% were in work, four fifths of them part time. Of the mothers with partners, 86% of partners were working. This also represents a big shift into work. Alan Marsh's large-scale study of this phenomenon illustrates the extent to which the simple process of children growing up helps lone mothers into work (Marsh and Vegeris, 2004). However, among these mothers the process appears significantly faster, particularly in the North.

## Work incentives

New Labour policy aimed at combating social exclusion has included a focus on encouraging paid work, for example through the new tax credits for working families with children (Working Families Tax Credit and Children's Tax Credit, later combined into the Child Tax Credit) and through the New Deal employment programmes. How have these policies impacted on the families in this study? The new tax credits may have played a role in the interviewees' increasing engagement in paid work, as the percentage of interviewees claiming these new tax credits has risen substantially. In Round One (2000), 15% of the working interviewees were claiming Working Families Tax Credit in the North; by Round Five, 70% of those in work were claiming (see also Mumford and Power, 2003, p 108).

Many interviewees had negative views on the new tax credits; fully half talked about problems they had experienced with the procedure of claiming the new tax credits (see also Mumford and Power, 2003, p 108):

"[I've] sent off forms for new versions. We don't like them. They don't answer the phone." (L041)

"We get them. They're absolutely useless, keep sending me giros and I want it in my bank." (L054)

"I had Working Family Tax Credit of £45 a week, I had a child tax code on my wages in April, when they changed it over to Child Tax Credit. I still haven't got my award to say how much I am getting because I was £250 a week worse off and, despite ringing up, you can never get through. It's horrendous. I looked on the website and found a number for the press officer and couldn't get through to the normal bit so rang the press bit and I spoke to a very nice young man who said he'd ring back the next day. He didn't. But one of their PR guys from the Inland Revenue did and said it has been sorted and will be in my bank today." (L033)

Thus, while the new tax credits might have had a real impact in encouraging the families in the study to take up paid employment, the families also highlighted administrative problems within the system that they have to deal with. This fits with wider reports of success in reducing the poverty trap, but problems in making the system run smoothly. There would possibly be even higher take-up of work if people felt they could rely on the system.

### New Deal programmes

In contrast to tax credits, government employment programmes seem to have played a very small direct role in increasing participation in paid employment (see also Lupton, 2003b, pp 197-202; see Millar, 2000, for more positive findings on this). None of the families in The Valley had any experience of New Deal employment programmes, and in Kirkside East only two interviewees' partners and one young adult had done so. In East London, only 5% of parents said their children had experienced the New Deal for Young People. More (16%) said that their children had experienced Connexions, the young people's advice service linked to work.

One mother felt very negative as a result of her son's experience of the New Deal. Another had met people who had not benefited from the programme:

> "He's on New Deal now.... He hasn't had any work through them." (L027)

> "I wouldn't advise it [going on New Deal] having worked with people who've done it." (L041)

There is no suggestion here that New Deal employment programmes have had much impact on the families in the North, on facilitating paid employment for the interviewees, their partners or their children of working age.

In London, the picture is a little more mixed, with both negative and positive experiences reported:

> "I think my eldest son had to keep going to the job centre and the New Deal gave him a job allowance while he was looking for a job. All they did was send him information, and sent him to the career office to find work." (N022)

> "Yes, we've seen leaflets, but we're not allowed to work." (H039, Kosovan family seeking asylum)

"My brother got his job on the New Deal, he's a pool cleaner. I've advised people to go on the New Deal, it's good for local people." (H002)

"Yes, they are great. They never made me apply for a job in the six years I was on benefits and they paid for training courses. I gave a lot of voluntary work for the New Deal. Loads of good stuff, but it's impossible for people to access anything." (H007)

## Education policy: schools

There was overall a very positive opinion of schools in the four neighbourhoods at the beginning of the study (see Bowman, 2001; Mumford, 2001). In the Round One interviews in Kirkside East and The Valley (in 2000), 49% of the parents in both areas were very satisfied with the schools their children attended, 31% were fairly satisfied and 6% were satisfied (a combined figure of 86% satisfied). Those who chose local schools often highlighted the positive aspects of their school, for example, their neighbourhood character, good facilities, friendly environment, cultural mix, positive approach to children, clear rewards and controls over behaviour and links between the school and the local community. Interviewees were also aware of the poor reputation of local schools both in the area and in the city more widely. Parents knew the local schools were underperforming in national terms but preferred their children to attend local schools and liked the security and ease of contact this brought, especially at primary level.

In the two London neighbourhoods, 44% of the interviewees in West City and 54% in East Docks thought that the primary schools were getting better, while 48% in both neighbourhoods thought that the secondary schools were getting better. Being part of an Education Action Zone (East Docks) was a plus. Other improvements that parents noticed included the introduction of homework, more reading, writing and sums, after-school and holiday clubs, a 'trouble shooter' head and the expulsion of bullies. Many parents in all four neighbourhoods shared the generally positive view of change and progress in schools.

In Round Two (2000/01), when we asked parents what they felt about their area for schools, over half of the interviewees (almost 50% in Kirkside East, over 50% in West City and over 60% in East Docks) felt that their neighbourhood was good for schools. However, in The Valley there was a definite drop in confidence in the local schools, with only a fifth of the interviewees (20%) feeling that their neighbourhood was good for schools (see Table 13.1).

By Round Five (2003), tiny numbers of parents felt that their children's primary schools had got worse since Round Three/Four (2002), while two thirds to three quarters felt, depending on the area, that the schools had either stayed the same or got better. The numbers are significantly lower for secondary schools.

The interviewees' comments about their children's schools were mingled with

**Table 13.1: Percentage of interviewees who feel their area is good for schools, Round Two (2001)**

|  | Kirkside East | The Valley | West City | East Docks |
|---|---|---|---|---|
| Very good | 12 | 4 | 8 | 11 |
| Fairly good | 36 | 16 | 51 | 58 |
| Total | 48 | 20 | 59 | 69 |

*Note:* The survey covers 50 respondents in each of four areas, that is, a maximum of 200 families. For some questions a small number of respondents did not give replies, so the percentages quoted relate to a somewhat smaller number than this.

their views on other related issues that they raised, including school leadership, homework, discipline and morale. Of those who commented, many spoke very positively:

> "Everybody has got a reading partner – from an older class. It is good. Everyday." (NO15, Round Three)

> "They're reading at an earlier stage and I think that will come through a lot stronger in the next few years." (L031, Round Three/Four)

> "The year six SATS results have improved in the area of literature and maths." (N005, Round Three)

> "It's small [the school] and there's not so many [in a class] so they cope with them and do more one-to-one." (S044, Round Three/ Four)

> "They are good at teaching. If they get stuck, they help them. Her reading and maths are great." (L051, Round Five)

> "I think it's the homework, the English and maths, and the communication between the parents and teachers [that I'm most pleased with]." (S001, Round Five)

This suggests that some New Labour education policies, such as smaller class sizes, literacy and numeracy hours and Key Stage testing, have been well received. However, some mothers spoke negatively about schooling:

> "It's slowly declining. Literacy/numeracy – it's all they do, it's wrong, it's important but it's just a skill and they need to develop the person. They should do more creative things and sports." (L041, Round Three/ Four)

"I don't feel the head has got any interest, he's losing interest.... I got the parent report from governors to parents – SATS results 40% for maths only 23% for English and I think that's atrocious for 11 year olds....The only time they ever get it (homework) is when OFSTED are due in and they get it in the two weeks before and during.They hardly ever bring reading books home either." (L012, Round Three/ Four)

Many interviewees had complex and mixed views about their children's schools, which this mother illustrates:

"I think it (literacy and numeracy) is important at that school.They just had league tables and they came third bottom. A lot of children have English as a second language and it is going to matter for them. I don't like the emphasis on SATS and I think they can get carried away and I find myself getting carried away for them. My mum used to say, 'You can only do what you can', and I find myself saying it to calm them down. I try to keep a lid on it." (S042, Round Three/ Four)

Some parents have themselves started studying since Round One of the interviews. While the numbers doing so are not large in any of the four neighbourhoods, the incremental picture is positive, year on year (see Table 13.2).

## Area-based regeneration

Having examined how two general policies related to family income and education played out in the eyes of the 200 mothers, we now look at more area-specific policies such as regeneration and renewal programmes (Bowman, 2001; Mumford, 2001).The interviewees in Round One (1999/2000) identified some positive things happening in their areas, including new investment through regeneration programmes. Government regeneration initiatives were targeting all areas, including Sure Start in three areas (both Yorkshire areas and East Docks) and New Deal for Communities in two areas (The Valley and West City). In

**Table 13.2: Percentage of interviewees who started studying since the last interview**

| Interview round | Kirkside East | The Valley | West City | East Docks |
|---|---|---|---|---|
| Two | 4 | 0 | 8 | 4 |
| Three | 0 | 6 | 6 | 4 |
| Four | – | – | 2 | – |
| Five | 4 | 2 | – | – |

*Note:* Rounds Three and Four interviews were combined in the North.

Kirkside East, a local community forum, in West City a New Deal Trust, and in The Valley a New Deal Community Forum were actively working to improve conditions, change the image of the area and upgrade the local environment through the involvement of residents. By the end of Round One (October 2000), there were five Sure Start bases around Kirkside East and some parents already active in schools were becoming involved in the development of Sure Start in all three areas with a programme. Interviewees generally welcomed the initiatives, telling us early on that New Labour interventions such as Sure Start and New Deal for Communities were among the most positive things happening in the areas. However, since this was early in the life of these programmes, some were untouched by them and preferred to "keep themselves to themselves".

What has been the impact over time on the interviewees and their families of these initiatives? This section first focuses on Sure Start and its evolution in the two Yorkshire areas and East Docks.

*Sure Start*

By Round Four (2002), quite a high percentage of interviewees in the Northern neighbourhoods had had contact with Sure Start – 38% in Kirkside East and 50% in The Valley, but only 12% in East Docks (a further 30% having heard of it). Very few of these parents had attended Sure Start meetings; only 4% in East Docks, and almost none in the other two neighbourhoods. So direct involvement with Sure Start discussions is unusual, but attending activity sessions and using Sure Start services is common, at least in the Northern areas.

The most recent findings from Kirkside East and The Valley, where involvement is high, tell us more about the actual impact of Sure Start on the lives of families. Many mothers with pre-school children – just over half in Kirkside East (57%) and just under half in The Valley (44%) – felt that Sure Start had made a difference to them. The numbers are lower in East Docks.

Overall, contact with Sure Start and the provision of facilities for children elicited a positive response from 50% of the families. In Round Five, we asked interviewees what they would focus on if they were in charge of managing their neighbourhood. Facilities for children, such as Sure Start provides, were the most popular choice for half of the interviewees.

The positive aspects of Sure Start which families describe illustrate why Sure Start has made a difference to half the families. One-to-one contact and home visits, youth work, events for children under age four, health care specialists and the way that Sure Start helps people to be less cut off are all praised. These positive aspects contribute directly to the quality of life of many of the families and their children, and the parents' overall view of the programme was supportive.

Some of the things that made Sure Start popular are highlighted by the following quotes:

"I know it's positive. I know from my friend who goes there – that the aim is how they can improve services for the under fours and how they can support families." (N01, Round Three)

"The Sure Start workers who are there for one-to-one help if you need them – I've had one and they were brilliant." (S002, Round Three)

"I don't think much was available before. Now Sure Start does home help and taking new buggies out and picking up children from school – I never had that." (S006, Round Three)

"There are more links with parents with children under four – more things available. They come round and visit and give packs with clothes in and they're looking out for mums that need that little bit of support." (S008, Round Three)

"I go to the homeopath twice a year and it's cured the asthma and the digestive problem was resolved by the osteopath.... The osteopath and homeopath I see through Sure Start." (L012, Round Five)

"It's a lot better for young children because of Sure Start and now they're doing youth work." (L022, Round Five)

"Sure Start has made a difference as in more events going on for under fours." (S034, Round Five)

*Interviewer:* "What sorts of things about this neighbourhood help people be less cut off?"
*Interviewee:* "Sure Start and mother and toddler groups, things like that." (S062, Round Five)

*Interviewer:* "Is there anything about this area that you feel helps you as a parent?"
*Interviewee:* "Yes, all the Sure Start stuff, clubs and services for children like homework clubs." (S067, Round Five)

Mothers also highlighted some problems with Sure Start. These include weak publicity, divisions arising from Sure Start funding and rigid but disputed boundaries. (Only those living within a demarcated area can access Sure Start services, a measure intended to ensure Sure Start is targeted on deprived families but without creating stigma or dividing a local community.) One parent thought the whole concept of helping vulnerable parents was offensive by implying poor parenting in targeted areas:

"The boundaries are a bit odd – they are set up for deprived areas but if you live three streets away you can't use it." (N021, Round Three)

"They were trying with Sure Start and the toy library but I don't know if it works. I felt the people who really needed the help weren't getting it." (S029, Round Three)

"I think the whole concept is offensive. I think it's terrible setting up something that is inherently critical. By saying you want children to have a Sure Start you're implying that that's not happening already." (S017, Round Three)

"I do think it's taking a long time to get off the ground and they need to find ways of involving parents from a greater cross-section of the community." (S034, Round Three)

"I only got to know it [Sure Start] via Mums and Tots Group. It isn't well publicised." (L061, Round Five)

"There is a division when different groups apply for New Deal or Sure Start money." (S019, Round Five)

### New Deal for Communities

Soon after coming to power, the new government announced 17 new style regeneration programmes in which the community was to play a decisive role in running the programme. Both West City and The Valley were to become New Deal for Communities areas. By Round Three of the interviews, a strikingly large majority of the interviewees in both of these neighbourhoods had heard of or had contact with this initiative – 70% of the interviewees in West City and 74% in The Valley. New Deal for Communities is clearly working in both neighbourhoods. The wide ranging achievements (some ongoing) include redeveloping a local park, a get-into-places-free scheme, groups for minority ethnic communities, adult learning opportunities and help with housing problems:

"We get some money for the school from the New Deal. I know they are redeveloping the local park. The redevelopment will be good if it's being done well. I think it's New Deal money." (H031, Round Three)

"Last summer they had a thing where they would give you a card so you could get into things free that were to do with the New Deal, eg a circus over the local park. Had to go to the New Deal office and show them your book and then they would give you a card." (H010, Round Three)

"I am being taught to drive through them [the local New Deal Trust]. They are paying for it." (H033, Round Four)

"The nursery is part of it [New Deal]." (H040, Round Four)

"Yes, I have contact [with the local New Deal trust]. I go to meetings sometimes, every two weeks, they teach me how to do things like filing and adviser training. My English is getting better." (H047, Round Four)

"I've been there [to the local New Deal Trust] to complain about the heating. They made an appointment for me to see the area manager." (H051, Round Four)

"[T]hey help sometimes, the local New Deal. Housing leaflets are useful." (H047, Round Four)

"There's a company around the market, the New Deal, and they've managed to put central heating in on the estate and are redoing windows and door frames." (H010, Round Four)

"A lot of New Deal stuff is going round. We've still got the homework club. I've been told by the main coordinator that it is being linked in with New Deal with four other groups. There's a Somali group and the Asian girls' group and two other groups." (S006, Round Four)

"I think it is probably making non-visible differences like doing adult learning and employment things." (S070, Round Five)

However, some interviewees made very negative comments about New Deal for Communities in their neighbourhood, suggesting that it does not have a wholly positive impact. One of the criticisms voiced was that New Deal for Communities seems in some ways to have increased divisions and segregation along ethnic lines within communities. In addition, some people feel 'messed around' over funding, in-fighting and misinformation, which wastes community time and produces slow or no results:

"New Deal and the big partnership groups are excluding, they're dividing and ruling. Why are they separating people off when the translation services can be there? People like being involved. Segregation is easier for them – telling you what they want you to know.... They shouldn't divide, they're supposed to be building a community. There's enough racism and separation without dividing black and black. I could take four friends and we'd have to go to different meetings." (S035, Round Four)

"There is a division when people in different groups apply for New Deal or Sure Start money." (S019, Round Five)

"I'm involved in the adventure playground locally and we've been messed around by New Deal. They insist we get matched funding and we got £2,500 from the Children's Fund and New Deal messed around so much we're going over the deadline and need to get an extension and we've been told we can't – so now it's a headache." (S017, Round Four)

"[N]ot enough people go [to consultation meetings to get New Deal money], and consultations mean agendas already have been decided anyway." (S019, Round Five)

"Yes, heard of it [New Deal for Communities] and tried to contact them for a grant for setting up an education group but I couldn't get through to them." (S065, Round Five)

"New Deal is a load of rubbish, a community with a lack of opportunities and low achievement at school and all of a sudden a few months to apply for £50 million and everything ends up in chaos, meetings are chaos, it leads to groups fighting, and it is a waste of community time. You see a few new flowerpots and £50 here and there and that is it. And what of the communities who don't get New Deal?" (S066, Round Five)

"The meeting was about New Deal evaluation, what they haven't got, their goals since years ago, like banks and supermarkets. So it was about no difference as yet." (S067, Round Five)

These harsh criticisms have to be balanced against the positive impacts. The quotes underline just how complex community conditions and relations are in these very mixed areas, and how important it is to collect local feedback. The polarised views we picked up are balanced by some interviewees recognising both positive and negative aspects of New Deal for Communities:

"In terms of finding out what is going on they [housing meetings run by New Deal] are useful, but not in terms of you having any input." (S012, Round Five)

"They have to [make a difference to the area] in that they have invested in the area, New Deal type things, but it is slow." (S071, Round Five)

"The way I feel varies as much with my life and my mood. I feel marginally better and not quite as neglected as I did a couple of years ago. But there's still not much sign of New Deal money. Who knows what's happened to that £52 million. What's been done so far is not New Deal. They've not renewed the temporary contracts and redone the board. So there's a lot of politicking and in-fighting." (S042, Round Four)

Overall New Deal seems to bring direct benefits, but these do not seem to match up to the scale of funding. On the other hand, they contribute to the ongoing effort to respond to needs, as this mother explains:

"I became a Home Start volunteer when we moved here and then worked for Sure Start, and then New Deal came along, and I've just been to a community meeting, and the same things are lacking as when we came and New Deal came along and said what it would do. But there is more for children, more services and centres and after-school clubs." (S067, Round Five)

The overall view of regeneration from the perspective of the families could be summed up as a generally positive attempt to meet local needs in the face of much bigger and wider problems. Without targeted initiatives such as Sure Start and New Deal for Communities, these areas would be poorer, more neglected and inevitably more removed from mainstream conditions. Unsurprisingly most parents recognised and valued the commitment these programmes represented.

## Crime and policing

One of the overriding problems that the government has tried to combat, particularly in poor areas, is crime. It has increasingly done this through more proactive policing. This certainly reflects a major concern among the families. First, we discuss the parents' views of crime, and then their response to specific area policing. Parents expressed a high fear of crime in Round One of the interviews in all four neighbourhoods (Bowman, 2001; Mumford, 2001). Drugs were a dominant worry for parents in all of the neighbourhoods, and particularly in East Docks and The Valley. In Kirkside East, vandalism, car theft and burning, violence and threatening behaviour were often mentioned. In The Valley, serious violence was a very live issue. In West City, mothers talked more generally about feeling unsafe. In both London neighbourhoods, crime problems were very serious indeed. Car crime was especially prevalent in East Docks.

In Round Two (2001), there was still a high fear of crime in all neighbourhoods

**Table 13.3: Percentage of interviewees who feel that crime is a problem in their area, Round Two (2001)**

|  | Kirkside East | The Valley | West City | East Docks |
|---|---|---|---|---|
| Serious problem | 44 | 50 | 57 | 64 |
| Problem but not serious | 20 | 12 | 28 | 11 |
| Problem in some parts of the area | 6 | 16 | 0 | 0 |
| Problems at different times | 2 | 2 | 0 | 0 |
| Problem but not experienced | 0 | 2 | 0 | 0 |
| Not a problem | 22 | 14 | 13 | 22 |
| Don't know | 6 | 4 | 2 | 2 |

(see Mumford and Power, 2003, pp 197-201). Over three quarters of all interviewees felt crime was a problem. Furthermore, over half of all interviewees felt that crime was a serious problem. The problem was clearly worse for London families. Table 13.3 shows this.

### Community policing and neighbourhood wardens

By Round Five (2003), community policing and neighbourhood wardens were established in the four neighbourhoods. What impact, if any, have such policies had on the neighbourhoods and the families?

In Kirkside East and The Valley, there was a slight increase in the experience of crime between Rounds Three and Five. This raises questions about the impact on the neighbourhoods of community police or neighbourhood wardens, although a greater police presence and public confidence can lead to increased reporting. Reported crime in The Valley more than doubled between Rounds Two and Five, from 6% to 14%. This could possibly be linked to the introduction of regeneration-funded community police and neighbourhood wardens, suggesting a positive impact on the families. However, in Kirkside East, reporting to the police fell slightly. Furthermore, in both neighbourhoods, less than half of those who reported a crime were satisfied with how it was handled. In the London areas, crime was still a very big problem but satisfaction with police responses was surprisingly high.

By Round Five of the study, only 6% in Sheffield and 14% in Leeds felt there were fewer police, and over a quarter of interviewees felt that there were more police in their neighbourhood than there were at the start of the study – 28% of the interviewees in Kirkside East, 34% in The Valley and 25% in London. This could suggest at least the beginnings of success for the community police. In London, fully 68% said there were policemen on the beat in their area. However, overall, more interviewees felt that there were the same numbers of police in their neighbourhood, and in The Valley many were critical of the fact that, although they saw more police, they were mostly in cars.

Six mothers in Kirkside East and five in The Valley said that the community police do make a difference to their neighbourhood. Often local contact and local knowledge are the main reasons for success:

> "Yes, they are good, because it makes it easier to report crimes and remain anonymous." (L017)

> "I think it does [make a difference to the neighbourhood] because they tend to get to know the villains and they seem to take notice of him [the Community Police Officer]. I mean, they're still villains, but if he comes around they will move on." (L033)

> "I think it does [make a difference to the neighbourhood] because it makes kids more aware." (L035)

> "I think if they are seen enough they help, as a deterrent." (L055)

> "They are here 24 hours, looking out for crime." (S062)

However, many mothers stressed that community police make no difference to their neighbourhood, or that some do and some do not. One critical problem appears to be that they are not visible or proactive enough:

> "I know they've got new community police via New Deal, who are supposed to respond more quickly than the other police, but they don't seem to be having an effect around here." (S066)

> "No [they don't make a difference in the neighbourhood], because you never see them." (L004)

> "They are in cars, aren't doing a lot. Would be better on foot." (S026)

> "They say they can only report things, so they can't see things through." (S067)

> We have New Deal dedicated police in the community. They wrote to us and asked us to give names of the problem youths and I didn't get that at all, that method, as some of us are trying to work with them, and I just haven't seen differences from their presence." (S018)

> "Whenever I've contacted them, they've not responded to me. Full-stop, unresponsive." (S071)

Overall, only 12% of respondents in Kirkside East and just 10% in The Valley felt that the community police made a difference to their area. These findings strongly suggest that the initiative has had too little impact so far. In London, the effect appears to be stronger: 27% thought they were making a difference and there was also positive feedback on beat policing.

A similar finding emerges from the neighbourhood warden schemes. These have been set up in three of the areas. In both Kirkside East and The Valley, three quarters of the interviewees thought that there were no wardens in their area. The general problem is similar to policing – lack of visibility due to insufficient numbers to overcome fears and worries about the lack of policing. In London, wardens are more conspicuous and in general more useful: 40% recognised neighbourhood wardens in the area.

The comments families made about the warden scheme in Kirkside East tell us something about the workings of this initiative. Perceived problems include wardens' lack of protection, working hours, the police not always working with them and their focus on property repairs rather than crime. However, positive views were also voiced:

> "They are quite good. Yeah, but it is like, we went to a meeting once and they want them to work in the area but they've got no protection from a gang of youths or a drunk man." (L002)

> "[T]hey finish at 5.30 which is when kids start up." (L025)

> "[They are] more to do with community property repairs." (L048)

> "I think he is alright. I don't see him that often. He is there to tell police what he sees. But once he rang the police when a car was being burnt out and they didn't come. He works normal hours and not at night. He pops in here [community centre]. I don't see him driving around. No, he doesn't really make a difference to the area." (L006)

> "I think they make a difference because they cycle about in summer, people know who they are, they chat to them in the street, they are a link, really, aren't they? And less of a threat than if a policeman is on the beat." (L001)

> "I think he does try and stop most of what kids are doing, because he's seen kids doing it a few times. The police come straight away if he rings. So I think it does make a difference if he's around and catches them." (L004)

> "He's really good. He'll get burnt out cars removed and stuff." (L016)

Parents valued the fact that wardens are known faces, they talk to people, they are less threatening than the police, they work with the police and they deal with one of the most prevalent, visible and threatening crimes in the neighbourhood – kids stealing, driving and then burning out cars:

> "People like this, to see someone trying to do something. It makes us feel better." (N051)

> "Getting better, but slowly. [In what ways?] The wardens, for a start. There are children hanging around setting cars on fire, hanging around in groups. But with the wardens it's better." (H020)

> "The new wardens walking around. It's something reassuring. Someone is walking around checking the area." (H008)

> "Yes. If there is crime going on, they are always around and also they are somewhat of a deterrence as there is a definite police presence in the area." (H045)

Neighbourhood wardens are more visible and more regular than community policemen, but more limited in their powers. So far, neither approach seems a match for the problem, and it may be that much more concerted interventions are essential in high crime areas. This is beginning in West City at least, where many parents commented on the much higher visibility of the police and wardens in recent months and their reassuring presence on the streets. From the parents' observations we conclude that visible frequent beat policing and street supervision are wanted but that they require a consistent continuous presence and proactive role if they are to make families feel comfortable. The policy shift in this direction is recognised by parents but does not yet go far enough.

## Community participation and neighbourhood change

There are many aspects of New Labour policy that apply particularly to low-income neighbourhoods, and to the mothers who live in them. Participation, leading to influence and control over events, is particularly important as programmes such as Sure Start, New Deal for Communities, neighbourhood wardens and school improvements all rely heavily on community involvement. The families we interviewed had quite complicated and sometimes contradictory experiences of involvement (see also Lupton, 2003b, pp 167-9). Over half the families interviewed in Round Three felt they had no influence at all, but fully a quarter of London families say they have been able to influence schools – a surprisingly positive response given the hierarchical nature of schools. Leeds City Council canvassed tenants' opinions on the creation of an arm's length management organisation for its housing stock, and Kirkside East, a large council estate, was strongly targeted. We found that nearly two thirds of Kirkside East families said they had influenced local developments in housing.

Almost all families knew about fun community events and a large majority attended some. There is warm praise for the sense of community and shared enjoyment these generate. Parents specifically highlighted the interracial contact and community mixing these events engendered. Far fewer attended community meetings, but an impressive one quarter to one third of all mothers belong to a community group, often linked to children, even though only a quarter feel they can make a difference. Most parents want to be involved as a way of meeting other people and gaining some 'ownership' of events that affect their lives, but are sceptical about whether they can really make a difference.

This brings us on to the families' views of area change. Only a minority of mothers in London were satisfied with their neighbourhood as a place to bring up children, less than in the North. Over time an increasing number of families wanted to move away from the area, even though there had been a noticeable improvement in conditions. The East London families had very mixed views and many more wanted to move out than in the Northern neighbourhoods. In spite of this, a majority of mothers in our latest interviews feel their children have better prospects than they themselves had when they were growing up and many feel that their neighbourhoods are improving in some ways, if not in others.

One of the most important conclusions we draw is that family life and experience within poor neighbourhoods is complex and each family's views contain contradictions and ambiguities, so it is a mistake to expect a simple area improvement pattern. This is shown very clearly in the case of Becky, a lone mother in Kirkside East with three boys, who lives in a pleasant semi-detached council house with a garden. When asked about the neighbourhood environment, she explains her dislike of "gardens not being maintained":

> "Up near the community centre it's always been ropey and it hasn't got any better, apart from the people clearing rubbish out of the gardens.... I've not seen anything changing for the better ... [but] just lately ... they've been clearing up the gardens."

Her overall impression is that the environment is still a mess, but actually she has noticed the beginnings of an improvement, not yet complete, and therefore not sufficient to dislodge her previous view. This problem of 'unfinished agendas' helps to explain some of the contradictions we have highlighted in this chapter around policing, regeneration, schools and participation. More importantly, some New Labour policies help families while others are not yet working, leading to complex and sometimes contradictory reactions to neighbourhood conditions and interventions among parents, for example the mixed experience of support targeted at narrowly defined groups or areas and different feelings about various aspects of education. Since multiple problems interact and reinforce each other in poor areas, it is difficult for any single intervention to address adequately all the problems at once. At the same time, the concentrated poverty and constant movement in and out of such areas guarantees a continuing flow of new demands on services, and in effect a constant recreation of problems. This requires a high level of focused long-term effort.

It is hard to see how without special efforts through area-based initiatives, such neighbourhoods can hold up, let alone improve. It would seem a great mistake, in the light of our families' accounts of both negative and positive change, to dilute targeted efforts and assume that general programmes are enough. The barriers these families face in crime, low income, educational disadvantage and community dislocation are far higher than average; and it seems clear that government interventions have produced some real gains for the families – not least through offering greater opportunity, greater support and increased resources.

## Conclusion

Many different conclusions can be drawn from this short review of government policy based on one thousand hours spent listening to families in low-income neighbourhoods. There are some positive views of change in schools; there is a shift by some mothers into paid work; recognition of Sure Start and New Deal for Communities are dominant themes in the interview data; and there is strong support for fun community events.

However, it is also clear that there are many gaps in the programmes and a lot more to do – most significantly on the neighbourhood security and environmental front, but also in relaxing some of the boundary rules and brokering community tensions more carefully. There remains a worrying trend towards ethnic polarisation that these programmes have far more potential to combat than is currently realised. (See Mumford and Power, 2003, for a fuller discussion of the issue of race relations.)

Many of our findings underline how different experiences are for different families. Information percolates partially and imperfectly and some families miss out because they simply do not know what is going on. The families that are more involved tend to have a more positive view of what is happening, though this is not always so.

Most families experience both benefits and problems in programme delivery. This is almost inevitable in externally-funded, nationally-driven programmes, and it is one of the strongest drawbacks to the lack of local organisational control. So while a family benefits greatly from the increased income that tax credits bring, there may be many frightening pitfalls in the bureaucratic administration. And, while most families regard Sure Start as helpful and well focused, they also see it as too restrictive, based on national rules. These contradictions are part of family, neighbourhood and organisational reality, but they could undermine the credibility of programmes that seem generally beneficial and attractive to residents.

The real problem lies in the scale of the difficulties these neighbourhoods face. The policies reflect a serious attempt to reverse a pattern of decline, and in some ways this seems to be working, for instance, in schools and in job access. However, there is a sense that even holding the line is very difficult. For example, the parents' general lack of knowledge of community policing reflects the huge distance yet to be traversed between current conditions with a lot of crime, and a secure future where the government aims to be. It may be that the mothers' heightened consciousness of crime, and fears for their children's future, demand much stronger, longer, more pervasive interventions.

Interestingly, these major problems override North–South differences. While clearly many things are different in different parts of the country, there is an overall pattern to the experiences of these parents that is stronger than most of the differences. Many families do want to move away – 16% in Kirkside East in Round Five (2003), 22% in The Valley and more in London, where there is a more immediate prospect of upgrading by moving to a new neighbourhood. But many want to stay and will stay, in part because of continuous efforts to make the areas more 'liveable', more family and child oriented.

Interventions in particular areas can not answer all of society's wider problems and pressures. These pressures inevitably become concentrated in the most disadvantaged areas, thereby constantly replenishing the 'kitbag of troubles' that the programmes are designed to remove. As a result, at least for now, there is a need for four types of intervention to help families in poor neighbourhoods: locally focused programmes (such as Sure Start); universal targets (such as higher literacy and numeracy); radical policy shifts (such as tax credits to reduce poverty and inequality); and more concentrated, more consistent efforts in high crime areas (such as street policing).

These programmes chip away at the barriers families face in poor neighbourhoods. Success can also inspire more carefully focused and intensive action on outstanding problems.

## Note

[1] The four areas have invented names to protect anonymity: in East London, West City (in Hackney) and East Docks (in Newham); in Yorkshire, Kirkside East (in Leeds) and The Valley (in Sheffield). The five rounds of interviews were completed in London in 1999, 2000, 2001, 2002 and 2003. In Yorkshire, Round One was completed in 2000, Round Two in 2001, Rounds Three and Four (combined) in 2002, and Round Five in 2003.

# FOURTEEN

# Changes in poverty and inequality in the UK in international context

*Kitty Stewart*

## Introduction

The UK's concern about levels of poverty and social exclusion in recent years is not unique. The Lisbon Summit of the European Council (23-24 March 2000) placed poverty and social exclusion at centre stage for EU countries, asking member states to take steps to "make a decisive impact on the eradication of poverty" (Lisbon Summit Conclusions, para 32). Countries have had to publish National Action Plans for Social Inclusion and a set of target indicators are now published: for the first time, Europe has a scorecard for poverty, inequality and exclusion alongside those for inflation and interest rates.

Prior to this, several member states had already begun to increase the priority given to tackling deprivation. In many cases this was triggered by the election of a left-of-centre government: by 1999, 11 of the 15 EU countries had such a government in power, all of them elected after 1993[1]. For instance, the Netherlands has had an anti-poverty policy since 1996, which has included active labour market policies alongside measures to raise the incomes of the poorest. In Ireland, the National Anti-Poverty Stategy (NAPS) was adopted in 1997, leading to targets for persistent poverty and unemployment, and the introduction of the practice of 'poverty-proofing' all government policy from 1998. In France, a 'law against exclusion' was passed in 1998, followed by a series of initiatives including the 1999 Law on Universal Health Insurance Coverage, while Portugal introduced a guaranteed minimum income for the first time in 1996. The Social-Democrat/ Liberal coalition elected in Belgium in 1999 was an important force behind the establishment of common European social indicators, having made this a major priority for the Belgian presidency of the EU in 2001.

Other anglophone countries also saw reform during the 1990s. New Zealand has seen the first official set of major anti-poverty strategies since the early 1970s, initiated by the new Labour government in 1999, and including active labour market policies, increases in benefits for households with children and a primary healthcare strategy (Waldegrave et al, 2002). In the US, major welfare reforms were introduced by the Clinton administration, although in this case the main aim was to increase work and reduce benefit receipt rather than to tackle poverty (Dickens and Ellwood, 2003).

However, while poverty has clearly risen up the agenda in many parts of the industrialised world, few other countries have had strategies as wide-ranging or as ambitious as that in the UK. Few others, of course, needed to: the UK in 1997 found itself at or near the bottom of European and international league tables for child poverty, inequality and worklessness (as highlighted in Chapter One and elsewhere in this volume).

This chapter asks: have the UK's policies since 1997 made a difference to its international standing? Are the changes the Labour government has brought about large enough to begin to narrow the gaps with other countries? Where the answer is no, what are the possible explanations? Is it a question of scale – a need for more spending, higher benefits? Or are there substantive differences in demography and the labour market that set the UK apart?

The chapter begins in the next section by examining changes since 1997 in indicators of poverty and inequality themselves. The following three sections go on to look behind these measures at the factors that drive them, seeking possible explanations of persistent differences. The EU's subsidiarity principle and the 'Open Method of Coordination' underline the right of each member state to choose its own policy tools for addressing poverty and inequality, but an addendum to the 2003 Joint Inclusion Report points to four key aspects to successful anti-poverty policy (EC, 2003b, p 2): employment; support for those unable to work; public spending on services such as education and health; and support for children, to prevent the intergenerational inheritance of poverty. The chapter looks at each of the first three areas in turn, giving special consideration in each case to how policies affect children in particular.

## Poverty and inequality: is the UK narrowing the gap?

Figure 14.1 shows child poverty in the EU member states in 1997 and 2001, as calculated by the European Commission from the European Community Household Panel. (The ECHP collects data for the previous year in each round, so the analysis here really tells us about change between 1996 and 2000.) The poverty line is 60% of the household median with income treated before housing costs, but the UK numbers differ slightly from those presented elsewhere in the book due to the details of methodology as well as the different dataset used[2]. However, the proportionate change in poverty is similar to that derived from UK government statistics, once one takes account of differences in the time frames for data collection.

In 1997, the share of children living in poor households in the UK was higher than anywhere else in the EU, but by 2001 its relative position had improved to fifth from bottom. As the figure shows, in part this is due to a worsening situation in other high poverty countries: Italy, Ireland and Portugal all saw child poverty rise over this period. But the three percentage point fall in child poverty in the

**Figure 14.1: Child poverty in the EU 1997 and 2001: evidence from the ECHP**

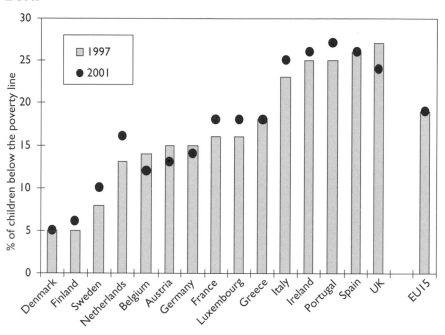

*Notes:* Poverty line is 60% of equivalised household median income.
*Source:* EC (2003a)

UK is unmatched elsewhere. Furthermore, these data reflect the situation before many of the government's tax–benefit changes came into effect. While the UK clearly has a long way to go to reach the average of the lowest three or four EU rates – the latest government interpretation of its pledge to eliminate child poverty (DWP, 2003c) – it has made a significant step in the right direction.

Available data for other anglophone countries are not plotted in the figure because they are from different sources and are not fully consistent. However, for comparison, it is interesting to note that in the US under Clinton the same relative child poverty measure fell by just under three percentage points to 35% – a similar drop to that in the UK but over a much longer period (Dickens and Ellwood, 2003). In New Zealand, child poverty rose from 20.5% to 24% between 1997 and 2000, although this would have been too early for the policies of the New Zealand Labour government to take effect (Waldegrave et al, 2002). In Canada, child poverty rose from 22.2% to 23.8% between 1994 and 1998 (Luxembourg Income Study Key Figures, 2004).

As we have seen in previous chapters of this volume, the fall in child poverty in the UK was not matched by developments for adults. In 1997, the UK's adult poverty ranking among EU countries was better than that for child poverty: 15% of UK over-16s lived in households below 60% of median income, the same as the EU average. In 2001, this number had not changed, and nor had the

UK's ranking, although adult poverty rates had converged across Europe: poverty among over-16s had risen in Scandinavia and fallen in Southern Europe. Figure 14.2 shows the percentage point change in adult poverty plotted against the change in child poverty between 1997 and 2001. Only one country, Austria, appears in the bottom left-hand quadrant, indicating that poverty fell over the period among both groups. In the other four countries in which adult poverty fell, all of them in Southern Europe, child poverty either rose or remained the same. The most populated quadrant is the top right: in Sweden, Finland, Ireland and Luxembourg, poverty rose among both groups.

Figure 14.3 shows European poverty rates for the retired population – a subset of the adults in Figure 14.2. Poverty among this group has risen in Spain, Austria, France, Belgium, Denmark, Greece and (most sharply) in Finland and Ireland (there is further comment on Ireland later in this chapter). Only three countries besides the UK have seen poverty fall for the retired: Luxembourg and Portugal in particular have seen substantial improvements.

The three figures presented so far show no evidence of especially good performance by other countries that have an explicit anti-poverty policy. In Belgium, poverty fell among children but rose among the elderly. Portugal, in contrast, has brought down poverty among adults and pensioners, but not children. In France, the Netherlands and Finland, poverty has been steady or rising among all groups, although in the Finnish case from a very low starting point. And in Ireland, despite the NAPS, relative poverty has risen over this period on all counts, especially among pensioners. Only Germany and the UK have seen all

**Figure 14.2: Percentage point change in poverty headcount for children (0 to 15) and adults (16 plus) 1997 and 2001: evidence from the ECHP**

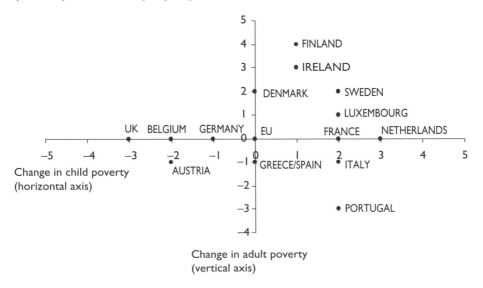

*Notes:* Poverty line is 60% of equivalised household median income.
*Source:* EC (2003a)

**Figure 14.3: Poverty among the retired population: evidence from the ECHP**

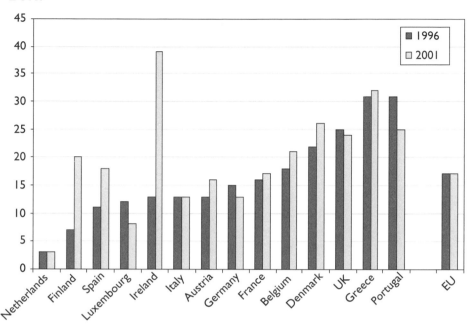

*Source:* 1996 from EC (2001); 2001 from EC (2003a)

three poverty measures fall or stay constant; Germany has had no specific anti-poverty policy.

Figure 14.4 shows the change in the poverty headcount from 1998 for the whole population taken together. The dark blocks show the percentage point change in the headcount measured against 60% of equivalised median income in each year, as in the previous figures. The UK's performance has been strongest overall, with a reduction of just under two points; at the other end of the spectrum, Finland and Ireland have seen increases in poverty of the same magnitude. However, the figure also shows us what has happened to poverty measured against a fixed poverty line of 60% of the 1998 median (the light blocks); that is, what has happened to the real (rather than relative) incomes of the poor. The UK's improvement of over five percentage points is still among the best in Europe, but Ireland, Spain and Portugal have also seen large reductions in poverty on this measure. Most strikingly, Ireland comes top when ranked on real income change, although it was bottom on relative change. Rapid economic growth has meant that the Irish poor have done better in one sense over this three-year period than the poor in any other EU country, but their incomes have not risen fast enough to keep pace with the median, resulting in higher relative poverty indicators. Those on incomes more closely linked to prices than earnings – such as the retired and the unemployed – are likely to have been hardest hit, helping explain the phenomenon in Figure 14.3.

**Figure 14.4: Percentage point change in poverty headcount between 1998 and 2001 measured against a constant (1998) and contemporary income poverty line**

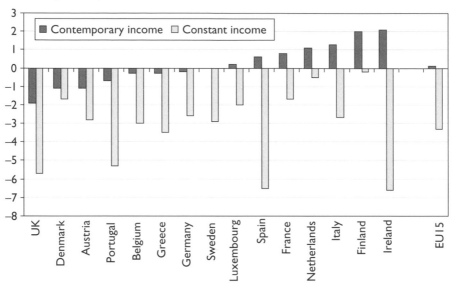

*Source:* EC (2003c, Figure 6)

Figure 14.5 presents income quintile share ratios from the ECHP – the inequality measure chosen by the EC for its set of social inclusion indicators. This is the ratio of the share of income received by the top 20% of the income distribution to that received by the bottom 20%. It therefore reflects changes in income at each end of the distribution, but not in the middle. Gini coefficients from the same source show a near identical pattern (the Gini also reflects the shape of the middle of the distribution).

The ECHP data show that the UK was unusual among higher inequality countries in having an income quintile share ratio that rose between 1997 and 2001. This was also true of all the more equal societies – Scandinavia, Luxembourg and the Netherlands – but Southern Europe and Ireland saw the ratio fall over this period. By 2001, the UK had overtaken Italy and Ireland and moved into fourth highest position; if the data reflect a trend, the UK may also soon have an income quintile share ratio higher than those in Spain and Greece.

It is striking that the inequality data present a very different picture to that given by the poverty headcount. Chapter Eleven of this volume points to divergent trends in poverty and inequality in the UK: we saw there that the bottom of the income distribution has made some gains on the middle since 1997 (resulting in a slight fall in the overall poverty rate), while the top has continued to move away from the middle (preventing inequality from falling). Now it appears as if contrasting trends in the two indicators is a common phenomenon. Ireland, Spain, Italy and France have all seen poverty rise but inequality fall in recent

**Figure 14.5: Income quintile share ratio 1997 and 2001: evidence from the ECHP**

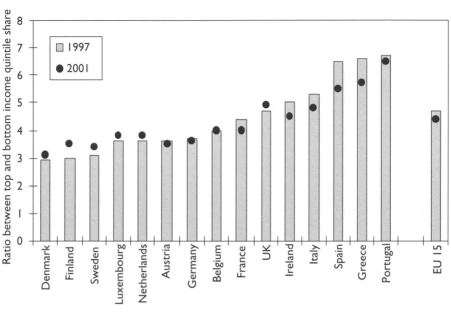

*Source:* EC (2003a)

years; Denmark has seen poverty fall but inequality rise a little – not unlike the UK. In addition, evidence from the Luxembourg Income Study points to rising inequality and falling poverty in the US between 1994 and 2000.

In sum, the UK has made a significant step on the road to bringing child poverty rates down towards average EU levels, although there remains a long way to go. The improvement in child poverty has come at a time when other high poverty countries within Europe have seen child poverty rise, as have other anglophone countries (although not the US). Poverty among the retired population has also come down very slightly against a static EU average (disguising sharp rises in poverty in some countries, and falls in others). However, poverty among adults in general has not moved. Looking at the overall poverty rate for the population as a whole, the UK's performance is the best in Europe, but this arguably says more about the lack of progress in other countries than about the scale of the UK's achievement.

On inequality, the story is very different, and the UK's relative position has deteriorated within Europe. This is the combined result of little change in the UK and improving performance in Ireland and Southern Europe, where inequality was highest.

The rest of this chapter explores differences across countries in some of the main factors driving poverty and inequality, and how these changed after Labour came to power.

## Employment, wages and in-work tax credits

The importance of a job lies at the heart of anti-poverty policy across Europe: every member state emphasises employment in the most recent round of National Action Plans for tackling social exclusion (EC, 2003c). In the US, raising employment has been the ultimate goal of welfare reform. This section considers how the UK has done at tackling unemployment and worklessness compared to other countries. It goes on to look at the 'making work pay' element of employment policy that is also common to most countries, examining changes in the market wage and in tax credits for the low paid.

### Unemployment and worklessness

Figure 14.6 shows that the UK has been very successful at keeping unemployment down in the face of economic downturns in Europe and the US. Unemployment in the UK is at its lowest level since the mid-1970s, and below the US rate.

Long-term unemployment (the share of the labour force unemployed for more than a year) is also very low in the UK: it was low by international standards when Labour came to power and has since fallen to 1.1%, compared to an EU average of 3%.

**Figure 14.6: Standardised unemployment rates for selected OECD countries**

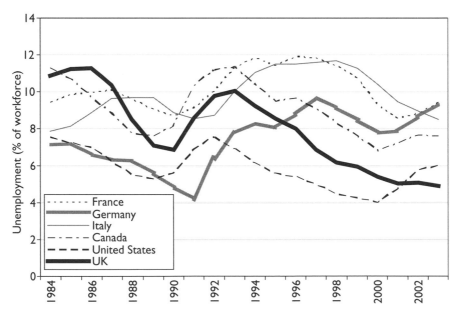

*Notes:* 2003 data for UK and Italy are for Q3 and are provisional.
*Source:* OECD Main Economic Indicators, 2004

However, the distribution of work across UK households looks rather different to that in other countries. Despite the strong record on unemployment, the share of UK households in which no adult had a job rose through the 1980s and 1990s. When Labour came to power, one in five children lived in a household with no job, far higher than the level in any other OECD country (Gregg et al, 1999). Partly this is explained by growing numbers of lone parent households, but polarisation of two-worker households into 'work-rich' and 'work-poor', perhaps due to falling demand for low-skilled labour, have had an even greater impact. Gregg et al (2002) find evidence of this polarisation in three other countries they examine (Germany, Spain and the US), but the rise has been much steeper in the UK than elsewhere.

As we have seen in previous chapters of this volume, the government has made progress in moving adults from workless households into work. The lone parent employment rate rose from 44% in 1997 to 53% in spring 2003 (HM Treasury, 2004a, p 88). In 2003, there were 400,000 fewer children in workless households than there had been in 1996 (see Chapter Seven, Table 7.5 in this volume). But as Figure 14.7 shows, this has only brought the UK down to the level at which its nearest neighbour, Ireland, began in 1995. The US and Australia, both with relatively high shares of children in workless households, also saw improvements between 1996 and 2000 (see Gregg and Wadsworth, 2003).

One of the factors keeping this indicator high in the UK is that lone parent employment rates, while moving upwards, still fall well short of those in most other countries. Figure 14.8 shows the share of families with children headed by a single parent along with employment rates for those households. The UK in 2001 has the third highest rate of lone parenthood and the fourth lowest lone parent employment rate. The figure shows that the government's aspiration for lone parents – 70% employed by 2010 – has precedents around the world: 14 countries out of 21 have employment rates of 65% or higher, with six clear above the 70% mark. In several cases, the numbers represent sharp recent increases: using different sources to that used in Figure 14.8, Millar (2003) finds that employment in the US rose from 57% of lone parents in 1994 to 70% in 2000, and in Norway from 53% in 1991 to 62% in 1999. In the Netherlands, employment rose from the 42% shown in the figure for 1997 to 54% in 2002 (Knijn and Van Berkel, 2003). In the Netherlands, as in the UK, lone mothers in receipt of benefits were only required to register for work in 1996, in contrast to policy in France and Scandinavia which had long treated this group as workers as well as mothers (Lewis, 2001).

Despite the precedent, some commentators have raised doubts about the likelihood of the UK reaching 70% given the story so far. There is evidence that the characteristics of lone parents in the UK differ from those in other countries in ways which present greater barriers to work: Bradshaw et al (1996) find that the education gap between single and married mothers is particularly large in the UK, while UK lone mothers are also younger and likely to have more children, including more children under age five. These differences are likely to have a

**Figure 14.7: Children in jobless households in selected EU countries**

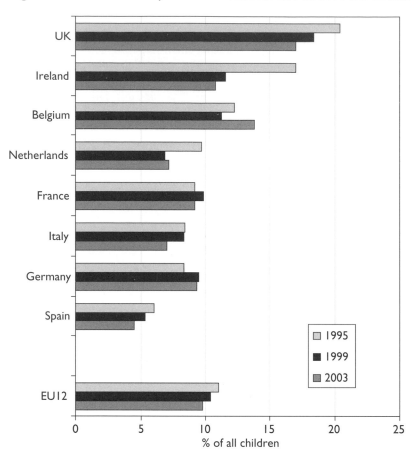

% of all children

*Notes:* All other EU countries for which data are available fall at or below the Spanish level. No household-based data are available from the Labour Force Surveys in Denmark, Finland and Sweden.
*Source:* EU Labour Force Survey data presented in EC (2003a)

greater impact on employment policy over time as the parents closest to the labour market will have been reached first: Gregg and Harkness (2003) suggest that the remaining non-working lone parents in the UK are increasingly less skilled, and are also more concentrated in social housing, making work incentives weaker. Differences in social and historical norms about combining work and motherhood may be equally important. Lewis (2001) cites evidence that an 'alternative moral rationality' underpins the commitment of British and Dutch lone mothers to family work: policies which make work pay financially may not be enough for everyone. As we saw in Chapter Seven of this volume, more than one third of non-working lone parents in the UK simply want to be at home with their children. Finally, employment rates in countries with generous parental leave may not be quite what they seem: many mothers classified as employed will in fact be at home on leave.

**Figure 14.8: Lone parenthood and employment in the late 1990s/ early 2000s**

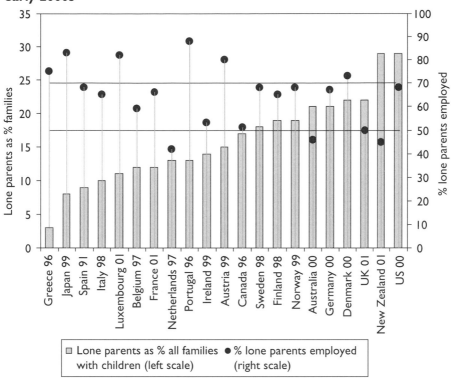

*Notes:* Years refer to data on employment; years for lone parent share may differ slightly.
*Source:* Bradshaw and Finch (2002, Tables 2.2, 2.5)

Nevertheless, it is also clear that there is a strong correlation across countries between the availability and affordability of childcare and employment rates for lone parents (Bradshaw et al, 1996). Hence continued expansion of childcare does seem very likely to result in further falls in household worklessness.

## The returns to work

But is work enough on its own to bring a family out of poverty? Poverty is still found among working households with no children, but it is low: in 2001, 6% of two-adult households with one worker classified as poor in the UK, compared to an EU average of 7%. Only Luxembourg, the Netherlands and Spain had lower rates of poverty for similar households. For single adult households, the rate was a little higher: 9% of single adults in work in the UK lived on less than 60% of median income, compared to 8% in the EU.

However, for households *with* children, poverty rates remain very high where the family relies on the wages of a single worker. Figure 14.9 shows poverty rates in 2001 for single parent households and households containing two adults and one or more children (but only one worker).

**Figure 14.9: Poverty among single worker households with children: EU 2001**

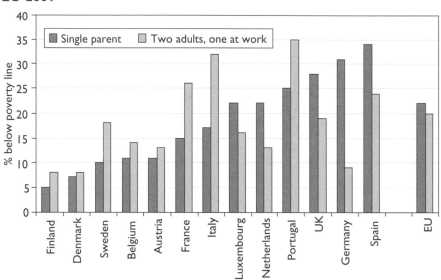

*Notes:* The unit of measurement in this figure is the household, not the child (rates of child poverty will be higher).
*Source:* EC (2003a, Table 14)

Twenty-eight per cent of UK households with a working single parent are poor, the third highest rate in Europe. Two adult families in the UK are better protected against the risks of poverty: wage earners in these households are more likely to work full time and (because more of them are men) in higher-paid jobs. But one in five of these households still lives below the poverty line.

However, it is interesting that, across Europe, two-parent households in work are not always less likely to be in poverty than those with single working parents. In fact, in the majority of the countries shown, poverty is higher among the two-adult households, with the difference particularly marked in Sweden, France, Italy and Portugal. These countries appear to offer stronger additional support for lone parent families, while assuming a two-worker model for families with two adults. As a result, while it is hardly impressive that 19% of two-adult families with one worker are poor in the UK (and this is at least twice the level in Denmark, Finland and Germany), it is still below the EU average and the rate for France, and close to the rate for Sweden.

There are three potential factors explaining differences in in-work poverty:

- the number of hours worked;
- the hourly wage; and
- the level of tax credits and benefits for employed families.

One reason for the high poverty rate among working lone parents in the UK may be the greater likelihood of part-time working. Bradshaw and Finch (2002, table 2.5) find that only 47% of employed lone mothers in the UK work 30+ hours a week, lower than any other country with data except the US (18%) and Ireland (45%). In contrast, in Finland, 83% of working lone mothers work more than 35 hours a week; in France 73% work 30+ hours. Furthermore, a significant number of employed lone mothers in the UK work fewer than 16 hours – 12%, compared to 2% in Ireland, 3% in Luxembourg and 0% in Portugal. Norway (12%) and France (17%) also have high shares of lone mothers working fewer than 16 hours, but most countries do not provide breakdowns of data that let us look at this low-hours group, perhaps itself an indication that it is not common practice.

Short working hours are therefore likely to be one factor contributing to high in-work poverty among lone parents. What about the working wage? Are more of these jobs low-wage jobs in the UK? There is evidence that women who work part time have much lower hourly wages than full-time workers in the UK, and that this is not true or is less true elsewhere (see, for example, Harkness and Waldfogel, 1999). Harkness and Waldfogel also find that full-time working mothers in the UK are lower paid relative to other working women than are mothers in any of the other six countries in their study.

In general, low-wage employment is also more prevalent in the UK than in many other countries. The OECD reports that, in most countries, employment grew more rapidly during the 1990s in high-paid industries and occupations than in those with average or below-average wages. It points to three exceptions. In Portugal, the strongest growth was in the medium-paid category, while the Netherlands and the UK saw relatively strong growth in the low-paid sector (OECD, 2003b, p 41). As a result, in the year 2000, just under 20% of UK full-time workers were earning less than two thirds of median gross earnings (OECD, 2003b, chart 1.A1.1); a substantially higher share than in all but four of the 14 other countries presented (the US, Canada, Hungary and Korea). In Belgium, only 8% were in this situation; in Germany 12%; and in Australia 15%. In the Netherlands, the share had been rising since the early 1980s but remained below 15%.

Table 14.1 shows the formal lower boundary for wages – the National Minimum Wage (NMW) per month and as a share of mean and median full-time wages for 17 countries in July 2001, as reported by Bradshaw and Finch (2002). It is a tribute to the Labour government that the UK features on this table at all, but at 35% of the median and 30% of the mean, the UK minimum in mid-2001 looks much lower relative to full-time earnings than anywhere else in Europe other than Spain. In fact, figures produced by the Low Pay Commission in the UK give a much more encouraging picture: they estimate that the NMW was 44% of the *male* median on its introduction (and hence would be a higher share of the overall median), rising to 46% by October 2003 (LPC, 2003, Table 6.3); while another UK source puts the 2003 wage at 37% of the mean (43% of the

**Table 14.1: Minimum wages in £ppp and as a share of the full-time wage (2001)**

|  | Minimum wage (£ppp/month) | % mean | % median |
|---|---|---|---|
| Denmark | 1,035 | 57 | – |
| Belgium | 828 | 52 | 59 |
| France | 765 | 51 | 62 |
| Italy | 728 | 51 | 61 |
| Australia | 869 | 48 | – |
| Ireland | 615 | 46 | – |
| Luxembourg | 851 | 44 | 51 |
| Netherlands | 798 | 44 | 57 |
| Portugal | 329 | 44 | – |
| Greece | 441 | 42 | 95 |
| Israel | 447 | 40 | 56 |
| New Zealand | 512 | 38 | – |
| UK | 561 | 30 | 35 |
| Canada | 559 | 28 | 32 |
| Spain | 366 | 28 | – |
| Japan | 432 | 24 | – |
| US | 507 | 24 | 30 |

*Notes:* – = no median earnings data available.
Austria, Finland, Germany, Norway and Sweden have no minimum wage legislation.
Data for Greece reported as in source.
*Source:* Bradshaw and Finch (2002, Table 2.7)

male median and 50% of the female median) (ONS, 2003b, Table E7.1). While these numbers might shift the UK away from the very bottom group in the table, however, they would still not be good enough to catch the Northern and Central EU countries. In Belgium, France, Italy, the Netherlands and (almost certainly) Denmark, the NMW is in the region of 60% of the median full-time wage. Only at this point is a full-time job likely to be enough to bring a household out of poverty.

Finally, what can be said about wage inequality between the bottom and the top? Chapter Eleven of this volume showed that wage growth for low earners in the UK has been keeping up with that for middle earners since the early 1990s (the 50:10 percentile ratio has stabilised), but that high earners continue to move ahead of the middle: the 90:10 ratio has continued to rise since 1997, having increased steadily from the late 1970s. In many other countries, including most of Western Europe and Japan, this ratio has remained roughly stable at substantially lower levels than the UK throughout this period (OECD, 2003b, chart 1.10). Among EU countries, only Austria, Ireland and Portugal had higher earnings dispersion between the top and the bottom than the UK in 2001, along with Canada and the US. In Ireland and France, the recent trend appears downwards, perhaps explaining some of the differing directions in income inequality change in Figure 14.5.

*Tax credits: the value of the take-home package for working households*

We have seen that shorter working hours and relative low wages may explain the higher levels of in-work poverty among lone parent households in the UK. This subsection considers the third possible contributing factor – differences in the generosity of the tax–benefit package.

Table 14.2 shows the results of model family analysis carried out by Bradshaw and Finch (2002) for households with children. The table shows the net package of benefits and services for two types of low-earning households: a two-adult household with two children aged seven and 14, in which a single worker earns half the mean male wage; and a lone parent household with one child aged seven, in which the parent earns half the mean female wage. The first column for each family type shows the net package of taxes and social security contributions, tax credits and benefits. In the second column this is combined with any costs or subsidies associated with housing, health, education or childcare for children of this age and in this income group, assuming the family uses services in the same way as the majority of people in that country. Clearly these are simplifications of the full picture, but they give us a broad idea of how countries compare[3].

It is striking that the English-speaking group do very well on this table; unexpected given the high child poverty rates in these countries. The UK ranks second or third out of 22 countries for both lone parents and couples on the basis of the tax–benefit package, falling to fifth or seventh rank when services and housing costs are included. For both the UK and the US, the generosity of the system is partly due to a strong degree of targeting of benefits and subsidies towards lower-income working families, compared to a stronger emphasis on universal services in some other countries. Bradshaw and Finch (2002) also calculate the value of the average package, for children from all income groups: the US in particular does much less well here, falling to 16th place, largely because of the high health care costs facing average earners (the US families represented in Table 14.2 are exempt from these costs). The UK falls towards the bottom of a second-ranking group of countries that includes France, Luxembourg, Sweden, Norway, Belgium, Germany, Denmark, Ireland and Australia; Austria and Finland are ahead in a league of their own (Bradshaw and Finch, 2002, Table 11.4). Bradshaw and Finch argue that this still represents a considerable improvement in the UK's relative position compared to earlier studies, a reflection of the first wave of changes to the child benefit package between 1999 and 2001, when this picture was taken.

Childcare support is one aspect of the child benefit package only partially reflected in Table 14.2, as the children in the model families shown there are of school age. This is another area where the UK's relative position has considerably improved, although this part of the package still falls well short of that in many other countries. Figure 14.10 shows the net cost in 2001 of full-time childcare for a child under three for two model families. In both cases, the cost is calculated as a share of half-average gross female earnings. For the UK lone parent family

**Table 14.2: Child benefit packages: taxes, cash benefits, housing costs and services (as share of average earnings) (July 2001)**

| | As % of average gross monthly earnings | | | | Ranks | | | |
|---|---|---|---|---|---|---|---|---|
| | One earner, two children, half-average male earnings | | Lone parent, one child, half-average female earnings | | One earner, two children, half-average male earnings | | Lone parent, one child, half-average female earnings | |
| | Taxes and benefits | Taxes, benefits, housing, services | Taxes and benefits | Taxes, benefits, housing, services | Taxes and benefits | Taxes, benefits, housing, services | Taxes and benefits | Taxes, benefits, housing, services |
| US | 28 | 33 | 15 | 17 | 1 | 1 | 8 | 8 |
| UK | 22 | 22 | 19 | 19 | 2 | 5 | 3 | 7 |
| Ireland | 21 | 17 | 35 | 31 | 3 | 9 | 1 | 2 |
| Luxembourg | 20 | 18 | 6 | 5 | 4 | 7 | 15 | 19 |
| Australia | 20 | 26 | 17 | 24 | 5 | 3 | 4 | 3 |
| Austria | 16 | 27 | 16 | 20 | 6 | 2 | 6 | 6 |
| New Zealand | 15 | 12 | 15 | 12 | 7 | 13 | 7 | 13 |
| Belgium | 14 | 12 | 6 | 6 | 8 | 15 | 16 | 18 |
| Italy | 14 | 13 | 9 | 8 | 9 | 12 | 13 | 15 |
| Finland | 13 | 25 | 6 | 21 | 10 | 4 | 17 | 4 |
| Sweden | 13 | 20 | 5 | 15 | 11 | 6 | 18 | 10 |
| Canada | 11 | 10 | 8 | 8 | 12 | 16 | 14 | 16 |
| Germany | 10 | 18 | 11 | 15 | 13 | 8 | 10 | 11 |
| Norway | 8 | 12 | 16 | 20 | 14 | 14 | 5 | 5 |
| Netherlands | 7 | 6 | 10 | 9 | 15 | 18 | 12 | 14 |
| France | 7 | 14 | 0 | 8 | 16 | 10 | 22 | 17 |
| Portugal | 6 | 6 | 3 | -3 | 17 | 17 | 19 | 22 |
| Denmark | 6 | 14 | 10 | 16 | 18 | 11 | 11 | 9 |
| Israel | 5 | 2 | 29 | 51 | 19 | 19 | 2 | 1 |
| Japan[a] | 3 | -4 | 13 | 13 | 20 | 22 | 9 | 12 |
| Greece | 2 | 2 | 1 | 1 | 21 | 20 | 21 | 21 |
| Spain | 0 | -1 | 2 | 1 | 22 | 21 | 20 | 20 |

Notes: Couple plus 2 children 7 and 14; difference from childless couple on same earnings. Lone parent with one child aged 7; difference from single childless person.
[a] In Japan, dependant's allowances and housing allowances paid on top of basic salary in the public sector and large private enterprises have not been included in earnings.
Source: Calculated from £PPPS figures given in Bradshaw and Finch (2002, Tables 9.8a, 9.8b, 9.9a, 9.9b) and national average earnings given in the same source, Table A.4

**Figure 14.10: Net costs of full-time childcare for a child under 3 after direct and indirect subsidies and taxes and benefits 2001, as a share of half-average female earnings**

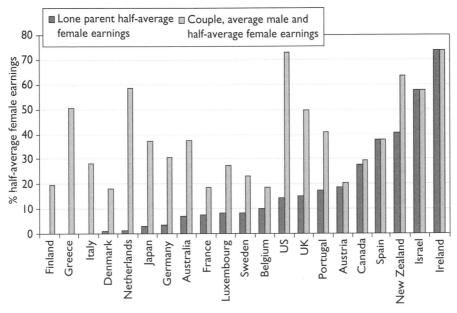

*Notes:* Most prevalent type of childcare in each country. For the UK at the time of analysis this was a childminder place.
*Source:* Calculated from Bradshaw and Finch (2002, Tables 5.6, B.3)

earning this amount, childcare comes to 15% of earnings. This represents a big improvement from 1997, when the absence of any support would have meant childcare costs of 50% of earnings, higher than anywhere else but Israel and Ireland. However, costs remain proportionately lower for low-earning lone parents in ten EU countries and in the US, Japan and Australia. (Furthermore, the figure over-represents the generosity of the UK system in assuming that everyone in the right income bracket receives the childcare tax credit. In fact, as discussed in Chapter Seven of this volume, this is far from true, largely because of the shortage of formal childcare places for which the credit can be used.) The two-earner household in the UK does not qualify for the childcare tax credit, and so this household does spend 50% of the female earner's wage on childcare. This only leads to a small deterioration in the UK's comparative position, down from rank 14 to 15 out of 21, as in almost all countries this second family type faces a substantially higher childcare bill than the first. In Ireland and the US, the couple family would need to spend over 70% of the female earner's wage. (This says nothing about differences in the quality of care provided, which would be expected to affect the market price of childcare across countries.)

In general, however, the UK's child benefit package now looks generous in international context, particularly for lower-earning families. Yet in-work child poverty remains high, especially among lone parent families. Other countries, such as Denmark and Finland, have much lower poverty rates among working households with children than might be expected on the basis of the level of child support. The relationship between working poverty and the generosity of the social transfer system is clearly far from perfect, drawing our attention back to the importance of market wage inequality as a factor driving in-work poverty. It is interesting that this was also the conclusion reached by an earlier study of cross-national differences in child poverty rates, based on pre-1997 data:

> The English-speaking countries other than the USA ... actually provide quite substantial income transfers to their most needy children. The living standards of these children, however, remain relatively low because of low labour-market incomes. (Bradbury and Jäntti, 2001, p 88)

## Security for those without work

Before the Labour government came to power, the UK compared badly in international studies examining the situation of individuals and families out of work. Table 14.3 shows poverty rates from an OECD source for children in workless households in the mid-1990s. Seventy per cent of children in workless single-parent households and 50% of those in two-adult workless households lived on less than 50% of median income (a less generous poverty line than that used earlier in the chapter). Only Canada, Italy and the US had more poverty among workless single parents; only these three countries and the Netherlands ranked lower on poverty among two-parent workless households.

Christina Behrendt's (2002) work uses model family analysis to examine the generosity of social assistance in the UK, Sweden and Germany in more detail.

**Table 14.3: Poverty rates among children in workless households (1995) (50% median poverty line)**

|  | Single parent | Two parents |
|---|---|---|
| Finland | 9.9 | 3.6 |
| Belgium | 22.8 | 16.1 |
| Sweden | 24.2 | 9.5 |
| Norway | 29.6 | 30.6 |
| Denmark | 34.2 | 6.0 |
| Greece | 36.8 | 22.0 |
| Netherlands | 41.3 | 51.4 |
| Australia | 42.1 | 18.3 |
| France | 45.1 | 37.5 |
| Germany | 61.8 | 44.8 |
| UK | 69.4 | 50.1 |
| Canada | 72.5 | 73.5 |
| Italy | 78.7 | 69.8 |
| US | 93.4 | 82.2 |

*Notes:* Data for 1995 except Italy 1993 and Denmark, Greece, Australia, France and Germany 1994.
*Source:* Oxley et al (2001, Table 15.5, using OECD data)

(This is just one aspect of security for those without work. Cross-national differences in unemployment benefit are not considered here because of space constraints, but are also likely to be important: earnings-related benefits continue to play a much more central role in most other EU countries than they do in the UK.) Some of Behrendt's results are presented in Figure 14.11, which shows that in Sweden in 1995 families of all types were entitled to social assistance benefits taking them well clear of a poverty line of 60% of equivalised median income. In Britain, in contrast, entitlements for most families fell between 45% and 55% of median income, with single parents at the upper end of this range and the elderly receiving a little more, but still short of 60%. In Germany, some types of family were able to live on social assistance without falling into poverty, while for other types the system was less generous: a lot of the difference appears due to much larger benefits available to families with babies. It should be emphasised that the figure points only to eligibility, not take-up, and Behrendt finds that take-up is much higher in the UK than in the other two countries[4]. But even if all UK families received the benefits to which they were entitled at that time, they did not come close to clearing the poverty line.

How have things changed since these snapshots were taken? Labour promised that a commitment to 'security for those who cannot' would run alongside the emphasis on employment, and during its first and second terms the government made substantial increases to income support and other benefits available to

**Figure 14.11: Level of social assistance entitlements as a proportion of equivalised median income: Sweden and Britain 1995 and Germany 1994**

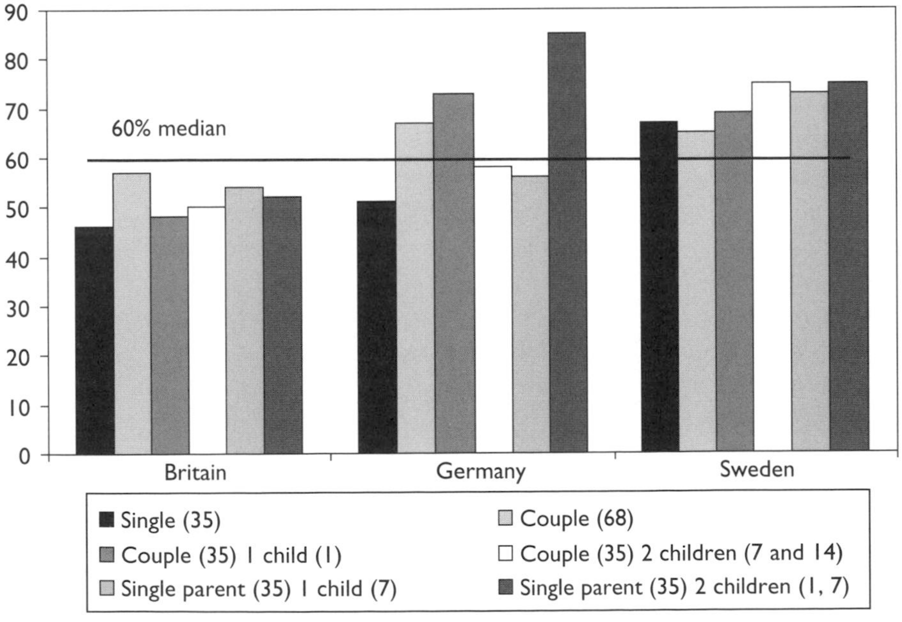

Source: Behrendt (2002, Figures 6.5, 6.6, 6.7). Median income calculated by Behrendt from LIS

workless families with children, as highlighted in Chapter Seven of this volume. This contrasts with the approach taken in America, where the welfare-to-work programme saw in-work benefits made more generous but benefits for those without work tightened, especially for single parents (Dickens and Ellwood, 2003). This tougher stance has not been restricted to the US: Kilkey and Bradshaw (2001, p 214) find that Norway and the Netherlands have both adopted measures leaving some lone parents "with no choice but to seek paid work". Indeed, of the six countries in their study (the others are the US, France and Australia), they argue that the UK has been working most intensively to improve the paid-work environment but has been least aggressive in pushing lone parents into paid work.

Has this translated into lower poverty rates for out-of-work families? Figure 14.12 recalculates the Behrendt figures for four years for the UK. The numbers differ from Behrendt's because of differences in methodology and data sources, but are internally consistent. (In particular, the McClements equivalence scale is used, which gives a low weight to young children; this is likely to explain why families with young children appear relatively better off in Figure 14.12 than in Figure 14.11.) The figure shows, surprisingly, that while between 1997/98 and 2004/05 income support grew as a share of median income for all family types except non-pensioner adults without children, in only one case was the increase enough to bring the family back up beyond the 1994/95 level. This family – a

**Figure 14.12: Income Support entitlements as a proportion of median income: UK (1994/95 to 2004/05)**

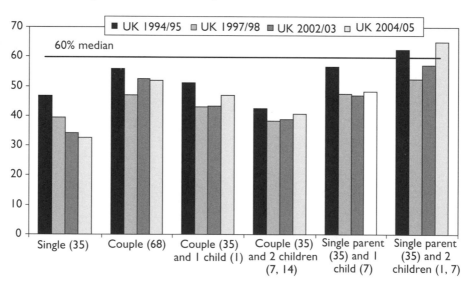

*Notes:* Income equivalised using the McClements scale. Median income for 2004/05 is predicted from 2002/03 incomes, assuming nominal growth of 4% per year. Children aged '1' are in fact assumed to be less than 1 for the full year.
*Source:* Author's calculations from DWP (2004a) and CPAG (2004) and earlier equivalents

single parent and two young children – cleared the poverty line in 2004/05 (although they are likely to slip back as soon as the youngest child becomes too old to qualify for the Baby Tax Credit introduced in 2003). No other case indicates substantial progress towards the line. The introduction of the Pension Credit from late 2003 does not appear to have helped the pensioner couple depicted (who are assumed to have no other income), although the new system will have made things easier for pensioners who have some additional pension provision. However, it is non-pensioner households without children who are clearly worst off: income for the single claimant shown has fallen steadily as a share of the median since 1994/95, down from 47% to 33%; relative income for childless couples (not shown) has fallen nearly as fast.

Figure 14.12 is somewhat partial: we must remember that real average income has grown rapidly since 1997/98 (the median is up 20% in real terms AHC, compared to a 7% increase over the earlier period). So the small changes in the figure disguise much greater growth in the real incomes of families living on income support. However, it remains the case that income support for households with children will need to reach the 60% line if child poverty is to be eradicated. Other European countries are managing to achieve this. Figure 14.12 illustrates the uphill task it will be to catch them up.

Figure 14.12 represents benefit entitlements. But what happened to actual poverty rates among households without work? Figure 14.13 shows poverty among unemployed adults for 11 EU countries. (For the UK this includes income

**Figure 14.13: Percentage of the unemployed with equivalised income below 60% contemporary median**

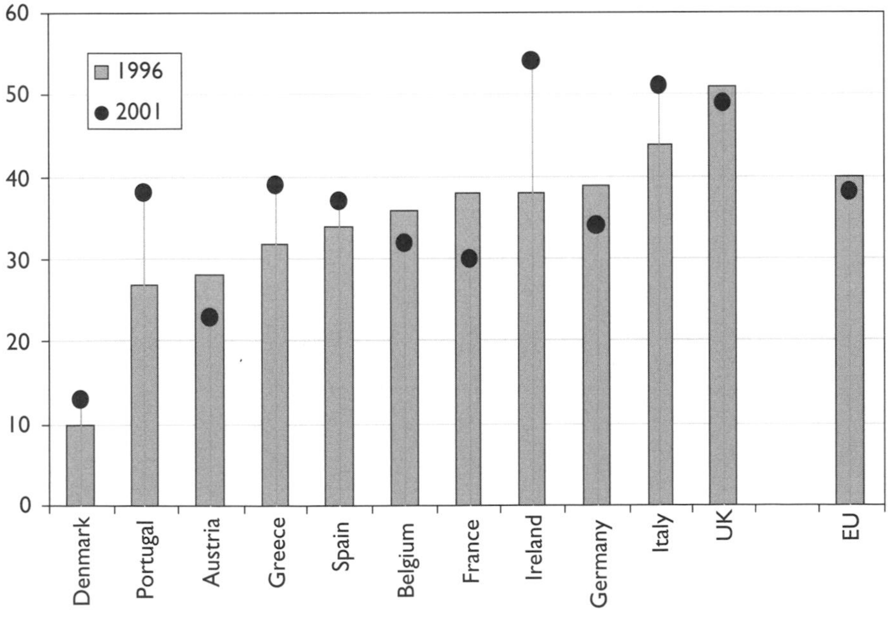

*Source:* 1996 from EC (2001); 2001 from EC (2003a)

support recipients as well as adults entitled to unemployment benefit or income-related Job Seekers' Allowance.) The UK started with a poverty rate of 51%, much higher than that in any other country, and over five times the rate in Denmark. By 2001, it had fallen very slightly to 49%, and the UK had also risen off the bottom rank due to sharp increases in relative poverty among the Irish and Italian unemployed. Poverty among inactive groups in the UK had at least stopped getting worse under the Labour government. However, Austria, France, Belgium and Germany had all managed much more substantial positive change.

## Public spending

After cuts in the first two years in office, the Labour government increased social expenditure from 22.9% of GDP in 1999/2000 to 25% in 2002/03 (HM Treasury, 2004b). How does this compare to levels of social spending in other countries? In 1998 – the most recent year available from the OECD social expenditure database – the UK ranked 13th out of 17 countries on its social expenditure share of GDP, ahead only of Canada, Ireland, the US and Japan (Hills, 2004a, Figure 6.8)[5]. Assuming no change in the spending share in other countries since then, the UK increase to 2002/03 would have pushed it up two places, ahead of Portugal and Spain, but still behind Greece. In 1998, Germany, Finland, Austria and France all spent between 30% and 35% of GDP on social expenditure; Sweden and Denmark spent over 35%. These differences are not surprising when one considers that the size of the government budget in the UK is far lower than in most other European countries. European Commission figures show that the taxation share of GDP grew from 35.4% in the UK in 1995 to 37.5% in 2001; this was a higher share than in Ireland, Spain, Portugal or Greece but lower than anywhere else in the EU, where the 2001 share ranged from 40% in the Netherlands through 45% in France to 54% in Sweden (EC, 2003d).

Figure 14.14 focuses on the areas given particular priority by Labour – health and education (the latter including spending on early years and childcare services). On the assumption again of no change elsewhere, recent increases in the UK's education budget have made a big difference to the rankings: the UK moved up six places, from fourth bottom to the middle of the chart. If education spending reaches 5.6% of GDP by 2005/06, as projected, the UK would find itself up another two positions, just behind Portugal. Increases in health spending have also moved the UK up from fourth bottom to among the higher spending countries.

On the other hand, even in 2005/06 education expenditure will still be significantly lower as a share of GDP than in France, Austria, New Zealand and Finland, and well below the rest of Scandinavia. Part of the difference is explained by much higher levels of spending in all these countries (with the exception of New Zealand) on childcare. The early years and childcare component of the UK budget increased by more than £1 billion between 1997/98 and 2002/03, but in the latter year it still amounted to just 0.3% of GDP, compared to between

**Figure 14.14: Expenditure on health, education and childcare as a share of GDP: OECD countries 1998; UK (1997/98 and 2002/03)**

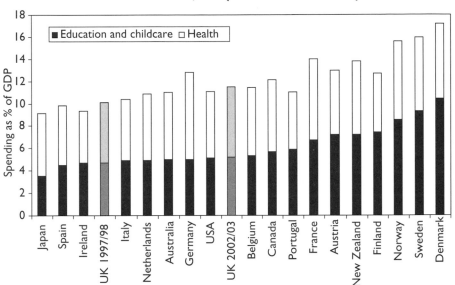

*Source:* OECD Social Expenditure Database 2001; HM Treasury (2004b)

0.7% and 0.9% on formal daycare in Austria and France in 1998, and between 1.2% and 2.1% in Scandinavia. Unfortunately, the explanation for the rest of the difference remains unclear, as we do not have any further breakdown of the budget. Clearly, the share spent on compulsory as opposed to post-compulsory education is important from a poverty perspective. Spending on UK schools increased from 53% of the education budget in 1996/97 to 62% in 2000/01 (see Chapter Three of this volume); it is quite likely, then, that the UK has made further progress up a ranking showing school expenditure as a share of GDP.

## Conclusion

The analysis in this chapter has shown the UK in a positive light in a number of ways:

- Efforts to bring down the rate of child poverty have had a positive impact on the UK's ranking in Europe, and the UK has also made the most progress of EU countries in bringing down the overall poverty rate (although changes elsewhere have arguably been less than impressive given the collective commitment to tackling the issue).
- Unemployment is at historically low levels and is resisting the downturn in other parts of Europe and the US; there is also evidence that 'make work pay' policies have been more successful (and less punitive) than elsewhere.

- The package of tax credits and benefits for lower-income households with children appears now to be among the most generous in the industrialised world.
- Recent increases in health and education expenditure have shifted the UK from among the very lowest spenders in the OECD to the middle rank.

However:

- Inequality remains very high and no progress has been made. Indeed, the UK's inequality ranking has got worse as the top of the distribution has moved away from the middle and as inequality has fallen in some other parts of Europe.
- Despite improvements, the level of worklessness among households with children remains the highest in Europe.
- The rate of in-work poverty among lone parent households also remains among the highest, in part due to shorter working hours (which may reflect parental preference) but in part to relative low wages.
- Almost all households dependent on income support are likely to remain well below the poverty line (in contrast to the situation in Sweden and Germany).
- Comparisons of overall social expenditure show that the UK remains alongside the Southern European countries and Ireland as a low-spending economy.

In sum, if the goal is not only to move off the bottom of poverty and inequality league tables, but to head to the top, a lot has been achieved but very much more remains to be done. This includes: (1) much more to tackle low market wages; (2) the expansion of good childcare to make work a real possibility for those who want it; (3) more support for those who do not work because they are unable to or choose to look after children; (4) continued investment in public services, in particular education; (5) an acceptance that income inequality cannot be addressed by concentrating solely on the bottom of the distribution.

Much of this will require increases in expenditure far beyond those introduced by the Labour government so far. It looks very unlikely that the lower poverty rates of Scandinavia, Benelux, France and Germany can be achieved without levels of spending – and taxation – closer to European levels.

## Notes

[1] Left-of-centre governments were elected in Denmark and Greece in 1993 (keeping power until 2001 and 2004 respectively); in the Netherlands and Sweden in 1994 (the Netherlands until 2003); in Portugal and Finland in 1995 (until 2002 and 2003); in Italy in 1996 (until 2001); in France and the UK in 1997 (France until 2002); in Germany in 1998 and in Belgium in 1999. In summer 2004, left-of-centre governments held power in Sweden, the UK, Germany, Belgium and Spain (elected 2004).

[2] For instance, the EC uses the modified OECD equivalence scale rather than the McClements scale traditionally used in the UK. After the 2003 consultation process on measuring child poverty, the UK government also decided to adopt the modified OECD scale, so in future the UK's own calculations should be closer to those of the EC (DWP, 2003c).

[3] Bradshaw and Finch (2002) present these figures in sterling purchasing power parities. They have been converted here to a share of average earnings to give a relative measure of the generosity of the system. In practice, the conversion does not lead to large differences in country rankings.

[4] Behrendt gives a number of possible reasons for this. Broadly, the UK system is simpler and more standardised than in the other two countries; it allows less room for the exercise of administrative discretion; its administration is better integrated with that of other benefits; and it is less rigorously means-tested than the Swedish system in particular, which allows no income disregards.

[5] United Kingdom data are from HM Treasury (2004b); OECD data are misleading for the UK in that they include private occupational pensions. Of course, similar problems could affect the data for other countries. An additional problem with these comparisons is highlighted by Adema (2000): some countries tax public transfers, so net spending is lower than gross spending. On Adema's calculations, once taxation is corrected for, social spending in the UK comes out ahead of Norway, the Netherlands and Italy but remains lower than in Sweden, Finland, Denmark and Germany.

# Part Four: Conclusion

# FIFTEEN

# A tide turned but mountains yet to climb?

*John Hills and Kitty Stewart*

## Introduction

In this chapter, we put evidence from earlier chapters within a common framework, and give an overview of what this shows about the impact of policies towards poverty, inequality and social exclusion under New Labour.

A first danger is timing. If the 1950s were still "too early to tell" the impact of the French Revolution according to Zhou Enlai, 2004 is far too early fully to assess policies that are still being implemented. The problem is not just of present preoccupations, but also of data. Statistics follow events with a lag. While there has been great improvement in the speed of key poverty and income distribution statistics, the most recent available to us are for 2002/03, with a mid-point in autumn 2002, before the major April 2003 tax credit changes, for instance. Other statistics have longer lags. More fundamentally, many measures are *designed* to have long-term effects: the impacts on adult outcomes of new policies towards children's early years and later education are inevitably still unknown.

Second, by focusing on specifics, we may miss the bigger picture. We have tried to avoid concentrating only on the government's own agenda, but there is often more to say when policy has been active than when it has not. Many data are from government sources, and relate to its own targets and priorities. It is impressive that there is now an annual progress report on poverty and social exclusion, *Opportunities for all* (DWP, 2003d) – and that it could report in 2003 that 33 of its 43 indicators had improved over the medium term (generally since New Labour came to power) while ten were steady and none had deteriorated. However, external views may be more convincing. For instance, the New Policy Institute's collection of indicators over a similar period shows 21 of its 44 indicators as improving, 16 steady, but seven deteriorating (Palmer et al, 2003). This is less rosy than the official collection but nonetheless encouraging, and contrasts with its earlier assessment of 'New Labour's inheritance', when they had found 19 indicators improving in the medium term, 11 steady, but 14 to have been deteriorating (Howarth et al, 1998).

Third, most evidence relates to trends over time and changes in them. But such trends may have been changing anyway. In many areas, continued good

croeconomic performance – for which the government argues that it can
 credit – has been the most important factor, not particular initiatives. There
is far more attention to evaluation and 'evidence-based policy' than there was
before 1997, but relatively few policies have been systematically evaluated.

Finally, an issue recurs throughout the book: assessments may differ depending
on whether the focus is on *absolute* changes for the most disadvantaged, or on
their *relative* position. This is obvious when discussing absolute and relative poverty,
but also applies in other areas. Even when considering differences between groups,
there are two kinds of gap: *absolute* and *proportionate*. These can easily move in
different ways – the absolute gap may be smaller, but the proportionate one
larger. It is not that one measure is 'right' and another 'wrong', but which is
appropriate depends on the precise question being asked.

## A framework for summary

The stories told in this volume's chapters are summarised below under four
headings:

- Were the key problems *recognised* as a priority and was attention devoted to
  *analysis*?
- Were appropriate *targets* set for improvement, and specific *policy changes* made
  to address them?
- What evidence is there of *impacts*, both in terms of *time trends*, and from specific
  *evaluations*?
- What are the main *problems and gaps* in the policy mix as it has evolved?

The material is organised into three sections:

1. *Evidence on poverty and inequality:* child poverty (Chapters Seven and Twelve),
   the working–age population (Chapter Eleven) and pensioners (Chapter Eight),
   together with trends in income inequality (Chapter Eleven).
2. *Broad policy areas:* employment (Chapter Two), education (Chapter Three),
   health (Chapter Four) and political participation (Chapter Five).
3. *Particular target groups:* poor neighbourhoods (Chapter Six), children in the
   early years (Chapter Seven), services for older people and longer–term prospects
   for pensioner incomes (Chapter Eight), ethnic inequalities (Chapter Nine)
   and vulnerable groups (Chapter Ten).

Evidence from international comparisons (Chapter Fourteen) and from the
experiences of families in low-income neighbourhoods (Chapter Thirteen) is
used throughout. Sources are given in the appropriate chapters, rather than
repeated here.

## Child poverty

*Recognition and analysis*

Child poverty emerged as a major New Labour preoccupation, the focus of its most prominent targets and of some of the Treasury's largest initiatives. A series of reviews and policy papers assessed a wide range of evidence on its causes and consequences.

*Targets and policies*

The pledge to "end child poverty" in a generation (eventually defined as being "among the best in Europe" in relative terms), and the specific targets of cutting relative poverty by a quarter by 2004/05 and by half by 2010/11 are among the most ambitious. Major reforms to tax and benefit policy created the new tax credit system. Special additional lone parent benefits were phased out, but non-working lone and two-parent families with children (particularly younger ones) have gained from the overall package as well as working families. Four fifths of all families with children have benefited to some extent. The package of support for low-income working families with children is now one of the most generous in the world.

*Impacts*

In relative terms, child poverty fell from 25% to 21% (before housing costs, BHC) or from 34% to 28% (after housing costs, AHC) between 1996/97 and 2002/03 (although it did not do so for all family types, rising slightly for children of two non-working parents). Simulation modelling suggests that changes in tax and transfer policies have had a substantial effect, and that the target of a cut by a quarter by 2004/05 should be hit on the BHC basis, and will be close to being hit after housing costs. Between the years up to 1997 and 2001, the UK moved from having the highest relative child poverty in the EU to fifth highest, its rate falling while others rose. As average incomes were growing steadily, against a US-style absolute poverty line, child poverty halved between 1996/97 and 2002/03. For lone parents, there were striking falls in indicators of material deprivation and financial stress between 1999 and 2002. Our new analysis of spending by low-income families with young children shows that they have increased spending disproportionately on goods for children (clothing, footwear, toys and games), but also on some adult goods (such as clothing) where they had lagged behind. Their spending on food increased, while it fell for other families; and their ownership of certain consumer durables caught up somewhat.

## Problems and gaps

Child poverty was so high initially that there is still far to go to reach the EU average, let alone the best in Europe. For benefits and tax credits there are two clear issues. First, most of their values are by default linked to price inflation, not general living standards (including the 'adult' elements of benefits for families with children). 'New' measures are needed every year, just to stand still against the moving target of a relative poverty line – and more to make progress. Second, the reforms have reduced the deepest parts of the 'poverty trap', but have extended means testing up the income range (Hills, 2004a, Figure 10.7). Pushing the strategy further means either widening or deepening the problem. Half of the low-income parents we spoke to reported frustration with administration of the new tax credits, and uncertainties about what they receive. Despite the tax credits, poverty rates for working lone parents remained high in European terms in 2001, partly reflecting low hours, but also low wages for women working part time.

# Working-age poverty

### Recognition and analysis

Policy has focussed on working-age poverty as a consequence of worklessness or parenthood, rather than on income poverty in itself. Most official analysis has concentrated on the labour market and the situation of low-income parents.

### Targets and policies

By contrast to children and pensioners, there is no specific target for working-age poverty. Policies have aimed at getting people into work and improvements in incomes for those in work through the National Minimum Wage and the Working Tax Credit, with some improvements in benefits for disabled people. On the other hand, Income Support for other single non-pensioner adults fell significantly as a percentage of the effective poverty line between 1997 and 2004.

### Impacts

There have been falls in poverty against an absolute line for the working-age population as a whole, but against a relative line it has fallen only slightly, much of this reflecting the improving position of parents. For working-age adults *without* children, relative poverty *increased* slightly (to a record level by 2002/03). Poverty rates for unemployed people remained among the worst of 11 EU countries with comparable data.

*Problems and gaps*

Although many employment measures have been successful, and registered unemployment has fallen substantially, significant numbers remain without work and dependent on state benefits. Successful welfare-to-work policies may reduce the numbers dependent on out-of-work benefits further, but those remaining will have real incomes steadily falling further behind the rest of the population.

## Pensioner poverty

*Recognition and analysis*

The overall structure of pensions and income levels for today's pensioners have been the focus of two Green Papers and part of the annual *Opportunities for all* analysis.

*Targets and policies*

Pensioner poverty followed child poverty as an explicit focus of policy, and has not had a high-profile target, but at the 2002 Labour Party Conference, Gordon Brown stated the aim of "ending pensioner poverty". The main policy has been to increase the means-tested minimum for pensioners and extend means-tested help higher up through the new Pension Credit. The basic pension has remained essentially linked to prices (although its real value has had a small increase). Special measures for all or some pensioners include winter fuel allowances, free eye tests, free TV licences and increased income tax allowances.

*Impacts*

Relative poverty for pensioners has followed a different course depending on how it is measured: BHC, it was no lower (21%) in 2002/03 than in 1996/97, but AHC, it fell from 27% to 21%. Simulation modelling suggests both measures may fall by a further two percentage points by 2004/05. Against a fixed real line, by 2002/03 pensioner poverty had fallen by approaching a half (BHC) or two thirds (AHC). This partly reflects the still favourable position of recent retirees compared to older cohorts, but changes in the real value of state benefits have had a substantial impact.

*Problems and gaps*

The clearest immediate problem is continued lack of take-up by all those entitled to the means-tested minimum, despite initiatives to encourage claims (it is too early to tell whether the administrative changes with the new Pension Credit system will do so). Non-claimants, for instance receiving only the basic pension, have fallen further behind relative poverty lines. More generally, the potential extended generosity of the Pension Credit will only be realised if those newly entitled claim it. The initial target was only for Pension Credit take-up to reach 72% by 2006, and the 2004 Spending Review's target for 2008 implies significant non-take-up to remain even then.

## Income inequality

### Recognition and analysis

Reducing *overall* income inequality has not been a New Labour aim. Inequalities between those with low incomes and the middle – relative poverty for children and pensioners and reduction of unemployment and worklessness – have been key concerns, as have unequal life chances and barriers to social mobility. However, inequality between the middle and the top of the income distribution has almost explicitly been ruled out as a concern.

### Targets and policies

The relevant targets have thus been those concerned with relative poverty and specific issues such as employment and education. However, at the Lisbon and Laeken EU summits, the UK agreed to its performance on social cohesion being judged against indicators including some of overall income inequality, notably the ratio between the incomes of the richest and poorest fifths of the population. Relevant policies have been those affecting child and pensioner poverty, incomes of the low paid in work, employment and education (including the potential impact of wider higher education in reducing the 'graduate premium' in wages), as well as those addressing long-term drivers of inequality. Following 1997 and 2001 General Election pledges, higher income tax rates have not increased.

### Impacts

What has happened to income inequality depends on whether measures include the very richest and very poorest[1]. Measures *excluding* these show inequality first increasing under New Labour, but then falling back by 2002/03 to similar levels to 1996/97. Except at the very top and very bottom, living standards for all income groups have risen by similar amounts, with those nearer the bottom doing slightly better than those nearer the top, contrasting with other recent periods of growth. However, a measure allowing for the highest incomes reached an all-time high by 2000/01, and was only a little lower by 2002/03, still above its 1996/97 level. Policy has clearly had an effect: had the tax and benefit system been left as it was in 1996/97, adjusted only for price inflation, this inequality measure would have been much higher. In these terms, New Labour can claim to have halted its growth. Overall relative poverty – a measure of inequality at the bottom – was only a little lower in the year up to 2001 than it had been in the year up to 1997, but this was still the greatest reduction in the EU. By contrast, the ratio between the incomes of the top and bottom fifths rose slightly over this period, in contrast to other high inequality EU countries.

## Problems and gaps

A key driver of overall inequality is that incomes and earnings at the very top continue to increase faster than others. Equally, incomes right at the bottom have not increased as fast as for other groups. While this is affected by data problems, it also reflects lack of take-up of improved benefits for some, and price-linking of benefits for others.

# Employment

### Recognition and analysis

Employment was New Labour's clearest priority when elected in 1997, and has remained so. Work, and the promotion of work, have been defining themes.

### Targets and policies

One of the five 1997 'early pledges' was to cut youth unemployment. There have been targets (now extended to 2008) for increasing the employment rates of disadvantaged groups (including lone parents, disabled people and minority ethnic groups) and for reducing the employment gap between disadvantaged groups and the overall rate, all under the slogans of "employment opportunity for all" and "work for those who can, security for those who cannot". Significant resources have gone into the New Deal programmes (particularly for young people), and tax credits for those in work (including help with childcare) intended (with the minimum wage) to reinforce the message that 'work pays'. The evolution of working-age social security begun before 1997 continued, with employment services and benefit delivery combined as part of the continuing move towards 'active' policies for the unemployed.

### Impacts

Registered unemployment has fallen to its lowest level in 30 years. Long-term unemployment is one of the lowest in Europe. Total employment is now at record levels, including increases in employment rates for lone parents and those aged between 50 and state pension age. However, economic inactivity rates have only fallen slowly for women, and have risen for men. The proportion of jobless households remains high in European terms, and the proportion of children living in them was still the highest in the EU in 2003, far higher than in most other countries. Most of these improvements relate to continued good macroeconomic performance, helped by employment measures allowing the economy to run at a faster rate without inflation than otherwise. Evaluations of specific employment measures show positive but relatively small impacts. Similarly, the net impact of the changes in tax and benefit structure on labour force participation has been positive, but not very large (although even this is a striking achievement, given increased incomes for some non-workers).

### Problems and gaps

Economic inactivity remains the biggest problem, particularly for prime-age men. There are also issues about the extent to which people are cycling through programmes, which may explain why unemployment rates for young workers have not fallen since 2000. The initial impact of the New Deal has slowed. Unemployment rates for 16- to 17-year-olds have not fallen. More fundamentally, there remains controversy about work as being the *only* policy towards reducing poverty for the working-age population.

## Education

### Recognition and analysis

Education famously represented all of Tony Blair's top three priorities in 1996, and inequalities in educational achievement have been extensively analysed. As well as school achievement, specific studies by the Social Exclusion Unit (SEU) included truancy and exclusions, the position of 16- to 17-year-olds outside education, lone parents and care leavers. Others major reports covered both further and higher education, and adult basic skills.

### Targets and policies

The most conspicuous targets relate to attainments at the end of the four 'Key Stages' (ages 7 to 16), including differences between areas and schools, as well as average achievement. Policies included smaller class sizes for 5- to 7-year olds, the literacy and numeracy hours, area-based policies such as Excellence in Cities, introduction of Education Maintenance Allowances and two waves of reforms to higher education funding. Education spending has risen as a share of GDP since its 1999 low point, and is moving up the international range.

### Impacts

At primary level, large class sizes have become less common, the numeracy and literacy hours have been positively evaluated, and attainment has not only risen overall (until 2001), but poorer schools have improved fastest. All this has been noticed and is popular with the parents we are interviewing in low-income neighbourhoods. At secondary level, the picture is more mixed. The overall proportion achieving 5+ 'good' GCSEs has increased, and social class differences have reduced, but remain large. Education Maintenance Allowances have been positively evaluated, and early evaluation of Excellence in Cities is also positive.

### Problems and gaps

Large social class differences remain, and may even have increased in terms of university access. Significant numbers of boys still reach age 16 with no graded results. Schools with large numbers of children from poor families continue to do badly at Key Stage 3 (age 14). There are natural tensions between the aims of improving average results and closing gaps in performance. In some cases, the targets used (such as concentration on A*-C grades at GCSE) may exacerbate this. Little has been done for further education despite the Kennedy report, and 'lifelong learning' dropped out of sight after the problems with Individual Learning Accounts. Although there has been progress on adult basic skills, there remains a long way to go.

## Health

### Recognition and analysis

Inequalities in health have been an unprecedented focus since commissioning of the Acheson report, with a cross-cutting review in 2002, and the 2003 publication, *Programme for action*. This analysis has emphasised the multiple drivers of health inequalities, including income levels and distribution.

### Targets and policies

However, the main thrust of policy has been concerned with overall levels of health and with increased public spending on health care. Such spending is disproportionately on those with low incomes (reflecting greater levels of need), and the formulae allocating NHS resources between areas have become more sensitively tuned to disadvantage. Some of the announced policies on health inequalities have been rather vague or limited, although there are specific national targets for reducing inequalities in infant mortality, life expectancy and death rates from heart disease, strokes and cancer.

### Impacts

Given the nature of health outcomes, it is too early to judge the results of recent policies. One overall survey found widespread recognition of the problems, but few improvements in health inequality outcomes attributable to policy. Many of the relevant time trends (such as for coronary heart disease or cancer) show absolute improvements for all socioeconomic groups, but little progress on gaps between them. In some cases, improvements for all have involved wider gaps (infant mortality rates and life expectancy for women), but in others there have been actual deteriorations at the bottom (low birthweight babies and numbers reporting 'not good health', although both measures need careful interpretation). Health Action Zones have been positively evaluated.

### Problems and gaps

As one official report put it, the challenge is now delivery and implementation, not further discussion. There are tensions – not always recognised – between the twin aims of overall improvement in health outcomes and closing gaps in them. Given the importance of factors such as child poverty and unemployment for health outcomes, the impact of other policies may have long-run effects on health gaps too.

## Political participation

### Recognition and analysis

Several aspects of participation have been a focus, including constitutional reform (such as devolution), 'modernising local government' and 'civil renewal'. The SEU's agenda for neighbourhood renewal has emphasised community self-help, while partnership, participation and consultation have been embodied into many parts of service delivery by central and local government.

### Targets and policies

Public Service Agreements for the Home Office and NHS include targets for community and voluntary sector 'participation' and 'patient accountability', while performance indicators for the 'Best Value' inspection regime for local authorities include consultation. Policies can be split between attempts to improve participation in formal politics – mayors, postal voting experiments – and less formal mechanisms (such as involvement in crime and disorder partnerships or 'capacity building' for tenant and community representatives).

### Impacts

Formal political participation has continued to decline (spectacularly so in turnout for the 2001 General Election), and social gaps in voting rates remain wide. However, postal voting experiments have increased voting rates, particularly for disadvantaged groups. Evidence on recent trends in volunteering shows that large socioeconomic differences remain. Evidence on the recognition by service providers of the need for and value of community participation and involvement is much more positive, particularly on the *quality* of participation (rather than its quantity, in terms of numbers involved).

### Problems and gaps

Despite changes by service providers, it is telling that more than half of the families we are talking to in low-income neighbourhoods feel that they have "no influence at all", even though most are connected to local groups in some way. This is not just a matter of the deficit in formal participation, but also reflects the way people are affected by key services such as social housing allocations. There are perceived conflicts between involvement and 'delivery', for instance in speeding the planning process and community involvement in decisions. Perhaps most importantly, what has been achieved has not led to any widespread excitement about the ideas of participation and involvement.

## Poor neighbourhoods

### Recognition and analysis

Problems of low-income neighbourhoods have been a major focus of consultation and analysis since 1997, culminating in the SEU's National Strategy for Neighbourhood Renewal.

### Targets and policies

The overall target for the strategy – that "within 10-20 years, no-one should be seriously disadvantaged by where they live" – is perhaps New Labour's most ambitious. It is backed up by targets for particular outcomes, notably 'floor targets' for achievement in the most disadvantaged areas in employment, education, crime, health and housing. Some policies have been for 'mainstream services', but others have been aimed at particular areas (particularly within England), such as neighbourhood wardens, Sure Start and Excellence in Cities.

### Impacts

At present, progress can only be measured at relatively aggregated levels (such as the most deprived fifth of local authorities as a whole). At this level, looking across services and outcomes, progress is being made, although not always quickly enough to reach the targets set, and still leaving substantial gaps between poor areas and others. In some cases, outcomes for poor areas are both improving and closing the gap on others (employment rates and teenage pregnancy), and in others this is being achieved, but not fast enough to meet targets (primary and secondary education). However, mortality differences are widening around an overall improvement, and crime outcomes are mixed. There are substantial differences between our own smaller-scale study areas, with some making significant progress but others not. Similarly, families living within these areas report mixed experiences, being positive about some initiatives (notably Sure Start and, for many, the New Deal for Communities), but less aware of others (such as neighbourhood wardens in some areas).

### Problems and gaps

Despite progress, substantial differences remain between areas, and not all poor neighbourhoods are improving. The biggest challenges are driving execution of policy down to lower levels, and making progress on the 'liveability' agenda: half of the families we spoke to felt that crime was a serious problem for them, and recent initiatives were only having slow effects. Equally, 'neighbourhood renewal' cannot be tackled only within individual neighbourhoods, but depends on broader policies and economic developments.

## Children and the early years

### Recognition and analysis

Early years policy has moved up the agenda. An early spending review resulted in the Sure Start programme, and the 2004 spending review included a cross-cutting study of the wider drivers and effects of child poverty. The emphasis on improving childcare provision has increased, linked to labour market policies, although issues around the quality of childcare and early education have tended to follow further behind.

### Targets and policies

There is an explicit target for increased childcare places (900,000 by 2004), for participation by all three- and four-year-olds in some nursery education (100% by September 2004) and a series of targets for Sure Start areas. Sure Start started as a programme targeted at certain low-income areas, but has gradually widened to include much of overall policy towards early years, accompanied by total spending rising by 80% between 1997/98 and 2002/03. Free part-time nursery places were guaranteed first for all four-year-olds, and then all three-year-olds. Tax credits can pay up to 70% of (registered) childcare costs for lower-income families. Maternity allowances have improved and last longer (for those previously working), and parents can now request flexible working patterns.

*Impacts*

Participation by three- and four-year-olds in early years education has increased, with the proportion benefiting from funded places reaching 88% and 98% respectively in 2003. Overall childcare places have increased, but the *net* increase looks likely to fall short of the 2004 target. While poorer areas appear to be catching up, this is accounted for by increased use of childminders, while their use in other areas is falling as a share of the total. By April 2004, a fifth of Working Tax Credit recipients received a credit for childcare costs, but this was a long way short of those potentially eligible. Both early evaluations of Sure Start and our own family interviews suggest that the programme is very popular indeed with parents. Its results against its formal targets are mixed, with, for instance, the proportion of babies with low birth weight not declining. However, it is not clear whether all such targets are appropriate, and a combined measure of 20 of its indicators does show a positive impact.

*Problems and gaps*

Despite recent increases, childcare provision and public spending on the early years are still low by comparison with elsewhere in Europe. The quality of childcare remains a major issue, as does the sustainability of an approach resting on demand-side subsidies.

## Older people – services and long-term incomes

*Recognition and analysis*

Long-term care for older people was the focus of New Labour's only Royal Commission. However, the commission produced majority and minority reports, the minority having more influence in England and the majority in Scotland. Care for the elderly has also been a focus of NHS reorganisation. An early Green Paper on pensions produced a new structure for the State Second Pension, a more recent one changes in the tax treatment of pensions and measures to allow flexible retirement, while the Independent Pensions Commission is looking at long-term prospects for pensions.

*Targets and policies*

The *Opportunities for all* targets include both the proportion of over-65s receiving care services at home, and of the working-age population contributing to private pensions. A National Service Framework set standards of care for older people in 2001. Free personal care has been introduced in Scotland, but not in England. More use of 'direct payments' is intended to give people more control over their own care. The State Second Pension reforms increase prospective pensions for the lower paid, and Stakeholder Pensions were introduced with the aim of increasing private pension provision for those around and below median earnings. While not a formal target, the government has talked of shifting the future balance of pension provision from 60% public to 60% private.

## Impacts

The total number of places for older people in residential care homes has continued to decline slowly since 1997. While overall hours of home care have increased, the proportion of over-75s receiving services has declined – the shift has been towards high intensity services, and to private sector provision. The proportion of those unable to walk outside unaided and living alone receiving public personal social services fell between 1994/95 and 2001/02. Since 2000, the stock market crash and the consequent underfunding of many private occupational schemes have dominated future pension prospects. While deficits are being filled for existing members, many new employees now have less valuable pension packages, with lower employer contributions. More people are working between age 50 and state pension age, continuing the trend since 1993.

## Problems and gaps

More services for the elderly are now means tested, with the risk that some fall outside the net. Tighter targeting on those with the most intense needs means that those with less intense or occasional needs are not being covered, with a risk of losing potential preventive effects. Concerns about being caught by future means testing as well as the sheer complexity of the emerging structure of state pensions leave very large question marks over whether private provision really will increase in the way envisaged by the government as a way of coping with an ageing population, particularly given the rapid switch of private occupational pensions towards riskier (and usually less valuable) 'defined contribution' models.

# Ethnic inequalities

## Recognition and analysis

In New Labour's first term, policy was framed by its response to the Macpherson Report, and its identification of 'institutional racism' within public services, leading to the 2000 Race Relations (Amendment) Act putting a statutory duty on public bodies to promote equality of opportunity. Ethnicity has generally been a sub-focus within more general studies of disadvantage, rather than a focus in its own right (although the Cabinet Office's work on employment is an exception).

## Targets and policies

Most policies and targets have aimed at disadvantage in general, implicitly assuming that, given their higher levels of disadvantage, minority ethnic groups will tend to be beneficiaries. There are some specific targets related to minority groups, such as raising employment rates and narrowing the gaps between these and the overall rate, and there have also been some policies specifically targeted at minority ethnic groups in Labour's second term, such as Ethnic Minority Achievement Grants to local authorities to improve educational achievement.

## Impacts

While it is too early to see effects of recent policies, evidence on trends in ethnic inequalities within some of the main service areas suggests diversity of experience between minority groups. In education, proportions achieving good GCSEs have increased in all ethnic groups, and the gap between minority groups and the white population narrowed between 1996 and 2002. School exclusions for Black Caribbean pupils fell between 1997/98 and 2000/01, but have since stabilised, still well above the national average. Differences in employment rates show no clear pattern, and while unemployment rates have fallen for all groups, there has been no convergence in relative unemployment rates. Incidence of low incomes shows varied patterns, with a clear decline in the proportion of the Indian population (especially children) and (more slowly) of black non-Caribbean people having incomes in the poorest fifth, but no decline in the very high proportion of the Pakistani and Bangladeshi population with low incomes.

## Problems and gaps

Despite evidence of improvement in many respects for most ethnic groups over the period, ethnic inequalities remain very large in many dimensions, with little evidence of policy success in reducing them so far. There appear to be tensions between some of New Labour's 'managerialist', target-driven policies, and the complexity of delivering services to diverse client groups. Area segregation remains a major issue.

# Vulnerable groups

## Recognition and analysis

A specific aim of the SEU established in 1997 was to focus on vulnerable groups, particularly those where current disadvantage was linked to later disadvantage, and where responsibilities fell between government departments. It has produced powerful analysis of the position of particular groups, notably teenage parents, ex-prisoners, children leaving care, pupils truanting or excluded from school,

16- to 18-year-olds not in education, employment or training (NEET) and rough sleepers. However, its coverage has been selective, and other vulnerable groups have not been subject to such attention.

### Targets and policies

For several of these groups, clear targets have been set, and policies have followed. These have included monitoring school exclusion policies, introduction of the Connexions service and Education Maintenance Allowances for 16- to 17-year-olds, and establishment of the Rough Sleepers Unit. But for other groups, there has been much less policy development, and in the case of asylum seekers, policy elsewhere in government has actively sought to *reduce* rights to income, employment and housing as part of the government's drive to reduce the numbers of new arrivals, running in the directly opposite direction to nearly all the other policies we have discussed.

### Impacts

For the targeted groups there is mixed evidence. In the three areas examined in Chapter Ten, permanent school exclusions first fell, but then rose again between 1999/2000 and 2001/02, while truancy fell, but not by enough to hit its target; teenage conception rates have fallen a little since 1998 and may hit the 2004 target (but are not on track for the 2010 target); and the number sleeping rough appear to have fallen substantially, meeting the target of a reduction by two thirds (although trends in less acute forms of homelessness are less clear).

### Problems and gaps

For some of the groups officially identified, the action that has followed appears less strong than warranted by the analysis. In some cases, there is a conflict in interest between those identified as vulnerable and others who may also be disadvantaged – for instance other pupils in classes with disruptive pupils. Other groups (for instance, older pensioners or disabled children) have come lower down the agenda. The example of asylum seekers shows that there are strict limits to the government's 'inclusion' agenda: some groups are clearly excluded from it.

## New Labour's record in perspective

A first overview is given by Figure 15.1, based on analysis by the Institute for Fiscal Studies. This contrasts what has happened to the net incomes (adjusted for family size) of those in successive fifths of the income distribution under the last three Prime Ministers (up to 2002/03 for Tony Blair).

The contrast is clear. While Mrs Thatcher was Prime Minister, incomes at the

**Figure 15.1: Real income growth by quintile group (% per year)**

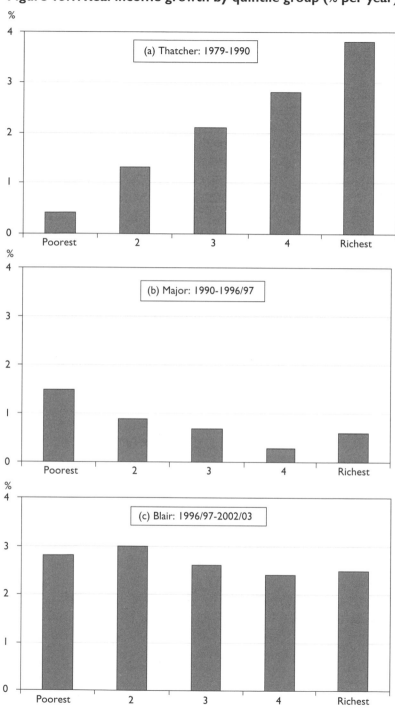

*Note:* The figures for each quintile group correspond to their mid-points (that is, the 10th, 30th, 50th, 70th and 90th percentiles of the income distribution). Incomes are before housing costs.
*Source:* Brewer et al (2004, Figure 2.3)

top grew rapidly. Lower down the distribution they grew much less fast, and at the bottom by very little. Average living standards grew, but income inequality widened rapidly, and the poor fell behind. During the Major years, the growth in inequality was partly reversed, but there was only slow growth in living standards for any of the groups. After 1997, all income groups enjoyed quite rapid growth in living standards. This did not mean much fall in *inequality*, and only a slow decline in relative poverty, but it did involve much faster growth in living standards for the poor than either of the earlier periods, and so resulted in rapid falls in absolute poverty.

For many concerned with disadvantage, the latest period is clearly preferable to the other two. Whether this makes it a 'success' depends on expectations. To illustrate this, Table 15.1 compares the position in the year Labour left three periods of office (or up to 2002/03 for New Labour) with that in the year before it came to office. It shows GDP growth, the change in real incomes for the two poorest tenths and the median, relative poverty for the whole population and for children (numbers with less than half-mean income) and income inequality (measured by the Gini coefficient).

In this light, the position when the Wilson government left office in 1970 now looks rather enviable. Inequality had fallen, incomes of the poorest fifth had grown rapidly in real terms over seven years, and overall relative poverty had fallen to below 10%. However, for those assessing its record closer to the time (with more limited data), this was not necessarily a success. For Townsend and Bosanquet (1972, pp 11, 288-9), summarising their edited review of *Labour and inequality*:

**Table 15.1: Trends in inequality, poverty and incomes during three periods of Labour government (%)**

|  | GDP per capita | Real incomes[a] | | | Relative poverty[b] | | Inequality[c] |
|---|---|---|---|---|---|---|---|
|  |  | Poorest tenth | Second tenth | Median | Children | All |  |
| 1963 | – | – | – | – | – | 11.7 | 26.9 |
| 1970 | – | – | – | – | – | 9.4 | 25.5 |
| Change | +18.4 | +29 | +20 | +16 | NA | –2.3 | –1.4 |
| 1973 | – | – | – | – | 10 | 9.7 | 25.5 |
| 1979 | – | – | – | – | 11 | 8.2 | 24.8 |
| Change | +9.5 | +7 | +4 | +4 | +1 | –1.5 | –0.7 |
| 1996-97 | – | – | – | – | 25 | 18.5 | 33.1 |
| 2002-03 | – | – | – | – | 22 | 18.1 | 34.3 |
| Change | +15.4 | +10 | +19 | +17 | –3 | –0.4 | +1.2 |

*Notes:* [a] Mid-points of each tenth by equivalent income (BHC);
[b] Percentage with income below half of population mean;
[c] Gini coefficient (BHC).
*Sources:* ONS (2003a, Table 1.5); Goodman and Webb (1994, Figures 2.4(a), 2.7, 2.2); Gregg, Harkness and Machin (1999b, Figure 1); DWP (2004a, Tables A1, D 7.2); Brewer et al (2004, Figure 2.9)

> Most of the authors have failed to find evidence of marked changes in the direction of fulfilling socialist objectives. Their analysis presents a gloomy picture.... The Government did not diminish inequalities of income, or did not reduce them very much.... Considerable poverty remained.... It is impossible not to feel a sense of dismay.

By such standards, the period since 1997 would hardly be judged a success either. Others were somewhat kinder to the Wilson government. In a survey of *The Labour government's economic record* at the same time, Stewart (1972, pp 110-1) concluded that:

> there was an improvement in the distribution of income, both vertical and horizontal, under the Labour government.... To have produced a measurable improvement in the distribution of income against the background of the deplorably slow rate of growth of output permitted by its macroeconomic policies was one of the Labour government's main achievements – though, ironically, one that has received very little recognition from Labour's own supporters. What might be achieved against the background of a reasonable growth rate? One day, perhaps we may see.

Clearly, expectations of growth change over time as well, given that the annual 2.4% growth rate over the six years since 1996/97 is seen as one of New Labour's major successes, but is identical to that between 1963 and 1970 deplored by Stewart.

Piachaud (1981, p 185) was rather kinder to the 1974 to 1979 Labour government:

> While poverty in Britain remains to the extent that it does, the Labour Government's record on social security cannot be a source of complacency or of pride. But it need not be a source of shame.

By 1979, both income inequality and relative poverty in Britain were at or near to their lowest ever levels. It is in the real income growth figures that the problems of the Wilson/Callaghan government and reasons for its demise are more apparent: overall living standards grew very slowly indeed.

## Conclusion

Some common points stand out from this analysis. First, there is no doubt that, since 1997, the government has taken poverty and social exclusion very seriously, in a way not done before. In almost all the areas we discuss, there is evidence of recognition of the range of problems faced by Britain in the mid-1990s, not just in the most relevant departments, but in the Treasury, and in Downing Street, to which the SEU initially reported.

Second, the issues have been recognised as multifaceted and interlinked. Policy debates have focused on cash incomes and services today, but also on long-term drivers of disadvantage and of life chances for children. This has partly followed from the impressive range of analysis on which the government has drawn, both newly commissioned (for instance resulting from pilots and evaluations), and assembled from other sources. Whether or not policies were really 'evidence-based', much evidence has been assembled and made publicly available. Again, the Treasury and the SEU have taken the lead in much of this, but there have been other major investigations, such as on health inequalities or long-term care.

Third, New Labour has been prolific in its use of targets, and poverty and social exclusion have been the subject of some of the most high profile. The two most prominent and ambitious have been the commitments to cut (relative) child poverty by a quarter by 2004/05, to halve it by 2010/11, and to "eradicate" it (or at least be among the best in Europe) within 20 years, and the aim of the neighbourhood renewal strategy, that within 10-20 years, no one should be seriously disadvantaged by where they live. Such targets involve the government holding itself to account in a way that few of its predecessors have done. The annual *Opportunity for all* reports contain an assessment of progress against a wide range of indicators of poverty and social exclusion. If it could *not* point to progress on most of these, it would be a source of major embarrassment, at least.

By their nature, targets have to focus on specific objectives, but there are conspicuous omissions – most obviously for working-age poverty (or for poverty of the population as a whole, as there is in Ireland), or for overall inequality (except in so far as it is monitored at EU level). In addition, a target is not in itself a policy, and there are areas where policy (let alone impact) appears to be lagging behind analysis and target-setting.

Fourth, for individual policy areas, there is much variation in the speed and scope of policy. Employment, education, child poverty, particular vulnerable groups (particularly of young people) and neighbourhood regeneration were early and continuing priorities, with substantial new resources. Children in the early years (particularly in terms of childcare) and pensioner poverty have become more important over time. But for others, while we identify a range of relevant initiatives, the scale of action looks less impressive by comparison with the challenge – ensuring that disadvantaged people have a real say over decisions that affect their own lives might be an example, tackling inequalities between ethnic groups another. Not only have some vulnerable groups been left out when it comes to special treatment, but there are others (notably asylum seekers) where government policy has actively *increased* exclusion in the terms applied to other groups. The inclusion agenda has, literally, had borders.

In looking at the impact of policy, there are some initiatives with explicit evaluations or where we can make our own assessment. Most such evaluations have been positive, although the effects identified are not always very large: the New Deals, literacy and numeracy hours in primary schools, Education Maintenance Allowances and some of the area-based initiatives. Simulation modelling shows that child poverty has been reduced by the tax and benefit reforms New Labour has introduced, and quickly enough to have a good chance of hitting its 2004/05 targets. Pensioner poverty should be falling by 2004/05, and overall income inequality has at least stopped growing as a result of tax and benefit policies, while it would otherwise have grown. Both our own analysis of spending patterns and the Families and Children Survey suggest that the income changes for parents with children are having clear benefits for their lives and standards of living. Our own study of twelve low-income areas and our interviews with parents point to improvements in several important outcomes (but not on a uniform basis) and to the popularity of particular initiatives (such as Sure Start and changes in primary schools).

But in many areas, no specific evaluations are available, and we depend on overall time trends. Two parts of the context for these may lead to contrasting overall judgements:

- The improvements we describe in many areas have taken place while the economy has been growing steadily, and indeed has been doing so for ten years. In some ways that makes it easier to achieve improvements, for instance in employment rates. In others, however, it makes it harder: achieving a reduction in relative poverty while general living standards are rising fast is harder than doing so when they are stagnating, particularly, of course, if benefit levels remain price-linked. Also, some of the groups now being reached out to are more deeply disadvantaged than those on the margins ten years ago.
- The starting point when New Labour came into office was in many respects very poor, with particularly high levels of relative poverty, area polarisation and income inequality, and with many indicators of exclusion having deteriorated. This also cuts two ways: is it relatively easy to cut poverty from a historically high level, or is it hard to start it moving in the right direction?

Finally, we have identified a number of recurring problems. In many areas there is an often unacknowledged conflict between government objectives of raising standards for all and of reducing differences between disadvantaged groups and others. For instance, much health policy has naturally enough aimed at improving the overall health of the population, but successes here have sometimes left the most disadvantaged lagging even further behind. Similarly, raising the proportion of children attaining five 'good' GCSEs has been a dominant aim, but reducing numbers with no qualifications or improving more basic skills have lagged behind.

By contrast, in other areas, there has been a growth in means testing or other forms of targeting, which have allowed limited resources to be focused on those in greatest need (for instance, incomes and services for older people). However, as side effects, this may lead to problems of complexity, of take-up and of widening (if milder) disincentives to work or save.

Third, while there has been action on a commendable variety of fronts, earlier chapters and the summaries above identify a number of gaps, and areas where people are still being left behind. Most prominently, the default policy for most social security benefits and tax credits is to link their values to prices, not to general living standards. In some cases, this has created the fiscal headroom for large real increases in selected elements of the system to create both a more generous but also more rational structure. Overall, the results have been more progressive than an alternative policy of simply earnings-linking all benefit levels without reform would have been. However, it has left gaps, the consequences of which are becoming apparent, for instance in the way in which relative poverty rates for those of working age *without* children had reached record levels (albeit still below those for other groups) by 2002/03. The speed with which some of this group have gained enough income from employment to escape poverty has not been fast enough to offset the way in which others are being left further behind.

Linked to this, the policies we have examined are the result of many specific initiatives, often fostered by the Treasury or the SEU. However, there is no overall strategy for doing what, for instance, the Irish government aims to do, in 'poverty-proofing' all policy initiatives, to ensure that policy against poverty and social exclusion is part of the mainstream objectives of all parts of government.

There are two possible overall assessments of policy since 1997 that the evidence we have assembled should dispel. First, that there has been little difference between the policies pursued in the years before 1997 and those pursued since. This is manifestly incorrect. In some of the most important areas, it is fair to say both that the tide has turned, and that policy has contributed to turning that tide. This is no mean achievement. A second reaction would be to go from this to conclude that policy has succeeded, and Britain has indeed already become a more equal society. In some respects it has, but in virtually all of the areas we have discussed in this book, there is still a very long way to go to reach an unambiguous picture of success, and sustained effort will be needed to make further progress.

## Note

[1] See Hills (2004a, Chapter 3) for a discussion of the increasing inequality of wealth since the mid-1990s.

# References

Abbas, T. (2002) 'The home and the school in the educational achievements of South Asians', *Race, Ethnicity and Education*, vol 5, no 3, pp 291-316.

ACU (Active Community Unit) (1999) *Report of the Policy Action Team on community self help*, London: Home Office.

ACU (2003) *Voluntary and community sector infrastructure: A consultation document*, London: Home Office.

Adema, W. (2000) *Revisiting real social spending across countries: A brief note*, Paris: OECD.

Age Concern/Fawcett Society (2003) *One in four*, London: Age Concern.

Aldbourne Associates and IRIS Consulting (2003) *Interim evaluation of tenant participation compacts*, London: ODPM.

Alexander, C. (forthcoming) 'Embodying violence: "riots", dis/order and the private lives of "the Asian gang"', in C. Alexander and C. Knowles (eds) *Making race matter: Bodies, space and identity*, Basingstoke: Palgrave Macmillan.

Ambler, M. (2004) *Costs and benefits of universal childcare: A preliminary economic analysis for the UK*, Policy Paper, PricewaterhouseCoopers for the Day Care Trust, London: Day Care Trust.

Amin, A. (2002) 'Ethnicity and the multicultural city: living with diversity', *Environment and Planning A*, vol 34, pp 959-80.

Anthias, F., Yuval-Davis, N. and Cain, H. (1993) *Racialized boundaries: Race, nation, gender, colour and class and the anti-racist struggle*, London: Routledge.

APHO (Association of Public Health Observatories) (2003) *Indications of public health in the English regions*, vol 1, no 1.

Arulampalam, W., Booth, A.L. and Taylor, M.P. (2000) 'Unemployment persistence', *Oxford Economic Papers*, 52, issue 1, pp 24-50.

Ashworth, K., Hardman, J., Hartfree, Y., Maguire, S., Middleton, S., Smith, D., Dearden, L., Emmerson, C., Frayne, C. and Meghir, C. (2002) 'Education Maintenance Allowance: the first two years. A quantitative evaluation', DfES research report 352, London: DfES.

Atkinson, A.B. (2002) *Top incomes in the United Kingdom over the twentieth century*, University of Oxford Discussion Papers in Economic and Social History, no 43, January, Oxford: University of Oxford.

Atkinson, A.B., Cantillon, B., Marlier, E. and Nolan, B. (2002) *Social indicators: The EU and social inclusion*, Oxford: Oxford University Press.

Atkinson, J., Evans, C., Willison, R., Lain, D. and van Gent, M. (2003) *New Deal 50plus: Sustainability of employment*, DWP Report WAE142, London: DWP.

Atkinson, R, and Moon, G. (1994) *Urban policy in Britain: The city, the state and the market*, London: Macmillan.

Attwood, C., Singh, G., Prime, D., Creasy, R. and others (2003) *2001 Home Office citizenship survey*, London: Home Office.

Audit Commission (1999) *Listen up! Effective community consultation*, London: Audit Commission.

Audit Commission (2002) *Policy focus: Neighbourhood renewal*, London: Audit Commission.

Audit Commission (2004) *Old virtues, new virtues: An overview of the changes in social care services over the seven years of joint reviews in England 1996-2003*, London: Audit Commission.

Back, L., Keith, M., Khan, A., Shukra, K. and Solomos, J. (2002) 'New Labour's white heart: politics, multiculturalism and the return of assimilation', *Political Quarterly*, vol 73, no 4, pp 445-54.

Bajekal, M., Purdon, S., Woodgate-Jones, G. and Davies, S. (2002) 'Healthy life expectancy at health authority level: comparing estimates from the General Household Survey and the Health Survey for England', *Health Statistics Quarterly*, no 16, pp 25-37.

Baker, D. and Middleton, E. (2003) 'Cervical screening and health inequality in England in the 1990s', *Journal of Epidemiology and Community Health*, vol 57, no 6, pp 417-23.

Ball, M. (2002) *Getting Sure Start started*, Nottingham: DfES.

Banks, E., Beral, V., Cameron, R., Hogg, A., Langley, N., Barnes, I., Bull, D., Reeves, G., English, R., Taylor, S., Elliman, J. and Harris, C.L. (2002) 'Comparison of various characteristics of women who do and do not attend for breast cancer screening', *Breast Cancer Research*, vol 4, pp R1-R6.

Bardasi, E. and Jenkins, S.P. (2002) *Income in later life: Work history matters*, Bristol/York: The Policy Press/Joseph Rowntree Foundation.

Barnes, M., Stoker, G. and Whiteley, P. (2003) 'Developing civil renewal: some lessons from research', *ESRC Seminar Series*, Swindon: ESRC.

Barnes, M., Sullivan, H. and Matka, E. (2001) *Building capacity for collaboration: The national evaluation of Health Action Zones*, Birmingham: University of Birmingham.

Bauld, L., Chesterman, J., Judge, K., Pound, E. and Coleman, T. (2003) 'Impact of UK National Health Service smoking cessation services: variations in outcomes in England', *Tobacco Control*, vol 12, pp 296-301.

Behrendt, C. (2002) *At the margins of the welfare state: Social assistance and the alleviation of poverty in Germany, Sweden and the United Kingdom*, Aldershot: Ashgate.

Bell, A. and Finch, S. (2004) *Sixth survey of parents of three and four year old children and their use of early years services*, Research Report 525, London: DfES.

Benzeval, M. and Meth, F. (2002) *Inequalities in health: A priority at the crossroads*, London: Queen Mary and Westfield College.

Berthoud, R. (1998) *The incomes of ethnic minorities*, ISER Report 98-1, Colchester: University of Essex Institute for Social and Economic Research.

Bhattarcharya, G., Ison, L. and Blair, M. (2003) *Minority ethnic attainment and participation in education and training: The evidence*, Research Topic Paper RTP01-03, London: DfES.

Birch, D. (2002) *Public Participation in local government: A survey of local authorities*, London: ODPM.

Birch, S. (1999) 'The 39 steps: the mystery of health inequalities in the UK', *Health Economics*, vol 8, pp 301-8.

Blair, T. (1994) *Socialism*, Fabian Pamphlet 565, London: Fabian Society.

Blair, T. (1996) 'My message to the Left', *The Independent on Sunday*, 28 July.

Blair, T. (1997a) Speech at the Aylesbury Estate, Southwark, 2 June.

Blair, T. (1997b) Speech on 'Bringing Britain together' at Stockwell Park School, South London, 8 December.

Blair, T. (1998a) *The Third Way: New politics for the new century*, Fabian Pamphlet 588, London: Fabian Society.

Blair, T. (1998b) *Leading the way: A new vision for local government*, London: Institute for Public Policy Research.

Blair, T. (1999) 'Beveridge revisited: a welfare state for the 21st century', in R. Walker (ed) *Ending child poverty: Popular welfare for the 21st century*, Bristol: The Policy Press.

Blair, T. (2002) Speech on tackling poverty and social exclusion, Anne Taylor Centre, Hackney, 18 September.

Blanden, J., Gregg, P. and Machin, S. (forthcoming) 'Changes in educational inequalities', Centre for Economics of Education Discussion Paper, London: London School of Economics and Political Science.

Blanden, J. and Machin, S. (2004) 'Educational inequality and the expansion of UK higher education', *Scottish Journal of Political Economy*, vol 51, no 2, pp 230-49.

Blundell, R., Dias, M., Meghir, C. and Van Reenen, J. (2001) 'Evaluating the impact of a mandatory job search assistance programme: the New Deal for Young People Gateway in the UK', Institute for Fiscal Studies (IFS) Working Paper, WP01/20, London: IFS.

Blundell, R., Reed, H., Van Reenen, J. and Shephard, A. (2003) 'The impact of the New Deal for Young People: a four-year assessment', in R. Dickens, P. Gregg and J. Wadsworth (eds) *The labour market under New Labour*, Basingstoke: Palgrave Macmillan.

Blunkett, D. (2003) *Active citizens, strong communities: Progressing civil renewal*, London: Home Office.

BMJ (1997) 'BMJ's question time', *British Medical Journal*, vol 314, p 1217.

Bourne, J. (2001) 'The life and times of institutional racism', *Race & Class*, vol 43, no 2, pp 7-22.

Bowling, B. (1999) *Violent racism: Victimization, policing and social context*, New York, NY: Oxford University Press.

Bowling, B. and Phillips, C. (2002) *Racism, crime and justice*, Harlow: Longman.

Bowling, B. and Phillips, C. (2003) 'Policing ethnic minority communities', in T. Newburn (ed) *Handbook of policing*, Cullompton: Willan, pp 528-55.

Bowman, H. (2001) *Talking to families in Leeds and Sheffield: A report on the first stage of the research*, CASEreport 18, London: London School of Economics and Political Science.

Bradbury, B. and Jäntti, M. (2001) 'Child poverty across 25 countries', in B. Bradbury, S.P. Jenkins and J. Micklewright (eds) *The dynamics of child poverty in industrialised countries*, Cambridge: Cambridge University Press, pp 62-91.

Bradshaw, J. (2000) 'Child poverty in comparative perspective', in D. Gordon and P. Townsend (eds) *Breadline Europe: The measurement of poverty*, Bristol: The Policy Press, pp 223-50.

Bradshaw, J. and Finch, N. (2002) *A comparison of child benefit packages in 22 countries*, DWP Research Report No 174, Leeds: Corporate Document Services.

Bradshaw, J., Kennedy, S., Kilkey, M., Hutton, S., Corden, A., Eardley, T., Holmes, H. and Neale, J. (1996) *The employment of lone parents: A comparison of policy in 20 countries*, London: Family Policy Studies Centre.

Bratti, M. (2002) *Parents' current income, long-term characteristics and children's education: Evidence from the 1970 British Cohort Study*, Warwick Economics Research Papers no 659, Coventry: University of Warwick.

Brewer, M. (2004) *Will the government hit its child poverty target in 2004-05?*, Briefing Note no 47, London: Institute for Fiscal Studies.

Brewer, M., Clark, T. and Goodman, A. (2003) 'What really happened to child poverty in the UK under Labour's first term?', *The Economic Journal*, vol 113, June, pp F240-F257.

Brewer, M., Goodman, A., Myck, M., Shaw, J. and Shephard, A. (2004) *Poverty and inequality in Britain: 2004*, Commentary 96, London: Institute for Fiscal Studies.

Bromley, C., Curtice, J. and Seyd, J. (2001) 'Political engagement, trust and constitutional reform,' in A. Park, J. Curtice, K. Thomson, L. Jarvis and C. Bromley (eds) *British social attitudes 18th report: Public policy, social ties*, London: Sage Publications, pp 199-225.

Bromley, C., Stratford, N. and Rao, N. (2000) *Revisiting public perceptions of local government: A decade of change?*, London: ODPM.

Bromley, C. (2003), 'Has Britain become immune to inequality?' in A. Park, J. Curtice, K. Thomson, L. Jarvis and C. Bromley (eds) *British social attitudes 20th report: Continuity and change over two decades*, London: Sage Publications, pp 71-92.

Brooks, R., Regan, S. and Robinson, P. (2002) *A new contract for retirement*, London: Institute for Public Policy Research.

Brown, G. (2004) NCVO (National Council for Voluntary Organisations) 2004 Annual Conference, keynote speech, London: NCVO.

Bunting, M. (2003) 'Citizens or consumers?', *The Guardian*, November 24.

Burchardt, T. (1999) *The evolution of disability benefits in the UK: Reweighting the basket*, CASEPaper 26, London: London School of Economics and Political Science.

Burchardt, T. (2000) *Enduring economic exclusion: Disabled people, income and work*, Joseph Rowntree Foundation Report, York: York Publishing Services.

Burchardt, T., Le Grand, J. and Piachaud, D. (2002) 'Degrees of exclusion: developing a dynamic, multidimensional measure,' in J. Hills, J. Le Grand and D. Piachaud (eds) *Understanding social exclusion*, Oxford: Oxford University Press, pp 30-43.

Burgess, S., Gregg, P., Hall, E., Meadows, S., Propper, C. and Washbrook, E. (2004) *Up to 5: Report to Department for Employment and Skills*, Bristol: Leverhulme Centre for Market and Public Organisation, University of Bristol.

Burgess, S., Wilson, D. and Lupton, R. (2004) 'Ethnic segregation across schools and neighbourhoods', Paper presented at the Education and the Neighbourhood Conference, School for Policy Studies, University of Bristol, 9 January.

Burnett, J. (2004) 'Community, cohesion and the state', *Race & Class*, vol 45, no 3, pp 1-18.

Burney, E. and Rose, G. (2002) *Racist offences – how is the law working? The implementation of the legislation on racially aggravated offences in the Crime and Disorder Act 1998*, Home Office Research Study 244, London: Home Office.

Burton, P. (2003) *Community involvement in neighbourhood regeneration*, Bristol: ESRC Centre for Neighbourhood Research, University of Bristol.

Cabinet Office (2001) *Ethnic minorities and the labour market: Interim analytical report*, London: Cabinet Office.

Cabinet Office (2002) *Social capital: A discussion paper*, London: Performance and Innovation Unit.

Cabinet Office (2003) *Ethnic minorities and the labour market: Final report*, London: Cabinet Office.

Callender, C. (2000) *The barriers to childcare provision*, Research Report 231, London: DfEE.

Callender, C. (2003) 'Student financial support in higher education: access and exclusion', in M. Tight (ed) *Access and exclusion: International perspectives on higher education research*, London: Elsevier Science.

Cameron, C., Candappa, M., McQuail, S., Mooney, A., Moss, P. and Petrie, P. (2003) *The workforce*, London: DfES.

Campbell, N. (1999) *The decline of employment among older workers in Britain*, CASEpaper 19, London: London School of Economics and Political Science.

Cantle, T. (2001) *Community cohesion: A report of the independent review team*, London: Home Office.

Carter, J. (2000) 'New public management and equal opportunities in the NHS', *Critical Social Policy*, vol 20, no 1, pp 61-83.

CASE (Centre for Analysis of Social Exclusion )/HM Treasury (1999) *Persistent poverty and lifetime inequality: The evidence*, CASEreport 5 and HM Treasury Occasional Paper No 10, London: London School of Economics and Political Science and HM Treasury.

Cashmore, E. (2001) 'The experiences of ethnic minority police officers in Britain: under-recruitment and racial profiling in a performance culture', *Ethnic and Racial Studies*, vol 24, no 4, pp 642-59.

Castles, S., Crawley, H. and Loughna, S. (2003) *States of conflict: Causes and patterns of forced migration to the EU and policy responses*, London: Institute for Public Policy Research.

CDG (Care Development Group) (2001) *Fair care for older people: Care Development Group Report*, Edinburgh: Scottish Executive.

CEMD (Confidential Enquiries into Maternal Deaths) (2001) *Why mothers die*, London: RCOG Press.

Chevalier, A. and Lanot, G. (2002) 'The relative effect of family and financial characteristics on educational achievement', *Education Economics*, vol 10, no 2, pp 165-81.

Chevalier, A. and Viitanen, T. (2003) 'The long-run labour market consequences of teenage motherhood in Britain', *Journal of Population Economics*, vol 16, pp 323-43.

Civil Renewal Unit (2003) *Building civil renewal: Government support for community capacity building and proposals for change*, London: Civil Renewal Unit, Home Office.

Clancy, A., Hough, M., Aust, R. and Kershaw, C. (2001) *Crime, policing and justice: The experience of ethnic minorities. Findings from the 2000 British Crime Survey*, Home Office Research Study 223, London: Home Office.

Clark, H., Gough, H. and Macfarlane, A. (2004) *It pays dividends: Direct payments and older people*, Bristol: The Policy Press.

Clark, T. and Taylor, J. (1999) 'Income inequality: a tale of two cycles', *Fiscal Studies*, vol 20, no 4, pp 387-400.

Cohen, S. (2002) 'The local state of immigration controls', *Critical Social Policy*, vol 22, no 3, pp 518-43.

Cole, I., Hickman, P., Millwood, L., Reid, B., Slocombe, L. and Whittle, S. (2000) *Tenant participation in England*, Sheffield: Centre for Regional Economic and Social Research, Sheffield Hallam University.

Coleman, M.P., Rachet, B., Woods, L.M., Mitry, E., Riga, M., Cooper, N., Quinn, M.J., Brenner, H. and Esteve, J. (2004) 'Trends and socioeconomic inequalities in cancer survival in England and Wales up to 2001', *British Journal of Cancer*, vol 90, pp 1367-73.

Collison, P. (ed) (1988) *Acceptable inequalities?*, London: The IEA Health Unit.

Coombes, M., Alderman, N. and Raybould, S. (2001) *Mapping grants to deprived areas*, London: Community Fund.

Cooper, Y. (2004) 'Left out or left behind', *The Guardian*, March 22.

Coulthard, M., Walker, A. and Morgan, A. (2002) *People's perceptions of their neighbourhood and community involvement*, London: The Stationery Office.

CPAG (Child Poverty Action Group) (2004) *Welfare benefits and tax credits handbook 2004/2005*, London: CPAG.

Crane, M. and Warnes, A. (2000) 'Policy and service responses to rough sleeping among older people', *Journal of Social Policy*, vol 29, no 1, pp 21-36.

CRE (Commission for Racial Equality) (1997) *Exclusion from school and racial equality: Good practice guide*, London: CRE.

Curry, C. and O'Connell, A. (2003) *The pensions landscape*, London: Pensions Policy Institute.

Daniel, W.W. (1968) *Racial discrimination in England*, Harmondsworth: Penguin.

Davey Smith, G., Morris, J.N. and Shaw, M. (1998) 'The independent inquiry into inequalities in health', *British Medical Journal*, vol 317, pp 1465-6.

Daycare Trust (2003) *Towards universal childcare*, London: Daycare Trust.

Deacon, A. (2003) '"Levelling the playing field, activating the players": New Labour and "the cycle of disadvantage"', *Policy & Politics*, vol 31, no 2, pp 123-37.

Dean, M. (2001) 'Looking good for do-gooders,' *The Guardian*, October 17.

Deaton, A. (2003) 'Health, inequality, and economic development', *Journal of Economic Literature*, vol 41, no 1, pp 113-58.

DCMS (Department for Culture, Media and Sport) (2000) *A sporting future for all*, London: DCMS.

DCMS (2004) *Leading the good life: Guidance on integrating cultural and community strategies*, London: DCMS.

DCMS and Department for the Environment, Transport and the Regions (DTLR) (2001) *The Historic environment: A force for our future*, London: DCMS.

Demack, S., Drew, D. and Grimsley, M. (2000) 'Minding the gap: Ethnic, gender and social class differences in attainment at 16, 1988-95', *Race, Ethnicity and Education*, vol 3, no 2, pp 117-43.

Denham, J. (2001) *Building cohesive communities: A report of the ministerial group on public order and community cohesion*, London: Home Office.

Dennis, N., Erdos, G. and Al-Shahi, A. (2000) *Racist murder and pressure group politics: The Macpherson report and the police*, London: Institute for the Study of Civil Society.

DETR (Department of the Environment, Transport and the Regions) (1998) *Modernising local government: Local democracy and community leadership*, London: The Stationery Office.

DETR (1999) *Towards an urban renaissance: Final report of the Urban Task Force*, London: DETR.

DETR (2000) *Our towns and cities: Delivering an urban renaissance*, London: DETR.

DETR (2001) *Preparing community strategies: Government guidance to local authorities*, London: DETR, p 5.

DfEE (Department for Education and Employment) (1998) *Meeting the childcare challenge*, London: DfEE.

DfEE (1999) *Improving literacy and numeracy: A fresh start*, London: DfEE.

DfES (Department for Education and Skills) (2001) *Improvements in provision for excluded pupils and in-school discipline as exclusions fall further in 1999-2000*. Press Notice 2001/0242, 4 May, London: DfES.

DfES (2002) *Removing the barriers: Raising achievement levels for minority ethnic pupils. Exploring good practice*, London: DfES.

DfES (2003a) *The Skills for Life Survey*, London: DfES.

DfES (2003b) *Departmental Annual Report 2003*, Cm 6006, London: DfES.

DfES (2003c) *Provision for children under five years of age in England: January 2003 (Provisional)*, Statistical First Release 15/2003, London: DfES.

DfES (2003d) *Autumn Performance Report 2003: Achievement against Public Service Agreement targets*, London: DfES.

DfES (2003e) *Pupil absence in schools in England 2002/3 (revised)*, London: DfES.

DfES (2004) *Five year strategy for children and learners* London: DfES, p 30.

DfES (2004a) *Participation in education, training and employment by 16-18 year olds in England: 2002 and 2003*, Statistical First Release 18/2004, London: DfES.

DfES (2004b) *GCE/VCE A/AS examination results for young people in England, 2002/3 (final)*, Statistical First Release 24/2004, London: DfES.

DfES (2004c) *Department for Education and Skills: Five year strategy for children and learners*, London: DfES.

DfES (2004d) *National Curriculum assessment and GCSE/GNVQ attainment by pupil characteristics in England, 2002 (final) and 2003 (provisional)*, Statistical First Release, 24 February. London: DfES (www.dfes.gov.uk/rsgateway/DB/SFR/s000448/table37-40.xls).

DfES (2004e) *Permanent exclusions from schools and exclusions appeals, England 2002/3 (provisional)*, London: DfES.

DH (Department of Health) (1991) *Health of the nation*, Cm 1523, London: HMSO.

DH (1997a) *The new NHS: Modern and dependable*, London: HMSO.

DH (1997b) *Better services for vulnerable people*, London: The Stationery Office.

DH (1998a) *Our healthier nation: A contract for health*, London: The Stationery Office.

DH (1998b) *Independent inquiry into inequalities in health report*, London: The Stationery Office.

DH (1998c) *Modernising social services: Promoting independence, improving protection, raising standards*, Cm 4169, London: The Stationery Office.

DH (1999) *Saving lives: Our healthier nation*, London: The Stationery Office.

DH (2001a) 'Health Secretary announces new plans to improve health in poorest areas', Press Release 2001/0108, London: DH

DH (2001b) *The NHS Plan*, London: The Stationery Office.

DH (2001c) *The National Service Framework for Older People*, London: DH.

DH (2002) *Health inequalities: national targets on infant mortality and life expectancy*, technical briefing, London: DH.

DH (2003a) *Tackling health inequalities: A programme for action*, London: DH.

DH (2003b) *Hutton announces crackdown on health cheats*, press release, London: DH.

DH (2003c) *Patient and Public Involvement (PPI): The new arrangements*, London: DH.

Dickens, R. and Ellwood, D.T. (2003) 'Child poverty in Britain and the United States', *The Economic Journal*, vol 113, pp F219-39.

Dickens, R., Gregg, P. and Wadsworth, J. (eds) *The labour market under New Labour*, Basingstoke: Palgrave Macmillan.

Dickens, R. and Manning, A. (2003) 'Minimum wage, minimum impact', in R. Dickens, P. Gregg and J. Wadsworth (eds) *The labour market under New Labour*, Basingstoke: Palgrave Macmillan.

Disney, R. (1999) 'Why have older men stopped working?', in P. Gregg and J. Wadsworth (eds) *The state of working Britain*, Manchester: Manchester University Press, pp 58-74.

Disney, R. and Hawkes, D. (2003) 'Why has employment recently risen among older workers in Britain?', in R. Dickens, P. Gregg and J. Wadsworth (eds) *The labour market under New Labour*, Basingstoke: Palgrave Macmillan, pp 53-69.

Dixon, A., Le Grand, J., Henderson, J., Murray, R. and Poteliakhoff, E. (2003) *Is the NHS equitable? A review of the evidence*, London School of Economics and Political Science Health and Social Care Discussion Paper no 11, London: London School of Economics and Political Science.

Dodd, V. and Hopkins, N. (2003) 'Momentum in fight against racism "wanes"', *The Guardian*, April 19.

Dolton, P. and O'Neill, D. (2002) 'The long-run effects of unemployment monitoring and work-search programs: experimental evidence from the UK', *Journal of Labour Economics*, vol 20, no 2, pp 391-403.

Dolton, P.J. and Vignoles, A. (2000) 'The effects of school quality on pupil outcomes: an overview', in H. Heijke and J. Muyksen (eds) *Education, training and employment in the knowledge based economy*, London: Macmillan.

Donaldson, C. and Gerard, K. (1993) *Economics of health care financing: The visible hand*, London: Macmillan.

Donkin, A., Goldblatt, P. and Lynch, K. (2002) 'Inequalities in life expectancy by social class, 1972-1999', *Health Statistics Quarterly*, no 15, pp 5-15.

Dorling, D. and Rees, P. (2003) 'A nation still dividing: the British Census and social polarisation, 1971-2001', *Environment and Planning A*, vol 35, pp 1287-313.

Dorling, D. and Simpson, L. (2001) 'The geography of poverty: a political map of poverty under New Labour', *New Economy*, vol 8, no 2, pp 87-91.

Drever, F. and Whitehead, M. (1997) *Health inequalities: Decennial supplement*, London: ONS.

DSS (Department of Social Security) (1998) *A new contract for welfare: Partnership in pensions*, Cm 4179, London: The Stationery Office.

DSS (1999) *Opportunity for all: Tackling poverty and social exclusion*, London: DSS.

DTI (Department of Trade and Industry) (2003) *Individual income series*, London: Women's Equality Unit, DTI.

DTI (2004) *Trends in union membership and union density: Labour Force Survey: Great Britain, 1989-2003*, London: DTI (www.dti.gov.uk/er/emar/trade_data03.pdf).

Duncan, G. and Brooks–Gunn, J. (eds) (1997) *The consequences of growing up poor*, New York, NY: Russell Sage Foundation.

Duncan, P. and Thomas, S. (2001) *Evaluation of the community champions and the Community Development Learning Fund*, Norwich: DfES.

Dustmann, C., Rajah, N. and van Soest, A. (2003) 'Class size, education, and wages', *Economic Journal*, vol. 113, no 485, pp F99-120.

DWP (Department for Work and Pensions) (2002a) *Opportunity for all: A summary of the Fourth Report 2002*, London: DWP.

DWP (2002b) *Simplicity, security and choice: Working and saving for retirement*, Cm 5677, London: The Stationery Office.

DWP (2003a) *Households below average income 1994/5-2001/2*, Leeds: Corporate Document Services.

DWP (2003b) *Opportunity for all: A summary of the Fifth Annual Report 2003*, London: DWP.

DWP (2003c) *Measuring child poverty*, London: DWP.

DWP (2003d) *Opportunity for all: Fifth Annual Report 2003*, Cm 5956, London: The Stationery Office.

DWP (2003e) *Abstract of statistics 2003*, London: DWP.

DWP (2004a) *Households below average income: An analysis of the income distribution 1994/5-2002/03*, Leeds: Corporate Document Services.

DWP (2004b) *Income related benefits: Estimates of takeup in 2001-02*, London: DWP.

DWP (2004c) *Pensioner income series 2002/3*, London: DWP Pensions Analysis Division.

DWP (2004d) *Income support quarterly statistical enquiry: November 2003*, London: DWP Analytical Services Division.

Eagle, A., Duff, L., Tah, C. and Smith, N. (2002) 'Asylum seekers' experiences of the voucher system in the UK: fieldwork report', Home Office Research Development and Statistics Directorate online report 02/02, London: Home Office (www.homeoffice.gov.uk/rds/pdfs2/asylumexp.pdf)

EC (European Commission) (2001) *The social situation in the European Union 2001*, Luxembourg: Office for Official Publications of the European Communities.

EC (2003a) *Draft joint inclusion report: Statistical annex, COM(2003)773 final*, Brussels: Commission of the European Communities.

EC (2003b) *Draft joint report on social inclusion: Frequently asked questions*, Brussels: Commission of the European Communities.

EC (2003c) *Joint report on social inclusion*, SEC(2003)1425, Brussels: Commission of the European Communities.

EC (2003d) *Structures of the taxation systems in the European Union*, Luxembourg: Office for Official Publications of the European Communities.

Electoral Commission, The (2002) *Modernising Elections – A strategic evaluation of the 2002 Electoral Pilot Schemes*, London, The Electoral Commission.

Electoral Commission, The (2003a) *Turnout factsheet*, London: The Electoral Commission.

Electoral Commission, The (2003b) *Absent voting in Great Britain*, London: The Electoral Commission

Ermisch, J. and Pevalin, D.J. (2003) *Does a 'teen birth' have longer-term impact on the mother? Evidence from the BCS70*, ISER working paper 2003/28, Colchester: University of Essex.

Ermisch, J., Francesconi, M. and Pevalin, D.J. (2001) *Outcomes for children of poverty*, DWP Research Report No 158, Leeds: Corporate Document Services.

Evandrou, M. (2000) 'Social inequalities in later life: the socio-economic position of older people from ethnic minority groups in Britain', *Population Trends*, no.101 pp 32-9, London: The Stationery Office.

Evandrou, M. and Falkingham, J. (1998) 'The personal social services', in H.Glennerster and J. Hills (eds) *The state of welfare* (2nd edn), Oxford: Oxford University Press, pp 188-256.

Evans, M., Eyre, J., Millar, J. and Sarre, S. (2003) *New Deal for Lone Parents: Second synthesis report*, DWP Research Report no 163, Sheffield: DWP.

Evans, M., Noble, M., Wright, G., Smith, G., Lloyd, M. and Dibben, C. (2002) *Growing together, growing apart*, Bristol/York: The Policy Press/Joseph Rowntree Foundation.

Exworthy, M. (2003) 'The 'second Black Report'? The Acheson Report as another opportunity to tackle health inequalities', in V. Berridge and S. Blume (eds) *Poor health: Social inequality before and after the Black Report*, London: Frank Cass.

Exworthy, M., Stuart, M., Blane, D. and Marmot, M. (2003) *Tackling health inequalities since the Acheson Inquiry*, Bristol: The Policy Press.

Faggio, G. and Nickell, S. (2003) 'The rise of inactivity among adult men', in R. Dickens, P. Gregg and J. Wadsworth (eds) *The labour market under New Labour*, Basingstoke: Palgrave Macmillan, pp 40-52.

Fairclough, N. (2000) *New Labour, new language?*, London: Routledge.

Farrell, C. and O'Connor, W. (2003) *Low-income families and household spending*, DWP Research Report no 192, Leeds Corporate Document Services.

FBU (Family Budget Unit) (2003) *Low cost but acceptable budget for pensioners* updated to April 2003, York: FBU.

Feinstein, L. (1998) *Pre-school educational inequality? British children in the 1970 cohort*, Centre for Economic Performance, Discussion Paper 404, London: London School of Economics and Political Science.

Feinstein, L. (2000) *The relative importance of academic, psychological and behavioural attributes developed in childhood*, Centre for Economic Performance Discussion Paper No 443, London: London School of Economics and Political Science.

Feinstein, L. (2003) 'Inequality in the early cognitive development of British children in the 1970 Cohort', *Economica*, vol 70, no 277, pp 73-97.

Fenton, S. (1996) 'Counting ethnicity: social groups and official categories', in R. Levitas and W. Guy (eds) *Interpreting official statistics*, London: Routledge.

Fieldhouse, E.A., Kalra, V.S. and Alam, S. (2002) 'A New Deal for Young People from minority ethnic communities in the UK', *Journal of Ethnic and Migration Studies*, vol 28, no 3, pp 499-513.

Finn, J.D. and Achilles, C.M. (1990) 'Answers about questions about class size: a statewide experiment', *American Educational Research Journal*, vol 27, pp 557-77.

FitzGerald, M. (1999) *Final report into stop and search*, London: Metropolitan Police.

FitzGerald, M. and Sibbitt, R. (1997) *Ethnic monitoring in police forces: A beginning*, Home Office Research Study 173, London: Home Office.

Ford, R. and Millar, J. (eds) (1998) *Private lives and public responses: Lone parenthood and future policy in the UK*, London: Policy Studies Institute.

Gaffney, D., Pollock, A.M., Price, D. and Shaoul, J. (1999) 'The private finance initiative: the politics of the private finance initiative and the new NHS', *British Medical Journal*, vol 319, pp 249-53.

Galindo-Rueda, F., Marcenaro-Gutierrez, O. and Vignoles, A. (2004) 'The widening socio-economic gap in UK higher education', Centre for the Economics of Education Discussion Paper, London: London School of Economics and Political Science.

Gaventa, J. (2004) *Representation, community leadership and participation*, draft for Neighbourhood Renewal Unit, London: ODPM.

Gibbons, S. (2002) 'Geography, resources and primary school performance', Centre for Economics of Education Discussion Paper 25, London: London School of Economics and Political Science.

Gibbons, S. and Machin, S. (2001) 'Valuing primary schools', Centre for Economics of Education Discussion Paper 15, London: London School of Economics and Political Science.

Gibson, T. (2004) *Making ends meet to make it happen*, London: Radical Economics.

Gillborn, D. (1998) 'Race and ethnicity in compulsory schooling', in T. Modood and T. Acland (eds) *Race and higher education*, London: Policy Studies Institute, pp 11-23.

Gillborn, D. (2001) 'Racism, policy and the (mis)education of black children', in R. Majors (ed) *Educating our black children: New directions and radical approaches*, London: Routledge Palmer, pp 13-27.

Gillborn, D. and Mirza, H. (2000) *Educational inequality: Mapping race, class and gender – a synthesis of research evidence*, London: DfES.

Ginn, J. and Arber, S. (2001) 'Pension prospects of minority ethnic groups: inequality by gender and ethnicity', *British Journal of Sociology*, vol 52, no 3, pp 519-39.

Glennerster, H. (1997) *Paying for welfare: Towards 2000*, Hemel Hempstead: Prentice Hall.

Glennerster, H. (2001) *United Kingdom education 1997-2001*, CASEpaper 50, London: London School of Economics and Political Science.

Glennerster, H. and Hills J. (1998) *The state of welfare: The economics of social spending*, Oxford: Oxford University Press.

Goddard, M. and Smith, P. (2001) 'Equity of access to health care services', *Social Science and Medicine*, vol 53, no 9, pp 1149-62.

Goodman, A., Johnson, P. and Webb, S. (1997) *Inequality in the UK*, Oxford: Oxford University Press.

Goodman, A., Myck, M. and Shephard, A. (2003) *Sharing in the nation's prosperity? Pensioner poverty in Britain*, Commentary 93, London: Institute for Fiscal Studies.

Goodman, A. and Webb, S. (1994) *For richer, for poorer: The changing distribution of income in the United Kingdom, 1961-1991*, Commentary 41, London: Institute for Fiscal Studies.

Gordon, D., Levitas, R., Pantazis, C., Patsios, D., Payne, S., Townsend, P., Adelman, L., Ashworth, K., Middleton, S., Bradshaw, J. and Williams, J. (2000) *Poverty and social exclusion in Britain*, York: Joseph Rowntree Foundation.

Gordon, D., Lloyd, E., Senior, M., Shaw, M. and Ben Shlomo, Y. (2001) *Wales NHS resource allocation review*, Cardiff: The National Assembly for Wales.

Graham, H. (2000) 'The challenge of health inequalities', in H. Graham (ed) *Understanding health inequalities*, Buckingham: Open University Press.

Greenaway, D. and Haynes, M. (2000) *Funding universities to meet national and international challenges*, School of Economics policy report, Nottingham: University of Nottingham.

Gregg, P., Hansen, K. and Wadsworth, J. (1999) 'The rise of the workless household', in P. Gregg and J. Wadsworth (eds) *The state of working Britain*, Manchester: Manchester University Press, pp 75-89.

Gregg, P. and Harkness, S. (2003) 'Welfare reform and the employment of lone parents', in R. Dickens, P. Gregg and J. Wadsworth (eds) *The labour market under New Labour*, Basingstoke: Palgrave Macmillan, pp 98-115.

Gregg, P., Harkness, S. and Machin, S. (1999a) 'Poor kids: trends in child poverty in Britain, 1968-96', *Fiscal Studies*, vol 20, no 2, pp 163-187.

Gregg, P., Harkness, S. and Machin, S. (1999b) *Child development and family income*, York: Joseph Rowntree Foundation.

Gregg, P. and Wadsworth, J. (eds) (1999) *The state of working Britain*, Manchester: Manchester University Press.

Gregg, P. and Wadsworth, J. (2001) 'Everything you ever wanted to know about measuring worklessness and polarization at the household level but were afraid to ask', *Oxford Bulletin of Economics and Statistics*, vol 63, Special Issue, pp 777-806.

Gregg, P. and Wadsworth, J. (2002) *Why we should (also) measure worklessness at the household level: Theory and evidence from Britain, Spain, Germany and the United States*, CMPO Working Paper 53, Bristol: University of Bristol.

Gregg, P. and Wadsworth, J. (2003) 'Workless households and the recovery', in R. Dickens, P. Gregg and J. Wadsworth (eds) *The labour market under New Labour*, Basingstoke: Palgrave Macmillan, pp 32-9.

Gregg, P. and Washbrook, E. (2003) *The effects of early maternal employment on child development in the UK*, CMPO Working Paper no 03/070, Bristol: University of Bristol.

Haddock, M. (2003) *Summary report on Community Cohesion Initiatives in Oldham primary schools* (www.oldham.gov.uk/housing/cohesion/ oldham_schools_cohesion.report.pdf).

Haezewindt, P. (2003) 'Investing in each other and the community: the role of social capital', in C. Summerfield and P. Babb (eds) *Social Trends no 33*, London: The Stationery Office, pp 19-27.

Hall, P. A. (1999) 'Social capital in Britain', *British Journal of Political Science*, vol 29, pp 417-61.

Hallam, S. and Castle, F. (2001) 'Exclusion from school: what can help prevent it?' *Educational Review*, vol 53, no 2, pp 169-79.

Harkness, S. and Waldfogel, J. (1999) *The family gap in pay: Evidence from seven industrialised countries*, CASEpaper 30, London: London School of Economics and Political Science.

Harrison, M. and Phillips, D. (2003) *Housing and black and minority ethnic communities: Reviewing the evidence base*, London: ODPM.

Hasluck, C., Elias, P. and Green, A. (2003) *The wider labour market impact of employment zones*, DWP Report WAE 175, Sheffield: DWP.

Hawksworth, J. (2002) 'UK state pensions policy at the crossroads: a review of the potential long-term costs and benefits of alternative options', in R. Brooks, S. Regan and P. Robinson (eds) A *new contract for retirement: Modelling policy options to 2050*, London: Institute for Public Policy Research, pp 9-34.

Heath, A., Jowell, R. and Curtice, J. (1994) 'Can Labour win?', in A. Heath, R. Jowell and J. Curtice with B. Taylor (eds) *Labour's last chance?*, Aldershot: Dartmouth, pp 275-99.

Heath, A., Jowell, R. and Curtice, J. (2001) *The rise of New Labour: Party policies and voter choices*, Oxford: Oxford University Press.

Her Majesty's Inspectorate of Constabulary (2000) *Winning the race: Embracing diversity*, Consolidation Inspection of Police Community and Race Relations 2000, London: Home Office.

Hibbert, A., Fogelman, K. and Maoner, O. (1990) 'Occupational outcomes of truancy', *British Journal of Educational Psychology*, vol 60, no 1, pp 23-6.

Hill, D. (2000) *Urban policy and politics in Britain*, London: Macmillan.

Hills, J. (1995) *Inquiry into income and wealth*, vol 2, York: Joseph Rowntree Foundation.

Hills, J. (2002) 'Social security policy and public attitudes since 1997', *Fiscal Studies*, vol 23, no 4, pp 539-58.

Hills, J. (2004a) *Inequality and the state*, Oxford: Oxford University Press.

Hills, J. (2004b) 'Inclusion or insurance? National Insurance and the future of the contributory principle', *Journal of Social Policy*, vol 33, pp 347-72.

Hills, J. and Sutherland, H. (2004) 'Ending child poverty in a generation? Policies and prospects in the UK', Paper presented at Conference on Supporting Children: English Speaking Countries in International Perspective, Princeton University, New Jersey, January.

Hirst, A., Tarling, R., Lefaucheux, M., Rowland, B., McGregor, A., Glass, A., Trinh, T., Simm, C., Shaw, H. and Engineer, R. (2002) *Qualitative evaluation of employment zones: A study of local delivery agents and area case studies*, DWP Report WAE 124, Sheffield: DWP.

HM Treasury (1997) 'Employment opportunity for all: a new approach', HM Treasury Press Release, 27 Novemeber (http://archive.treasury.gov.uk/pub/html/prebudgetNov97/hmt8.html)

HM Treasury (1999) *Tackling poverty and extending opportunity: The modernisation of Britain's tax and benefit system Number Four*, London: HM Treasury.

HM Treasury (2000) *Spending Review 2000*, London: The Stationery Office.

HM Treasury (2001) *Tackling child poverty: Giving every child the best possible start in life*, pre-budget report document, London: HM Treasury.

HM Treasury (2002) *Tax and the environment: Using economic instruments*, London: HM Treasury.

HM Treasury (2004c) *Child poverty review*, London: The Stationery Office.

HM Treasury (2004a) *Economic and fiscal strategy Report: Budget 2004*, London: HM Treasury.

HM Treasury (2004b) *Public expenditure statistical analyses 2004*, London: HM Treasury.

Hobcraft, J. (1998) *Intergenerational and life-course transmission of social exclusion: Influences of childhood poverty, family disruption, and contact with the police*, CASEpaper 13, London: London School of Economics and Political Science.

Hobcraft, J. and Kiernan, K. (2001) 'Childhood poverty, early motherhood and adult social exclusion', *British Journal of Sociology*, vol 52, no 3, pp 495-517.

Hodge, M. (2000) 'Equality and New Labour', *Renewal*, vol 8, no 3, pp 34-41.

Holtermann, S., Brannen, J., Moss, P. and Owen, C. (1999) *Lone parents and the labour market: Results from the Labour Force Survey and review of research*, ESR23, Sheffield: Employment Service.

Home Office (1997) *Race and the criminal justice system 1994*, London: Home Office.

Home Office (1998a) *Statistics on race and the criminal justice system: A Home Office publication under Section 95 of the Criminal Justice Act 1991*, London: Home Office.

Home Office (1998b) *Fairer, faster and firmer: A modern approach to immigration*, Cm 4019, London: The Stationery Office.

Home Office (1999) *Stephen Lawrence Inquiry: Home Secretary's action plan*, London: Home Office.

Home Office (2002) *Guidance on community cohesion*, London: Home Office.

Home Office (2003a) *Statistics on race and the criminal justice system 2002*, London: Home Office.

Home Office (2003b) *Community Cohesion Pathfinder Programme: The first six months*, London: Home Office.

Home Office (2004) *Asylum statistics: 4th quarter 2003, United Kingdom*, London: Home Office.

Hosie, A. (2003) 'Re-engagement and re-integration of pregnant young women and young mothers of school age', Briefing Paper, Newcastle: University of Newcastle upon Tyne.

House of Commons (2000) *Minutes of evidence taken before the Health Committee*, Thursday 16 November, London: House of Commons.

House of Commons (2001) *Select Committee on public administration, First Report, Public participation: issues and innovations*, London: House of Commons.

House of Commons (2003) *Hansard*, Oral Answers, Mr Andrew Smith, Secretary of State for Work and Pensions, 7 July: column 735.

Howarth, C., Kenway, P., Palmer, G. and Street, C. (1998) *Monitoring poverty and social exclusion: Labour's inheritance*, York: Joseph Rowntree Foundation.

IAP (Inter-Agency Partnership) (2004) *The impact of Section 55 on the Inter-Agency Partnership and the asylum seekers it supports*, London: Refugee Council.

Illsley, R. and Le Grand, J. (1987) 'The measurement of inequality in health', in A. Williams (ed) *Health and economics*, Basingstoke: Macmillan.

Inland Revenue (2003) *Annual Report*, Cm 6050, London: The Stationery Office

Inland Revenue (2004) *Child and Working Tax Credits: Quarterly statistics April 2004*, London: Inland Revenue.

Institute for Volunteering Research (2002) *UK-wide evaluation of the Millennium Volunteers Programme*, Research Brief 357, Nottingham: DfES.

Institute for Social Research (2003) *Social science in the public interest*, vol 2, no 3, Ann Arbor: University of Michigan.

Irvine, B. and Ginsberg, I. (2004) *England vs Scotland: Does more money mean better health?*, London: Civitas.

Jenkins, S.P. and Schluter, C. (2002) *The effect of family income during childhood on later-life attainment: Evidence from Germany*, ISER Working Paper 2002-20, University of Essex.

Johnson, M. (2003) 'Asylum seekers in dispersal: healthcare issues', Home Office Research Development and Statistics online report 13/03, London: Home Office (www.homeoffice.gov.uk/rds/pdfs2/rdsolr1303.pdf)

Johnston, D. and Campbell-Jones, C. (2003) *Skills for regeneration: Learning by community champions*, Research Report RR441, Norwich: DfES.

Johnston, M. and Jowell, R. (2001) 'How robust is British civil society?' in A. Park, J. Curtice, K. Thomson, L. Jarvis and C. Bromley (eds) *British social attitudes 18th Report: Public policy, social ties*, London: SAGE Publications, pp 175-96.

Jolliffe, A. (2003) 'You've got to be Einstein to understand pensions', *Financial Times, FT Money & Business*, 11 October, p 29.

Jones, T. (1993) *Britain's ethnic minorities*, London: Policy Studies Institute.

Jordan, B. and Düvell, F. (2002) *Irregular migration: The dilemmas of trans-national mobility*, Cheltenham: Edward Elgar.

Kalra, V.S. (2002) 'Extended view: riots, race and reports: Denham, Cantle, Oldham and Burnley Inquiries', *Sage Race Relations Abstracts*, vol 27, no 4, pp 20-30.

Karlsen, S. and Nazroo, J.Y. (2000) 'Identity and structure: rethinking ethnic inequalities in health', in H. Graham (ed) *Understanding health inequalities*, Buckingham: Open University Press.

Karn, V. and Phillips, D. (1998) 'Race and ethnicity in housing: a diversity of experience', in T. Blackstone, B. Parekh and P. Sanders (eds) *Race relations in Britain: A developing agenda*, London: Routledge, pp 128-57.

Kasparova, D., Marsh, A., Vegeris, S. and Perry, J. (2003) *Families and children 2001: Work and childcare*, DWP Research Report no 191, Leeds: Corporate Document Services.

Kawachi, I. (1999) 'Social capital and community effects on population and individual health', *Annals of the New York Academy of Science*, vol 896, pp 120-30.

Kendall, L., Morris, M. and Stoney, S. (2002) *Overall impact of Excellence in Cities: Preliminary findings*, London: DfES.

Kenway, P. (2003) *Eradicating poverty: A target for the Labour movement. A Paper for the Fabian Society*, London: Fabian Society.

Kilkey, M. and Bradshaw, J. (2001) 'Making work pay policies for lone parents', in J. Millar and K. Rowlingson (eds) *Lone parents, employment and social policy*, Bristol: The Policy Press, pp 211-31.

Klein, R. (2003) 'Making policy in a fog', in A. Oliver (ed) *Health inequalities: Evidence, policy and implementation, proceedings from a meeting of the Health Equity Network*, London: Nuffield Trust.

Knijn, T. and Van Berkel, R. (2003) 'Again revisited: employment and activation policies for lone parents on social assistance in the Netherlands', in J. Millar and M. Evans (eds) *Lone parents and employment: International comparisons of what works*, Sheffield: DWP.

Krishnamurthy, A., Prime, D. and Zimmeck, M. (2001) *Voluntary and community activities: Findings from the 2000 British Crime Survey*, London: Home Office Research, Development and Statistics Directorate.

Krueger, A.B. and Whitmore, D.M. (2001) 'The effect of attending a small class in the early grades on college-test taking and middle school test results: evidence from Project Star', *Economic Journal*, vol 111, no 468, pp 1-28.

Kundnani, A. (2001) 'From Oldham to Bradford: the violence of the violated', *Race & Class*, vol 43, no 2, pp 105-10.

Labour Party (1997) *Labour Party Manifesto: New Labour because Britain deserves better*, London: Labour Party.

Labour Party (2001) *Ambitions for Britain: Labour's manifesto 2001*, London: Labour Party.

Lakey, J. (1997) 'Neighbourhoods and housing', in T. Modood, R. Berthoud, J. Lakey, J. Nazroo, P. Smith, S. Virdee and S. Beishon (eds) *Ethnic minorities in Britain: Diversity and disadvantage*, London: Policy Studies Institute, pp 184-223.

Le Grand, J. and Vizard, P. (1998) 'The National Health Service: crisis, change, or continuity?', in H. Glennerster and J. Hills (eds) *The state of welfare*, Oxford: Oxford University Press.

Leonard, M. (2000) 'Introduction', in B. Hombach (ed) *The new centre*, Cambridge: Polity Press, pp xi-xxix.

Lessof, C., Miller, M., Phillips, M., Pickering, K., Purdon, S. and Hales, J. (2003) *New Deal for Lone Parents evaluation: Findings from the quantitative survey*, DWP Report WAE147, Sheffield: DWP.

Levitas, R. (1998) *The inclusive society? Social exclusion and New Labour*, Basingstoke: Macmillan.

Levitas, R. (2000) 'What is social exclusion?', in D. Gordon and P. Townsend (eds) *Breadline Europe: The measurement of poverty*, Bristol: The Policy Press, pp 357-83.

Lewis, J. (2001) 'Orientations to work and the issue of care', in J. Millar and K. Rowlingson (eds) *Lone parents, employment and social policy: Cross-national comparisons*, Bristol: The Policy Press, pp 153-68.

LGA (Local Government Association) (2000) *The only way is up! Increasing turnout in local government elections*, London: LGA.

Lister, R. (1998) 'Fighting social exclusion with one hand tied behind our back', *New Economy*, vol 5, no 1, London: Institute for Public Policy Research.

Lister, R. (2001a) 'Doing good by stealth: the politics of poverty and inequality under New Labour', *New Economy*, vol 8, no 2, pp 65-70.

Lister, R. (2001b) 'New Labour: a study of ambiguity from a position of ambivalence', *Critical Social Policy*, vol 21, no 4, pp 425-47.

Lister, R. and Moore, R. (1997) 'Government must reconsider its strategy for more equal society', *The Financial Times*, 1 October.

Loumidis, J., Stafford, B., Young, R., Green, A., Arthur, S., Legard, R., Lessof, C., Lewis, J., Walker, R., Corden, A., Thornton, P. and Sainsbury, R. (2001) *Evaluation of the New Deal for Disabled People Personal Adviser Service pilot*, DSS Research Report no 144, Leeds: Corporate Document Services.

Lowndes, V. and Wilson, D. (2001) 'Social capital and local governance: exploring the institutional design variable,' *Political Studies*, vol 49, issue 4, pp 629-47.

Lowndes, V., Pratchett, L. and Stoker, G. (2001) 'Trends in public participation: Part 1 – government perspectives,' *Public Administration*, vol 79, no 1, pp 205-22.

LPC (Low Pay Commission) (2000) *The National Minimum Wage: The story so far*, second report of the LPC, London: The Stationery Office.

LPC (2003) *The National Minimum Wage: Building on success*, Fourth Report, London: The Stationery Office.

LPC (2004) *Protecting young workers: The National Minimum Wage*, LPC report, London, The Stationery Office.

Lundberg, S., Pollack, R. and Wales, T. (1997) 'Do husbands and wives pool their resources? Evidence from the United Kingdom Child Benefit', *Journal of Human Resources*, vol 32, no 3, pp 463-80.

Lupton, R. (2003a) 'Secondary schools in disadvantaged areas: the impact of context on school processes and quality', PhD thesis, Department of Social Policy, London School of Economics and Political Science.

Lupton, R. (2003b) *Poverty Street: The dynamics of neighbourhood decline and renewal*, Bristol: The Policy Press.

Lupton, R. and Power, A. (2002) 'Social exclusion and neighbourhoods', in J. Hills, J. Le Grand and D. Piachaud (eds) *Understanding social exclusion*, Oxford: Oxford University Press, pp 118-40.

Lupton, R. and Power, A. (forthcoming) *Minority ethnic groups in Britain's cities 1991-2001*, CASE-Brookings Census Briefs no 2, London: London School of Economics and Political Science.

Machin, S. (2003) 'Wage inequality since 1975', in R. Dickens, P. Gregg and J. Wadsworth (eds) *The labour market under New Labour*, Basingstoke: Palgrave Macmillan.

Machin, S. and McNally, S. (2004) *The literacy hour*, IZA Discussion Paper no 1005, Bonn: Institute for the Study of Labour (IZA).

Machin, S., McNally, S. and Meghir, C. (2003) *Excellence in cities: Evaluation of an education policy in disadvantaged areas*, report produced for the DfES, March 2003 (www.nfer.ac.uk/research/documents/EIC/CEPIF.doc).

Machin, S., McNally, S. and Meghir, C. (2004) 'Improving pupil performance in English secondary schools: Excellence in Cities', *Journal of the European Economic Association*, vol 2, issue 2, pp 396-405.

Macintyre, S. (1999) 'Reducing health inequalities: an action report', *Critical Public Health*, vol 9, no 4, pp 347-50.

Mackenbach, J.P. and Bakker, M.J. (2003) 'Tackling socioeconomic inequalities in health: analysis of European experiences', *The Lancet*, vol 362, pp 1409-14.

Macpherson, W. (1999) *The Stephen Lawrence Inquiry: Report of an Inquiry by Sir William Macpherson of Cluny*, London: Home Office.

Mandelson, P. (1997) *Labour's next steps: Tackling social exclusion*, Fabian Pamphlet 581, London: Fabian Society.

Marmot, M., Adelsten, A.M. and Bulusu, L. (1984) *Immigrant mortality in England and Wales 1970-78. Causes of death by country of birth*, London: HMSO.

Marsh, A. and Vegeris, S. (2004) *The British lone parent cohort and their children 1991 to 2001*, DWP Research Report no 209, Leeds: Corporate Document Services.

Mason, D. (1982) 'After Scarman: a note on the concept of "institutional racism"', *New Community*, vol 10, no 1, pp 38-45.

Maynard, W. and Read, T. (1997) *Policing racially motivated incidents*, Police Research Series 84, London: Home Office.

Mayor of London (2004) *Destitution by design: Withdrawal of support from in-country asylum applicants: an impact assessment for London*, London: Greater London Authority.

McKay, S. and Collard, S. (2003) *Developing deprivation questions for the Family Resources Survey*, Personal Finance Research Centre, Bristol: University of Bristol.

McKnight, A., Elias, P. and Wilson, R. (1998) *Low pay and the National Insurance system: A statistical picture*, Equal Opportinites Commission, Research Discussion Series, Manchester: EOP.

McKnight, A. (2000) 'Transitions off Income Support: estimating the impact of New Deal for Lone Parents using administrative data', in C. Hasluck, A. McKnight and P. Elias (eds) *Evaluation of the New Deal for Lone Parents: Early lessons from the Phase One prototype – cost-benefit and econometric analysis*, DSS Research Report no 110, Leeds: Corporate Document Services, pp 51-85.

McKnight, A. (2002) 'From childhood poverty to labour market disadvantage', in J. Bynner, P. Elias, A. McKnight, H. Pan and G. Pierre (eds) *Young people's changing routes to independence*, York: York Publishing Services.

Middleton, E. and Baker, D. (2003) 'Comparison of social distribution of immunisation with measles, mumps, and rubella vaccine, England, 1991 2001', *British Medical Journal*, vol 326, p 854.

Middleton, S., Ashworth, K. and Braithwaite, I. (1997) *Small fortunes: Spending on children, childhood poverty, and parental sacrifice*, York: Joseph Rowntree Foundation.

Miles, R. and Brown, M. (2003) *Racism* (2nd edn), London: Routledge.

Millar, J. (2000) *Keeping track of welfare reform: The New Deal programmes*, York: Joseph Rowntree Foundation.

Millar, J. (2003) 'Employment policies for lone parents', in J. Millar and M. Evans (eds) *Lone parents and employment: International comparisons of what works*, Sheffield: DWP.

Miller, J., Quinton, P. and Bland, N. (2000) *Police stops and searches: Lessons from a programme of research*, Briefing Note, London: Home Office.

Modood, T., Berthoud, R., Lakey, J., Nazroo, J., Smith, P., Virdee, S. and Beishon, S. (eds) (1997) *Ethnic minorities in Britain: Diversity and disadvantage*, London: Policy Studies Institute.

MORI (2003) *Attitudes towards voting and the political process in 2003*, London: The Electoral Commission.

Moser, K., Li, L. and Power, C. (2003) 'Social inequalities in low birth weight in England and Wales: trends and implications for future population health', *Journal of Epidemiology and Community Health*, vol 57, no 9, pp 687-91.

Moss, N. and Arrowsmith, J. (2003) *A review of 'what works' for clients aged over 50*, DWP Report no 174, Leeds: Corporate Document Services.

Mumford, K. (2001) *Talking to families in East London: A report on the first stage of the research*, CASEreport 9, London: London School of Economics and Political Science.

Mumford, K. and Power, A. (2003) *East Enders: Family and community in East London*, Bristol: The Policy Press.

Munton, T. and Zurawan, A. (2004) *Active communities: Headline findings from the 2003 Home Office Citizenship Survey*, London: Home Office.

NACAB (National Association of Citizens' Advice Bureaux) (2002a) *Process error: CAB clients' experience of the National Asylum Support service*, London: NACAB.

NACAB (2002b) *Distant voices: CAB clients' experience of continuing problems with the National Asylum Support service*, London: NACAB.

NAO (National Audit Office) (2004) *Early years: Progress in developing high quality childcare and early education accessible to all*, HC 268, London: The Stationery Office.

NAPF (National Association of Pension Funds) (2001) *Annual Survey of occupational pension schemes*, London: NAPF.

Narendranathan, W. and Stewart, M. (1993) 'How does the benefit effect vary as unemployment spells lengthen?', *Journal of Applied Econometrics*, vol 8, no 4, pp 361-82.

Naylor, R., Smith, J. and McKnight, A. (2002) *Sheer class? The extent and sources of variation in the UK graduate earnings premium*, CASEpaper 54, London: London School of Economics and Political Science.

Nazroo, J.Y. (2003) 'The structuring of ethnic inequalities in health: Economic position, racial discrimination and racism', *American Journal of Public Health*, vol 93, no 2, pp 277-84.

NESS (National Evaluation of Sure Start) (2004) *'The impact of Sure Start local programmes on child development and family functioning: A report on preliminary findings'*, Institute for the Study of Children, Families and Social Issues, Birkbeck College, University of London.

Neuburger, J. (2001) 'How far is dispersal led by the availability of housing? What impact has this had on asylum seekers' experiences of dispersal?', dissertation for MSc/Diploma in Housing, London School of Economics and Political Science.

Newburn, T. and Jones, T. (2002) *Consultation by crime and disorder partnerships*, London: Home Office.

NHF (National Housing Federation) (2004) *Stock Transfer Briefing No 5*, London: NHF.

Nickell, S. (2003) 'Poverty and worklessness', *Centre Piece: The Magazine of the Centre for Economic Performance*, vol 8, issue 3.

Nickell, S. and Quintini, G. (2002) 'The consequences of the decline in public sector pay in Britain: a little bit of evidence', *Economic Journal*, vol 112 (February), pp F107-18.

NOF (New Opportunities Fund) and Community Fund (2003) *Fair share – one year on: Update for the Department of Culture, Media and Sport*, London: NOF and Community Fund.

NRU (Neighbourhood Renewal Unit) (2004) *Neighbourhood management pathfinder programme national evaluation: Annual review 2002/03 research report*, London: ODPM.

Nye, B.A., Boyd-Zaharias, J., Fulton, D. and Wallenhorst, M.P. (1992) 'Smaller class sizes really are better', *The American School Board Journal*, May, pp 31-3.

O'Connell, A. (2004) *State pension reform: The consultation response*, London: Pensions Policy Institute.

ODPM (Office of the Deputy Prime Minister) (2002) *Living places: Cleaner, safer, greener*, London: ODPM.

ODPM (2003a) *Sustainable communities: Building for the future*, London: ODPM.

ODPM (2003b) *Rough sleeping estimates in England*, London: ODPM.

ODPM (2003c) *English House Condition Survey 2001*, London: The Stationery Office.

ODPM (2004a) *Consultation paper on Planning Policy Statement 1: Creating sustainable communities*, London: ODPM, p 11.

ODPM (2004b) *Safer places: The planning system and crime prevention*, London: ODPM, p 48.

OECD (Organisation for Economic Co-operation and Development) (1998) *Employment outlook*, Paris: OECD.

OECD (2001a) *OECD Employment outlook 2001*, Paris: OECD.

OECD (2001b) *Starting strong: Early childhood education and care*, Paris: OECD.

OECD (2003a) *Education at a glance*, Paris: OECD.

OECD (2003b) *Employment outlook*, Paris: OECD.

OFSTED (Office for Standards in Education) (2002) *Achievement of black caribbean pupils: Three successful primary schools*, HMI 447, London: OFSTED.

OFSTED (2003) *Excellence in Cities and Education Action Zones: Management and impact*, London: OFSTED.

Oliver, A. and Nutbeam, D. (2003) 'Addressing health inequalities in the United Kingdom: A case study', *Journal of Public Health Medicine*, vol 25, pp 281-7.

ONS (Office for National Statistics) (1997) *Adult literacy in Britain*, London: HMSO.

ONS (1999) 'Trade union membership and recognition 1997-98: an analysis of data from the Certification Officer and the Labour Force Survey', *Labour Market Trends*, July, pp 343-53.

ONS (2002a) *Social capital matrix of surveys (update)*, London: ONS.

ONS (2002b) *Health Statistics Quarterly*, no 15, Autumn 2002, London: The Stationery Office.

ONS (2003a) *Economic Trends Annual Supplement 2003*, London: The Stationery Office.

ONS (2003b) *Labour Market New Earnings Survey 2003: Data for 2003*, analyses by region, county and small areas, London: ONS.

ONS (2004a) *Focus on ethnicity and identity*, web-based publication, 4 January (www.statistics.gov.uk).

ONS (2004b) *Population trends*, no 115, Spring 2004, London: The Stationery Office.

ONS (2004c) *Labour Force Survey Quarterly Supplement*, no 24, Autumn, London: ONS.

Osler, A. and Starkey, M. (2001) 'Citizenship, education and national identities in France and England: inclusive or exclusive', *Oxford Review of Education*, vol 27, pp 287-305.

Osler, A., Watling, R., Busher, H., Cole, T. and White, A. (2001) *Reasons for exclusion from school*, DfEE Research Report 244, London: DfEE.

Oxfam (2000) *Token gestures: The effects of the voucher scheme on asylum seekers and organisations in the UK*, Oxford: Oxfam GB.

Oxley, H., Dang, T-T., Förster, M.F. and Pellizzari, M. (2001) 'Income inequalities and poverty among children and households with children in selected OECD countries', in K. Vleminckx and T. M. Smeeding (eds) *Child well-being, child poverty and child policy in modern nations: What do we know?*, Bristol: The Policy Press, pp 371-406.

Palmer, G., North, J., Carr, J. and Kenway, P. (2003) *Monitoring poverty and social exclusion 2003*, York: Joseph Rowntree Foundation.

Parekh, B. (2000) *The future of multi-ethnic Britain*. London: Profile Books.

Parker, H. (ed) (2001) *Low cost but acceptable: A minimum income standard for households aged 65-74 years, April 2001 prices*, London: Age Concern England.

Parker, H. (ed) (2002) *Modest but adequate budget for pensioners, April 2002 prices*, London: Age Concern England.

Peach, C. (ed) (1996) *Ethnicity in the 1991 Census. Volume Two: The ethnic minority populations of Great Britain*, London: HMSO.

Peters, J., Soukas, A. and Green, G. (2002) *Tackling health inequalities in Sheffield*, Sheffield: Sheffield Health Action Zone.

Petrou, S., Kupek, E., Vause, S. and Maresh, M. (2001) 'Clinical, provider and sociodemographic determinants of antenatal visits in England and Wales', *Social Science and Medicine*, vol 52, pp 1123-34.

Phillips, C. and Bowling, B. (2003) 'The experiences of crime and criminal justice among minority ethnic groups: a review of the literature', unpublished report, London: Criminal Justice System Race Unit.

Piachaud, D. (1981) 'Social security', in N. Bosanquet and P. Townsend (eds) *Labour and equality*, London: Heinemann, pp 171-85.

Pleace, N. (2000) 'The new consensus, the old consensus and the provision of services for people sleeping rough', *Housing Studies*, vol 15, no 4, pp 581-94.

Policy Commission on Public Services (2004) *Making public services personal*, London: National Consumer Council.

Pollock, A.M. (1999) 'Devolution and health: challenges for Scotland and Wales', *British Medical Journal*, vol 318, pp 1195-8.

Pollock, A.M., Price, D., Talbot-Smith, A. and Mohan, J. (2003) 'NHS and the Health and Social Care Bill: end of Bevan's vision?', *British Medical Journal*, vol 327, no 7421, pp 982-5.

Powell, M. (ed) (1999) *New Labour, new welfare state? The 'third way' in British social policy*, Bristol: The Policy Press.

Power, A. (2004) *Sustainable communities and sustainable development: A review of the sustainable communities plan*, London: CASE and the Sustainable Development Commission.

Power, A. and Mumford, K. (1999) *The slow death of great cities: Urban abandonment or urban renaissance*, York: Joseph Rowntree Foundation.

Programme Committee on Socio-Economic Inequalities in Health (2001) *Reducing socio-economic inequalities in health*, The Hague: Ministry of Health, Welfare and Sports.

Radice, G. (1992) *Southern discomfort*, Fabian Pamphlet 555, London: Fabian Society.

Rake, K., Falkingham, J. and Evans, M. (2000) 'British pension policy in the 21st century: a partnership in pensions or a marriage to the means test?', *Social Policy and Administration*, vol 34, no 3, pp 296-317.

Rallings, C. and Thrasher, M. (eds) (2000) *British electoral facts 1832-1999*, Dartmouth: Parliamentary Research Services.

Rallings, C. and Thrasher, M. (2002) *NDC Elections: A study in community engagement*, London: ODPM.

Rallings, C., Thrasher, M. and Cowling, D. (2002) 'Mayoral referendums and elections', *Local Government Studies*, vol 28, no 4, pp 67-90.

Randall, G. and Brown, S. (1999) *Homes for street homeless people: An evaluation of the Rough Sleepers Initiative*, London: DETR.

Randall, G. and Brown, S. (2002) *Helping rough sleepers off the streets: A report to the Homelessness Directorate*, London: ODPM.

Ratcliffe, P., Harrison, M., Hogg, R., Line, B., Phillips, D., Tomlins, R. and Power, A. (2001) *Breaking down the barriers: Improving Asian access to social rented housing*, Coventry: Chartered Institute of Housing.

Richardson, L. and Le Grand, J. (2002) 'Outsider and insider expertise: the response of residents of deprived neighbourhoods to an academic definition of social exclusion', *Social Policy and Administration*, vol 36, no 5, pp 496-515.

Riley, R. and Young, G. (2001a) 'Does welfare to work policy increase employment: Evidence from the UK New Deal for Young People', National Institute for Economic and Social Research, Discussion Paper no 183, London: NIESR.

Riley, R. and Young, G. (2001b) 'The macroeconomic effect of the New Deal for Young People', National Institute for Economic and Social Research Discussion Paper no 184, London: NIESR.

Roberts, K. (1995) *Youth and employment in modern Britain*, Oxford: Oxford University Press.

Roberts, K. and Harris, J. (2002) *Disabled refugees in Britain*, York: Social Policy Research Unit, University of York.

Robinson, P. (2003) 'Some are more unequal than others', *The Guardian*, 17 November.

Robinson, V. and Segrott, J. (2002) *Understanding the decision-making of asylum seekers*, Home Office Research Study no 243, London: Home Office.

Rolfe, H., Metcalfe, H., Anderson, T. and Meadows, P. (2003) *Recruitment and retention of childcare, early years and play workers: Research study*, Research Report no 409, London: DfES.

Sales, R. (2002) 'The deserving and the undeserving? Refugees, asylum seekers and welfare in Britain', *Critical Social Policy*, vol 22, no 3, pp 456-78.

Sassi, F., Carrier, J. and Weinberg, J. (2004) 'Affirmative action: the lessons for health care', *British Medical Journal*, vol 328, pp 1213-4.

Sassi, F., Le Grand, J. and Archard, L. (2001) 'Equity versus efficiency: a dilemma for the NHS. If the NHS is serious about equity it must offer guidance when principles conflict', *British Medical Journal*, vol 323, pp 762-3.

Saxena, S., Eliahoo, J. and Majeed, A. (2002) 'Socioeconomic and ethnic group differences in self-reported health status and use of health services by children and young people in England: cross sectional study', *British Medical Journal*, vol 325, pp 520-5.

Schmitt, J. and Wadsworth, J. (2002) *Give pcs a chance: Personal computer ownership and the digital divide in the United States and Great Britain*, Centre for Economic Performance Discussion Paper 0526, London: London School of Economics and Political Science.

Sefton, T. (2002) *Recent Changes in the Distribution of the Social Wage*, CASEpaper 62, London: London School of Economics and Political Science.

Selman, P., Richardson, D., Speak, S. and Hosie, A. (2001) *Monitoring of the Standards Fund Grant: Teenage pregnancy*, Newcastle: Newcastle upon Tyne.

SEU (Social Exclusion Unit) (1998a) *Truancy and school exclusion*, Cm 3957, London: The Stationery Office.

SEU (1998b) *Rough sleeping*, Cm 4008, London: The Stationery Office.

SEU (1998c) *Bringing Britain together: A national strategy for neighbourhood renewal*, London: SEU.

SEU (1999) *Teenage pregnancy*, Cm 4342, London: The Stationery Office.

SEU (2000) *Minority ethnic issues in social exclusion and neighbourhood renewal*, London: SEU.

SEU (2001) *New commitment to neighbourhood renewal: National strategy action plan*, London: Cabinet Office.

SEU (2004) *Tackling social exclusion: Taking stock and looking to the future. Emerging findings*, London: ODPM.

Sewell, T. (1997) *Black masculinities and schooling: How black boys survive modern schooling*, London: Trentham Books.

Seyd, P. (1998) 'Tony Blair and New Labour', in A. King, D. Denver, I. McLean, P. Norris, P. Norton, D. Sanders and P. Seyd (eds) *New Labour triumphs: Britain at the polls*, Chatham, NJ: Chatham House, pp 49-74.

Shaw, M., Dorling, D., Gordon, D. and Davey Smith, G. (1999) *The widening gap: Health inequalities and policy in Britain*, Bristol: The Policy Press.

Shaw, R. and Smith, P. (2001) *Allocating health care resources to reduce health inequalities*, London: The King's Fund.

Shelter (2001) *Street homelessness*, London: Shelter.

Shifrin, T. (2003) 'TimeBank wins 500k lottery cash,' *The Guardian*, 8 October.

Shropshire, J. and Middleton, S. (1999) *Small expectations: Learning to be poor?*, York: Joseph Rowntree Foundation.

Smith, A. (2002) 'The new ethnicity classification in the Labour Force Survey', *Labour Market Trends*, vol 110, no 12, pp 657-66.

Smith, A., Youngs, R., Ashworth, K., McKay, S., Walker, R., Elias, P. and McKnight, A. (2000) *Understanding the impact of Jobseeker's Allowance*, DSS report No 111, Leeds: Corporate Document Services.

Smith, D.J. (1977) *Racial disadvantage in Britain*, Harmondsworth: Penguin.

Smith, J.D. (1998) *1997 National Survey for Volunteering in the UK*, London: Institute for Volunteering Research.

Smith, J., McKnight, A. and Naylor, R. (2000) 'Graduate employability: policy and performance in higher education in the UK', *Economic Journal*, vol 110, pp 382-411.

Spencer, P. (1996) 'Reactions to a flexible labour market', in R. Jowell, J. Curtice, A. Park, L. Brook and K. Thomson (eds) *British social attitudes: The 13th report*, Aldershot: Dartmouth.

Sport England (2004) '£20m investment for community sports clubs', press release, 14 April, London: Sport England.

Stalker, P. (2002) 'Migration trends and migration policy in Europe', *International Migration*, vol 40, no 5, pp 151-79.

Stewart, M. (1972) 'The distribution of income', in W. Beckerman (ed) *The Labour government's economic record: 1964-1970*, London: Duckworth.

Stoker, G. and Bottom, K.A. (2003) 'Community capacity building', Paper given to Municipal Association of Victoria Conference, Lorne, 25-27 July.

Strategy Unit (2002) *Inter-departmental childcare review: Delivering for children and families*, London: Strategy Unit.

Stratford, N., Finch, S. and Pethick, J. (1997) *Survey of parents of three and four year old children and their use of early years services*, Research Report no 31, London: DfEE.

Straw, J. (1999) 'Full text of Jack Straw's statement to Parliament', *The Guardian*, 24 February.

Summerfield, C. and Babb, P. (eds) (2004) *Social Trends 34*, London: The Stationery Office.

Sutherland, H. (2004) *Poverty in Britain: The impact of government policy since 1997. An update to 2004-5 using microsimulation*, Cambridge: Microsimulation Unit, University of Cambridge.

Sutherland, H., Sefton, T. and Piachaud, D. (2003) *Poverty in Britain: The impact of government policy since 1997*, York: Joseph Rowntree Foundation.

Sutherland, S. (1999) *With respect to old age: Long term care – rights and responsibilities: A report by the Royal Commission on Long Term Care*, Cm 4192-I, London: The Stationery Office.

Sutton, M., Gravelle, H., Morris, D., Leyland, A., Windmeijer, F., Dibben, C. and Muirhead, M. (2002) *Allocation of resources to English areas: Individual and small area determinants of morbidity and use of health care resources*, Edinburgh: Information and Services Division.

Swann Report (1985) *Education for all: The Report of the Committee of Inquiry into the Education of Children from Ethnic Minority Groups*, Cmnd 9453, London: HMSO.

Sylva, K., Melhuish, E., Sammons, P., Siraj-Blatchford, I., Taggart, B. and Elliot, K. (2003) *The Effective Provision Of Pre-School Education (EPPE) Project: Findings from the pre-school period*, Research Brief no RBX 15-03, London: DfES.

Taylor, M. (1995) *Unleashing the potential*, York: Joseph Rowntree Foundation.

Teenage Pregnancy Unit (2003) *Implementation of the Teenage Pregnancy Strategy: Progress report December 2003*, London: DfES.

Thomas Coram Research Unit (2002) *Research on ratios, group size and staff qualifications and training in early years and childcare settings*, Research Report 320, London: DfES.

Tikly, L., Osler, A., Hill, J. and Vincent, K. (2002) *Ethnic Minority Achievement Grant: Analysis of LEA action plans*, Research Report 371, London: DfES.

Tomlinson, S. (1998) 'New inequalities? Educational markets and ethnic minorities [1]', *Race, Ethnicity and Education*, vol 1, no 2, pp 207-23.

Tomlinson, S. (2001) 'Ethnic minorities and education: new disadvantages', in H. Goulbourne (ed) *Race and ethnicity: Critical concepts in sociology*, London: Routledge, pp 15-34.

Townsend, P. (2001) *Targeting poor health*, Cardiff: The National Assembly for Wales.

Townsend, P. and Bosanquet, N. (eds) (1972) *Labour and inequality: Sixteen Fabian essays*, London: Fabian Society.

Townsend, P., Davidson, N., Whitehead, M. (1992) *Inequalities in health: The Black Report and the health divide*, London: Penguin Books.

Toynbee, P. and Walker, D. (2001) *Did things get better? An audit of Labour's successes and failures*, London: Penguin Books.

TUC (Trades Union Congress) (2002) *Pensions in peril: The decline of the final salary pension scheme*, London: TUC.

TUC (2003) *A briefing on Employment Zones: Fourth edition*, TUC Welfare Reform series no 11, London: TUC.

UNHCR (United Nations High Commissioner for Refugees) (2003) *Refugees by numbers 2003*, Geneva: UNHCR.

UNHCR (2004) *Asylum levels and trends: Europe and non-European industrialized countries, 2003*, Geneva: UNHCR.

UNICEF (United Nations Children's Fund) (2000) *A league table of child poverty in rich nations*, Innocenti Report Card no 1, Florence: UNICEF Innocenti Research Centre.

Van Reenen, J. (2004) 'Active labor market policies and the British New Deal for unemployed youth in context', in R. Blundell, D. Card and R. Freeman (eds) *Seeking a premier league economy*, Chicago, IL: University of Chicago Press.

Vegeris, S. and Perry, J. (2003) *Families and children 2001: Living standards and the children*, DWP Research Report 190, London: The Stationery Office.

Vulliamy, G. and Webb, R. (2001) 'The social construction of school exclusion rates: implications for evaluation methodology', *Educational Studies*, vol 27, no 3, pp 357-70.

Wadsworth, J. (2003) 'The labour market performance of ethnic minorities in the recovery', in R. Dickens, P. Gregg and J. Wadsworth (eds) *The labour market under New Labour: the state of working Britain*, Basingstoke: Palgrave Macmillan, pp 116-33.

Waldegrave, C., Stephens, R. and King, P. (2002) *Assessing the progress on poverty reduction*, New Zealand Poverty Measurement Project, Wellington, NZ: Family Centre Social Policy Research Unit.

Waldfogel, J. (1998) *Early childhood interventions and outcomes*, CASEpaper 21, London: London School of Economics and Political Science.

Wanless, D. (2002) *Securing our future health: Taking a long-term view*, London: HM Treasury.

Wanless, D. (2004) *Securing good health for the whole population*, London: HM Treasury.

Warde A., Tampubolon, G., Longhurst, B., Ray, K., Savage, M. and Tomlinson, M. (2003) 'Trends in social capital: membership of associations in Great Britain, 1991-98', *British Journal of Political Science*, vol 33, pp 515-34.

Wellings, K. and Kane, R. (1999) 'Trends in teenage pregnancy in England and Wales: how can we explain them?', *Journal of the Royal Society of Medicine*, vol 92, pp 277-82.

West, A. and Pennell, H. (2003) *Underachievement in schools*, London: Routledge.

Whiteley, P. (2004) *Civic renewal and participation in Britain*, Essex: University of Essex.

Wilkinson, R. (1996) *Unhealthy societies: The afflictions of inequality*, London: Routledge.

Williams, C.C. (2002) 'Cultures of community engagement', *Local Governance*, vol 28, no 4, pp 263-71.

Wilson, V. (2002) *Does small really make a difference? A review of the literature on the effects of class size on teaching practice and pupils' behaviour and attainment*, SCRE Research Report no 107, Glasgow: University of Glasgow.

Wincott, D. (2004) 'Learning from devolution: making childcare Labour's "big idea"', *Devolution and Constitutional Change*, Briefing no 4 (www.devolution.ac.uk/publications2.htm#Briefings July 2004).

Woodland, S., Miller, M. and Tipping, S. (2002) *Repeat study of parents' demand for childcare*, Research Report 348, London: DfES.

Work and Pensions Committee (2004) *Child poverty in the UK Volume I*, London: The Stationery Office.

Zaidi, A. and Burchardt, T. (2003) *Comparing incomes when needs differ: Equivalisation for the extra costs of disability in the UK*, CASEpaper 64, London: London School of Economics and Political Science.

Zetter, R., Griffiths, D., Ferretti, S. and Pearl, M. (2003) *An assessment of the impact of asylum policies, 1990-2000*, Home Office Research Study no 259, London: Home Office.

# Index

Page references for figures and tables are in *italics*; those for notes are followed by n